THE
GREAT INSTAURATION
AND THE
NOVUM ORGANUM

Partial Contents: The Interpretation of Nature; The Empire of Man; The Reign of Man; Natural and Experimental History; Phenomena of the Universe; The Names of the Winds; Sympathy and Antipathy of Things; Sulfur, Mercury and Salt; Life and Death; Scaling the Ladder of Intellect; plus much more!

Francis Bacon

ISBN 1-56459-638-9

CONTENTS

H

THE GREAT INSTAURATION

OF LORD BACON.

PART II.

NOVUM ORGANUM.

EDITOR'S PREFACE.

The following is a TRANSLATION of the "Instauratio Magna," excepting the first book, the Treatise "De Augmentis Scientiarum."

BOOK II. NOVUM ORGANUM.

The first edition of this work was published in folio, in 1620, when Lord Bacon was chancellor. Editions in 12mo. were published in Holland in 1645, 1650, and 1660. An edition was published in 1779; "Wirceburgi, apud Jo. Jac. Stahel:" and an edition was published at Oxford in 1813. No assistance to this, or, as I am aware, to any part of Lord Bacon's works, has been rendered by the University of Cambridge.

Parts of the Novum Organum have, at different periods, been translated.

In Watts's translation, in 1640, of the Treatise De Augmentis, there is a translation of the Introductory Tract prefixed to the Novum Organum.

In the third edition of the Resuscitatio, published in 1671, there are three translated tracts from the Novum Organum, viz., 1. The Natural and Experimental History of the Form of Hot Things. 2. Of the several kinds of Motion or of the Active Virtue. 3. A Translation of the Parasceve, which is the beginning of the third part of the Instauration, but is annexed to the Novum Organum in the first edition. This translation of the Parasceve is by *a well wisher to his lordship's writings.*

In the tenth edition of the Sylva Sylvarum, there is an abridged translation of the Novum Organum. The following is a copy of the title page: *The Novum Organum of Sir Francis Bacon, Baron of Verulam, Viscount St. Albans Epitomiz'd: for a clearer understanding of his Natural History. Translated and taken out of the Latine by M. D. B. D. London: Printed for Thomas Lee, at the Turk's-head in Fleet Street*, 1676. As this tenth edition of the Sylva was published 1671, and Dr. Rawley died 1667, it must not, from any document now known, be ascribed to him. It is not noticed in the Baconiana published in 1679.

In 1733, Peter Shaw, M. D., published a translation of the Novum Organum.

Dr. Shaw, who was a great admirer of Lord Bacon, seems to have laboured under a diseased love of arrangement, by which he was induced to deviate from the order of the publications by Lord Bacon, and to adopt his own method. This may be seen in almost every part of his edition, but particularly in his edition of the Essays, and of the Novum Organum, which is divided and subdivided into sections, with a perplexing alteration, without an explanation of the numbers of the Aphorisms; this will appear at the conclusion of his first section, where he passes from section thirty-seven to section one.

His own account of his translation is as follows :—"The design of these volumes is to give a methodical English edition of his philosophical works, fitted for a commodious and ready perusal; somewhat in the same manner as the philosophical works of Mr. Boyle were, a few years since, fitted, in three quarto volumes.

"All the author's pieces, that were originally written in Latin, or by himself translated into Latin, are here new done from those originals; with care all along to collate his own English with the Latin, where the pieces were extant in both languages.

"The method observed in thus rendering them into English, is not that of a direct translation, (which might have left them more obscure than they are; and no way suited this design;) but a kind of open version, which endeavours to express, in modern English, the sense of the author, clear, full, and strong; though without deviating from him, and, if possible, without losing of his spirit, force, or energy. And though this attempt may seem vain, or bold, it was doubtless better to have had the view, than willingly to have aimed at second prizes.

"The liberty sometimes taken, not of abridging, (for just and perfect writings are incapable of abridgment,) but of dropping, or leaving out, some parts of the author's writings, may require greater excuse. But this was done in order to shorten the works, whose length has proved one discouragement to their being read. And regard has been had to omit none of the philosophical matter; but only certain personal addresses, compliments, exordiums, and the like; for, as the reasons and ends, for which these were originally made, subsist no longer, it was thought superfluous to continue such particularities, in a work of this general nature."

In the year 1810 the Novum Organum was translated into Italian. The following is a copy of the title-page: *Nuovo Organo Delle Scienze di Francesco Bacone, Di Verulamio, Traduzione in Italiano del can. Antonio Pellizzari, Edizione seconda arricchita di un Indice e di Annotazioni. Bassano, Tipografia Remondiniana*, 1810.

For the translation of the Novum Organum contained in this volume, I am indebted to my friend William Wood: excepting the translation of the Catalogue of Particular Histories, for which I am indebted to my friend and pupil, William G. Glen.

BOOK III. NATURAL AND EXPERIMENTAL HISTORY.

THE HISTORY OF THE WINDS.

The translation was published in 1671, in the third edition of the Resuscitatio. It is "translated into English by R. G., gentleman." Of this tract Archbishop Tennison, says, in his Baconiana: "The second section is the History of Winds, written in Latin by the author, and by R. G., gentleman, turned into English. It was dedicated to King Charles, then Prince, as the first-fruits of his lordship's Natural History; and as a grain of mustard-seed, which was, by degrees, to grow into a tree of experimental science. This was the birth of the first of those six months, in which he determined (God assisting him) to write six several histories of natural things. To wit, of Dense and Rare Bodies; of Heavy and Light Bodies; of Sympathy and Antipathy; of Salt, Sulphur, and Mercury; of Life and Death; and (which he first perfected) that of Winds, which he calls the Wings, by which men fly on the sea, and the besoms of the air and earth. And he rightly observeth, concerning those postnati, (for, as he saith, they are not a part of the six days' work or primary creatures,) that the generation of them has not been well understood, because men have been ignorant of the nature and power of the air, on which the winds attend, as Æolus on Juno.

"The English translation of this book of Winds is printed in the second part of the Resuscitatio, as it is called, though improperly enough; for it is rather a collection of books already printed, than a resuscitation of any considerable ones, which before slept in private manuscript."

The translations of the Histories of Density and Rarity; of Heavy and Light: of Sympathy and Antipathy; of Sulphur, Mercury, and Salt, are from the third edition of the Resuscitatio, published in 1671; which contains also a translation of the Entrance to the History of Life and Death.

The translation of the History of Life and Death is taken from the seventh edition of the Sylva Sylvarum, published in 1658. Of this translation, Archbishop Tennison thus speaks in his Baconiana: "The sixth section is the History of Life and Death, written by his lordship in Latin, and first turned into English by an injudicious translator, and rendered much better a second time, by an abler pen, made abler still by the advice and assistance of Dr. Rawley.

"This work, though ranked last amongst the six monthly designations, yet was set forth in the second place. His lordship (as he saith) inverting the order, in respect of the prime use of this argument, in which the least loss of time was by him esteemed very precious. The subject of this book, (which Sir Henry Wotton calleth none of the least of his lordship's works,) and the argument of which some had before undertaken, but to much less purpose, is the first of those which he put in his Catalogue of the Magnalia Naturæ. And, doubtless, his lordship undertook both a great and a most desirable work, of making art short, and life easy and long. 'And it was his lordship's wish that the nobler sort of physicians might not employ their times wholly in the sordidness of cures, neither be honoured for necessity only; but become coadjutors and instruments of the Divine omnipotence and clemence, in prolonging and renewing the life of man; and in helping Christians, who pant after the land of promise, so to journey through this world's wilderness, as to have their shoes and garments (these of their frail bodies) little worn and impaired.'"

BOOK IV. OF THE SCALING LADDER OF THE INTELLECT.

For this translation I am indebted to my dear friend, the Reverend Archdeacon Wrangham, with whom, after an uninterrupted friendship of more than forty years, I am happy to be associated in this work.

Archbishop Tennison thus speaks of this fourth book: "The fourth part of the Instauration designed, was Scala Intellectus.

"To this there is some sort of entrance in his lordship's distribution of the Novum Organum, and in a page or two under that title of Scala, published by Gruter. But the work itself passed not beyond the model of it in the head of the noble author.

"That which he intended was, a particular explication and application of the second part of the Instauration, (which giveth general rules for the interpretation of nature,) by gradual instances and examples.

"He thought that his rules, without some more sensible explication, were like discourses in geometry or mechanics, without figures and types of engines. He therefore designed to select certain subjects in nature or art; and, as it were, to draw to the sense a certain scheme of the beginning and progress of philosophical disquisition in them; showing, by degrees, where our consideration takes root, and how it spreadeth and advanceth. And some such thing is done by those who, from the Cicatricula, or from the Punctum Saliens, observe and register all the phenomena of the animal unto its death, and after it, also, in the medical, or culinary, or other use of its body; together with all the train of the thoughts occasioned by those phenomena, or by others in compare with them.

"And because he intended to exhibit such observations, as they gradually arise, therefore, he gave to that designed work the title of the Scale, or Ladder of the Understanding. He also expressed the same conceit by another metaphor, advising students to imitate men who, by going by degrees, from several eminences of some very high mountain, do at length arrive at the top, or pike of it."

FIFTH BOOK, OR ANTICIPATIONS OF THE SECOND PHILOSOPHY.

For this translation I am also indebted to my friend, Archdeacon Wrangham. Of this tract Archbishop Tennison thus speaks: "The fifth part of the Instauration designed, was what he called Prodromi sive Anticipationes Philosophiæ Secundæ. To this we find a very brief entrance in the Organum, and the Scripta, published by Gruter. And, though his lordship is not known to have composed any part of this work by itself, yet something of it is to be collected from the axioms and greater observations interspersed in his Natural Histories, which are not pure but mixed writings. The anticipations he intended to pay down as use, till he might furnish the world with the principal."

FRANCIS OF VERULAM

THOUGHT THUS,

AND SUCH IS THE METHOD HE WITHIN HIMSELF PURSUED, WHICH HE THOUGHT IT CONCERNED BOTH THE LIVING AND POSTERITY TO BECOME ACQUAINTED WITH.

SEEING he was satisfied that the human understanding creates itself labour, and makes not a judicious and convenient use of such real helps as are within man's power, whence arise both a manifold ignorance of things, and innumerable disadvantages, the consequence of such ignorance; he thought that we ought to endeavour, with all our might, either (if it were possible) completely to restore, or, at all events, to bring to a better issue that free intercourse of the mind with things, nothing similar to which is to be met with on earth, at least as regards earthly objects. But that errors which have gained firm ground, and will forever continue to gain ground, would, if the mind were left to itself, successively correct each other, either from the proper powers of the understanding, or from the helps and support of logic, he entertained not the slightest hope. Because the primary notions of things, which the mind ignorantly and negligently imbibes, stores up, and accumulates, (and from which every thing else is derived,) are faulty and confused, and carelessly abstracted from the things themselves; and in the secondary and following notions, there is an equal wantonness and inconsistency. Hence it happens that the whole system of human reasoning, as far as we apply it to the investigation of nature, is not skilfully consolidated and built up, but resembles a magnificent pile that has no foundation. For while men admire and celebrate the false energies of the mind, they pass by, and lose sight of the real; such as may exist if the mind adopt proper helps, and act modestly towards things instead of weakly insulting them. But one course was left, to begin the matter anew with better preparation, and to effect a restoration of the sciences, arts, and the whole of human learning, established on their proper foundation. And, although, at the first attempt, this may appear to be infinite, and above the strength of a mere mortal, yet will it, in the execution, be found to be more sound and judicious than the course which has hitherto been pursued. For this method admits at least of some termination, whilst, in the present mode of treating the sciences, there is a sort of whirl, and perpetual hurry round a circle. Nor has he forgotten to observe that he stands alone in this experiment, and that it is too bold and astonishing to obtain credit. Nevertheless, he thought it not right to desert either the cause or himself, by not exploring and entering upon the only way, which is pervious to the human mind. For it is better to commence a matter which may admit of some termination, than to be involved in perpetual exertion and anxiety about that which is interminable. And, indeed, the ways of contemplation nearly resemble those celebrated ways of action; the one of which, steep and rugged at its commencement, terminates in a plain, the other, at the first view smooth and easy, leads only to by-roads and precipices. Uncertain, however, whether these reflections would ever hereafter suggest themselves to another, and, particularly, having observed, that he has never yet met with any person disposed to apply his mind to similar meditations, he determined to publish whatsoever he had first time to conclude. Nor is this the haste of ambition, but of his anxiety, that if the common lot of mankind should befall him, some sketch and determination of the matter his mind had embraced might be extant, as well as an earnest of his will being honourably bent upon promoting the advantage of mankind. He assuredly looked upon any other ambition as beneath the matter he had undertaken; for that which is here treated of is either nothing, or it is so great that he ought to be satisfied with its own worth, and seek no other return.

T0

OUR MOST SERENE AND MIGHTY PRINCE AND LORD

JAMES,

BY THE GRACE OF GOD, KING OF GREAT BRITAIN, FRANCE, AND IRELAND, DEFENDER OF THE FAITH, ETC.

MOST SERENE AND MIGHTY KING:

Your majesty will, perhaps, accuse me of theft, in that I have stolen from your employments time sufficient for this work. I have no reply, for there can be no restitution of time, unless, perhaps, that which has been withdrawn from your affairs might be set down as devoted to the perpetuating of your name and to the honour of your age, were what I now offer of any value. It is at least new, even in its very nature; but copied from a very ancient pattern, no other than the world itself, and the nature of things, and of the mind. I myself (ingenuously to confess the truth) am wont to value this work rather as the offspring of time than of wit. For the only wonderful circumstance in it is, that the first conception of the matter, and so deep suspicions of prevalent notions should ever have entered into any person's mind; the consequences naturally follow. But, doubtless, there is a chance, (as we call it,) and something as it were accidental in man's thoughts, no less than in his actions and words. I would have this chance, however, (of which I am speaking,) to be so understood, that if there be any merit in what I offer, it should be attributed to the immeasurable mercy and bounty of God, and to the felicity of this your age; to which felicity I have devoted myself whilst living with the sincerest zeal, and I shall, perhaps, before my death have rendered the age a light unto posterity, by kindling this new torch amid the darkness of philosophy. This regeneration and instauration of the sciences is with justice due to the age of a prince surpassing all others in wisdom and learning. There remains for me to but to make one request, worthy of your majesty, and very especially relating to my subject, namely, that, resembling Solomon as you do in most respects, in the gravity of your decisions, the peacefulness of your reign, the expansion of your heart, and, lastly, in the noble variety of books you have composed, you would further imitate the same monarch in procuring the compilation and completion of a Natural and Experimental History, that shall be genuine and rigorous, not that of mere philologues, and serviceable for raising the superstructure of philosophy, such, in short, as I will in its proper place describe: that, at length, after so many ages, philosophy and the sciences may no longer be unsettled and speculative, but fixed on the solid foundation of a varied and well considered experience. I for my part have supplied the instrument, the matter to be worked upon must be sought from things themselves. May the great and good God long preserve your majesty in safety.

Your majesty's

Most bounden and devoted,

FRANCIS VERULAM, Chancellor

FRANCIS OF VERULAM'S

GREAT INSTAURATION.

PREFACE.

ON THE STATE OF LEARNING.—THAT IT IS NEITHER PROSPEROUS NOR GREATLY ADVANCED, AND THAT AN ENTIRELY DIFFERENT WAY FROM ANY KNOWN TO OUR PREDECESSORS MUST BE OPENED TO THE HUMAN UNDERSTANDING, AND DIFFERENT HELPS BE OBTAINED, IN ORDER THAT THE MIND MAY EXERCISE ITS JURISDICTION OVER THE NATURE OF THINGS.

IT appears to me that men know not either their acquirements or their powers, and trust too much to the former, and too little to the latter. Hence it arises that, either estimating the arts they have become acquainted with at an absurd value, they require nothing more, or forming too low an opinion of themselves, they waste their powers on trivial objects, without attempting any thing to the purpose. The sciences have thus their own pillars, fixed as it were by fate,* since men are not roused to penetrate beyond them either by zeal or hope: and inasmuch as an imaginary plenty mainly contributes to a dearth, and from a reliance upon present assistance, that which will really hereafter aid us is neglected, it becomes useful, nay, clearly necessary, in the very outset of our work, to remove, without any circumlocution or concealment, all excessive conceit and admiration of our actual state of knowledge, by this wholesome warning not to exaggerate or boast of its extent or utility. For, if any one look more attentively into that vast variety of books which the arts and sciences are so proud of, he will everywhere discover innumerable repetitions of the same thing, varied only by the method of treating it, but anticipated in invention; so that although at first sight they appear numerous, they are found, upon examination, to be but scanty. And with regard to their utility I must speak plainly. That philosophy of ours which we have chiefly derived from the Greeks, appears to me but the childhood of knowledge, and to possess the peculiarity of that age, being prone to idle loquacity, but weak and unripe for generation; for it is fruitful of controversy and barren of effects. So that the fable of Scylla seems to be a lively image of the present state of letters; for she exhibited the countenance and expression of a virgin, but barking monsters surrounded and fastened themselves to her womb. Even thus, the sciences to which we have been accustomed have their flattering and specious generalities, but when we come to particulars, which, like the organs of generation, should produce fruit and effects, then spring up altercations and barking questions, in the which they end, and bring forth nothing else. Besides, if these sciences were not manifestly a dead letter, it would never happen, as for many ages has been the case in practice, that they should adhere almost immovably to their original footing, without acquiring a growth worthy of mankind: and this so completely, that frequently not only an assertion continues to be an assertion, but even a question to be a question, which, instead of being solved by discussion, becomes fixed and encouraged; and every system of instruction successively handed down to us brings upon the stage the characters of master and scholar, not those of an inventor and one capable of adding some excellence to his inventions. But we see the contrary happen in the mechanical arts. For they, as if inhaling some life-inspiring air, daily increase, and are brought to perfection; they generally in the hands of the inventor appear rude, cumbrous, and shapeless, but afterwards acquire such additional powers and facility, that sooner may men's wishes and fancies decline and change, than the arts reach their full height and perfection. Philosophy and the intellectual sciences on the contrary, like statues, are adored and celebrated, but are not made to advance: nay, they are frequently most vigorous in the hands of their author, and thenceforward degenerate. For since men have voluntarily surrendered themselves, and gone over in crowds to the opinion of their leader, like those silent senators of Rome,† they add nothing to the extent of learning themselves, but perform the servile duty of illustrating and waiting upon particular authors. Nor let any one allege that learning, slowly springing up, attained by degrees its full stature, and from that time took up its abode in the works of a few, as having performed its predetermined course; and that, as it is impossible to discover any further improvement, it only

---

* Alluding to the frontispiece of the original work, which represents a vessel passing beyond the Pillars of Hercules.
† Pedarii Senatores

remains for us to adorn and cultivate that which has been discovered. It were indeed to be wished that such were the case; the more correct and true statement, however, is, that this slavery of the sciences arises merely from the impudence of a few, and the indolence of the rest of mankind. For, no sooner was any particular branch of learning (diligently enough, perhaps) cultivated and laboured, than up would spring some individual confident in his art, who would acquire authority and reputation from the compendious nature of his method, and, as far as appearances went, would establish the art, whilst in reality he was corrupting the labours of his ancestors. Yet will this please succeeding generations, from the ready use they can make of his labour, and their wearisome impatience of fresh inquiry. But if any one be influenced by an inveterate uniformity of opinion, as though it were the decision of time—let him learn that he is relying on a most fallacious and weak argument. For not only are we, in a great measure, unacquainted with the proportion of arts and sciences that has been discovered and made its way to the public in various ages and regions, (much less with what has been individually attempted and privately agitated,) neither the births nor the abortions of time being extant in any register; but also that uniformity itself, and its duration are not to be considered of any great moment. For, however varied the forms of civil government may be, there is but one state of learning, and that ever was and' ever will be the democratic. Now with the people at large, the doctrines that most prevail are either disputatious and violent, or specious and vain, and they either ensnare or allure assent. Hence, without question, the greatest wits have undergone violence in every age, whilst others of no vulgar capacity and understanding have still, from consulting their reputation, submitted themselves to the decision of time and the multitude. Wherefore, if more elevated speculations have perchance anywhere ·burst forth, they have been from time to time blown about by the winds of public opinion, and extinguished; so that time, like a river, has brought down all that was light and inflated, and has sunk what was weighty and solid. Nay, those very leaders who have usurped, as it were, a dictatorship in learning, and pronounce their opinion of things with so much confidence, will yet, when they occasionally return to their senses, begin to complain of the subtility of nature, the remoteness of truth, the obscurity of things, the complication of causes, and the weakness of human wit. They are not, however, more modest in this than in the forme rinstances, since they prefer framing an excuse of the common condition of men and things, to confessing their own defects. Besides, it is generally their practice, if some particular art fail to accomplish any object, to conclude that it cannot be accomplished by that art. But yet the art cannot be condemned, for she herself deliberates and decides the question; so that their only aim is to deliver their ignorance from ignominy. The following statement exhibits sufficiently well the state of knowledge delivered down and received by us. It is barren in effects, fruitful in questions, slow and languid in its improvement, exhibiting in its generality the counterfeit of perfection, but ill filled up in its details, popular in its choice, but suspected by its very promoters, and therefore bolstered up and countenanced with artifices. Even those who have been determined to try for themselves, to add their support to learning, and to enlarge its limits, have not dared entirely to desert received opinions, nor to seek the springhead of things. But they think they have done a great thing if they intersperse and contribute something of their own, prudently considering that by their assent they can save their modesty, and by their contributions their liberty. Whilst consulting, however, the opinions of others, and good manners, this admired moderation tends to the great injury of learning: for it is seldom in our power both to admire and surpass our author, but, like water, we rise not higher than the springhead whence we have descended. Such men, therefore, amend some things, but cause little advancement, and improve more than they enlarge knowledge. Yet there have not been wanting some, who, with greater daring, have considered every thing open to them, and, employing the force of their wit, have opened a passage for themselves and their dogmas by prostrating and destroying all before them; but this violence of theirs has not availed much, since they have not laboured to enlarge philosophy and the arts, both in their subject-matter and effect; but only to substitute new dogmas, and to transfer the empire of opinion to themselves. with but small advantage; for opposite errors proceed mostly from common causes. Even if some few, who, neither dogmatise nor submit to dogmatism, have been so spirited as to request others to join them in investigation, yet have such, though honest in their zeal, been weak in their efforts. For they seem to have followed only probable reasoning, and are hurried in a continued whirl of arguments, till, by an indiscriminate license of inquiry, they have enervated the strictness of investigation. But not one has there been found of a disposition to dwell sufficiently on things themselves and experience. For some again, who have committed themselves to the waves of experience, and become almost mechanics, yet in their very experience employ an unsteady investigation, and war not with it by fixed rules. Nay, some have only proposed to themselves a few paltry tasks, and think it a great thing if they can work out one single discovery, a plan no less beggarly than unskilful. For no one examines thoroughly or successfully the nature of any thing in the thing itself, but after a laborious variety of experiments, instead of pausing there, they set out upon some further inquiry. And we must by no means omit observing, that all the industry displayed in experiment, has, from the very first, caught with a too hasty and intemperate zeal at some determined effect; has sought (I say) productive rather than enlightening experiments, and has not imitated the Divine method, which on the first day created light alone, and assigned it one whole day, producing no material works thereon, but descending to their creation on the following days. Those who have attributed the pre-eminence to logic, and have thought that it afforded the safest support to learning, have seen very correctly and properly that man's understanding, when left to itself, is deservedly to be suspected. Yet the remedy is even weaker than the disease; nay, it is not itself free from disease. For the common system of logic, although most properly applied to civil matters, and such arts as lie in discussion and opinion, is far from reaching the subtility of nature, and, by catching at that which it cannot grasp, has done more to confirm, and, as it were, fasten errors upon us, than to open the way to truth.

To sum up, therefore, our observations, neither reliance upon others, nor their own industry, appear hitherto to have set forth learning to mankind in her best light, especially as there is little aid in such demonstrations and experiments as have yet reached us. For the fabric of this universe is like a labyrinth to the contemplative mind, where doubtful paths, deceitful imitations of things and their signs, winding and intricate folds and knots of nature everywhere present themselves, and a way must constantly be made through the forests of experience and particular natures, with the aid of the uncertain light of the senses, shining and disappearing by fits. But the guides who offer their services are (as has been said) themselves confused, and increase the number of wanderings and of wanderers. In so difficult a matter we must despair of man's unassisted judgment, or even of any casual good fortune: for neither the excellence of wit, however great, nor the die of experience, however frequently cast, can overcome such disadvantages. We must guide our steps by a clue, and the whole path, from the very first perceptions of our senses, must be secured by a determined method. Nor must I be thought to say, that nothing whatever has been done by so many and so much labour; for I regret not our discoveries, and the ancients have certainly shown themselves worthy of admiration in all that requires either wit or abstracted meditation. But, as in former ages, when men at sea used only to steer by their observations of the stars, they were indeed enabled to coast the shores of the Continent, or some small and inland seas; but before they could traverse the ocean and discover the regions of the new world, it was necessary that the use of the compass, a more trusty and certain guide on their voyage, should be first known; even so, the present discoveries in the arts and sciences are such as might be found out by meditation, observation, and discussion, as being more open to the senses and lying immediately beneath our common notions: but before we are allowed to enter the more remote and hidden parts of nature, it is necessary that a better and more perfect use and application of the human mind and understanding should be introduced.

We, for our part at least, overcome by the eternal love of truth, have committed ourselves to uncertain, steep, and desert tracks, and trusting and relying on Divine assistance, have borne up our mind against the violence of opinions, drawn up as it were in battle array, against our own internal doubts and scruples, against the mists and clouds of nature, and against fancies flitting on all sides around us: that we might at length collect some more trustworthy and certain indications for the living and posterity. And if we have made any way in this matter, no other method than the true and genuine humiliation of the human soul has opened it unto us. For all who before us have applied themselves to the discovery of the arts, after casting their eyes a while upon things, instances, and experience, have straightway invoked, as it were, some spirits of their own to disclose their oracles, as if invention were nothing but a species of thought. But we, in our subdued and perpetual intercourse with things, abstract our understanding no farther from them than is necessary to prevent the confusion of the images of things with their radiation, a confusion similar to that we experience by our senses: and thus but little is left for the powers and excellence of wit. And we have in teaching continued to show forth the humility, which we adopt in discovering. For we do not endeavour to assume or acquire any majestic state for these our discoveries, by the triumphs of confutation, the citing of antiquity, the usurpation of authority, or even the veil of obscurity, which would easily suggest themselves to one endeavouring to throw light upon his own name, rather than the minds of others. We have not, I say, practised either force or fraud on men's judgments, nor intend we so to do; but we conduct them to things themselves and the real connexion of things, that they may themselves behold what they possess, what they prove, what they add, and what they contribute to the common stock. If, however, we have in any matter given too easy credit, or slumbered and been too inadvertent, or have mistaken our road, and broken off inquiry, yet we exhibit things plainly and openly, so that our errors can be noted and separated before they corrupt any further the mass of sciences, and the continuation of our labours is rendered easy and unembarrassed. And we think that by so doing we have established forever the real and legitimate union of the empiric and rational faculties, whose sullen and inauspicious divorces and repudiations have disturbed every thing in the great family of mankind.

Since, therefore, these matters are beyond our control, we in the beginning of our work pour forth most humble and ardent prayers to God the Father, God the Word, and God the Spirit, that, mindful of the cases of man, and of his pilgrimage through this life, in which we wear out some few and evil days, they would vouchsafe through our hands to endow the family of mankind with these new gifts; and we moreover humbly pray that human knowledge may not prejudice divine truth, and that no incredulity and darkness in regard to the divine mysteries may arise in our minds upon the disclosing of the ways of sense, and this greater kindling of our natural light; but rather that, from a pure understanding, cleared of all fancies and vanity, yet no less submitted to, nay, wholly prostrate before the divine oracles, we may render unto faith the tribute due unto faith. And, lastly, that being freed from the poison of knowledge, infused into it by the serpent, and with which the human soul is swoln and puffed up, we may neither be too profoundly nor immoderately wise, but worship truth in charity.

Having thus offered up our prayers, and turning our thoughts again towards man, we propound some salutary admonitions, and some just requests. First, then, we admonish mankind to keep their senses within the bounds of duty as regards divine objects. For the senses, like the sun, open the surface of the terrestrial globe, but close and seal up that of the celestial; next, that, whilst avoiding this error, they fall not into the contrary, which will surely be the case, if they think the investigation of nature to be in any part denied as if by interdict. For it was not that pure and innocent knowledge of nature, by which Adam gave names to things from their properties, that was the origin or occasion of the fall, but that ambitious and imperious appetite for moral knowledge, distinguishing good from evil, with the intent that man might revolt from God and govern himself, was both the cause and means of temptation. With regard to the sciences that contemplate nature, the sacred philosopher declares it to be "the glory of God to conceal a thing, but of the king to search it out,"* just as if the Divine Spirit were wont to be pleased with the innocent and gentle sport of children, who hide themselves that they may be found; and had chosen the human soul as a playmate out of his indulgence and goodness towards man. Lastly, we would in general admonish all to consider the true ends of knowledge, and not to seek it for the gratifications of their minds, or for disputation, or that they may despise others, or for emolument, or fame, or power, or such low objects, but for its intrinsic merit and the purposes of life, and that they would perfect and regulate it by charity. For from the desire of power the angels fell, and men from that of knowledge; but there is no excess in charity, and neither angel nor man was ever endangered by it.

The requests we make are three. Of ourselves we say nothing; but for the matter which we treat, we desire men not to regard it as an opinion, but as a work, and to hold it for certain that we are not laying the foundation of any sect or theory, but of that which will profit and dignify mankind. In the next place, that they should fairly consult their common advantage, laying aside the jealousies and prejudices of opinions, and themselves participate in the remaining labours, when they have been rescued by us from the errors and impediments of the road, and furnished with our defence and assistance. Moreover, that they should be strong in hope, and should not pretend or imagine that our instauration is an infinite work, surpassing human strength, since it is really an end and legitimate termination of infinite error, yet that they should still recollect the mortal lot of man, and not trust that the matter can be altogether perfected within the course of one age, but deliver it over to succeeding ages, and, finally, that they should not arrogantly search for the sciences in the narrow cells of human wit, but humbly in the greater world. That, however, which is empty is commonly vast, whilst solid matter is generally condensed, and lies in a small space. Lastly, we must require (lest any one should be disposed to injustice towards us in the very point on which our subject turns) that men would consider how far they imagine they can be permitted to comment and pass judgment on our work, after considering what it is necessary for us to claim for ourselves, if we would preserve any consistency, seeing we reject all human methods that are premature, anticipating, carelessly and too rapidly abstracted from things as regards the investigation of nature, considering them to be changeable, confused, and badly constructed; nor is it to be required that we should be judged by that which we ourselves arraign.

* Prov. xxv. 2.

THE DISTRIBUTION OF THE WORK.

IT CONSISTS OF SIX PARTS.

1. DIVISIONS OF THE SCIENCES.
2. NOVUM ORGANUM; OR, PRECEPTS FOR THE INTERPRETATION OF NATURE.
3. PHENOMENA OF THE UNIVERSE; OR, NATURAL AND EXPERIMENTAL HISTORY ON WHICH TO FOUND PHILOSOPHY.

4. SCALE OF THE UNDERSTANDING.
5. PRECURSORS OR ANTICIPATIONS OF THE SECOND PHILOSOPHY.
6. SOUND PHILOSOPHY, OR ACTIVE SCIENCE.

THE ARGUMENTS OF THE SEVERAL PARTS.

ONE point of our design is, that every thing should be set out as openly and clearly as possible. For this nakedness, as once that of the body, is the companion of innocence and simplicity. The order and method of the work, therefore, shall first be explained. We divide it into six parts. The first part exhibits a summary, or universal description of such science and learning as mankind is, up to this time, in possession of. For we have thought fit to dwell a little even on received notions, with a view the more easily to perfect the old, and approach the new; being nearly equally desirous to improve the former and to attain the latter. This is of avail also towards our obtaining credit: according to the text, "The unlearned receives not the words of knowledge, unless you first speak of what is within his own heart."* We will not, therefore, neglect coasting the shores of the now received arts and sciences, and importing thither something useful on our passage.

But we also employ such a division of the sciences as will not only embrace what is already discovered and known, but what has hitherto been omitted and deficient. For there are both cultivated and desert tracts in the intellectual as in the terrestrial globe. It must not, therefore, appear extraordinary if we sometimes depart from the common divisions. For additions, whilst they vary the whole, necessarily vary the parts, and their subdivisions, but the received divisions are only adequate to the received summary of the sciences, such as it now exists.

With regard to what we shall note as omitted, we shall not content ourselves with offering the mere names and concise proofs of what is deficient: for if we refer any thing to omissions, of a high nature, and the meaning of which may be rather obscure, (so that we may have grounds to suspect that men will not understand our intention, or the nature of the matter we have embraced

* Prov xviii. 2. "A fool hath no delight in understanding but that his hea t may discover itself." Bacon quotes from the Vulgate.

in our conception and contemplation,) we will always take care to subjoin to an instance of the whole, some precepts for perfecting it, or perhaps a completion of a part of it by ourselves. For, we consider it to concern our own character as well as the advantage of others, that no one may imagine a mere passing idea of such matters to have crossed our mind, and that what we desire and aim at resembles a wish; whilst in reality it is in the power of all men, if they be not wanting to themselves, and we ourselves are actually masters of a sure and clear method. For we have not undertaken to measure out regions in our mind, like augurs for divination, but like generals to invade them for conquest.—

And this is the first part of the work.

Having passed over the ancient arts, we will prepare the human understanding for pressing on beyond them. The object of the Second Part, then, is the doctrine touching a better and more perfect use of reasoning in the investigation of things, and the true helps of the understanding; that it may by this means be raised, as far as our human and mortal nature will admit, and be enlarged in its powers so as to master the arduous and obscure secrets of nature. And the art which we employ (and which we are wont to call the interpretation of nature) is a kind of logic. For common logic professes to contrive and prepare helps and guards for the understanding, and so far they agree. But ours differs from the common, chiefly in three respects, namely, in its end, the order of demonstration, and the beginning of the inquiry.

For the end of our science is not to discover arguments, but arts, nor what is agreeable to certain principles, but the principles themselves, nor probable reasons, but designations and indications of effects. Hence, from a diversity of intention follows a diversity of consequences. For, in in the one an opponent is vanquished and constrained by argument, in the other, nature by effects.

And the nature and order of the demonstrations agree with this end. For in common logic almost our whole labour is spent upon the syllogism

338

The logicians appear scarcely to have thought seriously of induction, passing it over with some slight notice, and hurrying on to the formulæ of dispute. But we reject the syllogistic demonstration, as being too confused, and letting nature escape from our hands. For, although nobody can doubt that those things which agree with the middle term agree with each other, (which is a sort of mathematical certainty,) nevertheless, there is this source of error, namely, that a syllogism consists of propositions, propositions of words, and words are but the tokens and signs of things. If, therefore, the notions of the mind (which are as it were the soul of words, and the basis of this whole structure and fabric) are badly and hastily abstracted from things, and vague, or not sufficiently defined and limited, or, in short, faulty (as they may be) in many other respects, the whole falls to the ground. We reject, therefore, the syllogism, and that not only as regards first principles, (to which even the logicians do not apply them,) but also in intermediate propositions, which the syllogism certainly manages in some way or other to bring out and produce, but then they are barren of effects, unfit for practice, and clearly unsuited to the active branch of the sciences. Although we would leave therefore to the syllogism, and such celebrated and applauded demonstrations, their jurisdiction over popular and speculative arts, (for here we make no alteration,) yet; in every thing relating to the nature of things, we make use of induction, both for our major and minor propositions. For we consider induction to be that form of demonstration which assists the senses, closes in upon nature, and presses on, and, as it were, mixes itself with action.

Hence also the order of demonstration is naturally reversed. For at present the matter is so managed, that from the senses and particular objects they immediately fly to the greatest generalities, as the axes round which their disputes may revolve : all the rest is deduced from them intermediately, by a short way we allow, but an abrupt one, and impassable to nature, though easy and well suited to dispute. But, by our method, axioms are raised up in gradual succession, so that we only at last arrive at generalities. And that which is most generalized, is not merely national but well defined, and really acknowledged by nature as well known to her, and cleaving to the very pith of things.

By far our greatest work, however, lies in the form of induction and the judgment arising from it. For the form of which the logicians speak, which proceeds by bare enumeration, is puerile, and its conclusions precarious, is exposed to danger from one contrary example, only considers what is habitual, and leads not to any final result.

The sciences, on the contrary, require a form of induction capable of explaining and separating experiments, and coming to a certain conclusion by a proper series of rejections and exclusions. If, however, the common judgment of the logicians has been so laborious, and has exercised such great wits, how much more must we labour in this which is drawn not only from the recesses of the mind, but the very entrails of nature.

Nor is this all, for we let down to a greater depth, and render more solid the very foundations of the sciences, and we take up the beginning of our investigation from a higher part than men have yet done, by subjecting those matters to examination which common logic receives upon the credit of others. For the logicians borrow the principles of one science from another, in the next place they worship the first formed notions of their minds, and, lastly, they rest contented with the immediate information of the senses, if well directed. But we have resolved that true logic ought to enter upon the several provinces of the sciences with a greater command than is possessed by their first principles, and to force those supposed principles to an account of the grounds upon which they are clearly determined. As far as relates to the first notions of the understanding, not any of the materials which the understanding, when left to itself, has collected, is unsuspected by us, nor will we confirm them unless they themselves be put upon their trial and be judged accordingly. Again, we have many ways of sifting the information of the senses themselves : for the senses assuredly deceive, though at the same time they disclose their errors : the errors, however, are close at hand, whilst their indication must be sought at a greater distance.

There are two faults of the senses : they either desert or deceive us. For in the first place there are many things which escape the senses, however well directed and unimpeded, owing either to the subtilty of the whole body, or the minuteness of its parts, or the distance of place, or the slowness or velocity of motion, or the familiarity of the object, or to other causes. Nor are the apprehensions of the senses very firm, when they grasp the subject; for the testimony and information of the senses bears always a relation to man and not to the universe, and it is altogether a great mistake to assert that our senses are the measure of things.

To encounter these difficulties, we have everywhere sought and collected helps for the senses with laborious and faithful service, in order to supply defects and correct errors : and that not so much by means of instruments, as by experiments. For experiments are much more delicate than the senses themselves, even when aided by instruments, at least if they are skilfully and scientifically imagined and applied to the required point. We attribute but little, therefore, to the immediate and proper perception of the senses.

but reduce the matter to this, that *they* should decide on the experiment, and the experiment on the subject of it. Wherefore, we consider that we have shown ourselves most observant priests of the senses, (by which all that exists in nature must be investigated if we would be rational,) and not unskilful interpreters of their oracles: for others seem to observe and worship them in word alone, but we in deed. These then are the means which we prepare for kindling and transmitting the light of nature: which would of themselves be sufficient, if the human understanding were plain and like a smoothed surface. But since the minds of men are so wonderfully prepossessed, that a clear and polished surface for receiving the true rays of things is wholly wanting, necessity urges us to seek a remedy for this also.

The images or idols by which the mind is preoccupied are either adventitious or innate. The adventitious have crept into the minds of men either from the dogmas and sects of philosophers, or the perverted rules of demonstration. But the innate are inherent to the very nature of the understanding, which appears to be much more prone to error than the senses. For however men may be satisfied with themselves, and rush into a blind admiration and almost adoration of the human mind, one thing is most certain, namely, that as an uneven mirror changes the rays proceeding from objects according to its own figure and position, so the mind when affected by things through the senses does not act in the most trustworthy manner, but inserts and mixes her own nature into that of things, whilst clearing and recollecting her notions.

The first two species of idols are *with difficulty* eradicated, the latter can never be so. We can only point them out, and note and demonstrate that insidious faculty of the mind, lest new shoots of error should happen to spring up, from the destruction of the old, on account of the mind's defective structure; and we should then find ourselves only exchanging instead of extinguishing errors; whilst it ought on the other hand to be eternally resolved and settled, that the understanding cannot decide otherwise than by induction and by a legitimate form of it. Wherefore the doctrine of the purifying of the understanding, so as to fit it for the reception of truth, consists of three reprehensions; the reprehension of the schemes of philosophy, the reprehension of methods of demonstration, and the reprehension of natural human reason. But when these have been gone through, and it has at last been clearly seen, what results are to be expected from the nature of things and the nature of the mind, we consider that we shall have prepared and adorned a nuptial couch for the mind and the universe; the divine goodness being our bridemaid. But let the prayer of our epithalamium be this; that from this union may spring assistance to man,

and a race of such discoveries as will in some measure overcome his wants and necessities.—

And this is the second part of the work.

It is our intention not only to open and prepare the way, but also to enter upon it. The third part, therefore, of our work embraces the phenomena of the universe; that is to say, experience of every kind, and such a natural history as can form the foundation of an edifice of philosophy. For there is no method of demonstration, or form of interpreting nature, so excellent as to be able to afford and supply *matter* for knowledge, as well as to defend and support the mind against error and failure. But those who resolve not to conjecture and divine, but to discover and know, not to invent buffooneries and fables about worlds, but to inspect, and, as it were, dissect the nature of this real world, must derive all from things themselves. Nor can any substitution or compensation of wit, meditation, or argument, (were the whole wit of all combined in one,) supply the place of this labour, investigation, and personal examination of the world; our method then must necessarily be pursued, or the whole forever abandoned. But men have so conducted themselves hitherto, that it is little to be wondered at if nature do not disclose herself to them.

For in the first place the defective and fallacious evidence of our senses, a system of observation slothful and unsteady, as though acting from chance, a tradition vain and depending on common report, a course of practice intent upon effects, and servile, blind, dull, vague, and abrupt experiments, and lastly our careless and meagre natural history, have collected together, for the use of the understanding, the most defective materials as regards philosophy and the sciences.

In the next place, a preposterous refinement, and, as it were, ventilation of argument, is attempted as a late remedy for a matter become clearly desperate, and neither makes any improvement, nor removes errors. There remains no hope therefore of greater advancement and progress, unless by some restoration of the sciences.

But this must commence entirely with natural history. For it is useless to clean the mirror if it have no images to reflect, and it is manifest that we must prepare proper matter for the understanding as well as steady support. But our history, like our logic, differs in many respects, from the received, in its end or office, in its very matter and compilation, in its nicety, in its selection, and in its arrangements relatively to what follows.

For, in the first place, we begin with that species of natural history which is not so much calculated to amuse by the variety of its objects, or to offer immediate results by its experiments, as to throw a light upon the discovery of causes, and to present, as it were, its bosom as the first nurse of philosophy. For, although we regard principally effects and the active division of the sciences, yet we wait for the time of harvest, and do not go about to reap moss and a green crop : being sufficiently aware that well formed axioms draw whole crowds of effects after them, and do not manifest their effects partially, but in abundance. But we wholly condemn and banish that unreasonable and puerile desire of immediately seizing some pledges as it were of new effects, which, like the apple of Atalanta, retard our course—such then is the office of our natural history.

With regard to its compilation, we intend not to form a history of nature at liberty and in her usual course, when she proceeds willingly and acts of her own accord, (as for instance the history of the heavenly bodies, meteors, the earth and sea, minerals, plants, animals,) but much rather a history of nature constrained and perplexed, as she is seen when thrust down from her proper rank and harassed and modelled by the art and contrivance of man. We will therefore go through all the experiments of the mechanical and the operative part of the liberal arts, and all those of different practical schemes which have not yet been put together so as to form a peculiar art: as far as we have been able to investigate them and it will suit our purpose. Besides, (to speak the truth,) without paying any attention to the pride of man, or to appearances, we consider this branch of much more assistance and support than the other: since the nature of things betrays itself more by means of the operations of art than when at perfect liberty.

Nor do we present the history of bodies alone, but have thought it moreover right to exert our diligence in compiling a separate history of properties : we mean those which may be called the cardinal properties of nature, and of which its very elements are composed, namely, matter with its first accidents and appetites, such as density, rarity, heat, cold, solidity, fluidity, weight, levity, and many others.

But, with regard to the nicety of natural history, we clearly require a much more delicate and simple form of experiments than those which are obvious. For we bring out and extract from obscurity many things which no one would have thought of investigating, unless he were proceeding by a sure and steady path to the discovery of causes ; since they are in themselves of no great use, and it is clear that they were not sought for on their own account, but that they bear the same relation to things and effects, that the letters of the alphabet do to discourse and words, being useless indeed in themselves, but the elements of all language.

In the selection of our reports and experiments, we consider that we have been more cautious for mankind than any of our predecessors. For we admit nothing but as an eyewitness, or at least upon approved and rigorously examined testimony ; so that nothing is magnified into the miraculous, but our reports are pure and unadulterated by fables and absurdity. Nay, the commonly received and repeated falsehoods, which by some wonderful neglect have held their ground for many ages and become inveterate, are by us distinctly proscribed and branded, that they may no longer molest learning. For, as it has been well observed, that the tales, superstitions, and trash which nurses instil into children, seriously corrupt their minds, so are we careful and anxious whilst managing and watching over the infancy, as it were, of philosophy committed to the charge of natural history, that it should not from the first become habituated to any absurdity. In every new and rather delicate experiment, although to us it may appear sure and satisfactory, we yet publish the method we employed, that, by the discovery of every attendant circumstance, men may perceive the possibly latent and inherent errors, and be roused to proofs of a more certain and exact nature, if such there be. Lastly, we intersperse the whole with advice, doubts, and cautions, casting out and restraining, as it were, all phantoms by a sacred ceremony and exorcism.

Finally, since we have learned how much experience and history distract the powers of the human mind, and how difficult it is (especially for young or prejudiced intellects) to become at the first acquainted with nature, we frequently add some observations of our own, by way of showing the first tendency, as it were, and inclination or aspect of history towards philosophy ; thus assuring mankind that they will not always be detained in the ocean of history, and also preparing for the time when we shall come to the work of the understanding. And by such a natural history as we are describing, we think that safe and convenient access is opened to nature, and solid and ready matter furnished to the understanding.

But after furnishing the understanding with the most surest helps and precautions, and having completed, by a rigorous levy, a complete host of divine works, nothing remains to be done but to attack Philosophy herself. In a matter so arduous and doubtful, however, a few reflections must necessarily be here inserted, partly for instruction and partly for present use.

The first of these is, that we should offer some examples of our method and course of investigation and discovery, as exhibited in particular subjects ; preferring the most dignified subjects of our inquiry, and such as differ the most from each other, so that in every branch we may have an example. Nor do we speak of those examples, which are added to particular precepts and rules by way of illustration, (for we have furnished them abundantly in the second part of our work,) but we mean actual types and models, calculated to place, as it were, before our eyes the whole process of the mind, and the continuous frame and order of discovery in particular subjects, selected for their variety and importance. For we recollected that in mathematics, with the diagram before our eyes, the demonstration easily and clearly followed, but without this advantage every thing appeared intricate and more subtile than was really the case. We devote, therefore, the FOURTH PART of our work to such examples, which is in fact nothing more than a particular and fully developed application of the second part.

But the FIFTH PART is only used for a temporary purpose, whilst the rest are being perfected, and is paid down as interest, until the principal can be raised. For we rush not so blindly to our object, as to neglect any thing useful on our way. We compose this fifth part of the work therefore of those matters which we have either discovered, tried, or added; without, however, employing our own method and rules for interpretation, but merely making the same use of our understanding as others are wont to do in their investigations and discoveries. For, from our constant intercourse with nature, we both anticipate greater results from our meditations than the mere strength of our wit would warrant; and yet such results as have been mentioned may also serve as inns upon the road for the mind to repose itself a while on its way to more certain objects. We protest, in the mean time, against any great value being set upon that which has not been discovered or proved by the true form of interpretation. There is no reason, however, for any one to be alarmed at such suspense of judgment in our method of teaching, which does not assert absolutely that nothing can be known, but that nothing can be known without a determined order and method; and in the mean time has settled some determined gradations of certitude, until the mind can repose in the full developement of causes. Nor were those schools of philosophers, who professed absolute skepticism, inferior to the others which took upon themselves to dogmatise. They did not, however, prepare helps for the senses and understanding, as we have done, but at once abolished all belief and authority, which is totally different, nay, almost opposite matter.

Lastly, the SIXTH PART of our work (to which the rest are subservient and auxiliary) discloses and propounds that philosophy which is reared and formed by the legitimate, pure, and strict method of investigation previously taught and prepared. But it is both beyond our power and expectation to perfect and conclude this last part. We will, however, furnish no contemptible beginning, (if our hopes deceive us not,) and men's good fortune will furnish the result; such, perhaps, as men cannot easily comprehend or define in the present state of things and the mind. For we treat not only of contemplative enjoyment, but of the common affairs and fortune of mankind, and of a complete power of action. For man, as the minister and interpreter of nature does, and understands, as much as he has observed of the order, operation, and mind of nature; and neither knows nor is able to do more. Neither is it possible for any power to loosen or burst the chain of causes, nor is nature to be overcome except by submission. Therefore those two objects, human knowledge and power, are really the same; and failure in action chiefly arises from the ignorance of causes. For every thing depends upon our fixing the mind's eye steadily in order to receive their images exactly as they exist, and may God never permit us to give out the dream of our fancy as a model of the world, but rather in his kindness vouchsafe to us the means of writing a revelation and true vision of the traces and stamps of the Creator on his creatures.

May thou, therefore, O Father, who gavest the light of vision as the first-fruits of creation, and hast inspired the countenance of man with the light of the understanding as the completion of thy works, guard and direct this work, which, proceeding from thy bounty, seeks in return thy glory. When thou turnedst to look upon the works of thy hands, thou sawest that all were very good, and restedst. But man, when he turned towards the works of his hands, saw that they were all vanity and vexation of spirit, and had no rest. Wherefore, if we labour in thy works, thou wilt make us partakers of that which thou beholdest and of thy rest. We humbly pray that our present disposition may continue firm, and that thou mayest be willing to endow thy family of mankind with new gifts through our hands, and the hands of those to whom thou wilt accord the same disposition.

The First Part of the Instauration, which comprehends the Divisions of the Sciences, is wanting. But they can be partly taken from the Second Book, "On the Progress to be made in Divine and Human Learning."

Next followeth the Second Part of the Instauration, which exhibits the Art of interpreting Nature and of making a right Use of the Understanding; not, however, imbodied in a regular Treatise, but only summarily digested in Aphorisms.

THE SECOND PART OF THE WORK WHICH IS CALLED

NOVUM ORGANUM;

OR,

TRUE SUGGESTIONS FOR THE INTERPRETATION OF NATURE.

PREFACE.

They who have presumed to dogmatize on Nature, as on some well-investigated subject, either from self-conceit or arrogance, and in the professorial style, have inflicted the greatest injury on philosophy and learning. For they have tended to stifle and interrupt inquiry exactly in proportion as they have prevailed in bringing others to their opinion: and their own activity has not counterbalanced the mischief they have occasioned by corrupting and destroying that of others. They again who have entered upon a contrary course, and asserted that nothing whatever can be known, whether they have fallen into this opinion from their hatred of the ancient sophists, or from the hesitation of their minds, or from an exuberance of learning, have certainly adduced reasons for it which are by no means contemptible. They have not, however, derived their opinion from true sources, and, hurried on by their zeal, and some affectation, have certainly exceeded due moderation. But the more ancient Greeks (whose writings have perished) held a more prudent mean, between the arrogance of dogmatism, and the despair of skepticism; and though too frequently intermingling complaints and indignation at the difficulty of inquiry, and the obscurity of things, and champing, as it were, the bit, have still persisted in pressing their point, and pursuing their intercourse with nature: thinking, as it seems, that the better method was not to dispute upon the very point of the possibility of any thing being known, but to put it to the test of experience. Yet they themselves, by only employing the power of the understanding, have not adopted a fixed rule, but have laid their whole stress upon intense meditation, and a continual exercise and perpetual agitation of the mind.

Our method, though difficult in its operation, is easily explained. It consists in determining the degrees of certainty, whilst we, as it were, restore the senses to their former rank, but generally reject that operation of the mind which follows close upon the senses, and open and establish a new and certain course for the mind from the first actual perceptions of the senses themselves. This no doubt was the view taken by those who have assigned so much to logic; showing clearly thereby that they sought some support for the mind, and suspected its natural and spontaneous mode of action. But this is now employed too late as a remedy, when all is clearly lost, and after the mind, by the daily habit and intercourse of life, has become prepossessed with corrupted doctrines, and filled with the vainest idols. The art of logic therefore being (as we have mentioned) too late a precaution, and in no way remedying the matter, has tended more to confirm errors, than to disclose truth. Our only remaining hope and salvation is to begin the whole labour of the mind again; not leaving it to itself, but directing it perpetually from the very first, and attaining our end as it were by mechanical aid. If men, for instance, had attempted mechanical labours with their hands alone, and without the power and aid of instruments, as they have not hesitated to carry on the labours of their understanding with the unaided efforts of their mind, they would have been able to move and overcome but little, though they had exerted their utmost and united powers. And, just to pause a while on this comparison, and look into it as a mirror; let us ask, if any obelisk of a remarkable size were perchance required to be moved, for the purpose of gracing a triumph or any similar pageant, and men were to attempt it with their bare hands, would not any sober spectator avow it to be an act of the greatest madness? And if they should increase the number of workmen, and imagine that they could thus succeed, would he not think so still more? But if they chose to make a selection, and to remove the weak, and only employ the strong and vigorous, thinking by this means, at any rate, to achieve their object, would he not say that they were more fondly deranged? Nay, if, not content with this, they were to determine on consulting the athletic art, and were to give orders for all to appear with their hands, arms, and muscles regularly oiled and prepared, would he not exclaim that they were taking pains to rave by method and design? Yet men are hurried on with the same senseless energy and useless combination in intellectual matters, so long as they expect great results either from the number and agreement, or the excellence and acuteness of their wits; or even strengthen their minds with logic, which may be considered as an athletic prepara- tion, but yet do not desist (if we rightly consider the matter) from applying their own understandings merely with all this zeal and effort. Whilst nothing is more clear, than that in every great work executed by the hand of man without machines or implements, it is impossible for the strength of individuals to be increased, or for that of the multitude to combine.

Having premised so much, we lay down two points on which we would admonish mankind, lest they should fail to see or to observe them. The first of these is: that it is our good fortune, (as we consider it,) for the sake of extinguishing and removing contradiction and irritation of mind, to leave the honour and reverence due to the ancients untouched and undiminished, so that we can perform our intended work, and yet enjoy the benefit of our respectful moderation. For if we should profess to offer something better than the ancients, and yet should pursue the same course as they have done, we could never, by any artifice, contrive to avoid the imputation of having engaged in a contest or rivalry as to our respective wits, excellences, or talents; which, though neither inadmissible or new, (for why should we not blame and point out any thing that is imperfectly discovered or laid down by them, of our own right, a right common to all,) yet, however just and allowable, would perhaps he scarcely an equal match, on account of the disproportion of our strength. But, since our present plan leads us to open an entirely different course to the understanding, and one unattempted and unknown to them, the case is altered. There is an end to party zeal, and we only take upon our- selves the character of a guide, which requires a moderate share of authority and good fortune, rather than talents and excellence. This first admonition relates to persons, the next to things.

We make no attempt to disturb the system of philosophy that now prevails, or any other which may or will exist, either more correct or more complete. For we deny not that the received system of philosophy, and others of a similar nature, encourage discussion, embellish harangues, are em- ployed and are of service in the duties of the professor, and the affairs of civil life. Nay, we openly express and declare that the philosophy we offer will not be very useful in such respects. It is not obvious, nor to be understood in a cursory view, nor does it flatter the mind in its preconceived notions, nor will it descend to the level of the generality of mankind, unless by its advantages and effects.

Let there exist then (and may it be of advantage to both) two sources, and two distributions of learning, and in like manner two tribes, and as it were kindred families of contemplators or philoso- phers, without any hostility or alienation between them; but rather allied and united by mutual assistance. Let there be, in short, one method of cultivating the sciences, and another of discovering them. And as for those who prefer and more readily receive the former, on account of their haste, or from motives arising from their ordinary life, or because they are unable from weakness of mind to comprehend and embrace the other, (which must necessarily be the case with by far the greater number,) let us wish that they may prosper as they desire in their undertaking, and attain what they pursue. But if any individual desire and is anxious not merely to adhere to and make use of present discoveries, but to penetrate still further, and not to overcome his adversaries in disputes, but nature by labour, not, in short, to give elegant and specious opinions, but to *know* to a certainty and demonstration, let him, as a true son of science, (if such be his wish,) join with us; that when he has left the antechambers of nature trodden by the multitude, an entrance at last may be dis- covered to her inner apartments. And, in order to be better understood, and to render our meaning more familiar by assigning determinate names, we have accustomed ourselves to call the one method the anticipation of the mind, and the other the interpretation of nature.

We have still one request left. We have at least reflected and taken pains in order to render our propositions not only true, but of easy and familiar access to men's minds, however wonderfully prepossessed and limited. Yet it is but just that we should obtain this favour from mankind, (espe- cially in so great a restoration of learning and the sciences,) that whosoever may be desirous of forming any determination upon an opinion of this our work, either from his own perceptions, or the crowd of authorities, or the forms of demonstrations, he will not expect to be able to do so in a cursory manner, and whilst attending to other matters; but in order to have a thorough knowledge of the subject, will himself by degrees attempt the course which we describe and maintain; will become accustomed to the subtilty of things which is manifested by experience; and will correct the depraved and deeply rooted habits of his mind by a seasonable and as it were just hesitation : and then finally (if he will) use his judgment when he has begun to be master of himself.

SUMMARY OF THE SECOND PART,

DIGESTED IN APHORISMS.

APHORISMS ON THE INTERPRETATION OF NATURE AND THE EMPIRE OF MAN.

1. MAN, as the minister and interpreter of nature, does and understands as much as his observations on the order of nature, either with regard to things or the mind, permit him, and neither knows nor is capable of more.

2. The unassisted hand, and the understanding left to itself, possess but little power. Effects are produced by the means of instruments and helps, which the understanding requires no less than the hand. And as instruments either promote or regulate the motion of the hand, so those that are applied to the mind prompt or protect the understanding.

3. Knowledge and human power are synonymous, since the ignorance of the cause frustrates the effect. For nature is only subdued by submission, and that which in contemplative philosophy corresponds with the cause, in practical science becomes the *rule*.

4. Man, whilst operating, can only apply or withdraw natural bodies; nature, internally, performs the rest.

5. Those who become practically versed in nature, are the mechanic, the mathematician, the physician, the alchymist, and the magician; but all (as matters now stand) with faint efforts and meagre success.

6. It would be madness, and inconsistency, to suppose that things which have never yet been performed, can be performed without employing some hitherto untried means.

7. The creations of the mind and hand appear very numerous, if we judge by books and manufactures: but all that variety consists of an excessive refinement, and of deductions from a few well known matters; not of a number of axioms.

8. Even the effects already discovered are due to chance and experiment, rather than to the sciences. For our present sciences are nothing more than peculiar arrangements of matters already discovered, and not methods for discovery, or plans for new operations.

9. The sole cause and root of almost every defect in the sciences is this; that whilst we falsely admire and extol the powers of the human mind, we do not search for its real helps.

10. The subtilty of nature is far beyond that of sense or of the understanding: so that the specious meditations, speculations, and theories of mankind, are but a kind of insanity, only there is no one to stand by and observe it.

11. As the present sciences are useless for the discovery of effects, so the present system of logic is useless for the discovery of the sciences.

12. The present system of logic rather assists in confirming and rendering inveterate the errors founded on vulgar notions, than in searching after truth; and is therefore more hurtful than useful.

13. The syllogism is not applied to the principles of the sciences, and is of no avail in intermediate axioms, as being very unequal to the subtilty of nature. It forces assent, therefore, and not things.

14. The syllogism consists of propositions, propositions of words, words are the signs of notions. If, therefore, the notions (which form the basis of the whole) be confused and carelessly abstracted from things, there is no solidity in the superstructure. Our only hope, then, is in genuine induction.

15. We have no sound notions either in logic or physics; substance, quality, action, passion, and existence are not clear notions; much less, weight, levity, density, tenuity, moisture, dryness, generation, corruption, attraction, repulsion, element, matter, form, and the like. They are all fantastical and ill defined.

16. The notions of less abstract natures, as man, dog, dove; and the immediate perceptions of sense, as heat, cold, white, black, do not deceive us materially, yet even these are sometimes confused by the mutability of matter and the intermixture of things. All the rest, which men have hitherto employed, are errors; and improperly abstracted and deduced from things.

17. There is the same degree of licentiousness and error in forming axioms, as in abstracting notions: and that in the first principles, which depend on common induction. Still more is this the case in axioms and inferior propositions derived from syllogisms.

18. The present discoveries in science are such as lie immediately beneath the surface of common notions. It is necessary, however, to penetrate

the more secret and remote parts of nature, in order to abstract both notions and axioms from things, by a more certain and guarded method.

19. There are and can exist but two ways of investigating and discovering truth. The one hurries on rapidly from the senses and particulars to the most general axioms; and from them as principles and their supposed indisputable truth derives and discovers the intermediate axioms. This is the way now in use. The other constructs its axioms from the senses and particulars, by ascending continually and gradually, till it finally arrives at the most general axioms, which is the true but unattempted way.

20. The understanding when left to itself proceeds by the same way as that which it would have adopted under the guidance of logic, namely, the first. For the mind is fond of starting off to generalities, that it may avoid labour, and after dwelling a little on a subject is fatigued by experiment. But these evils are augmented by logic, for the sake of the ostentation of dispute.

21. The understanding when left to itself in a man of a steady, patient, and reflecting disposition, (especially when unimpeded by received doctrines,) makes some attempt in the right way, but with little effect; since the understanding, undirected and unassisted, is unequal to and unfit for the task of vanquishing the obscurity of things.

22. Each of these two ways begins from the senses and particulars, and ends in the greatest generalities. But they are immeasurably different; for the one merely touches cursorily the limits of experiment, and particulars, whilst the other runs duly and regularly through them; the one from the very outset lays down some abstract and useless generalities, the other gradually rises to those principles which are really the most common in nature.

23. There is no small difference between the *idols* of the human mind, and the *ideas* of the divine mind; that is to say, between certain idle dogmas, and the real stamp and impression of created objects, as they are found in nature.

24. Axioms determined upon in argument can never assist in the discovery of new effects: for the subtilty of nature is vastly superior to that of argument. But axioms properly and regularly abstracted from particulars, easily point out and define new particulars, and therefore impart activity to the sciences.

25. The axioms now in use are derived from a scanty handful, as it were, of experience, and a few particulars of frequent occurrence, whence they are of much the same dimensions or extent as their origin. And if any neglected or unknown instance occurs, the axiom is saved by some frivolous distinction, when it would be more consistent with truth to amend it.

26. We are wont, for the sake of distinction,

to call that human reasoning which we apply to nature, the anticipation of nature, (as being rash and premature;) and that which is properly deduced from things, the interpretation of nature.

27. Anticipations are sufficiently powerful in producing unanimity, for if men were all to become even uniformly mad, they might agree tolerably well with each other.

28. Anticipations again will be assented to much more readily than interpretations; because, being deduced from a few instances, and these principally of familiar occurrence, they immediately hit the understanding, and satisfy the imagination; whilst, on the contrary, interpretations, being deduced from various subjects, and these widely dispersed, cannot suddenly strike the understanding; so that, in common estimation, they must appear difficult and discordant, and almost like the mysteries of faith.

29. In sciences founded on opinions and dogmas, it is right to make use of anticipations and logic, if you wish to force assent rather than things.

30. If all the capacities of all ages should unite and combine and transmit their labours, no great progress will be made in learning by anticipations; because the radical errors, and those which occur in the first process of the mind, are not cured by the excellence of subsequent means and remedies.

31. It is in vain to expect any great progress in the sciences by the superinducing or engrafting new matters upon old. An instauration must be made from the very foundations, if we do not wish to revolve forever in a circle, making only some slight and contemptible progress.

32. The ancient authors, and all others, are left in undisputed possession of their honours. For we enter into no comparison of capacity or talent, but of method; and assume the part of a guide, rather than of a critic.

33. To speak plainly, no correct judgment can be formed, either of our method, or its discoveries, by those anticipations which are now in common use; for it is not to be required of us to submit ourselves to the judgment of the very method we ourselves arraign.

34. Nor is it an easy matter to deliver and explain our sentiments: for those things which are in themselves new can yet be only understood from some analogy to what is old.

35. Alexander Borgia said of the expedition of the French into Italy, that they came with chalk in their hands to mark up their lodgings, and not with weapons to force their passage. Even so do we wish our philosophy to make its way quietly into those minds that are fit for it, and of good capacity. For we have no need of contention where we differ in first principles, and our very notions, and even in our forms of demonstration.

36. We have but one simple method of deliver

ing our sentiments: namely, we must bring men to particulars, and their regular series and order, and they must for a while renounce their notions and begin to form an acquaintance with things.

37. Our method and that of the skeptics agree in some respects at first setting out: but differ most widely and are completely opposed to each other in their conclusion. For they roundly assert that nothing can be known; we, that but a small part of nature can be known by the present method. Their next step, however, is to destroy the authority of the senses and understanding, whilst we invent and supply them with assistance.

38. The idols and false notions which have already preoccupied the human understanding, and are deeply rooted in it, not only to beset men's minds, that they become difficult of access, but, even when access is obtained, will again meet and trouble us in the instauration of the sciences, unless mankind, when forewarned, guard themselves with all possible care against them.

39. Four species of idols beset the human mind: to which (for distinction's sake) we have assigned names: calling the first idols of the tribe; the second idols of the den; the third idols of the market; the fourth idols of the theatre.

40. The formation of notions and axioms on the foundation of true induction, is the only fitting remedy, by which we can ward off and expel these idols. It is, however, of great service to point them out. For the doctrine of idols bears the same relation to the interpretation of nature, as that of confutation of sophisms does to common logic.

41. The idols of the tribe are inherent in human nature, and the very tribe or race of man. For man's sense is falsely asserted to be the standard of things. On the contrary, all the perceptions, both of the senses and the mind, bear reference to man, and not to the universe, and the human mind resembles those uneven mirrors, which impart their own properties to different objects, from which rays are emitted, and distort and disfigure them.

42. The idols of the den are those of each individual. For everybody (in addition to the errors common to the race of man) has his own individual den or cavern, which intercepts and corrupts the light of nature; either from his own peculiar and singular disposition, or from his education and intercourse with others, or from his reading, and the authority acquired by those whom he reverences and admires, or from the different impressions produced on the mind, as it happens to be preoccupied and predisposed, or equable and tranquil, and the like: so that the spirit of man (according to its several dispositions) is variable, confused, and as it were ac-

tuated by chance; and Heraclitus said well that men search for knowledge in lesser worlds, and not in the greater or common world.

43. There are also idols formed by the reciprocal intercourse and society of man with man, which we call idols of the market, from the commerce and association of men with each other. For men converse by means of language; but words are formed at the will of the generality; and there arises from a bad and unapt formation of words a wonderful obstruction to the mind. Nor can the definitions and explanations, with which learned men are wont to guard and protect themselves in some instances, afford a complete remedy: words still manifestly force the understanding, throw every thing into confusion, and lead mankind into vain and innumerable controversies and fallacies.

44. Lastly, there are idols which have crept into men's minds from the various dogmas of peculiar systems of philosophy, and also from the perverted rules of demonstration, and these we denominate idols of the theatre. For we regard all the systems of philosophy hitherto received or imagined, as so many plays brought out and performed, creating fictitious and theatrical worlds. Nor do we speak only of the present systems, or of the philosophy and sects of the ancients, since numerous other plays of a similar nature can be still composed and made to agree with each other, the causes of the most opposite errors being generally the same. Nor, again, do we allude merely to general systems, but also to many elements and axioms of sciences, which have become inveterate by tradition, implicit credence, and neglect. We must, however, discuss each species of idols more fully and distinctly, in order to guard the human understanding against them.

45.* The human understanding, from its peculiar nature, easily supposes a greater degree of order and equality in things than it really finds; and although many things in nature be sui generis, and most irregular, will yet invent parallels and conjugates, and relatives, where no such thing is. Hence the fiction, that all celestial bodies were in perfect circles, thus rejecting entirely spiral and serpentine lines, (except as explanatory terms.) Hence, also, the element of fire is introduced with its peculiar orbit, to keep square with those other three which are objects of our senses. The relative rarity of the elements (as they are called) is arbitrarily made to vary in tenfold progression, with many other dreams of the like nature. Nor is this folly confined to theories, but it is to be met with even in simple notions.

46. The human understanding, when any proposition has been once laid down, (either from general admission and belief, or from the pleasure

* Hence to Aphorism 53 treats of the Idols of the tribe

it affords,) forces every thing else to add fresh support and confirmation; and although more cogent and abundant instances may exist to the contrary, yet either does not observe or despises them, or gets rid of and rejects them by some distinction, with violent and injurious prejudice, rather than sacrifice the authority of its first conclusions. It was well answered by him who was shown in a temple the votive tablets suspended by such as had escaped the peril of shipwreck, and was pressed as to whether he would then recognise the power of the gods, by an inquiry: "But where are the portraits of those who have perished in spite of their vows?" All superstition is much the same, whether it be that of astrology, dreams, omens, retributive judgment, or the like; in all of which the deluded believers observe events which are fulfilled, but neglect and pass over their failure, though it be much more common. But this evil insinuates itself still more craftily in philosophy and the sciences; in which a settled maxim vitiates and governs every other circumstance, though the latter be much more worthy of confidence. Besides, even in the absence of that eagerness and want of thought, (which we have mentioned,) it is the peculiar and perpetual error of the human understanding to be more moved and excited by affirmatives than by negatives, whereas it ought duly and regularly to be impartial; nay, in establishing any true axiom, the negative instance is the most powerful.

47. The human understanding is most excited by that which strikes and enters the mind at once and suddenly, and by which the imagination is immediately filled and inflated. It then begins almost imperceptibly to conceive and suppose that every thing is similar to the few objects which have taken possession of the mind; whilst it is very slow and unfit for the transition to the remote and heterogeneous instances, by which axioms are tried as by fire, unless the office be imposed upon it by severe regulations, and a powerful authority.

48. The human understanding is active and cannot halt or rest, but even, though without effect, still presses forward. Thus we cannot conceive of any end or external boundary of the world, and it seems necessarily to occur to us, that there must be something beyond. Nor can we imagine how eternity has flowed on down to the present day, since the usually received distinction of an infinity, *a parte ante* and *a parte post*, cannot hold good: for it would thence follow that one infinity is greater than another, and also that infinity is wasting away and tending to an end. There is the same difficulty in considering the infinite divisibility of lines, arising from the weakness of our minds, which weakness interferes to still greater disadvantage with the discovery of causes. For, although the greatest generalities in nature must be positive, just as they are found, and in fact not *causable*, yet, the human understanding, incapable of resting, seeks for something more intelligible. Thus, however, whilst aiming at further progress, it falls back to what is actually less advanced, namely, final causes; for they are clearly more allied to man's own nature than the system of the universe; and from this source they have wonderfully corrupted philosophy. But he would be an unskilful and shallow philosopher, who should seek for causes in the greatest generalities, and not be anxious to discover them in subordinate objects.

49. The human understanding resembles not a *dry light*, but admits a tincture of the will and passions, which generate their own system accordingly: for man always believes more readily that which he prefers. He, therefore, rejects difficulties for want of patience in investigation; sobriety, because it limits his hope; the depths of nature, from superstition; the light of experiment, from arrogance and pride, lest his mind should appear to be occupied with common and varying objects; paradoxes, from a fear of the opinion of the vulgar; in short, his feelings imbue and corrupt his understanding in innumerable and sometimes imperceptible ways.

50. But by far the greatest impediment and aberration of the human understanding proceeds from the dulness, incompetency, and errors of the senses: since whatever strikes the senses preponderates over every thing, however superior, which does not immediately strike them. Hence contemplation mostly ceases with sight; and a very scanty, or perhaps no regard is paid to invisible objects. The entire operation, therefore, of spirits enclosed in tangible bodies is concealed and escapes us. All that more delicate change of formation in the parts of coarser substances (vulgarly called alteration, but in fact a change of position in the smallest particles) is equally unknown; and yet, unless the two matters we have mentioned be explored and brought to light, no great effect can be produced in nature. Again, the very nature of common air, and all bodies of less density (of which there are many) is almost unknown. For the senses are weak and erring, nor can instruments be of great use in extending their sphere or acuteness; all the better interpretations of nature are worked out by instances, and fit and apt experiments, where the senses only judge of the experiment, the experiment of nature and the thing itself.

51. The human understanding is, by its own nature, prone to abstraction, and supposes that which is fluctuating to be fixed. But it is better to dissect than abstract nature; such was the method employed by the school of Democritus, which made greater progress in penetrating nature than the rest. It is best to consider matter, its

onformation, and the changes of that conforma-ion, its own action, and the law of this action or motion, for forms are a mere fiction of the human mind, unless you will call *the laws of action* by that name. Such are the idols of the tribe, which arise either from the uniformity of the constitution of man's spirit, or its prejudices, or its limited faculties, or restless agitation, or from the interference of the passions, or the incompetency of the senses, or the mode of their impressions.

53. The idols* of the den derive their origin from the peculiar nature of each individual's mind and body ; and also from education, habit, and accident. And although they be various and manifold, yet we will treat of some that require the greatest caution, and exert the greatest power in polluting the understanding.

54. Some men become attached to particular sciences and contemplations, either from supposing themselves the authors and inventors of them, or from having bestowed the greatest pains upon such subjects, and thus become most habituated to them. If men of this description apply themselves to philosophy and contemplations of an universal nature, they wrest and corrupt them by their preconceived fancies ; of which Aristotle affords us a signal instance, who made his natural philosophy completely subservient to his logic, and thus rendered it little more than useless and disputatious. The chymists, again, have formed a fanciful philosophy with the most confined views, from a few experiments of the furnace. Gilbert, too, having employed himself most assiduously in the consideration of the magnet, immediately established a system of philosophy to coincide with his favourite pursuit.

55. The greatest, and, perhaps, radical distinction between different men's dispositions for philosophy and the sciences is this ; that some are more vigorous and active in observing the differences of things, others in observing their resemblances. For a steady and acute disposition can fix its thoughts, and dwell upon, and adhere to a point, through all the refinements of differences ; but those that are sublime and discursive recognise and compare even the most delicate and general resemblances. Each of them readily falls into excess, by catching either at nice distinctions or shadows of resemblance.

56. Some dispositions evince an unbounded admiration of antiquity, others eagerly embrace novelty ; and but few can preserve the just medium, so as neither to tear up what the ancients have correctly laid down, nor to despise the just innovations of the moderns. But this is very prejudicial to the sciences and philosophy, and, instead of a correct judgment, we have but the factions of the ancients and moderns. Truth is not to be sought in the good fortune of any parti-

cular conjuncture of time, which is uncertain, but in the light of nature and experience, which is eternal. Such factions, therefore, are to be abjured, and the understanding must not allow them to hurry it on to assent.

57. The contemplation of nature and of bodies in their individual form distracts and weakens the understanding : but the contemplation of nature and of bodies in their general composition and formation stupifies and relaxes it. We have a good instance of this in the school of Leucippus and Democritus compared with others : for they applied themselves so much to particulars as almost to neglect the general structure of things, whilst the others were so astounded whilst gazing on the structure, that they did not penetrate the simplicity of nature. These two species of contemplation must therefore be interchanged, and each employed in its turn, in order to render the understanding at once penetrating and capacious, and to avoid the inconveniences we have mentioned, and the idols that result from them.

58. Let such, therefore, be our precautions in contemplation, that we may ward off and expel the idols of the den : which mostly owe their birth either to some predominant pursuit ; or, secondly, to an excess in synthesis and analysis ; or, thirdly, to a party zeal in favour of certain ages ; or, fourthly, to the extent or narrowness of the subject. In general, he who contemplates nature should suspect whatever particularly takes and fixes his understanding, and should use so much the more caution to preserve it equable and unprejudiced.

59. The idols* of the market are the most troublesome of all, those, namely, which have entwined themselves round the understanding from the associations of words and names. For men imagine that their reason governs words, whilst, in fact, words react upon the understanding ; and this has rendered philosophy and the sciences sophistical and inactive. Words are generally formed in a popular sense, and define things by those broad lines which are most obvious to the vulgar mind ; but when a more acute understanding, or more diligent observation is anxious to vary those lines, and to adapt them more accurately to nature, words oppose it. Hence the great and solemn disputes of learned men often terminate in controversies about words and names, in regard to which it would be better (imitating the caution of mathematicians) to proceed more advisedly in the first instance, and to bring such disputes to a regular issue by definitions. Such definitions, however, cannot remedy the evil in natural and material objects, because they consist themselves of words, and these words produce others ; so that we must necessarily have recourse to particular instances, and their regular

* Hence to Aphorism 59, treats of the Idols of the den.   * Hence to Aphorism 61, treats of the Idols of the market.
2 G

series and arrangement, as we shall mention when we come to the mode and scheme of determining notions and axioms.

60. The idols imposed upon the understanding by words are of two kinds. They are either the names of things which have no existence, (for, as some objects are from inattention left without a name, so names are formed by fanciful imaginations which are without an object,) or they are the names of actual objects, but confused, badly defined, and hastily and irregularly abstracted from things. Fortune, the primum mobile, the planetary orbits, the element of fire, and the like fictions, which owe their birth to futile and false theories, are instances of the first kind. And this species of idols is removed with greater facility, because it can be exterminated by the constant refutation or the desuetude of the theories themselves. The others, which are created by vicious and unskilful abstraction, are intricate and deeply rooted. Take some word for instance, as *moist ;* and let us examine how far the different significations of this word are consistent. It will be found that the word *moist* is nothing but a confused sign of different actions, admitting of no settled and defined uniformity. For it means that which easily diffuses itself over another body ; that which is indeterminable and cannot be brought to a consistency ; that which yields easily in every direction ; that which is easily divided and dispersed ; that which is easily united and collected ; that which easily flows and is put in motion ; that which easily adheres to and wets another body ; that which is easily reduced to a liquid state, though previously solid. When, therefore, you come to predicate or impose this name, in one sense flame is moist, in another air is not moist, in another fine powder is moist, in another glass is moist ; so that it is quite clear that this notion is hastily abstracted from water only, and common, ordinary liquors, without any due verification of it.

There are, however, different degrees of distortion and mistake in words. One of the least faulty classes is that of the names of substances, particularly of the less abstract and more defined species ; (those then of *chalk* and *mud* are good, of *earth,* bad ;) words signifying actions are more faulty, as to *generate,* to *corrupt,* to *change ;* but the most faulty are those denoting qualities, (except the immediate objects of sense,) as *heavy, light, rare, dense.* Yet in all of these there must be some notions a little better than others, in proportion as a greater or less number of things come before the senses.

61. The idols of the theatre* are not innate, nor do they introduce themselves secretly into the understanding ; but they are manifestly instilled and cherished by the fictions of theories and

* Hence to Aphorism 68, treats of the Idols of the theatre.

depraved rules of demonstration. To attempt, however, or undertake their confutation, would not be consistent with our declarations. For, since we neither agree in our principles nor our demonstrations, all argument is out of the question. And it is fortunate that the ancients are left in possession of their honours. We detract nothing from them, seeing our whole doctrine relates only to the path to be pursued. The lame (as they say) in the path outstrip the swift, who wander from it, and it is clear that the very skill and swiftness of him who runs not in the right direction, must increase his aberration.

Our method of discovering the sciences is such as to leave little to the acuteness and strength of wit, and indeed rather to level wit and intellect. For, as in the drawing of a straight line or accurate circle by the hand, much depends upon its steadiness and practice, but if a ruler or compass be employed there is little occasion for either ; so it is with our method. Although, however, we enter into no individual confutations, yet a little must be said, first, of the sects and general divisions of these species of theories ; secondly, something further to show that there are external signs of their weakness, and, lastly, we must consider the causes of so great a misfortune, and so long and general a unanimity in error, that we may thus render the access to truth less difficult, and that the human understanding may the more readily be purified, and brought to dismiss its idols.

62. The idols of the theatre or of theories are numerous, and may and perhaps will be still more so. For, unless men's minds had been now occupied for many ages in religious and theological considerations, and civil governments (especially monarchies) had been averse to novelties of that nature, even in theory, (so that men must apply to them with some risk and injury to their own fortunes, and not only without reward, but subject to contumely and envy,) there is no doubt that many other sects of philosophers and theorists would have been introduced, like those which formerly flourished in such diversified abundance amongst the Greeks. For, as many imaginary theories of the heavens can be deduced from the phenomena of the sky, so it is even more easy to found many dogmas upon the phenomena of philosophy ; and the plot of this our theatre resembles those of the poetical, where the plots which are invented for the stage are more consistent, elegant, and pleasurable than those taken from real history.

In general, men take for the groundwork of their philosophy either too much from a few topics, or too little from many ; in either case their philosophy is founded on too narrow a basis of experiment and natural history, and decides on too scanty grounds. For the theoretic philosopher seizes various common circumstances by experiment, without reducing them to certainty, or examining and frequently considering them, and relies for the rest upon meditation and the activity of his wit.

There are other philosophers who have diligently and accurately attended to a few experiments, and have thence presumed to deduce and invent systems of philosophy, forming every thing to conformity with them.

A third set, from their faith and religious veneration, introduce theology and traditions; the absurdity of some amongst them having proceeded so far as to seek and derive the sciences from spirits and genii. There are, therefore, three sources of error and three species of false philosophy; the sophistic, empiric, and superstitious.

· 63. Aristotle affords the most eminent instance of the first; for he corrupted natural philosophy by logic: thus, he formed the world of categories, assigned to the human soul, the noblest of substances, a genus determined by words of secondary operation, treated of density and rarity (by which bodies occupy a greater or lesser space) by the frigid distinctions of action and power, asserted that there was a peculiar and proper motion in all bodies, and that if they shared in any other motion, it was owing to an external moving cause, and imposed innumerable arbitrary distinctions upon the nature of things; being everywhere more anxious as to definitions in teaching, and the accuracy of the wording of his propositions, than the internal truth of things. And this is best shown by a comparison of his philosophy with the others of greatest repute among the Greeks. For the similar parts of Anaxagoras, the atoms of Leucippus and Democritus, the heaven and earth of Parmenides, the discord and concord of Empedocles, the resolution of bodies into the common nature of fire, and their condensation, according to Heraclitus, exhibit some sprinkling of natural philosophy, the nature of things, and experiment, whilst Aristotle's physics are mere logical terms, and he remodelled the same subject in his metaphysics under a more imposing title, and more as a realist than a nominalist. Nor is much stress to be laid on his frequent recourse to experiment in his books on animals, his problems, and other treatises; for he had already decided, without having properly consulted experience as the basis of his decisions and axioms, and after having so decided, he drags experiment along, as a captive constrained to accommodate herself to his decisions; so that he is even more to be blamed than his modern followers, (of the scholastic school,) who have deserted her altogether.

64. The empiric school produces dogmas of a more deformed and monstrous nature than the sophistic or theoretic school: not being founded in the light of common notions, (which, however poor and superficial, is yet in a manner universal and of a general tendency,) but in the confined obscurity of a few experiments. Hence this species of philosophy appears probable and almost certain to those who are daily practised in such experiments, and have thus corrupted their imagination, but incredible and futile to others. We have a strong instance of this in the alchymists and their dogmas; it would be difficult to find another in this age, unless, perhaps, in the philosophy of Gilbert.* We could not, however, neglect to caution others against this school, because we already foresee and augur, that if men be hereafter induced by our exhortations to apply seriously to experiments, (bidding farewell to the sophistic doctrines,) there will then be imminent danger from empirics, owing to the premature and forward haste of the understanding, and its jumping or flying to generalities and the principles of things. We ought, therefore, already to meet the evil.

65. The corruption of philosophy by the mixing of it up with superstition and theology is of a much wider extent, and is most injurious to it, both as a whole and in parts. For the human understanding is no less exposed to the impressions of fancy, than to those of vulgar notions. The disputatious and sophistic school entraps the understanding, whilst the fanciful, bombastic, and, as it were, poetical school rather flatters it. There is a clear example of this among the Greeks, especially in Pythagoras, where, however, the superstition is coarse and overcharged, but it is more dangerous and refined in Plato and his school. This evil is found also in some branches of other systems of philosophy, where it introduces abstracted forms, final and first causes, omitting frequently the intermediate, and the like. Against it we must use the greatest caution; for the apotheosis of error is the greatest evil of all, and when folly is worshipped, it is, as it were, a plague-spot upon the understanding. Yet, some of the moderns have indulged this folly, with such consummate inconsiderateness, that they have endeavoured to build a system of natural philosophy on the first chapter of Genesis, the book of Job, and other parts of Scripture; seeking thus the dead amongst the living. And this folly is the more to be prevented and restrained, because not only fantastical philosophy but heretical religion spring from the absurd mixture of matters divine and human. It is, therefore, most wise soberly to render unto faith the things that are faith's.

66. Having spoken of the vicious authority of the systems founded either on vulgar notions, or on a few experiments, or on superstition, we must now consider the faulty subjects for contemplation, especially in natural philosophy. The

* It is thus the Vulcanists and Neptunians have framed their opposite theories in geology. Phrenology is a modern instance of hasty generalization.

human understanding is perverted by observing the power of mechanical arts, in which bodies are very materially changed by composition or separation, and is induced to suppose that something similar takes place in the universal nature of things. Hence the fiction of elements, and their co-operation in forming natural bodies. Again, when man reflects upon the entire liberty of nature, he meets with particular species of things, as animals, plants, minerals, and is thence easily led to imagine that there exist in nature certain primary forms which she strives to produce, and that all variation from them arises from some impediment or error which she is exposed to in completing her work, or from the collision or metamorphosis of different species. The first hypothesis has produced the doctrine of *elementary properties*, the second that of *occult properties and specific powers :* and both lead to trifling courses of reflection, in which the mind acquiesces, and is thus diverted from more important subjects. But physicians exercise a much more useful labour in the consideration of the secondary qualities of things, and the operations of attraction, repulsion, attenuation, inspissation, dilatation, astringency, separation, maturation, and the like; and would do still more if they would not corrupt these proper observations by the two systems I have alluded to, of elementary qualities and specific powers, by which they either reduce the secondary to first qualities, and their subtile and immeasurable composition, or at any rate neglect to advance by greater and more diligent observation to the third and fourth qualities, thus terminating their contemplation prematurely. Nor are these powers (or the like) to be investigated only among the medicines of the human body, but also in all changes of other natural bodies.

A greater evil arises from the contemplation and investigation rather of the stationary principles of things, *from which*, than of the active, *by which* things themselves are created. For the former only serve for discussion, the latter for practice. Nor is any value to be set on those common differences of motion which are observed in the received system of natural philosophy, as generation, corruption, augmentation, diminution, alteration, and translation. For this is their meaning: if a body, unchanged in other respects, is moved from its place, this is *translation ;* if the place and species be given, but the quantity changed, it is *alteration ;* but if, from such a change, the mass and quantity of the body do not continue the same, this is the motion of *augmentation* and *diminution ;* if the change be continued so as to vary the species and substance, and transfuse them to others, this is *generation* and *corruption.* All this is merely popular, and by no means penetrates into nature ; and these are but the measures and bounds of motion, and not dif-

ferent species of it; they merely suggest *how far.* and not *how* or *whence.* For they exhibit neither the affections of bodies, nor the process of their parts, but merely establish a division of that motion, which coarsely exhibits to the senses matter in its varied form. Even when they wish to point out something relative to the causes of motion, and to establish a division of them, they most absurdly introduce *natural* and *violent* motion, which is also a popular notion, since every violent motion is also in fact *natural,* that is to say, the external efficient puts nature in action in a different manner to that which she had previously employed.

But if, neglecting these, any one were for instance to observe, that there is in bodies a tendency of adhesion, so as not to suffer the unity of nature to be completely separated or broken, and a vacuum to be formed ; or that they have a tendency to return to their natural dimensions or tension, so that, if compressed or extended within or beyond it, they immediately strive to recover themselves, and resume their former volume and extent; or that they have a tendency to congregate into masses with similar bodies, the dense, for instance, towards the circumference of the earth, the thin and rare towards that of the heavens, these and the like are true physical genera of motions, but the others are clearly logical and scholastic, as appears plainly from a comparison of the two.

Another considerable evil is, that men in their systems and contemplations bestow their labour upon the investigation and discussion of the principles of things and the extreme limits of nature, although all utility and means of action consist in the intermediate objects. Hence men cease not to abstract nature till they arrive at potential and shapeless matter, and still persist in their dissection, till they arrive at atoms ; and yet, were all this true, it would be of little use to advance man's estate.

67. The understanding must also be cautioned against the intemperance of systems, so far as regards its giving or withholding its assent; for such intemperance appears to fix and perpetuate idols, so as to leave no means of removing them.

These excesses are of two kinds. The first is seen in those who decide hastily, and render the sciences positive and dictatorial. The other in those who have introduced skepticism, and vague, unbounded inquiry. The former subdues, the latter enervates the understanding. The Aristotelian philosophy, after destroying other systems (as the Ottomans do their brethren) by its disputations, confutations, decided upon every thing, and Aristotle himself then raises up questions at will, in order to settle them ; so that every thing should be certain and decided, a method now in use among his successors.

The school of Plato introduced skepticism, first, as it were, in joke and irony, from their dislike to Protagoras, Hippias, and others, who were ashamed of appearing not to doubt upon any subject. But the new academy dogmatized in their skepticism, and held it as their tenet. Although this method be more honest than arbitrary decision, (for its followers allege that they by no means confound all inquiry, like Pyrrho and his disciples, but hold doctrines which they can follow as probable, though they cannot maintain them to be true,) yet, when the human mind has once despaired of discovering truth, every thing begins to languish. Hence men turn aside into pleasant controversies and discussions, and into a sort of wandering over subjects, rather than sustain any rigorous investigation. But, as we observed at first, we are not to deny the authority of the human senses and understanding, although weak; but rather to furnish them with assistance.

68. We have now treated of each kind of idols, and their qualities; all of which must be abjured and renounced with firm and solemn resolution, and the understanding must be completely freed and cleared of them; so that the access to the kingdom of man, which is founded on the sciences, may resemble that to the kingdom of heaven, where no admission is conceded except to children.

69. Vicious demonstrations are the muniments and support of idols, and those which we possess in logic, merely subject and enslave the world to human thoughts, and thoughts to words. But demonstrations are, in some manner, themselves systems of philosophy and science. For such as *they* are, and accordingly as they are regularly or improperly established, such will be the resulting systems of philosophy and contemplation. But those which we employ in the whole process leading from the senses and things to axioms and conclusions, are fallacious and incompetent. This process is fourfold, and the errors are in equal number. In the first place the impressions of the senses are erroneous, for they fail and deceive us. We must supply defects by substitutions, and fallacies by their correction. 2dly. Notions are improperly abstracted from the senses, and indeterminate and confused when they ought to be the reverse. 3dly. The induction that is employed is improper, for it determines the principles of sciences by simple enumeration, without adopting the exclusions, and resolutions, or just separations of nature. Lastly, the usual method of discovery and proof, by first establishing the most general propositions, then applying and proving the intermediate axioms according to them, is the parent of error and the calamity of every science. But we will treat more fully of that which we now slightly touch upon, when we come to lay down the true way of interpreting nature, after having gone through the above expiatory process and purification of the mind.

70. But experience is by far the best demon-

stration, provided it adhere to the experiment actually made; for if that experiment be transferred to other subjects apparently similar, unless with proper and methodical caution, it becomes fallacious. The present method of experiment is blind and stupid. Hence men wandering and roaming without any determined course, and consulting mere chance, are hurried about to various points, and advance but little; at one time they are happy, at another their attention is distracted, and they always find that they want something further. Men generally make their experiments carelessly, and as it were in sport, making some little variation in a known experiment, and then, if they fail, they become disgusted and give up the attempt: nay, if they set to work more seriously, steadily, and assiduously, yet they waste all their time on probing some solitary matter; as Gilbert on the magnet, and the alchymists on gold. But such conduct shows their method to be no less unskilful than mean. For nobody can successfully investigate the nature of any object by considering that object alone; the inquiry must be more generally extended.

Even when men build any science and theory upon experiment, yet they almost always turn with premature and hasty zeal to practice, not merely on account of the advantage and benefit to be derived from it, but in order to seize upon some security in a new undertaking of their not employing the remainder of their labour unprofitably; and by making themselves conspicuous, to acquire a greater name for their pursuit. Hence, like Atalanta, they leave the course to pick up the golden apple, interrupting their speed, and giving up the victory. But, in the true course of experiment, and in extending it to new effects, we should imitate the Divine foresight and order. For God, on the first day, only created light, and assigned a whole day to that work, without creating any material substance thereon. In like manner, we must first, by every kind of experiment, elicit the discovery of causes and true axioms, and seek for experiments which may afford light rather than profit. Axioms, when rightly investigated and established, prepare us not for a limited but abundant practice, and bring in their train whole troops of effects. But we will treat hereafter of the ways of experience, which are not less beset and interrupted than those of judgment; having spoken at present of common experience only as a bad species of demonstration, the order of our subject now requires some mention of those external signs of the weakness in practice of the received systems of philosophy and contemplation,* which we referred to above, and of the causes of a circumstance at first sight so wonderful and incredible. For the knowledge of these external signs prepares the

* See Ax. 61, towards the end. This subject extends to Ax. 78.

way for assent, and the explanation of the causes removes the wonder; and these two circumstances are of material use in extirpating more easily and gently the idols from the understanding.

71. The sciences we possess have been principally derived from the Greeks: for the addition of the Roman, Arabic, or more modern writers are but few, and of small importance; and, such as they are, are founded on the basis of Greek invention. But the wisdom of the Greeks was professional and disputatious, and thus most adverse to the investigation of truth. The name, therefore, of sophists, which the contemptuous spirit of those who deemed themselves philosophers, rejected and transferred to the rhetoricians, Gorgias, Protagoras, Hippias, Polus, might well suit the whole tribe, such as Plato, Aristotle, Zeno, Epicurus, Theophrastus, and their successors, Chrysippus, Carneades, and the rest. There was only this difference between them, the former were mercenary vagabonds, travelling about to different states, making a show of their wisdom and requiring pay; the latter, more dignified and noble, in possession of fixed habitations, opening schools, and teaching philosophy gratuitously. Both, however, (though differing in other respects,) were professorial, and reduced every subject to controversy, establishing and defending certain sects and dogmas of philosophy: so that their doctrines were nearly (what Dionysius not unaptly objected to Plato) "the talk of idle old men to ignorant youths." But the more ancient Greeks, as Empedocles, Anaxagoras, Leucippus, Democritus, Parmenides, Heraclitus, Xenophanes, Philolaus, and the rest, (for I omit Pythagoras, as being superstitious,) did not (that we are aware) open schools; but betook themselves to the investigation of truth with greater silence, and with more severity and simplicity: that is, with less affectation and ostentation. Hence, in our opinion, they acted more advisedly, however their works may have been eclipsed in course of time by those lighter productions which better correspond with and please the apprehensions and passions of the vulgar: for time, like a river, bears down to us that which is light and inflated, and sinks that which is heavy and solid. Nor were even these more ancient philosophers free from the natural defect, but inclined too much to the ambition and vanity of forming a sect, and captivating public opinion; and we must despair of any inquiry after truth, when it condescends to such trifles. Nor must we omit the opinion or rather prophecy of an Egyptian priest with regard to the Greeks, "that they would for ever remain children, without any antiquity of knowledge or knowledge of antiquity." For they certainly have this in common with children, that they are prone to talking, and incapable of generation, their wisdom being loquacious, and unproductive of effects. Hence the external signs derived

from the origin and birthplace of our present philosophy are not favourable.

72. Nor are those much better which can be deduced from the character of the time and age, than the former from that of the country and nation. For in that age the knowledge both of time and of the world was confined and meagre, which is one of the worst evils for those who rely entirely on experience. They had not a thousand years of history, worthy of that name, but mere fables and ancient traditions. They were acquainted with but a small portion of the regions and countries of the world—for they indiscriminately called all nations situated far towards the north Scythians, all those to the west Celts; they knew nothing of Africa, but the nearest part of Ethiopia, or of Asia beyond the Ganges, and had not even heard any sure and clear tradition of the region of the new world. Besides, a vast number of climates and zones, in which innumerable nations live and breathe, were pronounced by them to be uninhabitable, nay, the travels of Democritus, Plato, and Pythagoras, which were not extensive, but rather mere excursions from home, were considered as something vast. But in our times many parts of the new world, and every extremity of the old are well known, and the mass of experiments has been infinitely increased. Wherefore, if external signs were to be taken from the time of the nativity or procreation, (as in astrology,) nothing extraordinary could be predicted of these early systems of philosophy.

73. Of all signs there is none more certain or worthy than that of the fruits produced: for the fruits and effects are the sureties and vouchers, as it were, for the truth of philosophy. Now, from the systems of the Greeks and their subordinate divisions in particular branches of the sciences during so long a period, scarcely one single experiment can be culled that has a tendency to elevate or assist mankind, and can be fairly set down to the speculations and doctrines of their philosophy. Celsus candidly and wisely confesses as much, when he observes that experiments were first discovered in medicine, and that men afterwards built their philosophical systems upon them, and searched for and assigned causes, instead of the inverse method of discovering and deriving experiments from philosophy and the knowledge of causes. It is not, therefore, wonderful that the Egyptians (who bestowed divinity and sacred honours on the authors of new inventions) should have consecrated more images of brutes than of men; for the brutes, by their natural instinct, made many discoveries, whilst men discovered but few from discussion and the conclusions of reason.

The industry of the alchymists has produced some effect, by chance, however, and casualty, or from varying their experiments, (as mechanics also do,) and not from any regular art or theory; the theory they have imagined rather tending to disturb than to assist experiment. Those, too, who have occupied themselves with natural magic, (as they term it,) have made but few discoveries, and those of small import, and bordering on imposture. For which reason, in the same manner as we are cautioned by religion to show our faith by our works, we may very properly apply the principle to philosophy, and judge of it by its works; accounting that to be futile which is unproductive, and still more so, if instead of grapes and olives it yield but the thistle and thorns of dispute and contention.

74. Other signs may be selected from the increase and progress of particular systems of philosophy and the sciences. For those which are founded on nature grow and increase, whilst those which are founded on opinion change, and increase not. If, therefore, the theories we have mentioned were not like plants torn up by the roots, but grew in the womb of nature and were nourished by her; that which for the last two thousand years has taken place would never have happened: namely, that the sciences still continue in their beaten track, and nearly stationary, without having received any important increase; nay, having, on the contrary, rather bloomed under the hands of their first author, and then faded away. But we see that the case is reversed in the mechanical arts, which are founded on nature and the light of experience, for they (as long as they are popular) seem full of life, and uninterruptedly thrive and grow, being at first rude, then convenient, lastly polished, and perpetually improved.

75. There is yet another sign, (if such it may be termed, being rather an evidence, and one of the strongest nature,) namely, the actual confession of those very authorities whom men now follow. For even they who decide on things so daringly, yet, at times, when they reflect, betake themselves to complaints about the subtilty of nature, the obscurity of things, and the weakness of man's wit. If they would merely do this, they might perhaps deter those who are of a timid disposition from further inquiry, but would excite and stimulate those of a more active and confident turn to further advances. They are not, however, satisfied with confessing so much of themselves, but consider every thing which has been either unknown or unattempted by themselves or their teachers, as beyond the limits of possibility; and thus, with most consummate pride and envy, convert the defects of their own discoveries into a calumny on nature, and a source of despair to every one else. Hence arose the new academy, which openly professed skepticism and consigned mankind to eternal darkness. Hence the notion that forms, or the true differences of things, (which are in fact the laws of simple action,) are beyond man's reach, and cannot possibly be discovered. Hence those notions in the active and operative

branches; that the heat of the sun and of fire are totally different, so as to prevent men from supposing that they can elicit or form, by means of fire, any thing similar to the operations of nature; and, again, that composition only is the work of man and mixture of nature, so as to prevent men from expecting the generation or transformation of natural bodies by art. Men will, therefore, easily allow themselves to be persuaded by this sign, not to engage their fortunes and labour in speculations, which are not only desperate, but actually devoted to desperation.

76. Nor should we omit the sign afforded by the great dissension formerly prevalent among philosophers, and the variety of schools, which sufficiently show that the way was not well prepared, that leads from the senses to the understanding, since the same groundwork of philosophy (namely, the nature of things) was torn and divided into such widely differing and multifarious errors. And although, in these days, the dissensions and differences of opinions with regard to first principles and entire systems are nearly extinct, yet there remain innumerable questions and controversies with regard to particular branches of philosophy. So that it is manifest that there is nothing sure or sound either in the systems themselves or in the methods of demonstration.

77. With regard to the supposition that there is a general unanimity as to the philosophy of Aristotle, because the other systems of the ancients ceased and became obsolete on its promulgation, and nothing better has been since discovered; whence it appears that it is so well determined and founded as to have united the suffrages of both ages; we will observe—1st. That the notion of other ancient systems having ceased after the publication of the works of Aristotle is false, for the works of the ancient philosophers subsisted long after that event, even to the time of Cicero and the subsequent ages. But at a later period, when human learning had, as it were, been wrecked in the inundation of barbarians into the Roman empire, then the systems of Aristotle and Plato were preserved in the waves of ages, like blanks of a lighter and less solid nature. 2d. The notion of unanimity on a clear inspection is found to be fallacious. For true unanimity is that which proceeds from a free judgment arriving at the same conclusion after an investigation of the fact. Now, by far the greater number of those who have assented to the philosophy of Aristotle, have bound themselves down to it, from prejudice and the authority of others, so that it is rather obsequiousness and concurrence than unanimity. But even if it were real and extensive unanimity, so far from being esteemed a true and solid confirmation, it should lead to a violent presumption to the contrary. For there is no worse augury in intellectual matters than that derived from unanimity, with the ex

reption of divinity and politics, where suffrages are allowed to decide. For nothing pleases the multitude, unless it strike the imagination or bind down the understanding, as we have observed above, with the shackles of vulgar notions. Hence we may well transfer Phocion's remark from morals to the intellect: "That men should immediately examine what error or fault they have committed, when the multitude concurs with and applauds them." This, then, is one of the most unfavourable signs. All the signs, therefore, of the truth and soundness of the received systems of philosophy and the sciences are unpropitious, whether taken from their origin, their fruits, their progress, the confessions of their authors, or from unanimity.

78. We now come to the causes of errors,* and of such perseverance in them for ages. These are sufficiently numerous and powerful to remove all wonder that what we now offer should have so long been concealed from and have escaped the notice of mankind, and to render it more worthy of astonishment, that it should even now have entered any one's mind or become the subject of his thoughts; and that it should have done so, we consider rather the gift of fortune than of any extraordinary talent, and as the offspring of time rather than wit. But, in the first place, the number of ages is reduced to very narrow limits on a proper consideration of the matter. For, out of twenty-five centuries, with which the memory and learning of man are conversant, scarcely six can be set apart and selected as fertile in science and favourable in its progress. For there are deserts and wastes in times as in countries, and we can only reckon up three revolutions and epochs of philosophy. 1. The Greek. 2. The Roman. 3. Our own, that is, the philosophy of the western nations of Europe: and scarcely two centuries can with justice be assigned to each. The intermediate ages of the world were unfortunate, both in the quantity and richness of the sciences produced. Nor need we mention the Arabs or the scholastic philosophy which, in those ages, ground down the sciences by their numerous treatises more than they increased their weight. The first cause, then, of such insignificant progress in the sciences is rightly referred to the small proportion of time which has been favourable thereto.

79. A second cause offers itself, which is certainly of the greatest importance; namely, that in those very ages in which men's wit, and literature flourished considerably, or even moderately, but a small part of their industry was bestowed on natural philosophy, the great mother of the sciences. For every art and science torn from this root may, perhaps, be polished and put into a serviceable shape, but can admit of little

growth. It is well known that after the Christian religion had been acknowledged and arrived at maturity, by far the best wits were busied upon theology, where the highest rewards offered themselves, and every species of assistance was abundantly supplied, and the study of which was the principal occupation of the western European nations during the third epoch; the rather because literature flourished about the very time when controversies concerning religion first began to bud forth. 2. In the preceding ages, during the second epoch, (that of the Romans,) philosophical meditation and labour was chiefly occupied and wasted in moral philosophy, (the theology of the heathens:) besides, the greatest minds in these times applied themselves to civil affairs, on account of the magnitude of the Roman empire, which required the labour of many. 3. The age during which natural philosophy appeared principally to flourish among the Greeks was but a short period, since in the more ancient times the seven sages (with the exception of Thales) applied themselves to moral philosophy and politics, and at a later period after Socrates had brought down philosophy from heaven to earth, moral philosophy became more prevalent, and diverted men's attention from natural. Nay, the very period during which physical inquiries flourished, was corrupted and rendered useless by contradictions and the ambition of new opinions. Since, therefore, during these three epochs, natural philosophy has been materially neglected or impeded, it is not at all surprising that men should have made but little progress in it, seeing they were attending to an entirely different matter.

80. Add to this that natural philosophy, especially of late, has seldom gained exclusive possession of an individual free from all other pursuits, even amongst those who have applied themselves to it, unless there may be an example or two of some monk studying in his cell, or some nobleman in his villa. She has rather been made a passage and bridge to other pursuits.

Thus has this great mother of the sciences been degraded most unworthily to the situation of an handmaid, and made to wait upon medicine or mathematical operations, and to wash the immature minds of youth, and imbue them with a first dye, that they may afterwards be more ready to receive and retain another. In the mean time let no one expect any great progress in the sciences, (especially their operative part,) unless natural philosophy be applied to particular sciences, and particular sciences again referred back to natural philosophy. For want of this, astronomy, optics, music, many mechanical arts, medicine itself, and (what perhaps is more wonderful) moral and political philosophy, and the logical sciences have no depth, but only glide over the surface and variety of things; because these sciences, when they have been once partitioned out and esta

* See end of Axiom 61. This subject extends to Axiom 93.

olished, are no longer nourished by natural philosophy, which would have imparted fresh vigour and growth to them from the sources and genuine contemplation of motion, rays, sounds, texture, and confirmation of bodies, and the affections and capacity of the understanding. But we can little wonder that the sciences grow not when separated from their roots.

81. There is another powerful and great cause of the little advancement of the sciences, which is this: it is impossible to advance properly in the course when the goal is not properly fixed. But the real and legitimate goal of the sciences is the endowment of human life with new inventions and riches. The great crowd of teachers know nothing of this, but consist of dictatorial hirelings: unless it so happen that some artisan of an acute genius and ambitious of fame gives up his time to a new discovery, which is generally attended with a loss of property. The majority, so far from proposing to themselves the augmentation of the mass of arts and sciences, make no other use of an inquiry into the mass already before them, than is afforded by the conversion of it to some use in their lectures, or to gain, or to the acquirement of a name and the like. But if one out of the multitude he found, who courts science from real zeal and on its own account, even he will be seen rather to follow contemplation and the variety of theories than a severe and strict investigation of truth. Again, if there even be an unusually strict investigator of truth, yet will he propose to himself as the test of truth the satisfaction of his mind and understanding, as to the causes of things long since known, and not such a test as to lead to some new earnest of effects, and a new light in axioms. If, therefore, no one have laid down the real end of science, we cannot wonder that there should be error in points subordinate to that end.

82. But, in like manner as the end and goal of science is ill defined, so, even were the case otherwise, men have chosen an erroneous and impassable direction. For it is sufficient to astonish any reflecting mind, that nobody should have cared or wished to open and complete a way for the understanding, setting off from the senses, and regular, well conducted experiment; but that every thing has been abandoned either to the mists of tradition, the whirl and confusion of argument, or the waves and mazes of chance, and desultory, ill-combined experiment. Now, let any one but consider soberly and diligently the nature of the path men have been accustomed to pursue in the investigation and discovery of any matter, and he will doubtless first observe the rude and inartificial manner of discovery most familiar to mankind: which is no other than this. When any one prepares himself for discovery, he first inquires and obtains a full account of all that has been said on the subject by others, then adds his

own reflections, and stirs up and, as it were, invokes his own spirit, after much mental labour, to disclose its oracles. All which is a method without foundation and merely turns on opinion.

Another perhaps calls in logic to assist him in discovery, which bears only a nominal relation to his purpose. For the discoveries of logic are not discoveries of principles and leading axioms, but only of what appears to accord with them. And when men become curious and importunate and give trouble, interrupting her about her proofs and the discovery of principles or first axioms, she puts them off with her usual answer, referring them to faith, and ordering them to swear allegiance to each art in its own department.

There remains but mere experience, which when it offers itself is called chance; when it is sought after, experiment. But this kind of experience is nothing but a loose faggot, and mere groping in the dark, as men at night try all means of discovering the right road, whilst it would be better and more prudent either to wait for day or procure a light and then proceed. On the contrary the real order of experience begins by setting up a light, and then shows the road by it, commencing with a regulated and digested, not a misplaced and vague course of experiment, and thence deducing axioms, and from those axioms new experiments: for not even the Divine Word proceeded to operate on the general mass of things without due order.

Let men therefore cease to wonder if the whole course of science be not run, when all have wandered from the path; quitting entirely and deserting experience, or involving themselves in its mazes, and wandering about, whilst a regularly combined system would lead them in a sure track through its wilds to the open day of axioms.

83. The evil, however, has been wonderfully increased by an opinion, or inveterate conceit, which is both vainglorious and prejudicial, namely, that the dignity of the human mind is lowered by long and frequent intercourse with experiments and particulars, which are the objects of sense and confined to matter; especially since such matters generally require labour in investigation, are mean subjects for meditation, harsh in discourse, unproductive in practice, infinite in number, and delicate in their subtilty. Hence we have seen the true path not only deserted, but intercepted and blocked up, experience being rejected with disgust, and not merely neglected or improperly applied.

84. Again, the reverence for antiquity and the authority of men who have been esteemed great in philosophy, and general unanimity, have retarded men from advancing in science, and almost enchanted them. As to unanimity, we have spoken of it above.

The opinion which men cherish of antiquity is altogether idle, and scarcely accords with the term. For the old age and increasing years of the world should in reality be considered as antiquity, and this is rather the character of our own times than of the less advanced age of the world in those of the ancients. For the latter, with respect to ourselves, are ancient and elder, with respect to the world, modern and younger. And as we expect a greater knowledge of human affairs and more mature judgment from an old man, than from a youth, on account of his experience, and the variety and number of things he has seen, heard, and meditated upon; so we have reason to expect much greater things of our own age, (if it knew.but its strength and would essay and exert it,) than from antiquity, since the world has grown older, and its stock has been increased and accumulated with an infinite number of experiments and observations. We must also take into our consideration that many objects in nature fit to throw light upon philosophy have been exposed to our view and discovered by means of long voyages and travels, in which our times have abounded. It would indeed be dishonourable to mankind, if the regions of the material globe, the earth, the sea, and stars should be so prodigiously developed and illustrated in our age, and yet the boundaries of the intellectual globe should be confined to the narrow discoveries of the ancients.

With regard to authority, it is the greatest weakness to attribute infinite credit to particular authors, and to refuse his own prerogative to time, the author of all authors, and, therefore, of all authority. For, truth is rightly named the daughter of time, not of authority. It is not wonderful, therefore, if the bonds of antiquity, authority, and unanimity, have so enchained the power of man, that he is unable (as if bewitched) to become familiar with things themselves.

85. Nor is it only the admiration of antiquity, authority, and unanimity, that has forced man's industry to rest satisfied with present discoveries, but also the admiration of the effects already placed within his power. For, whoever passes in review the variety of subjects, and the beautiful apparatus collected and introduced by the mechanical arts for the service of mankind, will certainly be rather inclined to admire our wealth than to perceive our poverty; not considering that the observations of man and operations of nature (which are the souls and first movers of that variety) are few, and not of deep research; the rest must be attributed merely to man's patience and the delicate and well regulated motion of the hand or of instruments. To take an instance, the manufactory of clocks is delicate and accurate, and appears to imitate the heavenly bodies in its wheels, and the pulse of animals in its regular oscillation, yet it only depends upon one or two axioms of nature.

Again, if one consider the refinement of the liberal arts, or even that exhibited in the preparation of natural bodies in mechanical arts and the like; as the discovery of the heavenly motions in astronomy, of harmony in music, of the letters of the alphabet (still unadopted by the Chinese) in grammar; or, again, in mechanical operations, the productions of Bacchus and Ceres, that is, the preparation of wine and beer, the making of bread, or even the luxuries of the table, distillation, and the like; if one reflect also and consider for how long a period of ages (for all the above, except distillation, are ancient) these things have been brought to their present state of perfection, and, as we instanced in clocks, to how few observations and axioms of nature they may be referred, and how easily, and, as it were, by obvious chance or contemplation they might be discovered, one would soon cease to admire and rather pity the human lot, on account of its vast want and dearth of things and discoveries for so many ages. Yet, even the discoveries we have mentioned were more ancient than philosophy, and the intellectual arts; so that, to say the truth, when contemplation and doctrinal science began, the discovery of useful works ceased.

But if any one turn from the manufactories to libraries, and be inclined to admire the immense variety of books offered to our view, let him but examine and diligently inspect the matter and contents of these books, and his astonishment will certainly change its object: for when he finds no end of repetitions, and how much men do and speak the same thing over again, he will pass from admiration of this variety to astonishment at the poverty and scarcity of matter, which has hitherto possessed and filled men's minds.

But if any one should condescend to consider such sciences as are deemed rather curious than sound, and take a full view of the operations of the alchymists or magi, he will perhaps hesitate whether he ought rather to laugh or to weep. For the alchymist cherishes eternal hope, and when his labours succeed not, accuses his own mistakes, deeming, in his self-accusation, that he has not properly understood the words of art, or of his authors; upon which he listens to tradition and vague whispers, or imagines there is some slight unsteadiness in the minute details of his practice, and then has recourse to an endless repetition of experiments: and, in the mean time, when in his casual experiments he falls upon something in appearance new, or of some degree of utility, he consoles himself with such an earnest, and ostentatiously publishes them, keeping up his hope of the final result. Nor can it be denied that the alchymists have made several discoveries, and presented mankind with useful inventions. But we may well apply to them the fable of the old man, who bequeathed to his sons some gold buried in his garden, pretending not to know the exact spot, whereupon they worked diligently in digging the vineyard, and though they found no gold, the vintage was rendered more abundant by their labour.

The followers of natural magic, who explain every thing by sympathy and antipathy, have assigned false powers and marvellous operations to things, by gratuitous and idle conjectures: and if they have ever produced any effects, they are rather wonderful and novel than of any real benefit or utility.

In superstitious magic, (if we say any thing at all about it,) we must chiefly observe, that there are only some peculiar and definite objects with which the curious and superstitious arts have in every nation and age, and even under every religion, been able to exercise and amuse themselves. Let us, therefore, pass them over. In the mean time we cannot wonder that the false notion of plenty should have occasioned want.

86. The admiration of mankind with regard to the arts and sciences, which is of itself sufficiently simple and almost puerile, has been increased by the craft and artifices of those who have treated the sciences and delivered them down to posterity. For they propose and produce them to our view so fashioned, and as it were masked, as to make them pass for perfect and complete. For, if you consider their method and divisions, they appear to embrace and comprise every thing which can relate to the subject. And although this frame be badly filled up, and resemble an empty bladder, yet it presents to the vulgar understanding the form and appearance of a perfect science.

The first and most ancient investigators of truth were wont, on the contrary, with more honesty and success, to throw all the knowledge they wished to gather from contemplation, and to lay up for use, into aphorisms, or short, scattered sentences, unconnected by any method, and without pretending or professing to comprehend any entire art. But, according to the present system, we cannot wonder that men seek nothing beyond that which is handed down to them as perfect, and already extended to its full complement.

87. The ancient theories have received additional support and credit, from the absurdity and levity of those who have promoted the new, especially in the active and practical part of natural philosophy. For there have been many silly and fantastical fellows who, from credulity or imposture, have loaded mankind with promises, announcing and boasting of the prolongation of life, the retarding of old age, the alleviation of pains, the remedying of natural defects, the deception of the senses, the restraint and excitement of the passions, the illumination and exaltation of the intellectual faculties, the transmutation of substances, the unlimited intensity and multiplication of motion, the impressions and changes of the air, the bringing into our power the management of celestial influences, the divination of future events, the representation of distant objects, the revelation of hidden objects and the like. One would not be very wrong in observing, with regard to such pretenders, that there is as much difference in philosophy, between their absurdity and real science, as there is in history between the exploits of Cæsar or Alexander, and those of Amadis de Gaul and Arthur of Britain. For those illustrious generals are found to have actually performed greater exploits, than such fictitious heroes are even pretended to have accomplished, by the means, however, of real action, and not by any fabulous and portentous power. Yet it is not right to suffer our belief in true history to be diminished, because it is sometimes injured and violated by fables. In the mean time we cannot wonder that great prejudice has been excited against any new propositions (especially when coupled with any mention of effects to be produced) by the conduct of impostors who have made a similar attempt, for their extreme absurdity and the disgust occasioned by it, has even to this day overpowered every spirited attempt of the kind.

88. Want of energy, and the littleness and futility of the tasks that human industry has undertaken, have produced much greater injury to the sciences: and yet (to make it still worse) that very want of energy manifests itself in conjunction with arrogance and disdain.

For, in the first place, one excuse, now from its repetition become familiar, is to be observed in every art, namely, that its promoters convert the weakness of the art itself into a calumny upon nature: and whatever it in their hands fails to effect, they pronounce to be physically impossible. But how can the art ever be condemned, whilst it acts as judge in its own cause? Even the present system of philosophy cherishes in its bosom certain positions or dogmas, which (it will be found on diligent inquiry) are calculated to produce a full conviction that no difficult, commanding, and powerful operation upon nature, ought to be anticipated through the means of art; we instanced * above, the alleged different quality of heat in the sun and fire, and composition and mixture. Upon an accurate observation, the whole tendency of such positions is wilfully to circumscribe man's power, and to produce a despair of the means of invention and contrivance, which would not only confound the promises of hope, but cut the very springs and sinews of industry, and throw aside even the chances of experience. The only object of such philosophers is, to acquire the reputation of perfection for their own art, and they are anxious to obtain the most silly and abandoned renown, by causing a belief that whatever has not yet been invented and understood, can never be so hereafter. But if any one attempt to give himself up to things, and to

_____
* See Axiom 75.

discover something new, yet he will only propose and destine for his object, the investigation and discovery of some one invention, and nothing more; as the nature of the magnet, the tides, the heavenly system and the like, which appear enveloped in some degree of mystery, and have hitherto been treated with but little success. Now, it is the greatest proof of want of skill, to investigate the nature of any object in itself alone; for that same nature, which seems concealed and hidden in some instances, is manifest and almost palpable in others; and excites wonder in the former, whilst it hardly attracts attention in the latter. Thus the nature of consistency is scarcely observed in wood or stone, but passed over by the term *solid*, without any further inquiry about the repulsion of separation, or the solution of continuity. But in water-bubbles the same circumstance appears matter of delicate and ingenious research, for they form themselves into thin pellicles, curiously shaped into hemispheres, so as for an instant to avoid the solution of continuity.

In general, those very things which are considered as secret, are manifest and common in other objects, but will never be clearly seen if the experiments and contemplation of man be directed to themselves only. Yet it commonly happens, that if, in the mechanical arts, any one bring old discoveries to a finer polish, or more elegant height of ornament, or unite and compound them, or apply them more readily to practice, or exhibit them on a less heavy and voluminous scale, and the like, they will pass off as new.

We cannot, therefore, wonder that no magnificent discoveries, worthy of mankind, have been brought to light, whilst men are satisfied and delighted with such scanty and puerile tasks, nay, even think that they have pursued or attained some great object in their accomplishment.

89. Nor should we neglect to observe that natural philosophy has, in every age, met with a troublesome and difficult opponent: I mean superstition, and a blind and immoderate zeal for religion. For we see that among the Greeks those who first disclosed the natural causes of thunder and storms to the yet untrained ears of man, were condemned as guilty of impiety towards the gods. Nor did some of the old fathers of Christianity treat those much better who showed by the most positive proofs (such as no one now disputes) that the earth is spherical, and thence asserted that there were antipodes.

Even in the present state of things, the condition of discussions on natural philosophy is rendered more difficult and dangerous by the summaries and methods of divines, who, after reducing divinity into such order as they could, and brought it into a scientific form, have proceeded to mingle an undue proportion of the contentious and thorny philosophy of Aristotle with the substance of religion.

The fictions of those who have not feared to deduce and confirm the truth of the Christian religion by the principles and authority of philosophers, tend to the same end, though in a different manner. They celebrate the union of faith and the senses as though it were legitimate, with great pomp and solemnity, and gratify men's pleasing minds with a variety, but, in the mean time, confound most improperly things divine and human. Moreover, in these mixtures of divinity and philosophy, the received doctrines of the latter are alone included, and any novelty, even though it be an improvement, scarcely escapes banishment and extermination.

In short, you may find all access to any species of philosophy, however pure, intercepted by the ignorance of divines. Some, in their simplicity, are apprehensive that a too deep inquiry into nature may penetrate beyond the proper bounds of decorum, transferring and absurdly applying what is said of sacred mysteries in holy writ against those who pry into divine secrets, to the mysteries of nature, which are not forbidden by any prohibition. Others, with more cunning, imagine and consider that if secondary causes be unknown, every thing may more easily be referred to the divine hand and wand; a matter, as they think, of the greatest consequence to religion, but which can only really mean that God wishes to be gratified by means of falsehood. Others fear from past example, lest motion and change in philosophy should terminate in an attack upon religion. Lastly, there are others who appear anxious lest there should be something discovered in the investigation of nature to overthrow, or at least shake religion, particularly among the unlearned. The two last apprehensions appear to resemble animal instinct, as if men were diffident, in the bottom of their minds, and secret meditations, of the strength of religion, and the empire of faith over the senses; and therefore feared that some danger awaited them from an inquiry into nature. But any one who properly considers the subject, will find natural philosophy to be, after the word of God, the surest remedy against superstition, and the most approved support of faith. She is therefore rightly bestowed upon religion as a most faithful attendant, for the one exhibits the will and the other the power of God. Nor was he wrong who observed, "Ye err, not knowing the Scriptures and the power of God;" thus uniting in one bond the revelation of his will, and the contemplation of his power. In the mean while it is not wonderful that the progress of natural philosophy has been restrained, since religion, which has so much influence on men's minds, has been led and hurried to oppose her through the ignorance of some and the imprudent zeal of others.

90. Again, in the habits and regulations of schools, universities, and the like assemblies, de-

stined for the abode of learned men, and the improvement of learning, every thing is found to be opposed to the progress of the sciences. For the lectures and exercises are so ordered, that any thing out of the common track can scarcely enter the thoughts and contemplations of the mind. If, however, one or two have perhaps dared to use their liberty, they can only impose the labour on themselves, without deriving any advantage from the association of others : and if they put up with this, they will find their industry and spirit of no slight disadvantage to them in making their fortune. For the pursuits of men in such situations are, as it were, chained down to the writings of particular authors, and if any one dare to dissent from them, he is immediately attacked as a turbulent and revolutionary spirit. Yet how great is the difference between civil matters and the arts; for there is not the same danger from new activity and new light. In civil matters even a change for the better is suspected on account of the commotion it occasions; for civil government is supported by authority, unanimity, fame, and public opinion, and not by demonstration. In the arts and sciences, on the contrary, every department should resound, as in mines, with new works and advances. And this is the rational, though not the actual view of the case : for that administration and government of science we have spoken of, is wont too rigorously to repress its growth.

91. And even should the odium I have alluded to be avoided, yet it is sufficient to repress the increase of science that such attempts and industry was unrewarded. For the cultivation of science and its reward belong not to the same individual. The advancement of science is the work of a powerful genius, the prize and reward belong to the vulgar or to princes, who (with a few exceptions) are scarcely moderately well informed. Nay, such progress is not only deprived of the rewards and beneficence of individuals, but even of popular praise : for it is above the reach of the generality, and easily overwhelmed and extinguished by the winds of common opinions. It is not wonderful, therefore, that little success has attended that which has been little honoured.

92. But by far the greatest obstacle to the advancement of the sciences and the undertaking of any new attempt or department is to be found in men's despair and the idea of impossibility. For men of a prudent and exact turn of thought are altogether diffident in matters of this nature, considering the obscurity of nature, and the shortness of life, the deception of the senses, and weakness of the judgment. They think, therefore, that in the revolutions of ages and of the world there are certain floods and ebbs of the sciences, and that they grow and flourish at one time, and wither and fall off at another, that

when they have attained a certain degree and condition they can proceed no further.

If, therefore, any one believe or promise greater things, they impute it to an uncurbed and immature mind, and imagine that such efforts begin pleasantly, then become laborious, and end in confusion. And since such thoughts easily enter the minds of men of dignity and excellent judgment, we must really take heed lest we should be captivated by our affection for an excellent and most beautiful object, and relax or diminish the severity of our judgment ! and we must diligently examine what gleam of hope shines upon us, and in what direction it manifests itself, so that, banishing her lighter dreams, we may discuss and weigh whatever appears of more sound importance. We must consult the prudence of ordinary life, too, which is diffident upon principle, and in all human matters augurs the worst. Let us then speak of hope, especially as we are not vain promisers, nor are willing to force or ensnare men's judgment, but would rather lead them willingly forward. And, although we shall employ the most cogent means of enforcing hope when we bring them to particulars, and especially those which are digested and arranged in our Tables of Invention, (the subject partly of the second, but principally of the fourth part of the Instauration,) which are indeed rather the very object of our hopes than hope itself; yet to proceed more leniently, we must treat of the preparation of men's minds, of which the manifestation of hope forms no slight part. For, without it, all that we have said tends rather to produce a gloom than to encourage activity or quicken the industry of experiment, by causing them to have a worse and more contemptuous opinion of things as they are than they now entertain, and to perceive and feel more thoroughly their unfortunate condition. We must therefore disclose and prefix our reasons for not thinking the hope of success improbable, as Columbus before his wonderful voyage over the Atlantic gave the reasons of his conviction that new lands and continents might be discovered besides those already known. And these reasons though at first rejected, were yet proved by subsequent experience, and were the causes and beginnings of the greatest events.

93. Let us begin from God, and show that our pursuit from its exceeding goodness clearly proceeds from him, the Author of good and Father of light. Now, in all divine works, the smallest beginnings lead assuredly to some result, and the remark in spiritual matters that "The kingdom of God cometh without observation," is also found to be true in every great work of divine Providence; so that every thing glides quietly on without confusion or noise, and the matter is achieved before men either think or perceive that it is commenced. Nor should we neglect to

mention the prophecy of Daniel of the last days of the world.* "Many shall run to and fro and knowledge shall be increased," thus plainly hinting and suggesting that Fate (which is Providence) would cause the complete circuit of the globe, (now accomplished, or at least going forward by means of so many distant voyages,) and the increase of learning, to happen at the same epoch.

94. We† will next give a most potent reason for hope deduced from the errors of the past, and the ways still unattempted. For well was an ill governed state thus reproved,‡ "That which is worst with regard to the past, should appear most consolatory for the future. For if you had done all that your duty commanded, and your affairs proceeded no better, you could not even hope for their improvement; but since their present unhappy situation is not owing to the force of circumstances, but to your own errors, you have reason to hope, that by banishing or correcting the latter, you can produce a great change for the better in the former." So, if men had, during the many years that have elapsed, adhered to the right way of discovering and cultivating the sciences without being able to advance, it would be assuredly bold and presumptuous to imagine it possible to improve; but if they have mistaken the way and wasted their labour on improper objects, it follows that the difficulty does not arise from things themselves, which are not in our power, but from the human understanding, its practice and application, which is susceptible of remedy and correction. Our best plan, therefore, is to expose these errors. For, in proportion as they impeded the past, so do they afford reason to hope for the future. And although we have touched upon them above, yet we think it right to give a brief, bare, and simple enumeration of them in this place.

95. Those who have treated of the sciences have been either empirics or dogmatical. The former like ants only heap up and use their store, the latter like spiders spin out their own webs. The bee, a mean between both, extracts matter from the flowers of the garden and the field, but works and fashions it by its own efforts. The true labour of philosophy resembles hers, for it neither relies entirely or principally on the powers of the mind, nor yet lays up in the memory, the matter afforded by the experiments of natural history or mechanics in its raw state, but changes

and works it in the understanding. We have good reason, therefore, to derive hope from a closer and purer alliance of these faculties, (the experimental and rational) than has yet been attempted.

96. Natural philosophy is not yet to be found unadulterated, but is impure and corrupted; by logic in the school of Aristotle, by natural theology in that of Plato, by mathematics in the second school of Plato, (that of Proclus and others,) which ought rather to terminate natural philosophy than to generate or create it. We may, therefore, hope for better results from pure and unmixed natural philosophy.

97. No one has yet been found possessed of sufficient firmness and severity, to resolve upon and undertake the task of entirely abolishing common theories and notions, and applying the mind afresh, when thus cleared and levelled, to particular researches. Hence our human reasoning is a mere farrago and crude mass, made up of a great deal of credulity and accident, and the puerile notions it originally contracted.

But if a man of mature age, unprejudiced senses, and clear mind, would betake himself anew to experience and particulars, we might hope much more from such a one. In which respect we promise ourselves the fortune of Alexander the Great, and let none accuse us of vanity till they have heard the tale, which is intended to check vanity.

For Æschines spoke thus of Alexander and his exploits: "We live not the life of mortals, but are born at such a period that posterity will relate and declare our prodigies." As if he considered the exploits of Alexander to be miraculous.

But in succeeding ages* Livy took a better view of the fact, and has made some such observation as this upon Alexander: "That he did no more than dare to despise insignificance." So in our opinion posterity will judge of us, "That we have achieved no great matters, but only set less account upon what is considered important." For the mean time (as we have before observed) our only hope is in the regeneration of the sciences, by regularly raising them on the foundation of experience and building them anew, which I think none can venture to affirm to have been already done or even thought of.

98. The foundations of experience (our sole resource) have hitherto failed completely or have been very weak; nor has a store and a collection of particular facts capable of informing the mind or in any way satisfactory, been either sought after or amassed. On the contrary, learned, but

---

* Daniel, c. xii. ver. 4.

† Hence to Aphorism 108 treats of the grounds of hope to be derived from correcting former errors.

‡ See Demosthenes's 3d Philippic near the beginning, τὸ χείριστον ἐν τοῖς παρεληλυθόσι, τοῦτο πρὸς τὰ μέλλοντα βέλτιστον ὑπάρχει. Τί οὖν ἐστὶ τοῦτο; ὅτι οὔτε μικρὸν, οὔτε μέγα οὐδὲν τῶν δεόντων ποιούντων ὑμῶν, κακῶς τὰ πράγματα ἔχει· ἐπείτοιγε εἰ πάνθ'ἃ προσήκει πραττόντων ὑμῶν, οὕτω διέκειτο οὐδ᾽ ἂν ἐλπὶς ἦν αὐτὰ γενέσθαι βελτίω, νῦν δὲ τῆς μὲν ῥᾳθυμίας τῆς ὑμετέρας καὶ τῆς ἀμελείας κεκράτηκε Φιλιππός, τῆς πόλεως δ᾽οὐ κεκράτηκεν.

* See Livy, lib. x. c. 17, where in a digression on the probable effect of a contest between Rome and Alexander the Great, he says: "Non cum Dario rem esse dixisset: quem mulierum ac spadonum agmen trahentem inter purpuram atque aurum, oneratum fortunæ apparatibus, prædam veriùs quam hostem, nihil aliud quam ausus vana contemnere, incruentus devicit."

idle and indolent men received some mere reports of experience, traditions, as it were, of dreams, as establishing or confirming their philosophy ; and have not hesitated to allow them the weight of legitimate evidence. So that a system has been pursued in philosophy with regard to experience, resembling that of a kingdom or state which would direct its councils and affairs according to the gossip of city and street politicians, instead of the letters and reports of ambassadors and messengers worthy of credit. Nothing is rightly inquired into, or verified, noted, weighed, or measured, in natural history. Indefinite and vague observation produces fallacious and uncertain information. If this appear strange or our complaint somewhat too unjust, (because Aristotle himself, so distinguished a man, and supported by the wealth of so great a king, has completed an accurate history of animals, to which others with greater diligence but less noise have made considerable additions, and others again have composed copious histories and notices of plants, metals, and fossils,) it will arise from a want of sufficiently attending to and comprehending our present observations. For a natural history compiled on its own account, and one collected for the mind's information as a foundation for philosophy, are two different things. They differ in several respects, but principally in this ; the former contains only the varieties of natural species without the experiments of mechanical arts. For as in ordinary life every person's disposition, and the concealed feelings of the mind and passions are most drawn out when they are disturbed ; so the secrets of nature betray themselves more readily when tormented by art, than when left to their own course. We must begin, therefore, to entertain hopes of natural philosophy then only, when we have a better compilation of natural history, its real basis and support.

99. Again, even in the abundance of mechanical experiments there is a very great scarcity of those which best inform and assist the understanding. For the mechanic, little solicitous about the investigation of truth, neither directs his attention nor applies his hand to any thing that is not of service to his business. But our hope of further progress in the sciences will then only be well founded, when numerous experiments shall be received and collected into natural history, which, though of no use in themselves, assist materially in the discovery of causes and axioms: which experiments we have termed enlightening, to distinguish them from those which are *profitable*. They possess this wonderful property and nature, that they never deceive, or fail you, for, being used only to discover the natural cause of some object, whatever be the result, they equally satisfy your aim by deciding the question.

100. We must not only search for and procure a greater number of experiments, but also introduce a completely different method, order, and progress of continuing and promoting experience For vague and arbitrary experience is (as we have observed) mere groping in the dark, and rather astonishes than instructs. But when experience shall proceed regularly and uninterruptedly by a determined rule, we may entertain better hopes of the sciences.

101. But after having collected and prepared an abundance and store of natural history, and of the experience required for the operations of the understanding, or philosophy ; still the un derstanding is as capable of acting on such materials of itself with the aid of memory alone, as any person would be of retaining and achieving by memory the computation of an almanac. Yet meditation has hitherto done more for discovery than writing, and no experiments have been committed to paper. We cannot, however, approve of any mode of discovery without writing, and when that comes into more general use we may have further hopes.

102. Besides this, there is such a multitude and host as it were of particular objects, and lying so widely dispersed, as to distract and confuse the understanding ; and we can therefore hope for no advantage from its skirmishing, and quick movements and incursions, unless we put its forces in due order and array by means of proper, and well arranged, and as it were living tables of discovery of these matters which are the subject of investigation, and the mind then apply itself to the ready prepared and digested aid which such tables afford.

103. When we have thus properly and regularly placed before the eyes a collection of particulars, we must not immediately proceed to the investigation and discovery of new particulars or effects, or, at least, if we do so, must not rest satisfied therewith. For, though we do not deny that by transferring the experiments from one art to another, (when all the experiments of each have been collected and arranged, and have been acquired by the knowledge and subjected to the judgment of a single individual,) many new experiments may be discovered, tending to benefit society and mankind, by what we term *literate experience ;* yet comparatively insignificant results are to be expected thence, whilst the more important are to be derived from the new light of axioms, deduced by certain method and rule from the above particulars, and pointing out and defining new particulars in their turn. Our road is not along a plain, but rises and falls, ascending to axioms and descending to effects.

104. Nor can we suffer the understanding to jump and fly from particulars to remote and most general axioms, (such as are termed the principles of arts and things,) and thus prove and make out their intermediate axioms according to the supposed unshaken truth of the former. This,

however, has always been done to the present time from the natural bent of the understanding, educated, too, and accustomed to this very method by the syllogistic mode of demonstration. But we can then only augur well for the sciences, when the ascent shall proceed by a true scale and successive steps, without interruption or breach, from particulars to the lesser axioms, thence to the intermediate, (rising one above the other,) and lastly to the most general. For the lowest axioms differ but little from bare experiment, the highest and most general (as they are esteemed at present) are notional, abstract, and of no real weight. The intermediate are true, solid, full of life, and upon them depend the business and fortune of mankind; beyond these are the really general, but not abstract, axioms, which are truly limited by the intermediate.

We must not then add wings, but rather lead and ballast to the understanding, to prevent its jumping or flying, which has not yet been done; but whenever this takes place we may entertain greater hopes of the sciences.

105. In forming axioms, we must invent a different form of induction from that hitherto in use; not only for the proof and discovery of principles, (as they are called,) but also of minor intermediate, and in short every kind of axioms. The induction which proceeds by simple enumeration is puerile, leads to uncertain conclusions, and is exposed to danger from one contradictory instance, deciding generally from too small a number of facts, and those only the most obvious. But a really useful induction for the discovery and demonstration of the arts and sciences should separate nature by proper rejections and exclusions, and then conclude for the affirmative, after collecting a sufficient number of negatives. Now, this has not been done, or even attempted, except perhaps by Plato, who certainly uses this form of induction in some measure, to sift definitions and ideas. But much of what has never yet entered the thoughts of man, must necessarily be employed in order to exhibit a good and legitimate mode of induction, or demonstration; so as even to render it essential for us to bestow more pains upon it than have hitherto been bestowed on syllogisms. The assistance of induction is to serve us not only in the discovery of axioms, but also in defining our notions. Much indeed is to be hoped from such an induction as has been described.

106. In forming our axioms from induction, we must examine and try, whether the axiom we derive, be only fitted and calculated for the particular instances from which it is deduced, or whether it be more extensive and general. If it be the latter, we must observe, whether it confirm its own extent and generality, by giving surety, as it were, in pointing out new particulars, so that we may neither stop at actual discoveries, nor with a careless grasp catch at shadows and abstract forms, instead of substances of a determinate nature; and as soon as we act thus, well authorized hopes may with reason be said to beam upon us.

107. Here, too, we may again repeat what we have said above, concerning the extending of natural philosophy, and reducing particular sciences to that one, so as to prevent any schism or dismembering of the sciences; without which we cannot hope to advance.

108. Such are the observations we would make, in order to remove despair and excite hope, by bidding farewell to the errors of past ages, or by their correction. Let us examine whether there be other grounds for hope. And, first, if many useful discoveries have occurred to mankind by chance or opportunity, without investigation or attention on their part, it must necessarily be acknowledged that much more may be brought to light by investigation and attention, if it be regular and orderly, not hasty and interrupted. For, although it may now and then happen that one falls by chance upon something that had before escaped considerable efforts and laborious inquiries, yet, undoubtedly, the reverse is generally the case. We may, therefore, hope for further, better, and more frequent results from man's reason, industry, method, and application, than from chance and mere animal instinct, and the like, which have hitherto been the sources of invention.

109. We may also derive some reason for hope, from the circumstance of several actual inventions being of such a nature, that scarcely any one could have formed a conjecture about them, previously to their discovery, but would rather have ridiculed them as impossible. For men are wont to guess about new subjects, from those they are already acquainted with, and the hasty and vitiated fancies they have thence formed: than which there cannot be a more fallacious mode of reasoning, because much of that which is derived from the sources of things, does not flow in their usual channel. If, for instance, before the discovery of cannon, one had described its effects in the following manner: "There is a new invention, by which walls and the greatest bulwarks can be shaken and overthrown from a considerable distance," men would have begun to contrive various means of multiplying the force of projectiles and machines, by means of weights and wheels, and other modes of battering and projecting. But it is improbable that any imagination or fancy would have hit upon a fiery blast expanding and developing itself so suddenly and violently, because none would have seen an instance at all resembling it, except perhaps in earthquakes or thunder, which they would have immediately rejected as the great operations of nature, not to be imitated by man.

So if, before the discovery of silk thread, any

one had observed, " that a species of thread had been discovered, fit for dresses and furniture, far surpassing the thread of worsted or flax in fineness, and at the same time in tenacity, beauty, and softness," men would have begun to imagine something about Chinese plants, or the fine hair of some animals, or the feathers or down of birds, but certainly would never have had an idea of its being spun by a small worm, in so copious a manner, and renewed annually. But if any one had ventured to suggest the silk worm, he would have been laughed at, as if dreaming of some new manufacture from spiders.

So, again, if before the discovery of the compass, any one had said, " that an instrument had been invented, by which the quarters and points of the heavens could be exactly taken and distinguished," men would have entered into disquisitions on the refinement of astronomical instruments, and the like, from the excitement of their imaginations; but the thought of any thing being discovered, which not being a celestial body, but a mere mineral or metallic substance, should yet in its motion agree with that of such bodies, would have appeared absolutely incredible. Yet were these facts, and the like (unknown for so many ages) not discovered at last, either by philosophy or reasoning, but by chance and opportunity; and (as we have observed) they are of a nature most heterogeneous, and remote from what was hitherto known, so that no previous knowledge could lead to them.

We* may, therefore, well hope that many excellent and useful matters are yet treasured up in the bosom of nature, bearing no relation or analogy to our actual discoveries, but out of the common track of our imagination, and still undiscovered; and which will doubtless be brought to light in the course and lapse of years, as the others have been before them; but in the way we now point out, they may rapidly and at once be both represented and anticipated.

110. There are moreover some inventions which render it probable that men may pass and hurry over the most noble discoveries which lie immediately before them. For, however the discovery of gunpowder, silk, the compass, sugar, paper, or the like, may appear to depend on peculiar properties of things and nature, printing at least involves no contrivance which is not clear and almost obvious. But from want of observing that although the arrangement of the types of letters required more trouble than writing with the hand, yet these types once arranged serve for innumerable impressions, whilst manuscript only affords one copy; and again, from want of observing that ink might be thickened so as to stain without running, (which was necessary, seeing the letters face upwards, and the impression is made from above,) this most beautiful invention (which assists so materially the propagation of learning) remained unknown for so many ages.

The human mind is often so awkward and ill regulated in the career of invention, that it is at first diffident, and then despises itself. For it appears at first incredible that any such discovery should be made, and when it has been made, it appears incredible that it should so long have escaped men's research. All which affords good reason for the hope that a vast mass of inventions yet remains, which may be deduced not only from the investigation of new modes of operation, but also from transferring, comparing, and applying these already known, by the method of what we have termed literate experience.

111. Nor should we omit another ground of hope. Let men only consider (if they will) their infinite expenditure of talent, time, and fortune, in matters and studies of far inferior importance and value: a small portion of which applied to sound and solid learning would be sufficient to overcome every difficulty. And we have thought right to add this observation, because we candidly own that such a collection of natural and experimental history as we have traced in our own mind, and as is really necessary, is a great, and, as it were, royal work, requiring much labour and expense.

112. In the mean time, let no one be alarmed at the multitude of particulars, but rather inclined to hope on that very account. For the particular phenomena of the arts and nature are in reality but as a handful, when compared with the fictions of the imagination, removed and separated from the evidence of facts. The termination of our method is clear, and I had almost said, near at hand; the other admits of no termination, but only of infinite confusion. For men have hitherto dwelt but little, or rather only slightly touched upon experience, whilst they have wasted much time on theories and the fictions of the imagination. If we had but any one who could actually answer our interrogations of nature, the invention of all causes and sciences would be the labour of but a few years.

113. We think some ground of hope is afforded by our own example, which is not mentioned for the sake of boasting, but as a useful remark. Let those who distrust their own powers observe myself, one who have amongst my contemporaries been the most engaged in public business, who am not very strong in health, (which causes a great loss of time,) and am the first explorer of this course, following the guidance of none, nor even communicating my thoughts to a single individual; yet having once firmly entered in the right

---

* This hope has been abundantly realized in the discovery of gravity, and the decomposition of light, strictly by the inductive method. To a better philosophy, we may also attribute the discovery of electricity, galvanism, and their mutual connexion with each other, and magnetism, the inventions of the air pump, steam engine, chronometer, &c.

way, and submitting the powers of my mind to things. I have somewhat advanced (as 1 make bold to think) the matter I now treat of. Then let others consider what may be hoped from men who enjoy abundant leisure, from united labours, and the succession of ages, after these suggestions on our part, especially in a course which is not confined, like theories, to individuals, but admits of the best distribution and union of labour and effect, particularly in collecting experiments. For men will then only begin to know their own power, when each performs a separate part, instead of undertaking in crowds the same work.

114. Lastly, though a much more faint and uncertain breeze of hope were to spring up from our new continent, yet we consider it necessary to make the experiment, if we would not show a dastard spirit. For the risk attending want of success is not to be compared with that of neglecting the attempt; the former is attended with the loss of a little human labour, the latter with that of an immense benefit. For these and other reasons, it appears to us that there is abundant ground to hope, and to induce not only those who are sanguine to make experiment, but even those who are cautious and sober to give their assent.

115. Such are the grounds for banishing despair, hitherto one of the most powerful causes of the delay and restraint to which the sciences have been subjected ; in treating of which, we have at the same time discussed the signs and causes of the errors, idleness, and ignorance, that have prevailed : seeing especially that the more refined causes, which are not open to popular judgment and observation, may be referred to our remarks on the idols of the human mind. Here, too, we should close the demolishing branch of our Instauration, which is comprised in three confutations. 1. The confutation of natural human reason left to itself. 2. The confutation of demonstration. 3. The confutation of theories, or received systems of philosophy and doctrines. Our confutation has followed such a course as was open to it, namely, the exposing of the signs of error, and the producing evidence of the causes of it: for we could adopt no other, differing, as we do, both in first principles and demonstrations from others.

It is time for us, therefore, to come to the art itself, and the rule for the interpretation of nature : there is, however, still something which must not be passed over. For the intent of this first book of aphorisms being to prepare the mind for understanding as well as admitting what follows, we must now, after having cleansed, polished, and levelled its surface, place it in a good position, and, as it were, a benevolent aspect towards our propositions ; seeing that prejudice in new matters may be produced not only by the strength of preconceived notions, but also by a false anticipation or expectation of the matter proposed. We shall, therefore, endeavour to induce good and correct

opinions of what we offer, although this be only necessary for the moment, and, as it were, laid *out at interest*, until the matter itself be well understood.

116. First, then, we must desire men not to suppose that we are ambitious of founding any philosophical sect, like the ancient Greeks, or some moderns, as Telesius,* Patricius,† and Severinus.‡ For, neither is this our intention, nor do we think that peculiar abstract opinions on nature and the principles of things, are of much importance to men's fortunes ; since it were easy to revive many ancient theories, and to introduce many new ones ; as, for instance, many *hypotheses* with regard to the *heavens* can be formed, differing in themselves, and yet sufficiently according with the phenomena.

We bestow not our labour on such theoretical and, at the same time, useless topics. On the contrary, our determination is that of trying whether we can lay a firmer foundation, and extend to a greater distance the boundaries of human power and dignity. And although, here and there, upon some particular points, we hold (in our own opinion) more true and certain, and I might even say, more advantageous tenets, than those in general repute, (which we have collected in the fifth part of our Instauration,) yet we offer no universal or complete theory. The time does not yet appear to us to be arrived, and we entertain no hope of our life being prolonged to the completion of the sixth part of the Instauration, (which is destined for philosophy discovered by the interpretation of nature,) but are content if we proceed quietly and usefully in our intermediate pursuit, scattering, in the mean time, the seeds of less adulterated truth for posterity, and, at least, commence the great work.

117. And, as we pretend not to found a sect, so do we neither offer nor promise particular effects : which may occasion some to object to us, that since we so often speak of effects, and consider every thing in its relation to that end, we ought also to give some earnest of producing them. Our course and method, however, as we have often said, and again repeat, is such as not to deduce effects from effects, nor experiments from experiments, (as the empirics do,) but in our capacity of legitimate interpreters of nature, to deduce causes and axioms from effects and

* Bernardino Telesio, a Neapolitan. He studied at Padua, and published his " De Rerum naturâ juxta propria principia" in 1565, in opposition to Aristotle. He applied mathematics to physics, and held some notions similar to those of Parmenides.

† Francesco Patrizio, born in Cherso, on the coast of Dalmatia, in 1529. He studied at Padua, and was afterwards professor of Platonic philosophy at Rome till his death in 1597. He impugned Aristotle's philosophy in his Nova de Universis Philosophia.

‡ Marco Aurelio Severini, a learned physician of Naples, who published an attack on Aristotle's Natural History, and several other works. He was born in 1580

experiments; and new effects and experiments from those causes and axioms.

And, although any one of moderate intelligence and ability will observe the indications and sketches of many noble effects in our tables of inventions, (which form the fourth part of the Instauration,) and also in the examples of particular instances cited in the second part, as well as in our observations on history, (which is the subject of the third part; yet we candidly confess that our present natural history, whether compiled from books or our own inquiries, is not sufficiently copious and well ascertained to satisfy, or even assist, a proper interpretation.

If, therefore, there be any one who is more disposed and prepared for mechanical art, and ingenious in discovering effects, than in the mere management of experiment, we allow him to employ his industry in gathering many of the fruits of our history and tables in his way, and applying them to effects, receiving them as interest till he can obtain the principal. For our own part, having a greater object in view, we condemn all hasty and premature rest in such pursuits, as we would Atalanta's apple (to use a common allusion of ours;) for we are not childishly ambitious of golden fruit, but use all our efforts to make the course of art outstrip nature, and we hasten not to reap moss or the green blade, but wait for a ripe harvest.

118. There will be some, without doubt, who, on a perusal of our history and tables of invention, will meet with some uncertainty, or perhaps fallacy, in the experiments themselves, and will thence, perhaps, imagine that our discoveries are built on false foundations and principles. There is, however, really nothing in this, since it must needs happen in beginnings. For it is the same as if in writing or printing one or two letters were wrongly turned or misplaced, which is no great inconvenience to the reader, who can easily by his own eye correct the error; let men in the same way conclude that many experiments in natural history may be erroneously believed and admitted, which are easily expunged and rejected afterwards by the discovery of causes and axioms. It is, however, true that if these errors in natural history and experiments become great, frequent, and continued, they cannot be corrected and amended by any dexterity of wit or art. If, then, even in our natural history, well examined and compiled with such diligence, strictness, and (I might say) reverential scruples, there be now and then something false and erroneous in the details, what must we say of the common natural history, which is so negligent and careless when compared with ours? or of systems of philosophy and the sciences based on such loose soil, or rather quicksand? Let none then be alarmed by such observations.

119. Again, our history and experiments will contain much that is light and common, mean and illiberal, too refined and merely speculative. and, as it were, of no use, and this, perhaps, may divert and alienate the attention of mankind. With regard to what is common; let men reflect, that they have hitherto been used to do nothing but refer and adapt the causes of things of rare occurrence to those of things which more frequently happen, without any investigation of the causes of the latter, taking them for granted and admitted.

Hence they do not inquire into the causes of gravity, the rotation of the heavenly bodies, heat, cold, light, hardness, softness, rarity, density, liquidity, solidity, animation, inanimation, similitude, difference, organic formation, but taking them to be self-evident, manifest, and admitted, they dispute and decide upon other matters of less frequent and familiar occurrence.

But we (who know that no judgment can be formed of that which is rare or remarkable, and much less any thing new brought to light, without a previous regular examination and discovery of the causes of that which is common, and the causes again of those causes) are necessarily compelled to admit the most common objects into our history. Besides, we have observed that nothing has been so injurious to philosophy as this circumstance, namely, that familiar and frequent objects do not arrest and detain men's contemplation, but are carelessly admitted, and their causes never inquired after; so that information on unknown subjects is not more often wanted than attention to those which are known.

120. With regard to the meanness or even the filthiness of particulars, for which (as Pliny observes) an apology is requisite, such subjects are no less worthy of admission into natural history than the most magnificent and costly: nor do they at all pollute natural history, for the sun enters alike the palace and the privy, and is not thereby polluted. We neither dedicate nor raise a capitol or pyramid to the pride of man, but rear a holy temple in his mind, on the model of the universe, which model therefore we imitate. For that which is deserving of existence is deserving of knowledge, the image of existence. Now, the mean and splendid alike exist. Nay, as the finest odours are sometimes produced from putrid matter, (such as musk and civet,) so does valuable light and information emanate from mean and sordid instances. But we have already said too much, for such fastidious feelings are childish and effeminate.

121. The next point requires a more accurate consideration, namely, that many parts of our history will appear to the vulgar, or even any mind accustomed to the present state of things, fantastically and uselessly refined. Hence we have in regard to this matter said from the first, and must again repeat, that we look for experi-

ments that shall afford light rather than profit, imitating the divine creation, which, as we have often observed, only produced light on the first day, and assigned that whole day to its creation, without adding any material work.

If any one then imagine such matters to be of no use, he might equally suppose light to be of no use, because it is neither solid nor material. For in fact the knowledge of simple natures, when sufficiently investigated and defined, resembles light, which though of no great use in itself, affords access to the general mysteries of effects, and with a peculiar power comprehends and draws with it whole bands and troops of effects, and the sources of the most valuable axioms. So, also, the elements of letters have of themselves separately no meaning, and are of no use, yet are they as it were the original matter in the composition and preparation of speech. The seeds of substances whose effect is powerful, are of no use except in their growth, and the scattered rays of light itself avail not unless collected.

But if speculative subtilties give offence, what must we say of the scholastic philosophers who indulged in them to such excess? And those subtilties were wasted on words, or at least common notions, (which is the same thing,) not on things or nature, and alike unproductive of benefit in their origin and their consequences: in no way resembling ours, which are at present useless, but in their consequences of infinite benefit. Let men be assured that all subtile disputes and discursive efforts of the mind are late and preposterous, when they are introduced subsequently to the discovery of axioms, and that their true or at any rate chief opportunity is when experiment is to be weighed and axioms to be derived from it. They otherwise catch and grasp at nature, but never seize or detain her: and we may well apply to nature that which has been said of opportunity or fortune, "that she wears a lock in front, but is bald behind."

In short, we may reply decisively to those who despise any part of natural history as being vulgar, mean, or subtle and useless in its origin, in the words of a poor woman to a haughty prince who had rejected her petition, as unworthy and beneath the dignity of his majesty: "then cease to reign;" for it is quite certain that the empire of nature can neither be obtained nor administered by one who refuses to pay attention to such matters as being poor and too minute.

122. Again, it may be objected to us as being singular and harsh, that we should with one stroke and assault, as it were, banish all authorities and sciences, and that too by our own efforts, without requiring the assistance and support of any of the ancients.

Now, we are aware, that had we been ready to act otherwise than sincerely, it was not difficult to refer our present method to remote ages, prior to those of the Greeks, (since the sciences in all probability flourished more in their natural state, though silently, than when they were paraded with the fifes and trumpets of the Greeks;) or even (in parts at least) to some of the Greeks themselves, and to derive authority and honour from thence; as men of no family labour to raise and form nobility for themselves in some ancient line, by the help of genealogies. Trusting, however, to the evidence of facts, we reject every kind of fiction and imposture: and think it of no more consequence to our subject, whether future discoveries were known to the ancients, and set or rose according to the vicissitudes of events and lapse of ages, than it would be of importance to mankind to know whether the new world be the island of Atlantis,* and known to the ancients, or be now discovered for the first time.

With regard to the universal censure we have bestowed, it is quite clear to any one who properly considers the matter, that it is both more probable and more modest than any partial one could have been. For if the errors had not been rooted in the primary notions, some well conducted discoveries must have corrected others that were deficient. But since the errors were fundamental, and of such a nature that men may be said rather to have neglected or passed over things than to have formed a wrong or false judgment of them, it is little to be wondered at, that they did not obtain what they never aimed at, nor arrive at a goal which they had not determined, nor perform a course which they had neither entered upon nor adhered to.

With regard to our presumption, we allow that if we were to assume a power of drawing a more perfect straight line or circle than any one else, by superior steadiness of hand or acuteness of eye, it would lead to a comparison of talent; but if one merely assert that he can draw a more perfect line or circle with a ruler or compasses, than another can by his unassisted hand or eye, he surely cannot be said to boast of much. Now this applies not only to our first original attempt, but also to those who shall hereafter apply themselves to the pursuit. For our method of discovering the sciences, merely levels men's wits, and leaves but little to their superiority, since it achieves every thing by the most certain rules and demonstrations. Whence, (as we have often observed,) our attempt is to be attributed to fortune rather than talent, and is the offspring of time rather than of wit. For a certain sort of chance has no less effect upon our thoughts than on our acts and deeds.

123. We may, therefore, apply to ourselves the joke of him who said, "that water and wine drinkers could not think alike," especially as it hits the matter so well. For others, both an-

* See Plato's Timæus.

rients and moderns, have, in the sciences, drank a crude liquor like water, either flowing of itself from the understanding, or drawn up by logic as the wheel draws up the bucket. But we drink and pledge others with a liquor made of many well ripened grapes, collected and plucked from particular branches, squeezed in the press, and at last clarified and fermented in a vessel. It is not, therefore, wonderful that we should not agree with others.

124. Another objection will, without doubt, be made, namely, that we have not ourselves established a correct, or the best goal or aim of the sciences, (the very defect we blame in others.) For, they will say, that the contemplation of truth is more dignified and exalted than any utility or extent of effects: but that our dwelling so long and anxiously on experience and matter, and the fluctuating state of particulars, fastens the mind to earth, or rather casts it down into an abyss of confusion and disturbance, and separates and removes it from a much more divine state, the quiet and tranquillity of abstract wisdom. We willingly assent to their reasoning, and are most anxious to effect the very point they hint at and require. For we are founding a real model of the world in the understanding, such as it is found to be, not such as man's reason has distorted. Now, this cannot be done without dissecting and anatomizing the world most diligently; but we declare it necessary to destroy completely the vain, little, and as it were apish imitations of the world, which have been formed in various systems of philosophy by men's fancies. Let men learn (as we have said above) the difference that exists between the idols of the human mind, and the ideas of the Divine mind. The former are mere arbitrary abstractions; the latter the true marks of the Creator on his creatures, as they are imprinted on, and defined in matter, by true and exquisite touches. Truth, therefore, and utility are here perfectly identical, and the effects are of more value as pledges of truth than from the benefit they confer on men.

125. Others may object that we are only doing that which has already been done, and that the ancients followed the same course as ourselves. They may imagine, therefore, that, after all this stir and exertion, we shall at last arrive at some of those systems that prevailed among the ancients: for that they, too, when commencing their meditations, laid up a great store of instances and particulars, and digested them under topics and titles in their commonplace books, and so worked out their systems and arts, and then decided upon what they discovered, and related now and then some examples to confirm and throw light upon their doctrine; but thought it superfluous and troublesome to publish their notes, minutes, and commonplaces, and, therefore, followed the example of builders, who remove

the scaffolding and ladders when the building is finished. Nor can we indeed believe the case to have been otherwise. But to any one, not entirely forgetful of our previous observations, it will be easy to answer this objection, or rather scruple. For, we allow that the ancients had a particular form of investigation and discovery, and their writings show it. But it was of such a nature, that they immediately flew from a few instances and particulars, (after adding some common notions, and a few generally received opinions most in vogue,) to the most general conclusions, or the principles of the sciences, and then by their intermediate propositions deduced their inferior conclusions, and tried them by the test of the immovable and settled truth of the first, and so constructed their art. Lastly, if some new particulars and instances were brought forward, which contradicted their dogmas, they either with great subtilty reduced them to one system, by distinctions or explanations of their own rules, or got rid of them clumsily as exceptions, labouring most pertinaciously in the mean time to accommodate the causes of such as were not contradictory to their own principles. Their natural history and their experience were both far from being what they ought to have been, and their flying off to generalities ruined every thing.

126. Another objection will be made against us, that we prohibit decisions, and the laying down of certain principles, till we arrive regularly at generalities by the intermediate steps, and thus keep the judgment in suspense and lead to uncertainty. But our object is not uncertainty, but fitting certainty, for we derogate not from the senses, but assist them, and despise not the understanding, but direct it. It is better to know what is necessary, and not to imagine we are fully in possession of it, than to imagine that we are fully in possession of it, and yet in reality to know nothing which we ought.

127. Again, some may raise this question rather than objection, whether we talk of perfecting natural philosophy alone according to our method, or the other sciences also, such as logic, ethics, politics. We certainly intend to comprehend them all. And as common logic, which regulates matters by syllogisms, is applied not only to natural, but also to every other science, so our inductive method likewise comprehends them all. For we form a history and tables of invention for anger, fear, shame, and the like, and also for examples in civil life, and the mental operations of memory, composition, division, judgment, and the rest, as well as for heat and cold, light, vegetation, and the like. But since our method of interpretation, after preparing and arranging a history, does not content itself with examining the operations and disquisitions of the mind, like common logic; but also inspects the nature of

things, we so regulate the mind that it may be enabled to apply itself in every respect correctly to that nature. On that account we deliver numerous and various precepts in our doctrine of interpretation, so that they may apply in some measure to the method of discovering the quality and condition of the subject-matter of investigation.

128. Let none even doubt whether we are anxious to destroy and demolish the philosophy, arts, and sciences, which are now in use. On the contrary, we readily cherish their practice, cultivation, and honour. For we by no means interfere to prevent the prevalent system from encouraging discussion, adorning discourses, or being employed serviceably in the chair of the professor or the practice of common life, and being taken, in short, by general consent, as current coin. Nay, we plainly declare, that the system we offer will not be very suitable for such purposes, not being easily adapted to vulgar apprehensions, except by effects and works. To show our sincerity in professing our regard and friendly disposition towards the received sciences, we can refer to the evidence of our published writings, (especially our books on the advancement of learning.) We will not, therefore, endeavour to evince it any further by words; but content ourselves with steadily and professedly premising, that no great progress can be made by the present methods, in the theory or contemplation of science, and that they cannot be made to produce any very abundant effects.

129. It remains for us to say a few words on the excellence of our proposed end. If we had done so before, we might have appeared merely to express our wishes, but now that we have excited hope and removed prejudices, it will perhaps have greater weight. Had we performed and completely accomplished the whole, without frequently calling in others to assist in our labours, we should then have refrained from saying any more, lest we should be thought to extol our own deserts. Since, however, the industry of others must be quickened, and their courage roused and inflamed, it is right to recall some points to their memory.

First, then, the introduction of great inventions appears one of the most distinguished of human actions; and the ancients so considered it. For they assigned divine honours to the authors of inventions, but only heroic honours to those who displayed civil merit, (such as the founders of cities and empires, legislators, the deliverers of their country from everlasting misfortunes, the quellers of tyrants, and the like.) And if any one rightly compare them, he will find the judgment of antiquity to be correct. For the benefits derived from inventions may extend to mankind in general, but civil benefits to particular spots alone; the latter, moreover, last but for a time,

the former forever. Civil reformation seldom is carried on without violence and confusion, whilst inventions are a blessing and a benefit, without injuring or afflicting any.

Inventions are, also, as it were, new creations and imitations of divine works; as was expressed by the poet:*

"Primum frugiferos fœtus mortalibus ægris
Dididerant quondam præstanti nomine Athenæ
Et recreuverunt vitam legesque rogarunt."

And it is worthy of remark in Solomon, that whilst he flourished in the possession of his empire, in wealth, in the magnificence of his works, in his court, his household, his fleet, the splendour of his name, and the most unbounded admiration of mankind, he still placed his glory in none of these, but declared,† "That it is the glory of God to conceal a thing, but the glory of a king to search it out."

Again, let any one but consider the immense difference between men's lives in the most polished countries of Europe, and in any wild and barbarous region of the New Indies, he will think it so great, that man may be said to be a god unto man, not only on account of mutual aid and benefits, but from their comparative states: the result of the arts, and not of the soil or climate.

Again, we should notice the force, effect, and consequences of inventions, which are nowhere more conspicuous than in those three which were unknown to the ancients; namely, printing, gunpowder, and the compass. For these three have changed the appearance and state of the whole world; first in literature, then in warfare, and lastly in navigation: and innumerable changes have been thence derived, so that no empire, sect, or star, appears to have exercised a greater power and influence on human affairs than these mechanical discoveries.

It will, perhaps, be as well to distinguish three species and degrees of ambition. First, that of men who are anxious to enlarge their own power in their country, which is a vulgar and degenerate kind; next, that of men who strive to enlarge the power and empire of their country over mankind, which is more dignified, but not less covetous; but if one were to endeavour to renew and enlarge the power and empire of mankind in general over the universe, such ambition (if it may so be termed) is both more sound and more noble than the other two. Now, the empire of man over things is founded on the arts and sciences alone, for nature is only to be commanded by obeying her.

* This is the opening of the sixth book of Lucretius. Bacon probably quoted from memory; the lines are,

Primæ frugiferos fœtus mortalibus ægris
Dididerunt quondam præclaro nomine Athenæ
Et recreaverunt, &c.

The teeming corn, that feeble mortals crave,
First, and long since, renowned Athens gave,
And cheered their life—then taught to frame their laws
† Prov. xxv 2.

Besides this, if the benefit of any particular invention has had such an effect as to induce men to consider him greater than a man, who has thus obliged the whole race ; how much more exalted will that discovery be, which leads to the easy discovery of every thing else ! Yet, (to speak the truth,) in the same manner as we are very thankful for light which enables us to enter on our way, to practise arts, to read, to distinguish each other, and yet sight is more excellent and beautiful than the various uses of light ; so is the contemplation of things as they are, free from superstition or imposture, error or confusion, much more dignified in itself than all the advantage to be derived from discoveries.

Lastly, let none be alarmed at the objection of the arts and sciences becoming depraved to malevolent or luxurious purposes and the like, for the same can be said of every worldly good ; talent, courage, strength, beauty, riches, light itself, and the rest. Only let mankind regain their rights over nature, assigned to them by the gift of God, and obtain that power, whose exercise will be governed by right reason and true religion.

130. But it is time for us to lay down the art of interpreting nature; to which we attribute no absolute necessity (as if nothing could be done without it) nor perfection, although we think that our precepts are most useful and correct. For we are of opinion, that if men had at their command a proper history of nature and experience, and would apply themselves steadily to it, and could bind themselves to two things ; 1. To lay aside received opinions and notions ; 2. To restrain themselves, till the proper season, from generalization, they might, by the proper and genuine exertion of their minds, fall into our way of interpretation without the aid of any art. For interpretation is the true and natural act of the mind, when all obstacles are removed: certainly, however, every thing will be more ready and better fixed by our precepts.

Yet do we not affirm that no addition can be made to them; on the contrary, considering the mind in its connexion with things, and not merely relatively to its own powers, we ought to be persuaded that the art of invention can be made to grow with the inventions themselves.

THE SECOND BOOK OF

APHORISMS,

ON THE

INTERPRETATION OF NATURE, OR THE REIGN OF MAN.

---

1. To generate and superinduce a new nature, or new natures, upon a given body, is the labour and aim of human power : whilst to discover the form or true difference of a given nature, or the nature* to which such nature is owing, or source from whence it emanates, (for these terms approach nearest to an explanation of our meaning,) is the labour and discovery of human knowledge. And, subordinate to these primary labours, are two others of a secondary nature and inferior stamp. Under the first must be ranked the transformation of concrete bodies from one to another, which is possible within certain limits : under the second, the discovery, in every species of generation and motion, of the latent and uninterrupted process, from the manifest efficient and manifest subject-matter up to the given form : and a like discovery of the latent conformation of bodies which are at rest, instead of being in motion.

2. The unhappy state of man's actual knowledge is manifested even by the common asser-

tions of the vulgar. It is rightly laid down, that " true knowledge is that which is deduced from causes." The division of four causes, also, is not amiss : *matter, form,* the *efficient,* and *end,* or final cause.* Of these, however, the latter is so far from being beneficial, that it even corrupts the sciences, except in the intercourse of man with man. The discovery of form is considered desperate. As for the *efficient cause,* and *matter,* (according to the present system of inquiry and the received opinions concerning them, by which they are placed remote from, and without any latent process towards form,) they are but desultory and superficial, and of scarcely any avail to real and active knowledge. Nor are we unmindful of our having pointed out and corrected above the error of the human mind, in assigning the first qualities of essence to forms.† For, although nothing exists in nature except individual bodies,

* Τὸ τί ἦν εἶναι, or ἡ οὐσία of Aristotle. See lib. 3. Metap.

* These divisions are from Aristotle's Metaphysics, where they are termed. 1, ὕλη ἤ τὸ ὑποκείμενον. 2, τὸ τί ἦν εἶναι. 3, ὅθεν ἤ ἀρχη τῆς κινέσεως. 4, τὸ οὗ ἑνέκεν—καὶ τὸ ἀγωυου.

† See Aphorism 51, and 2d paragraph of Aphorism 65, in the first book.

exhibiting clear individual effects according to particular laws :* yet, in each branch of learning, that very law, its investigation, discovery, and development, are the foundation both of theory and practice.† This, law, therefore, and its parallel in each science, is what we understand by the term *form*, adopting that word because it has grown into common use, and is of familiar occurrence.

3. He who has learned the cause of a particular nature, (such as whiteness or heat,) in particular subjects only, has acquired but an imperfect knowledge: as he who can induce a certain effect upon particular substances only, among those which are susceptible of it, has acquired but an imperfect power. But he who has only learned the efficient and material cause, (which causes are variable, and mere vehicles conveying form to particular substances,) may perhaps arrive at some new discoveries in matters of a similar nature, and prepared for the purpose, but does not stir the limits of *things*, which are much more deeply rooted: whilst he who is acquainted with *forms*, comprehends the unity of nature in substances apparently most distinct from each other. He can disclose and bring forward, therefore, (though it has never yet been done,) things which neither the vicissitudes of nature, nor the industry of experiment, nor chance itself, would ever have brought about, and which would forever have escaped man's thoughts. From the discovery of forms, therefore, results genuine theory and free practice.

4. Although there is a most intimate connection and almost an identity between the ways of human power and human knowledge; yet, on account of the pernicious and inveterate habit of dwelling upon abstractions, it is by far the safest method to commence and build up the sciences from those foundations which bear a relation to the practical division, and to let them mark out and limit the theoretical. We must consider, therefore, what precepts, or what direction or guide, a person would most desire, in order to generate and superinduce any nature upon a given body: and this not in abstruse, but in the plainest language.

For instance, if a person should wish to superinduce the yellow colour of gold upon silver, or an additional weight, (observing always the laws of matter,) or transparency on an opaque stone, or tenacity in glass, or vegetation on a substance which is not vegetable, we must (I say) consider what species of precept or guide this person would prefer. And, firstly, he will doubtless be anxious to be shown some method that will neither fail in effect, nor deceive him in the trial of it. Secondly, he will be anxious that the prescribed method should not restrict him and tie him down to peculiar means, and certain particular methods of acting. For he will, perhaps, be at a loss, and without the power or opportunity of collecting and procuring such means. Now, if there be other means and methods (besides those prescribed) of creating such a nature, they will perhaps be of such a kind as are in his power; yet, by the confined limits of the precept he will be deprived of reaping any advantage from them. Thirdly, he will be anxious to be shown something not so difficult as the required effect itself, but approaching more nearly to practice.

We will lay this down, therefore, as the genuine and perfect rule of practice; " That it should be certain, free, and preparatory, or having relation to practice." And this is the same thing as the discovery of a true *form*. For the form of any nature is such, that when it is assigned, the particular nature infallibly follows. It is, therefore, always present when that nature is present, and universally attests such presence, and is inherent in the whole of it. The same form is of such a character, that if it be removed, the particular nature infallibly vanishes. It is, therefore, absent whenever that nature is absent, and perpetually testifies such absence, and exists in no other nature. Lastly, the true form is such, that it deduces the particular nature from some source of essence existing in many subjects, and more known (as they term it) to nature, than the form itself.* Such, then, is our determination and rule with regard to a genuine and perfect theoretical axiom; " that a nature be found convertible with a given nature, and yet such as to limit the more known nature, in the manner of a real genus." But these two rules, the practical and theoretical, are in fact the same, and that which is most useful in practice is most correct in theory.

5. But the rule or axiom for the transformation of bodies is of two kinds. The first regards the body as an aggregate or combination of simple natures. Thus, in gold are united the following circumstances; it is yellow, heavy, of a certain weight, malleable and ductile to a certain extent; it is not volatile, loses part of its substance by fire, melts in a peculiar manner, is separated and dissolved by particular methods, and so of the other *natures* observable in gold. An axiom, therefore, of this kind deduces the subject from the *forms* of simple natures. For he who has acquired the forms and methods of superinducing

---

* Plato's *ideas* or *forms*, are the abstractions or generalizations of distinct species, which have no *real* existence, *individuals only existing*.

† Observe throughout, Bacon's term *form* means no more than law. See, further, third paragraph of Aphorism 17 of this book.

* Thus, to adopt Bacon's own illustration, motion is a property common to many subjects, from which must be deduced the form of heat, by defining a particular genus of motion convertible with heat. See the First Vintage in Aphorism 20, below.

yellowness, weight, ductility, stability, deliques-
cence, solution, and the like, and their degrees
and modes, will consider and contrive how to
unite them in any body, so as to* transform it
into gold. And this method of operating belongs
to primary action. For it is the same thing to
produce one or many simple natures, except that
man is more confined and restricted in his operations, if many be required, on account of the difficulty of uniting many natures together. It must,
however, be observed, that this method of operating (which considers natures as simple, though in
a concrete body) sets out from what is constant,
eternal, and universal in nature, and opens such
broad paths to human power, as the thoughts of
man can in the present state of things scarcely
comprehend or figure to itself. The second kind
of axiom (which depends on the discovery of the
latent process) does not proceed by simple natures,
but by concrete bodies, as they are found in nature, and in its usual course. For instance; suppose the inquiry to be, from what beginnings, in
what manner, and by what process gold or any
metal or stone is generated from the original
menstruum, or its elements, up to the perfect
mineral: or, in like manner, by what process
plants are generated, from the first concretion of
juices in the earth, or from seeds, up to the perfect
plant, with the whole successive motion, and
varied and uninterrupted efforts of nature; and
the same inquiry be made as to a regularly
deduced system of the generation of animals
from coition to birth, and so on of other bodies.

Nor is this species of inquiry confined to the
mere generation of bodies, but it is applicable to
other changes and labours of nature. For instance; where an inquiry is made into the whole
series, and continued operation of the nutritive
process, from the first reception of the food, to its
complete assimilation to the recipient: or into the
voluntary motion of animals, from the first impression of the imagination, and the continuous
effects of the spirits, up to the bending and motion of the joints; or into the free motion of the
tongue and lips, and other accessories which give
utterance to articulate sounds. For all these investigations relate to concrete or associated natures, artificially brought together, and take into
consideration certain particular and special habits
of nature, and not those fundamental and general
laws which constitute forms. It must, however,
be plainly owned, that this method appears more
prompt and easy, and of greater promise than the
primary one.

In like manner the operative branch, which an-
swers to this contemplative branch, extends and
advances its operation from that which is usually

observed in nature, to other subjects immediately
connected with it, or not very remote from such
immediate connexion. But the higher and radical operations upon nature, depend entirely on the
primary axioms. Besides, even where man has not
the means of acting, but only of acquiring knowledge, as in astronomy, (for man cannot act upon,
change, or transform the heavenly bodies,) the
investigation of facts or truth, as well as the
knowledge of causes and coincidences, must be
referred to those primary and universal axioms
that regard simple natures; such as the nature of
spontaneous rotation, attraction, or the magnetic
force, and many others which are more common
than the heavenly bodies themselves. For, let
no one hope to determine the question, whether
the earth or heaven revolve in the diurnal motion,
unless he have first comprehended the nature of
spontaneous rotation.

6. But the latent process, of which we speak,
is far from being obvious to men's minds, beset
as they now are. For, we mean not the measures, symptoms, or degrees of any process
which can be exhibited in the bodies themselves, but simply a continued process, which,
for the most part, escapes the observation of
the senses.

For instance; in all generations and transformations of bodies, we must inquire, what is in
the act of being lost and escaping, what remains,
what is being added, what is being diluted, what
is being contracted, what is being united, what is
being separated, what is continuous, what is
broken off, what is urging forward, what impedes,
what predominates, what is subservient, and
many other circumstances.

Nor are these inquiries again to be made in the
mere generation and transformation of bodies
only, but in all other alterations and fluctuations,
we must in like manner inquire; what precedes,
what succeeds, what is quick, what is slow,
what produces and what governs motion, and the
like. All which matters are unknown and unattempted by the sciences, in their present heavy
and inactive state. For, since every natural act is
brought about by the smallest efforts, or at least
such as are too small to strike our senses, let no
one hope that he will be able to direct or change
nature, unless he have properly comprehended
and observed these efforts.

7. In like manner, the investigation and discovery of the latent confirmation in bodies is no less
new, than the discovery of the latent process and
form. For, we as yet are doubtless only admitted
to the antechamber of nature, and do not prepare
an entrance into her presence-room. But nobody
can endue a given body with a new nature, or
transform it successfully and appropriately into a
new body, without possessing a complete knowledge of the body so to be changed or transformed.
For he will run into vain, or, at least, into difficult

---

* By the recent discoveries in electric magnetism, copper
wires, or, indeed, wires of any metal may be transformed
into magnets; the magnetic law or form having been to that
extent discovered.

and perverse methods, ill adapted to the nature of the body upon which he operates. A clear path, therefore, towards this object, also must be thrown open, and well supported.

Labour is well and usefully bestowed upon the anatomy of organized bodies, such as those of men and animals, which appears to be a subtile matter, and a useful examination of nature. This species of anatomy, however, is that of first sight, open to the senses, and takes place only in organized bodies. It is obvious, and of ready access, when compared with the real anatomy of latent conformation in bodies which are considered similar, particularly in specific objects and their parts: as those of iron, stone, and the similar parts of plants and animals, as the root, the leaf, the flower, the flesh, the blood, and bones, &c. Yet human industry has not completely neglected this species of anatomy: for we have an instance of it in the separation of similar bodies by distillation, and other solutions, which shows the dissimilarity of the compound, by the union of the homogeneous parts. These methods are useful, and of importance to our inquiry, although attended generally with fallacy: for many natures are assigned and attributed to the separate bodies, as if they had previously existed in the compound, which, in reality, are recently bestowed and superinduced by fire and heat, and the other modes of separation. Besides, it is, after all, but a small part of the labour of discovering the real conformation in the compound, which is so subtile and nice, that it is rather confused and lost by the operation of the fire, than discovered and brought to light.

A separation and solution of bodies, therefore, is to be effected, not by fire indeed, but rather by reasoning and true induction, with the assistance of experiment, and by a comparison with other bodies, and a reduction to those simple natures and their forms, which meet and are combined in the compound; and we must assuredly pass from Vulcan to Minerva, if we wish to bring to light the real texture and conformation of bodies, upon which every occult and (as it is sometimes called) specific property and virtue of things depends, and whence, also, every rule of powerful change and transformation is deduced.

For instance, we must examine what spirit is in every body, what tangible essence; whether that spirit is copious and exuberant, or meagre and scarce, fine or coarse, aeriform or igniform, active or sluggish, weak or robust, progressive or retrograde, abrupt or continuous, agreeing with external and surrounding objects, or differing from them, &c. In like manner must we treat tangible essence, (which admits of as many distinctions as the spirit,) and its hairs, fibres, and varied texture. Again, the situation of the spirit in the corporeal mass, its pores, passages, veins, and cells, and the rudiments or first essays of the organic body are subject to the same examination. In these, however, as in our former inquiries, and therefore in the whole investigation of latent conformation, the only genuine and clear light which completely dispels all darkness and subtile difficulties, is admitted by means of the primary axioms.

8. This method will not bring us to atoms,* which takes for granted the vacuum, and the immutability of matter, (neither of which hypotheses is correct;) but to the real particles, such as we discover them to be. Nor is there any ground for alarm at this refinement, as if it were inexplicable, for, on the contrary, the more inquiry is directed to simple natures, the more will every thing be placed in a plain and perspicuous light; since we transfer our attention from the complicated to the simple, from the incommensurable to the commensurable, from surds to rational quantities, from the indefinite and vague to the definite and certain: as when we arrive at the elements of letters, and the simple tones of concords. The investigation of nature is best conducted when mathematics are applied to physics. Again, let none be alarmed at vast numbers and fractions; for, in calculation, it is as easy to set down or to reflect upon a thousand as a unit, or the thousandth part of an integer as an integer itself.

9. From† the two kinds of axioms above specified arise the two divisions of philosophy and the sciences, and we will use the commonly adopted terms, which approach the nearest to our meaning, in our own sense. Let the investigation of forms, which (in reasoning at least, and after their own laws) are eternal and immutable, constitute *metaphysics*, and let the investigation of the efficient cause of matter, latent process, and latent conformation (which all relate merely to the ordinary course of nature, and not to her fundamental and eternal laws) constitute *physics*. Parallel to these let there be two practical divisions; to *physics* that of *mechanics*, and to *metaphysics* that of *magic*, in the purest sense of the term, as applied to its ample means and its command over nature.

10. The object of our philosophy being thus laid down, we proceed to precepts, in the most clear and regular order. The signs for the interpretation of nature comprehend two divisions: the first regards the eliciting or creating of axioms from experiment, the second the deducing or deriving of new experiments from axioms. The first admits of three subdivisions into *ministrations*. 1. To the senses. 2. To the memory.

---

* The theory of the Epicureans and others. The atoms are supposed to be indivisible, unalterable particles, endued with all the properties of the given body, and forming that body by their union. They must be separated of course, which either takes a vacuum for granted, or introduces a tertium quid into the composition of the body.

† Compare the three following aphorisms with the three last chapters of the third book of the De Augmentis Scientiarum

3. To the mind or reason. For we must first prepare as a foundation for the whole a complete and accurate natural and experimental history. We must not imagine or invent, but discover the acts and properties of nature.

But natural and experimental history is so varied and diffuse, that it confounds and distracts the understanding unless it be fixed and exhibited in due order. We must, therefore, form tables and co-ordinations of instances, upon such a plan, and in such order, that the understanding may be enabled to act upon them.

Even when this is done, the understanding, left to itself and its own operation, is incompetent and unfit to construct its axioms without direction and support. Our third ministration, therefore, must be true and legitimate induction, the very key of interpretation. We must begin, however, at the end, and go back again to the others.

11. The investigation of Forms proceeds thus: A nature being given, we must first present to the understanding all the known instances which agree in the same nature, although the subject-matter be considerably diversified. And this collection must be made as a mere history, and without any premature reflection, or too great degree of refinement. For instance: take the investigation of the form of heat.

Instances agreeing in the Form of Heat.

1. The rays of the sun, particularly in summer, and at noon.

2. The same reflected and condensed, as between mountains, or along walls, and particularly in burning mirrors.

3. Ignited meteors.

4. Burning lightning.

5. Eruptions of flames from the cavities of mountains, &c.

6. Flame of every kind.

7. Ignited solids.

8. Natural warm baths.

9. Warm or heated liquids.

10. Warm vapours and smoke: and the air itself, which admits a most powerful and violent heat if confined, as in reverberating furnaces.

11. Damp hot weather, arising from the constitution of the air, without any reference to the time of the year.

12. Confined and subterraneous air in some caverns, particularly in winter.

13. All shaggy substances, as wool, the skins of animals, and the plumage of birds, contain some heat.

14. All bodies, both solid and liquid, dense and rare, (as the air itself,) placed near fire for any time.

15. Sparks arising from the violent percussion of flint and steel.

16 All bodies rubbed violently, as stone, wood, cloth, &c., so that rudders, and axles of wheels, sometimes catch fire, and the West Indians obtain fire by attrition.

17. Green and moist vegetable matter confined and rubbed together; as roses, peas in baskets; so hay, if it be damp when stacked, often catches fire.

18. Quicklime sprinkled with water.

19. Iron, when first dissolved by acids in a glass, and without any application to fire; the same of tin, but not so intensely.

20. Animals, particularly internally; although the heat is not perceivable by the touch in insects, on account of their small size.

21. Horse dung, and the like excrement from other animals, when fresh.

22. Strong oil of sulphur and of vitriol exhibit the operation of heat in burning linen.

23. As does the oil of marjoram, and like substances, in burning the bony substance of the teeth.

24. Strong and well rectified spirits of wine exhibit the same effects; so that white of eggs when thrown into it, grows hard and white, almost in the same manner as when boiled, and bread becomes burnt and brown as if toasted.

25. Aromatic substances and warm plants, as the dracunculus [arum,] old nasturtium, &c.; which, though they be not warm to the touch, (whether whole or pulverized,) yet are discovered by the tongue and palate to be warm and almost burning when slightly masticated.

26. Strong vinegar and all acids, or any part of the body not clothed with the epidermis, as the eye, tongue, or any wounded part, or where the skin is removed, excite a pain differing but little from that produced by heat.

27. Even a severe and intense cold produces a sensation of burning.[*]

"Nam Boreæ penetrabile frigus adurit."

28. Other instances.

We are wont to call this a table of existence and presence.

12. We must next present to the understanding instances which do not admit of the given nature; for form (as we have observed) ought no less to be absent where the given nature is absent, than to be present where it is present. If, however we were to examine every instance, our labour would be infinite.

Negatives, therefore, must be classed under the affirmatives, and the want of the given nature must be inquired into more particularly in objects which have a very close connexion with those others in which it is present and manifest. And this we are wont to term a table of deviation or of absence in proximity.

[*] "Ne tenues pluviæ, rapidive potentia solis
Acrior, aut Boreæ penetrabile frigus adurnt."
Virg. Georg. l. v. 92, 93

Proximate Instances wanting the Nature of Heat.

First negative subjunctive instance to the first affirmative instances.

The rays of the moon, stars, and comets, are not found to be warm to the touch, nay, the severest cold has been observed to take place at the full of the moon. Yet the larger fixed stars are supposed to increase and render more intense the heat of the sun, as he approaches them; when the sun is in the sign of the lion, for instance, and in the dog-days.

Second negative to the second affirmative.

The rays of the sun in what is called the middle region of the air give no heat, to account for which the commonly assigned reason is satisfactory; namely, that that region is neither sufficiently near to the body of the sun, whence the rays emanate, nor to the earth, whence they are reflected. And the fact is manifested by snow being perpetual on the tops of mountains, unless extremely lofty. But it is observed on the other hand by some, that at the Peak of Teneriffe, and also among the Andes of Peru, the tops of the mountains are free from snow, which only lies in the lower part, as you ascend. Besides, the air on the summit of these mountains is found to be by no means cold, but only thin and sharp; so much so, that in the Andes, it pricks and hurts the eyes from its extreme sharpness, and even excites the orifice of the stomach and produces vomiting. The ancients also observed, that the rarity of the air on the summit of Olympus, was such, that those who ascended it, were obliged to carry sponges moistened with vinegar and water, and to apply them now and then to their nostrils, as the air was not dense enough for their respiration; on the summit of which mountain it is also related, there reigned so great a serenity and calm, free from rain, snow, or wind, that the letters traced upon the ashes of the sacrifices on the altar of Jupiter, by the fingers of those who had offered them, would remain undisturbed till the next year. Those even, who, at this day, go to the top of the Peak of Teneriffe, walk by night and not in the daytime, and are advised and pressed by their guides, as soon as the sun rises, to make haste in their descent, on account of the danger, (apparently arising from the rarity of the atmosphere,) lest their breathing should be relaxed and suffocated.

Third negative to the second affirmative.

The reflection of the solar rays in the polar regions is found to be weak and inefficient in producing heat; so that the Dutch, who wintered in Nova Zembla, and expected that their vessels would be freed about the beginning of July from the obstruction of the mass of ice which had blocked it up, were disappointed and obliged t·embark in their boat. Hence the direct rays of the sun appear to have but little power even on the plain, and when reflected, unless they are multiplied and condensed, which takes place when the sun tends more to the perpendicular: for then the incidence of the rays occurs at more acute angles, so that the reflected rays are nearer to each other, whilst, on the contrary, when the sun is in a very oblique position, the angles of incidence are very obtuse and the reflected rays at a greater distance. In the mean time it must be observed, that there may be many operations of the solar rays, relating too to the nature of heat, which are not proportioned to our touch, so that, with regard to us, they do not tend to produce warmth, but, with regard to some other bodies, have their due effect in producing it.

Fourth negative to the second affirmative.

Let the following experiment be made. Take a lens the reverse of a burning glass, and place it between the hand and the solar rays, and observe whether it diminish the heat of the sun, as a burning glass increases it. For it is clear, with regard to the visual rays, that, in proportion as the lens is made of unequal thickness in the middle and at its sides, the images appear either more diffused or contracted. It should be seen, therefore, if the same be true with regard to heat.

Fifth negative to the second affirmative.

Let the experiment be well tried, whether the lunar rays can be received and collected by the strongest and best burning-glasses, so as to produce even the least degree of heat. But if that degree be, perhaps, so subtile and weak, as not to be perceived or ascertained by the touch, we must have recourse to those glasses which indicate the warm or cold state of the atmosphere, and let the lunar rays fall through the burning glass on the top of this thermometer, and then notice if the water be depressed by the heat.*

Sixth negative to the second affirmative.

Let the burning-glass be tried on warm objects which emit no luminous rays, as heated, but not ignited iron or stone, or hot water, or the like; and observe whether the heat become increased and condensed, as happens with the solar rays.

Seventh negative to the second affirmative.

Let it be tried on common flame.

Eighth negative to the third affirmative.

The effect of comets, (if we can reckon them amongst meteors,) in augmenting the heat of the season, is not found to be constant or clear, although droughts have generally been observed to follow them. However, luminous lines, and pil

---

* For the construction of Bacon's thermometer see No. 38 in the table of the degrees of heat. It serves also as a barometer, but is inaccurate in both capacities.

lars, and openings, and the like, appear more often in winter than in summer, and especially with the most intense cold, but joined with drought. Lightning, and coruscations, and thunder, however, rarely happen in winter, and generally at the time of the greatest heats. The appearances we term falling stars, are generally supposed to consist of some shining and enflamed viscous substance, rather than of violently hot matter. But let this be further investigated.

Ninth negative to the fourth affirmative.

Some coruscations emit light without burning; but are never accompanied by thunder.

Tenth negative to the fifth affirmative.

Eructations and eruptions of flame are to be found in cold climates as well as in hot, as in Iceland and Greenland; just as the trees of cold countries are sometimes inflammable, and more pitchy and resinous than in warm; as the fir, pine, and the like. But the position and nature of the soil, where such eruptions are wont to happen, is not yet sufficiently investigated to enable us to subjoin a negative instance to the affirmative.

Eleventh negative to the sixth affirmative.

All flame is constantly more or less warm, and this instance is not altogether negative. Yet, it is said, that the ignis fatuus, (as it is called,) and which sometimes is driven against walls, has but little heat; perhaps it resembles that of spirits of wine, which is mild and gentle. That flame, however, appears yet milder, which, in some well authenticated and serious histories, is said to have appeared round the head and hair of boys and virgins, and instead of burning their hair, merely to have played about it. And it is most certain that a sort of flash, without any evident heat, has sometimes been seen about a horse when sweating at night, or in damp weather. It is also a well known fact,* and it was almost considered as a miracle, that, a few years since, a girl's apron sparkled when a little shaken or rubbed; which was, perhaps, occasioned by the alum or salts with which the apron was imbued, and which, after having been stuck together and incrusted rather strongly, were broken by the friction. It is well known that all sugar, whether candied or plain, if it be hard, will sparkle when broken or scraped in the dark. In like manner sea and salt water is sometimes found to shine at night when struck violently by the oar. The foam of the sea, when agitated by tempests, also sparkles at night, and the Spaniards call this appearance the sea's lungs. It has not been sufficiently ascertained what degree of heat attends the flame which the ancient sailors called Castor and Pollux, and the moderns call St. Ermus's fire.

* Was it a silk apron, which will exhibit electric sparks? but silk was then scarce.

Twelfth negative to the seventh affirmative.

Every ignited body that is red-hot is always warm, although without flame, nor is any negative instance subjoined to this affirmative. Rotten wood, however, approaches nearly to it, for it shines at night, and yet is not found to be warm; and the putrefying scales of fish, which shine in the same manner, are not warm to the touch, nor the body of the glow-worm, or of the fly called lucciola.*

Thirteenth negative to the eighth affirmative.

The situation and nature of the soil of natural warm baths has not been sufficiently investigated, and, therefore, a negative instance is not subjoined.

Fourteenth negative to the ninth affirmative.

To the instances of warm liquids we may subjoin the negative one of the peculiar nature of liquids in general. For no tangible liquid is known that is at once warm in its nature and constantly continues warm; but their heat is only superinduced as an adventitious nature for a limited time: so that those which are extremely warm in their power and effect, as spirits of wine, chymical aromatic oils, the oils of vitriol and sulphur, and the like, and which speedily burn, are yet cold at first to the touch, and the water of natural baths, poured into any vessel and separated from its source, cools down like water heated by the fire. It is, however, true, that oily substances are rather less cold to the touch than those that are aqueous, oil for instance than water, silk than linen; but this belongs to the table of degrees of cold.

Fifteenth negative to the tenth affirmative.

In like manner we may subjoin a negative instance to that of warm vapour, derived from the nature of vapour itself; as far as we are acquainted with it. For exhalations from oily substances, though easily inflammable, are yet never warm unless recently inhaled from some warm substance.

Sixteenth negative to the tenth affirmative.

The same may be said of the instance of air. For we never perceive that air is warm, unless confined or pressed, or manifestly heated by the sun, by fire, or some other warm body.

Seventeenth negative to the eleventh affirmative.

A negative instance is exhibited in weather by its coldness with an east or north wind, beyond what the season would lead us to expect; just as the contrary takes place with the south or west winds. An inclination to rain (especially in winter) attends warm weather, and to frost cold weather.

Eighteenth negative to the twelfth affirmative.

A negative instance as to air confined in caverns

* The Italian fire-fly.

may be observed in summer. Indeed we should make a more diligent inquiry into the nature of confined air. For, in the first place, the qualities of air in its own nature with regard to heat and cold, may reasonably be the subject of doubt. For air evidently derives its heat from the effects of celestial bodies, and possibly its cold from the exhalation of the earth, and in the mid region of air (as it is termed) from cold vapours and snow, so that no judgment can be formed of the nature of air by that which is out of doors and exposed, but a more correct one might be derived from confined air. It is necessary, however, that the air should be enclosed in a vessel of such materials as would not imbue it with heat or cold of themselves, nor easily admit the influence of the exterternal atmosphere. The experiment should be made therefore with an earthen jar, covered with folds of leather to protect it from the external air, and the air should be kept three or four days in this vessel well closed. On opening the jar, the degree of heat may be ascertained either by the hand or a graduated glass tube.

Nineteenth negative to the thirteenth affirmative.

There is a similar doubt as to whether the warmth of wool, skins, feathers, and the like, is derived from a slight inherent heat, since they are animal excretions, or from their being of a certain fat and oily nature that accords with heat, or merely from the confinement and separation of air which we spoke of in the preceding paragraph.* For all air appears to possess a certain degree of warmth when separated from the external atmosphere. Let an experiment be made, therefore, with fibrous substances of linen, and not of wool, feathers, or silk, which are animal excretions. For it is to be observed that all powders (where air is manifestly enclosed) are less cold than the substances when whole, just as we imagine froth (which contains air) to be less cold than the liquid itself.

Twentieth negative to the fourteenth affirmative.

We have here no exactly negative instance, for we are not acquainted with any body tangible or spirituous which does not admit of heat when exposed to the fire. There is, however, this difference, that some admit it more rapidly, as air, oil, and water, others more slowly, as stone and metals.† This, however, belongs to the table of degrees.

Twenty-first negative to the fifteenth affirmative.

No negative is here subjoined, except the re-

mark that sparks are not kindled by flint and steel, or any other hard substance, unless some small particles of the stone or metal are struck off, and that the air never forms them by friction, as is commonly supposed; besides, the sparks from the weight of the ignited substance, have a tendency to descend rather than to rise, and when extinguished become a sort of dark ash.

Twenty-second negative to the sixteenth affirmative.

We are of opinion that here again there is no negative. For we are not acquainted with any tangible body which does not become decidedly warm by friction, so that the ancients feigned that the gods had no other means or power of creating heat than the friction of air, by rapid and violent rotation. On this point, however, further inquiry must be made, whether bodies projected by machines (as balls from cannon) do not derive some degree of heat from meeting the air, which renders them somewhat warm when they fall. The air in motion rather cools than heats, as in the winds, the bellows, or breath when the mouth is contracted. The motion, however, in such instances is not sufficiently rapid to excite heat, and is applied to a body of air and not to its component parts, so that it is not surprising that heat should not be generated.

Twenty-third negative to the seventeenth affirmative.

We must make a more diligent inquiry into this instance. For herbs, and green and moist vegetables appear to possess a latent heat, so small, however, as not to be perceived by the touch in single specimens, but when they are united and confined, so that their spirit cannot exhale into the air, and they rather warm each other, their heat is at once manifested, and even flame occasionally in suitable substances.

Twenty-fourth negative to the eighteenth affirmative.

Here, too, we must make a more diligent inquiry. For quicklime, when sprinkled with water, appears to conceive heat, either from its being collected into one point, (as we observed of herbs when confined,) or from the irritation and exasperation of the fiery spirit by water, which occasions a conflict and struggle. The true reason will more readily be shown if oil be used instead of water, for oil will equally tend to collect the confined spirit, but not to irritate. The experiment may be made more general, both by using the ashes and calcined products of different bodies, and by pouring different liquids upon them.

Twenty-fifth negative to the nineteenth affirmative.

A negative instance may be subjoined of other metals which are more soft and soluble. For leaf gold dissolved by aqua regia, or lead by aqua fortis, are not warm to the touch whilst dissolving, no more is quicksilver, (as far as I remember,) but

---

* This last is found to be the real air not being a good conductor, and therefore not allowing the escape of heat. The confined air is disengaged when these substances are placed under an exhausted receiver.

† This is erroneous. Air, in fact, is one of the worst, and metals are the best conductors of heat.

silver excites a slight heat, and so does copper, and tin yet more plainly, and most of all, iron and steel, which excite not only a powerful heat, but a violent bubbling. The heat, therefore, appears to be occasioned by the struggle which takes place when these strong dissolvents penetrate, dig into, and tear asunder the parts of those substances, whilst the substances themselves resist. When, however, the substances yield more easily, scarcely any heat is excited:

Twenty-sixth negative to the twentieth affirmative.

There is no negative instances with regard to the heat of animals, except in insects, (as has been observed,) owing to their small size. For, in fishes, as compared with land animals, a lower degree rather than a deprivation of heat is observable. In plants and vegetables, both as to their exudations and pith when freshly exposed, there is no sensible degree of heat. But in animals there is a great difference in the degree, both in particular parts, (for the heat varies near the heart, the brain, and the extremities,) and in the circumstances in which they are placed, such as violent exercise and fevers.

Twenty-seventh negative to twenty-first affirmative.

Here again there is scarcely a negative instance. I might add that the excrements of animals, even when they are no longer fresh, possess evidently some effective heat, as is shown by their enriching the soil.

Twenty-eighth negative to the twenty-second and twenty-third affirmative.

Such liquids (whether oily or watery) as are intensely acrid, exhibit the effects of heat, by the separation and burning of bodies after some little action upon them, yet they are not at first warm to the touch. But they act according to their affinity and the pores of the substances to which they are applied. For aqua regia dissolves gold, but not silver, on the contrary, aqua fortis dissolves silver, but not gold; neither of them dissolves glass, and so of the rest.

Twenty-ninth negative to twenty-fourth affirmative.

Let spirits of wine be tried on wood, or butter, wax, or pitch, to see if this will melt them at all by their heat. For the 24th instance shows that they possess properties resembling those of heat in causing incrustation. Let an experiment also be made with a graduated glass or calendar,* concave at the top, by pouring well rectified spirits of wine into the cavity, and covering it up in order that they may the better retain their heat, then observe whether their heat make the water descend.

Thirtieth negative to twenty-fifth affirmative.

Spices and acrid herbs are sensibly warm to the

* See No 38, in the table of the degrees of heat.

palate, and still more so when taken internally. One should see, therefore, on what other substances they exhibit the effects of heat. Now, sailors tell us that when large quantities of spices are suddenly opened, after having been shut up for some time, there is some danger of fever and inflammation to those who stir them or take them out. An experiment might therefore be made whether such spices and herbs when produced will, like smoke, dry fish and meat hung up over them.

Thirty-first negative to twenty-sixth affirmative.

There is an acrid effect, and a degree of penetration in cold liquids, such as vinegar and oil of vitriol, as well as in warm, such as oil of marjoram and the like. They have, therefore, an equal effect in causing animated substances to smart, and separating and consuming inanimate parts. There is not any negative instance as to this, nor does there exist any animal pain unaccompanied by the sensation of heat.

Thirty-second negative to twenty-seventh affirmative.

There are many effects common to cold and heat, however different in their process. For, snow balls appear to burn boys' hands after a little time, and cold no less than fire preserves bodies from putrefaction, besides, both heat and cold contract bodies. But it is better to refer these instances and the like to the investigation of cold.

13. In the third place, we must exhibit to the understanding the instances in which that nature, which is the object of our inquiries, is present in a greater or less degree, either by comparing its increase and decrease in the same object, or its degree in different objects. For, since the form of a thing is its very essence, and the thing only differs from its form as the apparent from the actual object, or the exterior from the interior, or that which is considered with relation to man from that which is considered with relation to the universe; it necessarily follows that no nature can be considered a real form, which does not uniformly diminish and increase with the given nature. We are wont to call this our table of degrees or comparative instances.

Table of the Degrees or Comparative Instances of Heat.

We will first speak of those bodies which exhibit no degree of heat sensible to the touch, but appear rather to possess a potential heat, or disposition and preparation for it. We will then go on to others, which are actually warm to the touch, and observe the strength and degree of it.

1. There is no known solid or tangible body which is by its own nature originally warm For neither stone, metal, sulphur, fossils, wood water, nor dead animal carcasses, are found warm.

The warm springs in baths appear to be heated accidentally, by flame, subterraneous fire, (such as is thrown up by Etna and many other mountains,) or by the contact of certain bodies, as heat is exhibited in the dissolution of iron and tin. The degree of heat, therefore, in inanimate objects is not sensible to our touch, but they differ in their degrees of cold, for wood and metal are not equally cold. This, however, belongs to the table of degrees of cold.

2. But with regard to potential heat and predisposition to flame, we find many inanimate substances wonderfully adapted to it; as sulphur, naphtha, and saltpetre.

3. Bodies which have previously acquired heat, as horse-dung from the animal, or lime, and perhaps ashes or soot from fire, retain some latent portion of it. Hence distillations and separations of substances are effected by burying them in horse-dung, and heat is excited in lime by sprinkling it with water, (as has been before observed.)

4. In the vegetable world we know of no plant, nor part of any plant, (as the exudations or pith) that is warm to man's touch. Yet, as we have before observed, green weeds grow warm when confined, and some vegetables are warm and others cold to our internal touch, i. e. the palate and stomach, or even, after a while, to our external skin, (as is shown in plasters and ointments.)

5. We know of nothing in the various parts of animals, when dead or detached from the rest, that is warm to the touch. For horse-dung itself does not retain its heat, unless it be confined and buried. All dung, however, appears to possess a potential heat, as in manuring fields. So, also, dead bodies are endued with this latent and potential heat, to such a degree that, in cemeteries where people are interred daily, the earth acquires a secret heat which consumes any recently deposited body much sooner than pure earth : and they tell you that the people of the East are acquainted with a fine soft cloth, made of the down of birds, which can melt butter wrapt gently up in it by its own warmth.

6. Manures, such as every kind of dung, chalk, sea-sand, salt, and the like, have some disposition towards heat.

7. All putrefaction exhibits some slight degree of heat, though not enough to be perceptible by the touch. For, neither the substances, which by putrefaction are converted into animalculæ, as flesh and cheese, nor rotten wood, which shines in the dark, are warm to the touch. The heat, however, of putrid substances displays itself occasionally in a disgusting and strong scent.

8. The first degree of heat, therefore, in substances which are warm to the human touch, appears to be that of animals, and this admits of a great variety of degrees, for the lowest (as in insects) is scarcely perceptible, the highest scarcely equals that of the sun's rays in warm climates and weather, and is not so acute as to be insufferable to the hand. It is said, however, of Constantius, and some others of a very dry constitution and habit of body, that when attacked with violent fevers, they became so warm as to appear almost to burn the hand applied to them.

9. Animals become more warm by motion and exercise, wine and feasting, venery, burning fevers, and grief.

10. In the paroxysm of intermittent fevers the patients are at first seized with cold and shivering, but soon afterwards become more heated than at first; in burning and pestilential fevers they are hot from the beginning.

11. Let further inquiry be made into the comparative heat of different animals, as fishes, quadrupeds, serpents, birds : and also of the different species, as the lion, the kite, or man. For, according to the vulgar opinion, fishes are the least warm internally, and birds the most; particularly doves, hawks, and ostriches.

12. Let further inquiry be made as to the comparative heat in different parts and limbs of the same animal. For milk, blood, seed, and eggs are moderately warm, and less hot than the outward flesh of the animal when in motion or agitated. The degree of heat of the brain, stomach, heart, and the rest, has not yet been equally well investigated.

13. All animals are externally cold in winter and cold weather, but are thought to be internally warmer.

14. The heat of the heavenly bodies, even in the warmest climates and seasons, never reaches such a pitch as to light or burn the dryest wood or straw, or even tinder without the aid of burning-glasses. It can, however, raise vapour from moist substances.

15. Astronomers tell us that some stars are hotter than others. Mars is considered the warmest after the sun, then Jupiter, then Venus. The moon and, above all, Saturn are considered to be cold. Among the fixed stars, Sirius is thought the warmest, then Cor Leonis, or Regulus, then the lesser dog-star.

The sun gives out more heat as it approaches towards the perpendicular or zenith, which may be supposed to be the case with the other planets according to their degree of heat; for instance, that Jupiter gives out more heat when situated beneath Cancer or Leo, than when he is beneath Capricorn and Aquarius.

17. It is to be supposed that the sun and other planets give more heat in perigee, from their approximation to the earth, than when in apogee. But if in any country the sun should be both in its perigee and nearer to the perpendicular at the same time, it must necessarily give out more heat than in a country where it is also in perigee, but situated more obliquely. So that the comparative altitude of the planets should be observed, and

their approach to or declination from the perpendicular in different countries.

18. The sun* and other planets are thought also to give out more heat in proportion as they are nearer to the larger fixed stars; as when the sun is in Leo he is nearer Cor Leonis, Cauda Leonis, Spica Virginis, Sirius, and the lesser dog-star, than when he is in Cancer, where, however, he approaches nearer to the perpendicular.

It is probable also that the quarters of the heavens produce a greater heat (though not perceptibly) in proportion as they are adorned with a greater number of stars, particularly those of the first magnitude.

19. On the whole, the heat of the heavenly bodies is augmented in three ways: 1. The approach to the perpendicular; 2. Proximity or their perigee; 3. The conjunction or union of stars.

20. There is a very considerable difference between the degree of heat in animals, and even in the rays of the heavenly bodies, (as they reach us,) and the heat of the most gentle flame, and even of all ignited substances, nay, liquids, or the air itself, when unusually heated by fire. For the flame of spirit of wine, though diffused and uncollected, is yet able to set straw, linen, or paper on fire, which animal heat, or that of the sun, will never accomplish without a burning-glass.

21. There are, however, many degrees of strength and weakness in flame and ignited bodies: but no diligent inquiry has been made in this respect, and we must, therefore, pass it hastily over. Of all flames, that of spirits of wine appears to be the most gentle, except, perhaps, the ignis fatuus, or the flashes from the perspiration of animals. After this we should be inclined to place the flame of light and porous vegetables, such as straw, reeds, and dried leaves; from which the flame of hair or feathers differs but little. Then, perhaps, comes the flame of wood, particularly that which contains but little rosin or pitch, that of small wood, however, (such as is usually tied up in fagots,) is milder than that of the trunks or roots of trees. This can be easily tried in iron furnaces, where a fire of fagots or branches of trees is of little service. Next follows the flame of oil, tallow, wax, and the like oily and fat substances, which are not very violent. But a most powerful heat is found in pitch and rosin, and a still greater in sulphur, camphire, naphtha, saltpetre, and salts, (after they have discharged their crude matter,) and in their compounds; as in gunpowder, Greek fire, (vulgarly called wild fire,) and its varieties. which possess such a stubborn heat as scarcely to be extinguished by water.

22. We consider that the flame which results

from some imperfect metals is very strong and active: but on all these points further inquiry should be made.

23. The flame of vivid lightning appears to exceed all the above, so as sometimes to have melted even wrought iron into drops, which the other flames cannot accomplish.

24. In ignited bodies there are different degrees of heat, concerning which also a diligent inquiry has not been made. We consider the faintest heat to be that of tinder, touchwood, and dry rope match, such as is used for discharging cannon. Next follows that of ignited charcoal, or cinders, and even bricks, and the like; but the most violent is that of ignited metals, as iron, copper, and the like. Further inquiry, however, must be made into this also.

25. Some ignited bodies are found to be much warmer than some flames; for instance, red-hot iron is much warmer, and burns more than the flame of spirits of wine.

26. Some bodies even not ignited, but only heated by the fire, as boiling water, and the air confined in reverberatories, surpass in heat many flames and ignited substances.

27. Motion increases heat, as is shown in the bellows and the blow-pipe, for the harder metals are not dissolved or melted. by steady, quiet fire. without the aid of the blow-pipe.

28. Let an experiment be made with burning-glasses; in which respect I have observed, that if a glass be placed at the distance of ten inches, for instance, from the combustible object, it does not kindle or burn it so readily as if the glass be placed at the distance of five inches, (for instance,) and be then gradually and slowly withdrawn to the distance of ten inches. The cone and focus of the rays, however, are the same, but the mere motion increases the effect of the heat.

29. Conflagrations, which take place with a high wind, are thought to make greater way against than with the wind, because, when the wind slackens, the flame recoils more rapidly than it advances, when the wind is favourable.

30. Flame does not burst out or arise unless it have some hollow space to move and exert itself in, except in the exploding flame of gunpowder and the like, where the compression and confinement of the flame increases its fury.

31. The anvil becomes so hot by the hammer, that if it were a thin plate, it might probably grow red, like ignited iron, by repeated strokes. Let the experiment be tried.

32. But in ignited bodies that are porous, so as to leave room for the fire to move itself, if its motion be prevented by strong compression, the fire is immediately extinguished; thus it is with tinder, or the burning snuff of a candle or lamp. or even hot charcoal cinders, for when they are squeezed by snuffers, or the foot, and the like the effect of the fire instantly ceases.

---

* This notion is erroneous, but the sun is in Leo about August. when the earth has become heated by the accumulation of heat after the solstice. The maximum of heat in the day is not at noon, but about two o'clock, for the same reason.

33. The approach towards a hot body, increases heat in proportion to the approximation; a similar effect to that of light, for the nearer any object is placed towards the light, the more visible it becomes.

34. The* union of different heats increases heat, unless the substances be mixed. For a large and small fire in the same spot, tend mutually to increase each other's heat, but lukewarm water poured into boiling water cools it.

35. The continued neighbourhood of a warm body increases heat. For the heat, which perpetually passes and emanates from it, being mixed with that which preceded it, multiplies the whole. A fire, for instance, does not warm a room in half an hour as much as the same fire would in an hour. This does not apply to light, for a lamp or candle placed in any spot, gives no more light by remaining there, than it did at first.

36. The irritation of surrounding cold increases heat, as may be seen in fires during a sharp frost. We think that this is owing not merely to the confinement and compression of the heat, (which forms a sort of union;) but also by the exasperation of it, as when the air or a stick are violently compressed or bent, they recoil, not only to the point they first occupied, but still further back. Let an accurate experiment, therefore, be made with a stick, or something of the kind, put into the flame, in order to see whether it be not sooner burnt at the sides than in the middle of it.†

37. There are many degrees in the susceptibility of heat. And, first, it must be observed how much a low, gentle heat changes and partially warms even the bodies least susceptible of it. For even the heat of the hand imparts a little warmth to a ball of lead or other metal held a short time in it. So easily is heat transmitted and excited, without any apparent change in the body.

38. Of all bodies that we are acquainted with, air admits and loses heat the most readily, which is admirably seen in weather-glasses, whose construction is as follows. Take a glass with a hollow belly, and a thin and long neck; turn it upside down, and place it with its mouth downwards into another glass vessel containing water; the end of the tube touching the bottom of the vessel, and the tube itself leaning a little on the edge, so as to be fixed upright. In order to do this more readily, let a little wax be applied to the edge, not, however, so as to block up the orifice, lest by preventing the air from escaping, the motion, which

we shall presently speak of, and which is very gentle and delicate, should be impeded.

Before the first glass be inserted in the other, its upper part (the belly) should be warmed at the fire. Then upon placing it as we have described, the air, (which was dilated by the heat,) after a sufficient time has been allowed for it to lose the additional temperature, will restore and contract itself to the same dimensions as that of the external or common atmosphere at the moment of immersion, and the water will be attracted upwards in the tube to a proportionate extent. A long, narrow slip of paper should be attached to the tube, divided into as many degrees as you please. You will then perceive, as the weather grows warmer or colder, that the air contracts itself into a narrower space in cold weather, and dilates in the warm, which will be exhibited by the rising of the water as the air contracts itself, and its depression as the air dilates. The sensibility of the air with regard to heat or cold is so delicate and exquisite, that it far exceeds the human touch, so that a ray of sunshine, the heat of the breath, and, much more, that of the hand placed on the top of the tube, immediately causes an evident depression of the water. We think, however, that the spirit of animals possesses a much more delicate susceptibility of heat and cold, only that it is impeded and blunted by the grossness of their bodies.

39. After air we consider those bodies to be most sensible of heat, which have been recently changed and contracted by cold, as snow and ice; for they begin to be dissolved and melt with the first mild weather. Next, perhaps, follows quicksilver; then greasy substances, as oil, butter, and the like; then wood; then water; lastly, stones and metals, which do not easily grow hot, particularly towards their centre.* When heated, however, they retain their temperature for a very long time; so that a brick or stone, or hot iron plunged in a basin of cold water, and kept there for a quarter of an hour or thereabouts, retains such a heat as not to admit of being touched.

40. The less massive the body is, the more readily it grows warm at the approach of a heated body, which shows that heat with us is somewhat averse to a tangible mass.†

41. Heat, with regard to the human senses and touch, is various and relative, so that lukewarm

---

* The fires supply fresh heat, the water has only a certain quantity of heat, which being diffused over a fresh supply of cooler water, must be, on the whole, lowered.

† If condensation were the cause of the greater heat, Bacon concludes the centre of the flame would be the hotter part, and vice versa. The fact is, neither of the causes assigned by Bacon is the true one; for the fire burns more quickly only because the draught of air is more rapid, the cold, dense air pressing rapidly into the heated room and towards the chimney.

* Bacon appears to have confounded combustibility and fusibility with susceptibility of heat; for, though the metals will certainly neither dissolve as soon as ice or butter, nor be consumed as soon as wood, that only shows that different degrees of heat are required to produce similar effects on different bodies; but metals much more readily acquire and transmit the same degree of heat than any of the above substances. The rapid transmission renders them generally cold to the touch. The convenience of fixing wooden handles to vessels containing hot water illustrates these observations.

† Another singular error, the truth being that solid bodies are the best conductors; but of course where heat is diffused over a large mass, it is less in each part, than if that part alone received the whole quantum of heat.

water appears hot if the hand be cold, and cold if the hand be hot.

Aph. 14.

Any one may readily see how poor we are in history, since in the above tables, besides occasionally inserting traditions and report instead of approved history and authentic instances, (always, however, adding some note if their credit or authority be doubtful,) we are often forced to subjoin, " Let the experiment be tried."—" Let further inquiry be made."

15. We are wont to term the office and use of these three tables, the presenting a review of instances to the understanding; and when this has been done, induction itself is to be brought into action. For on an individual review of all the instances, a nature is to be found, such as always to be present and absent with the given nature, to increase and decrease with it, and as we have said, to form a more common limit of the nature. If the mind attempt this affirmatively from the first, (which it always will when left to itself,) there will spring up phantoms, mere theories and ill-defined notions, with axioms requiring daily correction. These will, doubtless, be better or worse, according to the power and strength of the understanding which creates them. But it is only for God, (the bestower and creator of forms,) and perhaps for angels and intelligences, at once to recognise forms affirmatively, at the first glance of contemplation: man at least is unable to do so, and is only allowed to proceed first by negatives, and then to conclude with affirmatives, after every species of exclusion.

16. We must therefore effect a complete solution and separation of nature; not by fire, but by the mind, that divine fire. The first work of legitimate induction, in the discovery of forms, is rejection, or the exclusive instances of individual natures, which are not found in some one instance, where the given nature is present, or are found in any one instance where it is absent, or are found to increase in any one instance where the given nature decreases, or the reverse. After an exclusion correctly effected, an affirmative form will remain as the residuum, solid, true, and well defined, whilst all volatile opinions go off in smoke. This is readily said, but we must arrive at it by a circuitous route. We shall, perhaps, however, omit nothing that can facilitate our progress.

17. The first and almost perpetual precaution and warning which we consider necessary is this: that none should suppose from the great part assigned by us to forms, that we mean such forms as the meditations and thoughts of men have hitherto been accustomed to. In the first place, we do not at present mean the concrete forms, which (as we have observed) are in the common course of things compounded of simple natures, as those of a lion, an eagle, a rose, gold, or the like. The moment for discussing these will arrive, when we come to treat of the latent process, and latent conformation and the discovery of them as they exist in what are called substances, or concrete natures.

Nor, again, would we be thought to mean (even when treating of simple natures) any abstract forms or ideas, either undefined or badly defined in matter. For when we speak of forms, we mean nothing else than those laws and regulations of simple action, which arrange and constitute any simple nature, such as heat, light, weight, in every species of matter, and in a susceptible subject. The form of heat, or form of light, therefore, means no more than the law of heat, or the law of light. Nor do we ever abstract or withdraw ourselves from things, and the operative branch of philosophy. When, therefore, we say, (for instance,) in our investigation of the form of heat, reject rarity, or rarity is not of the form of heat, it is the same as if we were to say, " Man can superinduce heat on a dense body," or the reverse, " Man can abstract or ward off heat from a rare body."

But if our forms appear to any one to be somewhat abstracted, from their mingling and uniting heterogeneous objects, (the heat, for instance, of the heavenly bodies, appears to be very different from that of fire; the fixed red of the rose and the like, from that which is apparent in the rainbow, or the radiation of opal or the diamond;* death by drowning, from that by burning, the sword, apoplexy, or consumption; and yet they all agree in the common natures of heat, redness, and death,) let him be assured that his understanding is enthralled by habit, by general appearances and hypotheses. For it is most certain that, however heterogeneous and distinct, they agree in the form or law which regulates heat, redness, or death; and that human power cannot be emancipated and freed from the common course of nature, and expanded and exalted to new efficients and new modes of operation, except by the revelation and invention of forms of this nature. But after† this union of nature, which is the principal point, we will afterwards, in its proper place, treat of the divisions and ramifications of nature, whether ordinary or internal, or more real.

18. We must now offer an example of the exclusion or rejection of natures, found by the tables of review, not to be of the form of heat; first, premising, that not only each table is sufficient for the rejection of any nature, but even each single instance contained in them. For it is clear from what has been said, that every contradictory

---

* This general law or form, has been well illustrated by Newton's discovery of the decomposition of colours.

† i. e. the common link or *form* which connects the various kinds of natures, such as the different hot or red natures enumerated above. See Aphorism 1 Part 2.

instance destroys an hypothesis as to the form. Still, however, for the sake of clearness, and in order to show more plainly the use of the tables, we redouble or repeat the exclusive.

An Example of the exclusive Table, or of the Rejection of Natures from the Form of Heat.

1. On account of the sun's rays reject elementary (or terrestrial) nature.

2. On account of common fire, and particularly subterranean fires, (which are the most remote and secluded from the rays of the heavenly bodies,) reject celestial nature.

3. On account of the heat acquired by every description of substances, (as minerals, vegetables, the external parts of animals, water, oil, air, &c.) by mere approximation to the fire or any warm body, reject all variety and delicate texture of bodies.

4. On account of iron and ignited metals, which warm other bodies, and yet neither lose their weight nor substance, reject the imparting or mixing of the substance of the heating body.

5. On account of boiling water and air, and also those metals and other solid bodies which are heated, but not to ignition, or red heat, reject flame or light.

6. On account of the rays of the moon and other heavenly bodies, (except the sun,) again reject flame or light.

7. On account of the comparison between red-hot iron and the flame of spirits of wine, (for the iron is more hot and less bright, whilst the flame of spirits of wine is more bright and less hot,) again reject flame and light.

8. On account of gold and other ignited metals, which are of the greatest specific density, reject rarity.

9. On account of air, which is generally found to be cold and yet continues rare, reject rarity.

10. On account of ignited iron,* which does not swell in bulk, but retains the same apparent dimension, reject the absolute expansive motion of the whole.

11. On account of the expansion of the air in thermometers, and the like, which is absolutely moved and expanded to the eye, and yet acquires no manifest increase of heat, again reject absolute or expansive motion of the whole.

12. On account of the ready application of heat to all substances, without any destruction or remarkable alteration of them, reject destructive nature or the violent communication of any new nature.

13. On account of the agreement and conformity of the effects produced by cold and heat, reject both expansive and contracting motion as regards the whole.

14. On account of the heat excited by friction,

* This is erroneous : all metals expand considerably when heated

reject principal nature, by which we mean that which exists positively, and is not caused by a preceding nature.

There are other natures to be rejected ; but we are merely offering examples, and not perfect tables.

None of the above natures are of the form of heat; and man is freed from them all in his operation upon heat.

Aph. 19.

In the exclusive table are laid the foundations of true induction, which is not, however, completed until the affirmative be attained. Nor is the exclusive table perfect, nor can it be so at first. For it is clearly a rejection of simple natures; but if we have not as yet good and just notions of simple natures, how can the exclusive table be made correct ? Some of the above, as the notion of elementary and celestial nature and rarity, are vague and ill-defined. We, therefore, who are neither ignorant nor forgetful of the great work which we attempt, in rendering the human understanding adequate to things and nature, by no means rest satisfied with what we have hitherto enforced ; but push the matter farther, and contrive and prepare more powerful aid for the use of the understanding, which we will next subjoin. And, indeed, in the interpretation of nature, the mind is to be so prepared and formed, as to rest itself on proper degrees of certainty, and yet to remember, (especially at first,) that what is present, depends much upon what remains behind.

20. Since, however, truth emerges more readily from error than confusion, we consider it useful to leave the understanding at liberty to exert itself, and attempt the interpretation of nature in the affirmative, after having constructed and weighed the three tables of preparation, such as we have laid them down, both from the instances there collected, and others occurring elsewhere. Which attempt we are wont to call the liberty of the understanding. or the commencement of interpretation, or the first vintage.

The first Vintage of the Form of Heat.

It must be observed that the form of any thing is inherent (as appears clearly from our premises) in each individual instance in which the thing itself is inherent, or it would not be a form. No contradictory instance, therefore, can be alleged. The form, however, is found to be much more conspicuous and evident in some instances than in others ; in those, for example, where its nature is less restrained and embarrassed, and reduced to rule by other natures. Such instances we are wont to term coruscations, or conspicuous instances. We must proceed then to the first vintage of the form of heat.

From the instances taken collectively, as well

as singly, the nature whose limit is heat appears to be *motion*. This is chiefly exhibited in flame, which is in constant motion, and in warm or boiling liquids, which are likewise in constant motion. It is also shown in the excitement or increase of heat by motion, as by bellows and draughts: for which see Inst. 29, Tab. 3, and by other species of motion, as in Inst. 28 and 31, Tab. 3. It is also shown by the extinction of fire and heat upon any strong pressure, which restrains and puts a stop to motion; for which see Inst. 30 and 32, Tab. 3. It is further shown by this circumstance, namely, that every substance is destroyed, or at least materially changed, by strong and powerful fire and heat: whence it is clear that tumult and confusion are occasioned by heat, together with a violent motion in the internal parts of bodies, and this gradually tends to their dissolution.

What we have said with regard to motion must be thus understood, when taken as the genus of heat: it must not be thought that heat generates motion, or motion heat, (though in some respects this be true,) but that the very essence of heat, or the *substantial self* * of heat, is motion and nothing else, limited, however, by certain differences which we will presently add, after giving some cautions for avoiding ambiguity.

Sensible heat is relative, and regards man, not the universe; and is rightly held to be merely the effect of heat on animal spirit. It is even variable in itself, since the same body (in different states of sensations) excites the feeling of heat and of cold; this is shown by Inst. 41, Tab. 3.

Nor should we confound the communication of heat or its transitive nature, by which a body grows warm at the approach of a heated body, with the form of heat. For *heat* is one thing, and *heating* another. Heat can be excited by friction without any previous heating body, and, therefore, *heating* is excluded from the form of heat. Even when heat is excited by the approach of a hot body, this depends not on the form of heat, but on another more profound and common nature; namely, that of assimilation and multiplication, about which a separate inquiry must be made.

The notion of fire is vulgar, and of no assistance; it is merely compounded of the conjunction of heat and light in any body, as in ordinary flame and red-hot substances.

Laying aside all ambiguity, therefore, we must lastly consider the true differences which limit motion and render it the form of heat.

I. The first difference is, that heat is an expansive motion, by which the body strives to dilate itself, and to occupy a greater space than before. This difference is principally seen in flame, where the smoke or thick vapour is clearly dilated and bursts into flame.

It is also shown in all boiling liquids, which swell, rise, and boil up to the sight, and the process of expansion is urged forward till they are converted into a much more extended and dilated body than the liquid itself, such as steam, smoke, or air.

It is also shown in wood, and combustibles where exudation sometimes takes place, and evaporation always.

It is also shown in the melting of metals, which, being very compact, do not easily swell and dilate, but yet their spirit, when dilated and desirous of further expansion, forces and urges its thicker parts into dissolution, and if the heat be pushed still farther, reduces a considerable part of them into a volatile state.

It is also shown in iron or stones, which, though not melted or dissolved, are, however, softened. The same circumstance takes place in sticks of wood, which become flexible when a little heated in warm ashes.

It is most readily observed in air, which instantly and manifestly expands with a small degree of heat, as in Inst. 38, Tab. 3.

It is also shown in the contrary nature of cold. For cold contracts and narrows every substance; so that, in intense frosts, nails fall out of the wall, and brass cracks, and heated glass, exposed suddenly to the cold, cracks and breaks. So the air by a slight degree of cold contracts itself, as in Inst. 38, Tab. 3. More will be said of this in the inquiry into cold.

Nor is it to be wondered at if cold and heat exhibit many common effects, (for which see Inst. 32, Tab. 2,) since two differences, of which we shall presently speak, belong to each nature: although in the present difference the effects be diametrically opposed to each other. For heat occasions an expansive and dilating motion, but cold a contracting and condensing motion.

II. The second difference is a modification of the preceding, namely, that heat is an expansive motion, tending towards the exterior, but at the same time bearing the body upwards. For there is no doubt that there be many compound motions; as an arrow or dart, for instance, has both a rotatory and progressive motion. In the same way the motion of heat is both expansive and tending upwards.

This difference is shown by putting the tongs or poker into the fire. If placed perpendicularly with the hand above, they soon burn it, but much less speedily if the hand hold them sloping or from below.

It is also conspicuous in distillations *per descensum*, which men are wont to employ with delicate flowers, whose scent easily evaporates. Their industry has devised placing the fire above instead of below, that it may scorch less. For not only flame but all heat has an upward tendency

Let an experiment be made on the contrary

* "Quid ipsum," the τὸ τί ἢν εἴναι of Aristotle.

nature of cold; whether its contraction be downwards, as the expansion of heat is upwards. Take, therefore, two iron rods or two glass tubes, alike in other respects, and warm them a little, and place a sponge, dipped in cold water, or some snow below the one and above the other. We are of opinion that the extremities will grow cold in that rod first where it is placed beneath; as the contrary takes place with regard to heat.

III. The third difference is this. That heat is not a uniform expansive motion of the whole, but of the small particles of the body; and this motion being at the same time restrained, repulsed, and reflected, becomes alternating, perpetually hurrying, striving, struggling, and irritated by the repercussion; which is the source of the violence of flame and heat.

But this difference is chiefly shown in flame and boiling liquids, which always hurry, swell, and subside again in detached parts.

It is also shown in bodies of such hard texture as not to swell or dilate in bulk, such as red-hot iron, in which the heat is most violent.

It is also shown by the fires burning most briskly in the coldest weather.

It is also shown by this; that when the air is dilated in the thermometer uniformly and equably, without any impediment or repulsion, the heat is not perceptible. In confined draughts also, although they break out very violently, no remarkable heat is perceived, because the motion affects the whole, without any alternating motion in the particles. For which reason try whether flame do not burn more at the sides than in its centre.

It is also shown in this, that all burning proceeds by the minute pores of bodies, undermining, penetrating, piercing, and pricking them as if with an infinite number of needlepoints. Hence all strong acids (if adapted to the body on which they act) exhibit the effects of fire from their corroding and pungent nature.

The difference of which we now speak is common also to the nature of cold, in which the contracting motion is restrained by the resistance of expansion, as in heat the expansive motion is restrained by the resistance of contraction.

Whether, therefore, the particles of matter penetrate inwards or outwards, the reasoning is the same, though the power be very different, because we have nothing on earth which is intensely cold.

IV. The fourth difference is a modification of the preceding; namely, that this stimulating or penetrating motion should be rapid and never sluggish, and should take place not in the very minutest particles, but rather in those of some tolerable dimensions.

It is shown by comparing the effects of fire with those of time. Time dries, consumes, undermines, and reduces to ashes as well as fire, and, perhaps, to a much finer degree, but as its motion is very slow, and attacks very minute particles, no heat is perceived.

It is also shown in a comparison of the dissolution of iron and gold. For gold is dissolved without the excitement of any heat, but iron with a vehement excitement of it, although almost in the same time: because, in the former, the penetration of the separating acid is mild, and gently insinuates itself, and the particles of gold yield easily, but the penetration of iron is violent, and attended with some struggle, and its particles are more obstinate.

It is partially shown also in some gangrenes and mortifications of flesh, which do not excite great heat or pain from the gentle nature of the putrefaction.

Let this suffice for a first vintage, or the commencement of the interpretation of the form of heat by the liberty of the understanding.

From this first vintage, the form or true definition of heat (considered relatively to the universe and not to the sense) is briefly thus. "Heat is an expansive motion, restrained and striving to exert itself in the smaller particles." The expansion is modified by " its tendency to rise though expanding towards the exterior;" and the effort is modified by its not being sluggish, but active and somewhat violent.

With regard to the operative definition, the matter is the same. "If you are able to excite a dilating or expansive motion in any natural body, and so to repress that motion and force it on itself as not to allow the expansion to proceed equally, but only to be partially exerted, and partially repressed, you will, beyond all doubt, produce heat;" without any consideration as to whether the body be of earth (or elementary, as they term it) or imbued with celestial influence, luminous or opaque, rare or dense, locally expanded or contained within the bounds of its first dimensions, verging to dissolution or remaining fixed, animal, vegetable, or mineral, water, or oil, or air, or any other substance whatever susceptible of such motion. Sensible heat is the same, but considered relatively to the senses. Let us now proceed to further helps.

21. After our tables of first review, our rejection or exclusive table and the first vintage derived from them, we must advance to the remaining helps of the understanding with regard to the interpretation of nature, and a true and perfect induction; in offering which we will take the examples of cold and heat where tables are necessary, but where fewer instances are required we will go through a variety of others; so as neither to confound investigation nor to narrow our doctrine.

In the first place, therefore, we will treat of prerogative instances; 2. Of the supports of induction; 3. Of the correction of induction; 4. Of varying the investigation according to the nature of the subject; 5. Of the prerogative natures with respect to investigation, or of what should be the first or last objects of our research ; 6. Of the limits of investigation, or a synopsis of all natures that exist in the universe; 7. Of the application to practical purposes, or of what relates to man; 8. Of the preparations for investigation; 9. And, lastly, of the ascending and descending scale of axioms.

22. Amongst the prerogative instances we will first mention *solitary* instances. Solitary instances are those which exhibit the required nature in subjects that have nothing in common with any other subject than the nature in question ; or which do not exhibit the required nature in subjects resembling others in every respect except that of the nature in question. For these instances manifestly remove prolixity, and accelerate and confirm exclusion, so that a few of them are of as much avail as many.

For instance: let the inquiry be the nature of colour: Prisms, crystalline gems, which yield colours not only internally but on the wall, dews, &c., are solitary instances. For they have nothing in common with the fixed colours in flowers and coloured gems, metals, woods, &c., except the colour itself. Hence we easily deduce that colour is nothing but a modification of the image of the incident and absorbed light, occasioned in the former case by the different degrees of incidence, in the latter by the various textures and forms of bodies.* These are solitary instances as regards *similitude.*

Again, in the same inquiry, the distinct veins of white and black in marble, and the variegated colours of flowers of the same species, are solitary instances: for the black and white of marble, and the spots of white and purple in the flowers of the stock, agree in every respect but that of colour. Thence we easily deduce that colour has not much to do with the intrinsic natures of any body, but depends only on the coarser, and, as it were, mechanical arrangement of the parts. These are solitary instances as regards *difference.* We call them both solitary or wild, to borrow a word from the astronomers.

23. In the second rank of prerogative instances we will consider *Migrating* instances. In these, the required nature passes towards generation, having no previous existence, or towards corruption, having first existed. In each of these divisions, therefore, the instances are always twofold, or rather, it is one instance, first in motion or on its passage, and then brought to the opposite conclusion. These instances not only hasten and confirm exclusion, but also reduce affirmation, or the form itself, to a narrow compass. For, the form must be something conferred by this migration, or, on the contrary, removed and destroyed by it.

* This very nearly approaches to Sir I. Newton's discovery of the decomposition of light by the prism.

And, although all exclusion advances affirmation, yet this takes place more directly in the same than in different subjects. But, if the form (as it is quite clear, from what has been advanced) exhibit itself in one subject, it leads to all. The more simple the migration is, the more valuable is the instance. These migrating instances are, moreover, very useful in practice, for, since they manifest the form, coupled with that which causes or destroys it, they point out the right practice in some subjects, and thence there is an easy transition to those with which they are most allied. There is, however, a degree of danger which demands caution, namely, lest they should refer the form too much to its efficient cause, and imbue, or, at least, tinge the understanding with a false notion of the form from the appearance of such cause; which is never more than a vehicle or conveyance of the form. This may easily be remedied by a proper application of exclusion.

Let us then give an example of a migrating instance. Let whiteness be the required nature. An instance which passes towards generation, is glass in its entire, and in its powdered state ; or water in its natural state, and when agitated to froth. For glass, when entire, and water, in its natural state, are transparent and not white, but powdered glass and the froth of water are white, and not transparent. We must inquire, therefore, what has happened to the glass or water in the course of this migration. For, it is manifest that the form of whiteness is conveyed and introduced by the bruising of the glass and the agitation of the water. But nothing is found to have been introduced but a diminishing of the parts of the glass and water, and the insertion of air. Yet this is no slight progress towards discovering the form of whiteness, namely, that two bodies, in themselves more or less transparent, (as air and water, or air and glass,) when brought into contact in minute portions, exhibit whiteness, from the unequal refraction of the rays of light.

But here we must also give an example of the danger and caution of which we spoke. For instance; it will readily occur to an understanding perverted by efficients, that air is always necessary for producing the form of whiteness, or that whiteness is only generated by transparent bodies, which suppositions are both false, and proved to be so by many exclusions. Nay, it will rather appear, (without any particular regard to air or the like,) that all bodies which are even in such of their parts as affect the sight, exhibit transparency, those which are uneven and of simple texture, whiteness, those which are uneven and of compound but regular texture, all the other colours except black, but those which are uneven and of a compound, irregular, and confused texture, exhibit blackness. An example has been given, therefore, of an instance migrating towards generation in the required nature of whiteness. An instance migrating towards corruption in the same nature, is that of dissolving froth, or snow, for they lose their whiteness, and assume the transparency of water in its pure state without air.

Nor should we by any means omit to state, that under migrating instances we must comprehend not only those which pass towards generation and destruction, but also those which pass towards increase or decrease, for they too assist in the discovery of the form, as is clear from our definition of a form, and the table of degrees. Hence, paper, which is white when dry, is less white when moistened, (from the exclusion of air and admission of water,) and tends more to transparency. The reason is the same as in the above instances.

24. In the third rank of prerogative instances, we will class *conspicuous* instances, of which we spoke in our first vintage of the form of heat, and which we are also wont to call coruscations, or free and predominant instances. They are such as show the required nature in its bare substantial shape, and at its height, or greatest degree of power, emancipated and free from all impediments, or, at least, overcoming, suppressing, and restraining them by the strength of its qualities. For, since every body is susceptible of many united forms of natures in the concrete, the consequence is, that they mutually deaden, depress, break, and confine each other, and the individual forms are obscured. But there are some subjects in which the required nature exists in its full vigour rather than in others, either from the absence of any impediment or the predominance of its quality. Such instances are eminently conspicuous. But, even in these, care must be taken, and the hastiness of the understanding checked, for, whatever makes a show of the form, and forces it forward, is to be suspected, and recourse must be had to severe and diligent exclusion.

For example; let heat be the required nature. The thermometer is a conspicuous instance of the expansive motion, which (as has been observed) constitutes the chief part of the form of heat. For, although flame clearly exhibit expansion, yet, from its being extinguished every moment, it does not exhibit the progress of expansion. Boiling water, again, from its rapid conversion into vapour, does not so well exhibit the expansion of water in its own shape: whilst red-hot iron and the like, are so far from showing this progress, that, on the contrary, the expansion itself is scarcely evident to the senses, on account of its spirit being repressed and weakened by the compact and coarse articles which subdue and restrain it. But the thermometer strikingly exhibits the expansion of the air, as being evident and progressive, durable, and not transitory.

Take another example. Let the required nature be weight. Quicksilver is a conspicuous instance of weight; for it is far heavier than any other substance except gold, which is not much heavier;

and it is a better instance than gold for the purpose of indicating the form of weight. For gold is solid and consistent, which qualities must be referred to density, but quicksilver is liquid, and teeming with spirit, yet much heavier than the diamond and other substances considered to be most solid. Whence it is shown that the form of gravity or weight predominates only in the quantity of matter, and not in the close fitting of it.

25. In the fourth rank of prerogative instances we will class *clandestine* instances; which we are also wont to call twilight instances. They are, as it were, opposed to the conspicuous instances; for they show the required nature in its lowest state of efficacy, and, as it were, its cradle and first rudiments, making an effort, and a sort of first attempt, but concealed and subdued by a contrary nature. Such instances are, however, of great importance in discovering forms, for, as the conspicuous tend easily to differences, so do the clandestine best lead to genera; that is, to those common natures of which the required natures are only the limits.

As an example: let consistency, or that which confines itself, be the required nature, the opposite of which is a liquid or flowing state. The clandestine instances are such as exhibit some weak and low degree of consistency in fluids, as a water bubble, which is a sort of consistent and bounded pellicle, formed out of the substance of the water. So eaves' droppings, if there be enough water to follow them, draw themselves out into a thin thread, not to break the continuity of the water, but if there be not enough to follow, the water forms itself into a round drop, which is the best form to prevent a breach of continuity: and at the moment the thread ceases, and the water begins to fall in drops, the thread of water recoils upwards to avoid such a breach. Nay, in metals, which, when melted, are liquid, but more tenacious, the melted drops often recoil and are suspended. There is something similar in the instance of the child's looking-glass, which little boys will sometimes form of spittle between rushes, and where the same pellicle of water is observable: and still more in that other amusement of children, when they take some water rendered a little more tenacious by soap, and inflate it with a pipe, forming the water into a sort of castle of bubbles, which assumes such consistency by the interposition of the air, as to admit of being thrown some little distance without bursting. The best example is that of froth and snow, which assume such consistency as almost to admit of being cut, although composed of air and water, both liquids. All these circumstances clearly show that the terms liquid and consistent are merely vulgar notions adapted to the sense, and that in reality all bodies have a tendency to avoid a breach of continuity, faint and weak in bodies composed of homogeneous parts, (as is the case with liquids,) but more vivid and powerful in those of heterogeneous parts: because the approach of heterogeneous matter binds bodies together, whilst the insinuation of homogeneous matter loosens and relaxes them.

Again, to take another example: let the required nature be attraction or the cohesion of bodies. The most remarkable conspicuous instance, with regard to its form, is the magnet. The contrary nature to attraction is non-attraction, though in a similar substance. Thus, iron does not attract iron, lead lead, wood wood, nor water water. But the clandestine instance is that of the magnet armed with iron, or rather that of iron in the magnet so armed. For its nature is such, that the magnet when armed does not attract iron more powerfully at any given distance, than when unarmed; but if the iron be brought in contact with the armed magnet, the latter will sustain a much greater weight than the simple magnet, from the resemblance of substance in the two portions of iron, a quality altogether clandestine and hidden in the iron, until the magnet was introduced. It is manifest, therefore, that the form of cohesion is something which is vivid and robust in the magnet, and hidden and weak in the iron. It is to be observed, also, that small wooden arrows without an iron point, when discharged from large mortars, penetrate further into wooden substances (such as the ribs of ships or the like) than the same arrows pointed with iron;* owing to the similarity of substance, though this quality was previously latent in the wood. Again, although in the mass air does not appear to attract air, nor water water, yet, when one bubble is brought near another, they are both more readily dissolved, from the tendency to contact of the water with the water, and the air with the air.† These clandestine instances (which are, as has been observed, of the most important service) are principally to be observed in small portions of bodies, for the larger masses observe more universal and general forms, as will be mentioned in its proper place.

26. In the fifth rank of prerogative instances we will class *constitutive* instances, which we are wont also to call collective instances. They constitute a species or lesser form, as it were, of the required nature. For since the real forms (which are always convertible with the given nature) lie

at some depth, and are not easily discovered, the necessity of the case and the infirmity of the human understanding require that the particular forms, which collect certain groups of instances (but by no means all) into some common notion, should not be neglected, but most diligently observed. For whatever unites nature, even imperfectly, opens the way to the discovery of the form. The instances, therefore, which are serviceable in this respect, are of no mean power, but endowed with some degree of prerogative.

Here, nevertheless, great care must be taken, that after the discovery of several of these particular forms, and the establishing of certain partitions or divisions of the required nature derived from them, the human understanding do not at once rest satisfied, without preparing for the investigation of the great or leading form, and, taking it for granted that nature is compound and divided from its very root, despise and reject any farther union as a point of superfluous refinement, and tending to mere abstraction.

For instance, let the required nature be memory or that which excites and assists memory. The constitutive instances are order or distribution, which manifestly assists memory; topics or commonplaces in artificial memory, which may be either places in their literal sense, as a gate, a corner, a window, and the like, or familiar persons and marks, or any thing else, (provided it be arranged in a determinate order,) as animals, plants, and words, letters, characters, historical persons, and the like; of which, however, some are more convenient than others. All these commonplaces materially assist memory, and raise it far above its natural strength. Verse, too, is recollected and learned more easily than prose. From this group of three instances, order, the commonplaces of artificial memory, and verses, is constituted one species of aid for the memory, which may be well termed a separation from infinity. For when a man strives to recollect or recall any thing to memory, without a preconceived notion or perception of the object of his search, he inquires about, and labours, and turns from point to point, as if involved in infinity. But if he have any preconceived notion, this infinity is separated off, and the range of his memory is brought within closer limits. In the three instances given above, the preconceived notion is clear and determined. In the first, it must be something that agrees with order; in the second, an image which has some relation or agreement with the fixed commonplaces; in the third, words which fall into a verse: and thus infinity is divided off. Other instances will offer another species, namely, that whatever brings the intellect into contact with something that strikes the sense, (the principal point of artificial memory,) assists the memory. Others again offer another species, namely, whatever excites an impression by any powerful pas

---

* Query ?

† The real cause of this phenomena is the attraction of the surface of the water in the vessel by the sides of the bubbles. When the bubbles approach, the sides nearest each other both tend to raise the small space of water between them, and consequently less water is raised by each of the nearer sides than by the exterior part of the bubble, and the greater weight of the water raised on the exterior parts pushes the bubbles together. In the same manner a bubble near the side of a vessel is pushed towards it; the vessel and bubble both drawing the water that is between them. The latter phenomena cannot be explained on Bacon's hypothesis.

sion, as fear, wonder, shame, delight, assists the memory. Other instances will afford another species: thus those impressions remain most fixed in the memory, which are taken from the mind when clear and least occupied by preceding or succeeding notions, such as the things we learn in childhood, or imagine before sleep, and the first time of any circumstance happening. Other instances afford the following species: namely, that a multitude of circumstances or handles assist the memory, such as writing in paragraphs, reading aloud or recitation. Lastly, other instances afford still another species: thus the things we anticipate, and which rouse our attention, are more easily remembered than transient events; as, if you read any work twenty times over, you will not learn it by heart so readily, as if you were to read it but ten times, trying each time to repeat it, and when your memory fails you, looking into the book. There are, therefore, six lesser forms, as it were, of things which assist the memory: namely, 1. The separation of infinity. 2. The connexion of the mind with the senses. 3. The impression in strong passion. 4. The impression on the mind when pure. 5. The multitude of handles. 6. Anticipation.

Again, for example's sake, let the required nature be taste or the power of tasting. The following instances are constitutive: 1. Those who do not smell, but are deprived by nature of that sense, do not perceive or distinguish rancid or putrid food by their taste; nor garlic from roses, and the like. 2. Again, those whose nostrils are obstructed by accident (such as a cold) do not distinguish any putrid or rancid matter from any thing sprinkled with rose-water. 3. If those who suffer from a cold, blow their noses violently at the very moment in which they have any thing fetid or perfumed in their mouth, or on their palate, they instantly have a clear perception of the fetor or perfume. These instances afford and constitute this species or division of taste; namely, that it is in part nothing else than an internal smelling passing and descending through the upper passages of the nostrils to the mouth and palate. But, on the other hand, those whose power of smelling is deficient, or obstructed, perceive what is salt, sweet, pungent, acid, rough, and bitter, and the like, as well as any one else: so that the taste is clearly something compounded of the internal smelling, and an exquisite species of touch, which we will not here discuss.

Again, as another example, let the required nature be the communication of quality, without intermixture of substance. The instance of light will afford or constitute one species of communication, heat and the magnet another. For the communication of light is momentary and immediately arrested upon the removal of the original light. But heat and the magnetic force, when once transmitted to, or excited in another body, remain fixed for a considerable time after the removal of the source.

In fine, the prerogative of constitutive instances is considerable, for they materially assist the definitions (especially in details) and the divisions or partitions of natures, concerning which Plato has well said, "He who can properly define and divide is to be considered a god."

27. In the sixth rank of prerogative instances we will place *similar* or *proportionate* instances, which we are also wont to call physical parallels, or resemblances. They are such as exhibit the resemblances and connexions of things, not in minor forms, (as the constitutive do,) but at once in the concrete. They are, therefore, as it were, the first and lowest steps towards the union of nature; nor do they immediately establish any axiom, but merely indicate and observe a certain relation of bodies to each other. But, although they be not of much assistance in discovering forms, yet, they are of great advantage in disclosing the frame of parts of the universe, upon whose members they practise a species of anatomy, and thence occasionally lead us gently on to sublime and noble axioms, especially such as relate to the construction of the world, rather than to simple natures and forms.

As an example; take the following similar instances: a mirror and the eye: the formation of the ear, and places which return an echo. From such similarity, besides observing the resemblance, (which is useful for many purposes,) it is easy to collect and form this axiom: That the organs of the senses, and bodies which produce reflections to the senses, are of a similar nature. Again, the understanding once informed of this, rises easily to a higher and nobler axiom; namely, that the only distinction between sensitive and inanimate bodies, in those points in which they agree and sympathise, is this; in the former, animal spirit is added to the arrangement of the body, in the latter it is wanting. So that there might be as many senses in animals as there are points of agreement with inanimate bodies, if the animated body were perforated, so as to allow the spirit to have access to the limb properly disposed for action, as a fit organ. And, on the other hand, there are, without doubt, as many motions in an inanimate, as there are senses in the animated body, though the animal spirit be absent. There must, however, be many more motions in inanimate bodies than senses in the animated, from the small number of organs of sense. A very plain example of this is afforded by pains. For, as animals are liable to many kinds and various descriptions of pains, (such as those of burning, of intense cold, of pricking, squeezing, stretching, and the like,) so is it most certain, that the same circumstances, as far as motion is concerned, happen to inanimate bodies, such as wood or stone, when burned, frozen, pricked, cut, bent bruised, and the like; although there be no sensation, owing to the absence of animal spirit. Again, wonderful as it may appear, the roots and branches of trees are similar instances. For every vegetable swells and throws out its constituent parts towards the circumference, both upwards and downwards. And there is no difference between the roots and branches, except that the root is buried in the earth, and the branches are exposed to the air and sun. For if one take a young and vigorous shoot, and bend it down to a small portion of loose earth, although it be not fixed to the ground, yet will it immediately produce a root, and not a branch. And, vice versâ, if earth be placed above, and so forced down with a stone or any hard substance, as to confine the plant and prevent its branching upwards, it will throw out branches into the air downwards. The gums of trees and most rock gems are similar instances; for both of them are exudations, and filtered juices, derived in the former instance from trees, in the latter from stones; the brightness and clearness of both arising from a delicate and accurate filtering. For nearly the same reason, the hair of animals is less beautiful and vivid in its colour, than the plumage of most birds, because the juices are less delicately filtered through the skin than through the quills.

The scrotum of males, and matrix of females, are also similar instances : so that the noble formation which constitutes the difference of the sexes, appears to differ only as to the one being internal and the other external ; a greater degree of heat causing the genitals to protrude in the male, whilst the heat of the female being too weak to effect this, they are retained internally.

The fins of fishes, and the feet of quadrupeds, or the feet and wings of birds, are similar instances ; to which Aristotle adds the four folds in the motion of serpents ;* so that, in the formation of the universe, the motion of animals appears to be chiefly effected by four joints or bendings.

The teeth of land animals, and the beaks of birds, are similar instances, whence it is clear, that in all perfect animals there is a determination of some hard substance towards the mouth. Again, the resemblance and conformity of man to an inverted plant is not absurd. For the head is the root of the nerves and animal faculties, and the seminal parts are the lowest, not including the extremities of the legs and arms. But, in the plant, the root (which resembles the head) is regularly placed in the lowest, and the seeds in the highest part.

Lastly, we must particularly recommend and suggest, that man's present industry in the investigation and compilation of natural history be entirely changed, and directed to the reverse of

the present system. For, it has hitherto been active and curious in noting the variety of things and explaining the accurate differences of animals, vegetables, and minerals, most of which are the mere sport of nature, rather than of any real utility as concerns the sciences. Pursuits of this nature are certainly agreeable, and sometimes of practical advantage, but contribute little or nothing to the thorough investigation, of nature. Our labour must, therefore, be directed towards inquiring into, and observing resemblances and analogies, both in the whole, and its parts, for, they unite nature, and lay the foundation of the sciences.

Here, however, a severe and rigorous caution must be observed, that we only consider as similar and proportionate instances, those which (as we first observed) point out physical resemblances: that is, real and substantial resemblances, deeply founded in nature, and not casual and superficial, much less superstitious or curious ; such as those which are constantly put forward by the writers on natural magic, (the most idle of men, and who are scarcely fit to be named in connection with such serious matters as we now treat of,) who, with much vanity and folly, describe, and sometimes, too, invent unmeaning resemblances and sympathies.

But, leaving such to themselves, similar instances are not to be neglected, in the greater portions of the world's conformation ; such as Africa and the Peruvian continent, which reaches to the Straits of Magellan ; both of which possess a similar isthmus and similar capes, a circumstance not to be attributed to mere accident.

Again ; the New and Old World are both of them broad and expanded towards the north, and narrow and pointed towards the south.

Again ; we have very remarkable similar instances in the intense cold, towards the middle regions (as it is termed) of the air, and the violent fires which are often found to burst from subterraneous spots, the similarity consisting in both being ends and extremes ; the extreme of the nature of cold, for instance, is towards the boundary of heaven, and that of the nature of heat towards the centre of the earth, by a similar species of opposition or rejection of the contrary nature.

Lastly, in the axioms of the sciences there is a similarity of instances worthy of observation. Thus, the rhetorical trope which is called *surprise*, is similar to that of music termed the declining of a cadence.

.Again ; the mathematical postulate, that "things which are equal to the same are equal to one another," is similar to the form of the syllogism in logic, which unites things agreeing in the middle term. Lastly : a certain degree of sagacity in collecting and searching for physical points of similarity, is very useful in many respects.

---

* Is not this a very hasty generalization? Do serpents move with four folds only? Observe also the motion of centipedes and other insects.

28. In the seventh rank of prerogative instances we will place singular instances, which we are also wont to call irregular or heteroclite, (to borrow a term from the grammarians.) They are such as exhibit bodies in the concrete, of an apparently extravagant and separate nature, agreeing but little with other things of the same species. For, whilst the similar instances resemble each other, those we now speak of are only like themselves. Their use is much the same with that of clandestine instances; they bring out and unite nature, and discover genera or common natures, which must afterwards be limited by real differences. Nor should we desist from inquiry until the properties and qualities of those things, which may be deemed miracles, as it were, of nature, be reduced to, and comprehended in, some form or certain law; so that all irregularity or singularity may be found to depend on some common form; and the miracle only consists in accurate differences, degree, and rare coincidence, not in the species itself. Man's meditation proceeds no farther at present, than just to consider things of this kind as the secrets and vast efforts of nature, without an assignable cause, and, as it were, exceptions to general rules.

As examples of singular instances, we have the sun and moon amongst the heavenly bodies; the magnet amongst minerals; quicksilver amongst metals; the elephant amongst quadrupeds; the venereal sensation amongst the different kinds of touch; the scent of sporting dogs amongst those of smell. The letter S, too, is considered by the grammarians as sui generis, from its easily uniting with double or triple consonants, which no other letter will. These instances are of great value, because they excite and keep alive inquiry, and correct an understanding depraved by habit, and the common course of things.

29. In the eighth rank of prerogative instances, we will place *deviating* instances; such as the errors of nature, or strange and monstrous objects, in which nature deviates and turns from her ordinary course. For the errors of nature differ from singular instances, inasmuch as the latter are the miracles of species, the former of individuals. Their use is much the same, for they rectify the understanding in opposition to habit, and reveal common forms. For, with regard to these, also, we must not desist from inquiry till we discern the cause of the deviation. The cause does not, however, in such cases, rise to a regular form, but only to the latent process towards such a form. For he who is acquainted with the paths of nature will more readily observe her deviations, and, vice versâ, he who has learnt her deviations, will be able more accurately to describe her paths.

They differ again from singular instances, by being much more apt for practice, and the operative branch. For it would be very difficult to generate new species, but less so to vary known species, and thus produce many rare and unusual results.* The passage from the miracles of nature to those of art is easy; for if nature be once seized in her variations, and the cause be manifest, it will be easy to lead her by art to such deviation as she was at first led to by chance; and not only to that, but others, since deviations on the one side lead and open the way to others in every direction. Of this we do not require any examples, since they are so abundant. For a compilation, or particular natural history, must be made of all monsters and prodigious births of nature; of every thing, in short, which is new, rare, and unusual in nature. This should be done with a rigorous selection, so as to be worthy of credit. Those are most to be suspected which depend upon superstition, as the prodigies of Livy, and those, perhaps, but little less which are found in the works of writers on natural magic, or even alchymy, and the like, for such men, as it were, are the very suitors and lovers of fables; but our instances should be derived from some grave and credible history, and faithful narration.

30. In the ninth rank of prerogative instances, we will place *bordering* instances, which we are also wont to term participants. They are such as exhibit those species of bodies which appear to be composed of two species, or to be the rudiments between the one and the other. They may well be classed with the singular or heteroclite instances; for, in the whole system of things, they are rare and extraordinary. Yet from their dignity they must be treated of and classed separately, for they point out admirably the order and constitution of things, and suggest the causes of the number and quality of the more common species in the universe, leading the understanding from that which is, to that which is possible.

We have examples of them in moss, which is something between putrescence and a plant; in some comets, which hold a place between stars and ignited meteors; in flying fishes, between fishes and birds; and in bats, between birds and quadrupeds.† Again,

"Simia quam similis turpissima bestia nobis."

We have also biformed fetus, mingled species, and the like.

31. In the tenth rank of prerogative instances, we will place the instances of *power*, or the fasces, (to borrow a term from the insignia of empire,) which we are also wont to call the wit or hands of man. These are such works as are most noble and perfect, and, as it were, the masterpieces in every art For since our principal object is to

* This is well illustrated in plants, for the gardener can produce endless varieties of any known species, but can never produce a new species itself.

† There is, however, no real approximation to birds in either the flying fish or bat, any more than a man approximates to a fish because he can swim. The wings of the flying fish and bat are mere expansions of skin, bearing no resemblance whatever to those of birds.

make nature subservient to the state and wants of man, it becomes us well to note and enumerate the works, which have long since been in the power of man, especially those which are most polished and perfect; because the passage from these, to new and hitherto undiscovered works, is more easy and feasible. For if any one, after an attentive contemplation of such works as are extant, be willing to push forward in his design with alacrity and vigour, he will undoubtedly either advance them, or turn them to something within their immediate reach, or even apply and transfer them to some more noble purpose. ·

Nor is this all: for as the understanding is elevated and raised by rare and unusual works of nature, to investigate and discover the forms which include them also; so is the same effect frequently produced by the excellent and wonderful works of art: and even to a greater degree, because, the mode of effecting and constructing the miracles of art, is generally plain, whilst that of effecting the miracles of nature is more obscure. Great care, however, must be taken, that they do not depress the understanding, and fix it as it were to earth.

For there is some danger, lest the understanding should be astonished and chained down, and, as it were, bewitched, by such works of art as appear to be the very summit and pinnacle of human industry, so as not to become familiar with them, but rather to suppose, that nothing of the kind can be accomplished, unless the same means be employed, with perhaps a little more diligence, and more accurate preparation.

Now, on the contrary, it may be stated as a fact, that the ways and means hitherto discovered and observed, of effecting any matter or work, are for the most part of little value, and that all really efficient power depends, and is really to be deduced from the sources of forms, none of which have yet been discovered.

Thus, (as we have before observed,) had any one meditated on balistic machines, and battering rams, as they were used by the ancients, whatever application he might have exerted, and though he might have consumed a whole life in the pursuit, yet would he never have hit upon the invention of flaming engines, acting by means of gunpowder: nor would any person, who had made woollen manufactories and cotton the subject of his observation and reflection, have ever discovered thereby the nature of the silk-worm, or of silk. ·

Hence all the most noble discoveries have (if you observe) come to light, not by any gradual improvement and extension of the arts, but merely by chance; whilst nothing imitates or anticipates chance (which is wont to act at intervals of ages) but the invention of forms. ·

There is no necessity for adducing any particu-

lar examples of these instances, since they are abundant. The plan to be pursued is this; all the mechanical, and even the liberal arts, (as far as they are practical) should be visited and thoroughly examined, and thence there should be formed a compilation or particular history of the great masterpieces, or most finished works in each, as well as of the mode of carrying them into effect.

Nor do we confine the diligence to be used in such a compilation to the leading works and secrets only of every art, and such as excite wonder; for wonder is engendered by rarity, since that which is rare, although it be compounded of ordinary natures, always begets wonder. On the contrary, that which is really wonderful, from some specific difference distinguishing it from other species, is carelessly observed, if it be but familiar. Yet the singular instances of art should be observed no less than those of nature, which we have before spoken of: and, as in the latter we have classed the sun, the moon, the magnet, and the like, all of them most familiar to us, but yet in their nature singular, so should we proceed with the singular instances of art.

For example; paper, a very common substance, is a singular instance of art. For, if you consider the subject attentively, you will find that artificial substances are either woven by straight and transverse lines, as silk, woollen, or linen cloth, and the like; or coagulated from concrete juices, such as brick, earthenware, glass, enamel, porcelain, and the like, which admit of a polish, if they be compact, but, if not, become hard without being polished; all which latter substances are brittle, and are not adherent or tenacious. On the contrary, paper is a tenacious substance, which can be cut and torn, so as to resemble, and almost rival the skin of any animal, or the leaf of vegetables, and the like works of nature; being neither brittle like glass, nor woven like cloth, but having fibres, and not distinct threads, just as natural substances, so that scarcely any thing similar can be found amongst artificial substances, and it is absolutely singular. And in artificial works we should certainly prefer those which approach the nearest to an imitation of nature, or, on the other hand, powerfully govern and change her course. Again, in these instances which we term the wit and hands of man, charms and conjuring should not be altogether despised, for although mere amusements, and of little use, yet they may afford considerable information.

Lastly, superstition and magic (in its common acceptation) are not to be entirely omitted; for, although they be overwhelmed by a mass of lies and fables, yet some investigation should be made, to see if there be really any latent natural operation in them; as in fascination, and the fortifying of the imagination, the sympathy of distant objects, the transmission of impressions from spirit to spirit, no less than from body to body, and the like.

32. From the foregoing remarks, it is clear that the five last species of instances (the similar, singular, deviating, and bordering instances, and those of power) should not be reserved for the investigation of any given nature, as the preceding and many of the succeeding instances must, but a collection of them should be made at once, in the style of a particular history; so that they may arrange the matter which enters the understanding, and correct its depraved habit, for it is necessarily imbued, corrupted, perverted, and distorted by daily and habitual impressions.

They are to be used, therefore, as a preparative, for the purpose of rectifying and purifying the understanding, for, whatever withdraws it from habit, levels and planes down its surface for the reception of the dry and pure light of true notions. These instances, moreover, level and prepare the way for the operative branch, as we will mention in its proper place, when speaking of the practical deductions.

33. In the eleventh rank of prerogative instances, we will place *accompanying and hostile* instances. These are such as exhibit any body or concrete, where the required nature is constantly found, as an inseparable companion, or, on the contrary, where the required nature is constantly avoided and excluded from attendance, as an enemy. From these instances may be formed certain and universal propositions, either affirmative or negative; the subject of which will be the concrete body, and the predicate the required nature. For particular propositions are by no means fixed, when the required nature is found to fluctuate and change in the concrete, either approaching and acquired, or receding and laid aside. Hence, particular propositions have no great prerogative, except in the case of migration, of which we have spoken above. Yet such particular propositions are of great use, when compared with the universal, as will be mentioned in its proper place. Nor do we require absolute affirmation or negation, even in universal propositions, for, if the exceptions be singular or rare, it is sufficient for our purpose.

The use of accompanying instances is to narrow the affirmative of form. For, as it is narrowed by the migrating instances, where the form must necessarily be something communicated or destroyed by the act of migration, so it is narrowed by accompanying instances, where the form must necessarily be something which enters into the concretion of the body, or, on the contrary, is repugnant to it, and one who is well acquainted with the constitution or formation of the body, will not be far from bringing to light the form of the required nature.

For example: let the required nature be heat. Flame is an accompanying instance. For, in water, air, stone, metal, and many other substances, heat is variable, and can approach or retire, but all flame is hot, so that heat always accompanies the concretion of flame. We have no hostile instance of heat. For the senses are unacquainted with the interior of the earth, and there is no concretion of any known body which is not susceptible of heat.

Again, let solidity be the required nature. Air is a hostile instance. For metals may be liquid or solid, so may glass; even water may become solid by congelation, but air cannot become solid or lose its fluidity.

With regard to these instances of fixed propositions, there are two points to be observed, which are of importance. First, that if there be no universal affirmative or negative, it be carefully noted as not existing. Thus, in heat, we have observed that there exists no universal negative, in such substances at least as have come to our knowledge. Again, if the required nature be eternity or incorruptibility, we have no universal affirmative within our sphere, for these qualities cannot be predicated of any bodies below the heavens, or above the interior of the earth. Secondly, To our general propositions as to any concrete, whether affirmative or negative, we should subjoin the concretes which appear to approach nearest to the non-existing substances; such as the most gentle or least burning flames in heat, or gold in incorruptibility, since it approaches nearest to it. For they all serve to show the limit of existence and non-existence, and circumscribe forms, so that they cannot wander beyond the conditions of matter.

34. In the twelfth rank of prerogative instances, we will class those *subjunctive* instances, of which we spoke in the last aphorism, and which we are also wont to call instances of extremity or limits; for they are not only serviceable when subjoined to fixed propositions, but also of themselves and from their own nature. They indicate with sufficient precision the real divisions of nature, and measures of things, and the "how far" nature effects or allows of any thing, and her passage thence to something else. Such are gold in weight, iron in hardness, the whale in the size of animals, the dog in smell, the flame of gunpowder in rapid expansion, and others of the like nature. Nor are we to pass over the extremes in defect as well as in abundance, as spirits of wine in weight, the touchstone in softness, the worms upon the skin in the size of animals, and the like.

35. In the thirteenth rank of prerogative instances, we will place those of *alliance* or union. They are such as mingle and unite natures held to be heterogeneous, and observed and marked as such in received classifications.

These instances show that the operation and

effect, which is considered peculiar to some one of such heterogeneous natures, may also be attributed to another nature styled heterogeneous; so as to prove that the difference of the natures is not real nor essential, but a mere modification of a common nature. They are very serviceable, therefore, in elevating and carrying on the mind from differences to genera, and in removing those phantoms and images of things, which meet it in disguise in concrete substances.

For example; let the required nature be heat. The classification of heat into three kinds, that of the celestial bodies, that of animals, and that of fire, appears to be settled and admitted: and these kinds of heat, especially one of them compared with the other two, are supposed to be different, and clearly heterogeneous in their essence and species, or specific nature; since the heat of the heavenly bodies and of animals generates and cherishes, whilst that of fire corrupts and destroys. We have an instance of alliance then in a very common experiment, that of a vine branch admitted into a building where there is a constant fire, by which the grapes ripen a whole month sooner than in the air; so that fruit upon the tree can be ripened by fire, although this appear the peculiar effect of the sun. From this beginning, therefore, the understanding rejects all essential difference, and easily ascends to the investigation of the real differences between the heat of the sun and that of fire, by which their operation is rendered dissimilar, although they partake of a common nature.

These differences will be found to be four in number. The heat of the sun is much milder and gentler in degree than that of fire. 2. It is much more moist in quality, especially as it is transmitted to us through the air. 3. Which is the chief point, it is very unequal, advancing and increased at one time, retiring and diminished at another; which mainly contributes to the generation of bodies. For Aristotle rightly asserted, that the principal cause of generation and corruption on the surface of the earth, was the oblique path of the sun in the zodiac, whence its heat becomes very unequal, partly from the alternation of night and day, partly from the succession of summer and winter. Yet must he immediately corrupt and prevent his discovery, by dictating to nature according to his habit, and dogmatically assigning the cause of generation to the approach of the sun and that of corruption to its retreat; whilst in fact each circumstance indifferently and not respectively contributes both to generation and corruption; for unequal heat tends to generate and corrupt, as equable heat does to preserve. 4. The fourth difference between the heat of the sun and fire is of great consequence; namely, that the sun, gradually, and for a length of time, insinuates its effects, whilst those of fire (urged by the impatience of man) are brought to a termination in a shorter space of time. But if any one were to pay attention to the tempering of fire, and reducing it to a more moderate and gentle degree, (which may be done in various ways,) and then were to sprinkle and mix a degree of humidity with it, and above all were to imitate the sun in its inequality, and lastly were patiently to suffer some delay, (not such, however, as is proportioned to the effects of the sun, but more than men usually admit of in those of fire,) he would soon banish the notion of any difference, and would attempt, or equal, or perhaps sometimes surpass the effect of the sun, by the heat of fire. A like instance of alliance is that of reviving butterflies, benumbed and nearly dead from cold, by the gentle warmth of fire, so that fire is no less able to revive animals than to ripen vegetables. We may also mention the celebrated invention of Fracastorius, of applying a pan considerably heated to the head in desperate cases of apoplexy, which clearly expands the animal spirits, when compressed and almost extinguished by the humours and obstructions of the brain, and excites them to action, as the fire would operate on water or air, and in the result produces life. Eggs are sometimes hatched by the heat of fire, an exact imitation of animal heat; and there are many instances of the like nature, so that no one can doubt that the heat of fire, in many cases, can be modified till it resemble that of the heavenly bodies and of animals.

Again, let the required natures be motion and rest. There appears to be a settled classification, grounded on the deepest philosophy, that natural bodies either revolve, move in a straight line, or stand still and rest. For there is either motion without limit, or continuance within a certain limit, or a translation towards a certain limit. The eternal motion of revolution appears peculiar to the heavenly bodies, rest to this our globe, and the other bodies (heavy and light, as they are termed, that is to say, placed out of their natural position) are borne in a straight line to masses or aggregates which resemble them, the light towards the heaven, the heavy towards the earth: and all this is very fine language.

But we have an instance of alliance in low comets, which revolve, though far below the heavens; and the fiction of Aristotle, of the comet being fixed to or necessarily following some star, has been long since exploded; not only because it is improbable in itself, but from the evident fact of the discursive and irregular motion of comets, through various parts of the heavens.

Another instance of alliance is that of the motion of air, which appears to revolve from east to west within the tropics, where the circles of revolution are the greatest.

The flow and ebb of the sea would perhaps be another instance, if the water were once found to have a motion of revolution, though slow and hardly perceptible, from east to west, subject, however, to a reaction twice a day. If this be so, it is clear that the motion of revolution is not confined to the celestial bodies, but is shared also by air and water.

Again; the supposed peculiar disposition of light bodies to rise, is rather shaken; and here we may find an instance of alliance in a water bubble. For if air be placed under water, it rises rapidly towards the surface, by that striking motion (as Democritus terms it) with which the descending water strikes the air, and raises it; not by any struggle or effort of the air itself: and when it has reached the surface of the water, it is prevented from ascending any further, by the slight resistance it meets with in the water, which does not allow an immediate separation of its parts, so that the tendency of the air to rise must be very slight.

Again; let the required nature be weight. It is certainly a received classification, that dense and solid bodies are borne towards the centre of the earth, and rare and light bodies to the circumference of the heavens, as their appropriate places. As far as relates to places, (though these things have much weight in the schools,) the notion of there being any determinate place is absurd and puerile. Philosophers trifle, therefore, when they tell you that if the earth were perforated, heavy bodies would stop on their arrival at the centre. This centre would indeed be an efficacious nothing or mathematical point, could it affect bodies or be sought by them, for a body is not acted upon except by a body.* In fact, this tendency to ascend and descend, is either in the conformation of the moving body, or in its harmony and sympathy with another body. But if any dense and solid body be found, which does not however, tend towards the earth, the classification is at an end. Now, if we allow of Gilbert's opinion, that the magnetic power of the earth, in attracting heavy bodies, is not extended beyond the limit of its peculiar virtue, (which operates always at a fixed distance and no further,)† and this be proved by some instance, such an instance will be one of alliance in our present subject. The nearest approach to it is that of waterspouts, frequently seen by persons navigating the Atlantic towards either of the Indies. For the force and mass of the water suddenly effused by waterspouts, appears to be so considerable, that the water must have been collected previously, and have remained fixed where it was formed, until it was afterwards forced down by some violent

cause, rather than made to fall by the natural motion of gravity: so that it may be conjectured, that a dense and compact mass, at a great distance from the earth, may be suspended as the earth itself is, and would not fall unless forced down. We do not, however, affirm this as certain. In the mean while, both in this respect and many others, it will readily be seen how deficient we are in natural history, since we are forced to have recourse to suppositions for examples, instead of ascertained instances.

Again; let the required nature be the discursive power of the mind. The classification of human reason, and animal instinct, appears to be perfectly correct. Yet there are some instances of the actions of brutes, which seem to show that they too can syllogize. Thus it is related, that a crow, which had nearly perished from thirst in a great drought, saw some water in the hollow trunk of a tree, but as it was too narrow for him to get into it, he continued to throw in pebbles, which made the water rise till he could drink, and it afterwards became a proverb.

Again; let the required nature be vision. The classification appears real and certain, which considers light as that which is originally visible, and confers the power of seeing; and colour as being secondarily visible, and not capable of being seen without light, so as to appear a mere image or modification of light. Yet there are instances of alliance in each respect; as in snow when in great quantities, and in the flame of sulphur; the one being a colour originally and in itself light, the other a light verging towards a colour.*

36. In the fourteenth rank of prerogative instances, we will place the instances *of the cross*, borrowing our metaphor from the crosses erected where two roads meet, to point out the different directions. We are wont also to call them decisive and judicial instances, and in some cases instances of the oracle, and of command. Their nature is as follows. When in investigating any nature the understanding is, as it were, balanced, and uncertain to which of two or more natures the cause of the required nature should be assigned, on account of the frequent and usual concurrence of several natures; the instances of the cross show that the union of one nature with the required nature is firm and indissoluble, whilst that of the other is unsteady and separable; by which means the question is decided, and the first is received as the cause, whilst the other is dismissed and rejected. Such instances therefore afford great light, and are of great weight, so that the course of interpretation sometimes terminates and is completed in them. Sometimes, however, they are found amongst the instances already observed, but they are generally new, being ex-

---

* But see Bacon's own corollary at the end of the instances of divorce, Aphorism 37.

† Since Newton's discovery of the law of gravitation, we find that the attractive force of the earth must extend to an infinite distance. Bacon himself alludes to the operation of his attractive force at great distances, in the instances of the rod. Aphorism 45.

* Snow reflects light, but is not a source of light.

pressly and purposely sought for and applied, and brought to light only by attentive and active diligence.

For example ; let the required nature be the flow and ebb of the sea, which is repeated twice a day, at intervals of six hours between each advance and retreat, with some little difference, agreeing with the motion of the moon. We have here the following cross-ways.

This motion must be occasioned either by the advancing and the retiring of the sea, like water shaken in a basin, which leaves one side while it washes the other ; or by the rising of the sea from the bottom, and its again subsiding like boiling water. But a doubt arises, to which of these causes we should assign the flow and ebb. If the first assertion be admitted, it follows, that when there is a flood on one side, there must at the same time be an ebb on another, and the question, therefore, is reduced to this. Now, Acosta, and some others, after a diligent inquiry, have observed that the flood tide takes place on the coast of Florida and the opposite coasts of Spain and Africa at the same time, as does also the ebb ; and that there is not, on the contrary, a flood tide at Florida when there is an ebb on the coasts of Spain and Africa. Yet, if one consider the subject attentively, this does not prove the necessity of a rising motion, nor refute the notion of a progressive motion. For the motion may be progressive, and yet inundate the opposite shores of a channel at the same time ; as if the waters be forced and driven together from some other quarter, for instance, which takes place in rivers, for they flow and ebb towards each bank at the same time, yet their motion is clearly progressive, being that of the waters from the sea entering their mouths. So it may happen, that the waters coming in a vast body from the eastern Indian Ocean, are driven together and forced into the channel of the Atlantic, and therefore inundate both coasts at once. We must inquire, therefore, if there be any other channel by which the waters can, at the same time, sink and ebb ; and the Southern Ocean at once suggests itself, which is not less than the Atlantic, but rather broader, and more extensive than is requisite for this effect.

We at length arrive, then, at an instance of the cross, which is this. If it be positively discovered, that when the flood sets in towards the opposite coasts of Florida and Spain in the Atlantic, there is at the same time a flood tide on the coasts of Peru, and the back part of China in the Southern Ocean, then assuredly, from this decisive instance, we must reject the assertion that the flood and ebb of the sea, about which we inquire, takes place by progressive motion ; for no other sea or place is left where there can be an ebb. But this may most easily be learned, by inquiring of the inhabitants of Panama and Lima, (where the two oceans are separated by a narrow isthmus,) whether the flood and ebb takes place on the opposite sides of the isthmus at the same time, or the reverse. This decision or rejection appears certain, if it be granted that the earth is fixed ; but if the earth revolves, it may, perhaps, happen, that from the unequal revolution (as regards velocity) of the earth, and the waters of the sea, there may be a violent forcing of the waters into a mass, forming the flood, and a subsequent relaxation of them, (when they can no longer bear the accumulation,) forming the ebb. A separate inquiry must be made into this. Even with this hypothesis, however, it remains equally true, that there must be an ebb somewhere, at the same time that there is a flood in another quarter.

Again, let the required nature be the latter of the two motions we have supposed, namely, that of a rising and subsiding motion, if it should happen that, upon diligent examination, the progressive motion be rejected. We have, then, three ways before us, with regard to this nature. The motion, by which the waters raise themselves and again fall back, in the floods and ebbs, without the addition of any other water rolled towards them, must take place in one of the three following ways. Either the supply of water emanates from the interior of the earth, and returns back again ; or there is really no greater quantity of water, but the same water (without any augmentation of its quantity) is extended or rarefied, so as to occupy a greater space and dimension, and again contracts itself ; or there is neither an additional supply nor any extension, but the same waters (with regard to quantity, density, or rarity) raise themselves and fall from sympathy, by some magnetic power attracting and calling them up, as it were, from above. Let us, then, (passing over the two first motions,) reduce the investigation to the last ; and inquire if there be any such elevation of the water, by sympathy or a magnetic force. And it is evident, in the first place, that the whole mass of water being placed in the trench or cavity of the sea, cannot be raised at once, because there would not be. enough to cover the bottom, so that, if there be any tendency of this kind in the water, to raise itself, yet it would be interrupted and checked by the cohesion of things, or (as the common expression is) that there may be no vacuum. The water, therefore, must rise on one side, and for that reason be diminished, and ebb on another. But it will again necessarily follow, that the magnetic power, not being able to operate on the whole, operates most intensely on the centre, so as to raise the waters there, which, when thus raised successively, desert and abandon the sides.

We at length arrive, then, at an instance of the cross, which is this : if it be found that, during the ebb, the surface of the waters at sea is more curved and round, from the waters rising in the middle, and sinking at the sides or coast, and if, during the flood, it be more even and level, from the waters returning to their former position, then, assuredly, by this decisive instance, the raising of them by a magnetic force can be admitted, if otherwise, it must be entirely rejected. It is not difficult to make the experiment (by sounding in straits) whether the sea be deeper towards the middle in ebbs than in floods. But it must be observed, if this be the case, that (contrary to common opinion) the waters rise in ebbs, and only return to their former position in floods, so as to bathe and inundate the coast.

Again, let the required nature be the spontaneous motion of revolution, and particularly, whether the diurnal motion, by which the sun and stars appears to us to rise and set, be a real motion of revolution in the heavenly bodies, or only apparent in them, and real in the earth. There may be an instance of the cross of the following nature. If there be discovered any motion in the ocean from east to west, though very languid and weak, and, if the same motion be discovered rather more swift in the air, (particularly within the tropics, where it is more perceptible, from the circles being greater,) if it be discovered, also, in the low comets, and be already quick and powerful in them, if it be found also in the planets, but so tempered and regulated as to be slower in those nearest the earth, and quicker in those at the greatest distance, being quickest of all in the heavens, then the diurnal motion should certainly be considered as real in the heavens, and that of the earth must be rejected, for it will be evident, that the motion from east to west is part of the system of the world, and universal; since it is most rapid in the height of the heavens, and gradually grows weaker, till it stops, and is extinguished in rest at the earth.

Again, let the required nature be that other motion of revolution, so celebrated amongst astronomers, which is contrary to the diurnal, namely, from west to east, and which the ancient astronomers assign to the planets, and even to the starry sphere, but Copernicus and his followers to the earth also, and let it be examined whether any such motion be found in nature, or it be rather a fiction and hypothesis for abridging and facilitating calculation, and for promoting that fine notion of effecting the heavenly motions by perfect circles. For there is nothing which proves such a motion in heavenly objects to be true and real, either in a planet's not returning in its diurnal motion to the same point of the starry sphere, or in the pole of the zodiac being different from that of the world, which two circumstances have occasioned this notion. For the first phenomenon is well accounted for by the spheres overtaking or falling behind each other, and the second by spiral lines, so that the inaccuracy of the re-

turn, and declination to the tropics, may be rather modifications of the one diurnal motion, than contrary motions, or about different poles. And, it is most certain, if we consider ourselves for a moment as part of the vulgar, (setting aside the fictions of astronomers and the school, who are wont, undeservedly, to attack the senses in many respects, and to affect obscurity,) that the apparent motion is such as we have said, a model of which we have sometimes caused to be represented by wires in a sort of machine.

We may take the following instances of the cross upon this subject. If it be found in any history, worthy of credit, that there has existed any comet, high or low, which has not revolved in manifest harmony (however irregularly) with the diurnal motion, then we may decide so far as to allow such a motion to be possible in nature. But, if nothing of the sort be found, it must be suspected, and recourse must be had to other instances of the cross.

Again, let the required nature be weight or gravity. Heavy and ponderous bodies must, either of their own nature, tend towards the centre of the earth by their peculiar formation; or must be attracted, and hurried, by the corporeal mass of the earth itself, as being an assemblage of similar bodies, and be drawn to it by sympathy.* But if the latter be the cause, it follows, that the nearer bodies approach to the earth, the more powerfully and rapidly they must be borne towards it, and the further they are distant, the more faintly and slowly, (as is the case in magnetic attractions,) and that this must happen within a given distance, so that if they be separated at such a distance from the earth that the power of the earth cannot act upon them, they will remain suspended like the earth, and not fall at all.

The following instance of the cross may be adopted. Take a clock, moved by leaden weights, and another by a spring, and let them be set well together, so that one be neither quicker nor slower than the other; then let the clock moved by weights, be placed on the top of a very high church, and the other be kept below, and let it be well observed, if the former move slower than it did, from the diminished power of the weights. Let the same experiment be made at the bottom of mines worked to a considerable depth, in order to see whether the clock move more quickly from the increased power of the weights.† But, if this power be found to diminish at a height, and to increase in subterraneous places, the at-

---

* A close approximation to the truth and the experiment pointed out, is very ingenious; indeed, the oscillations of the pendulum, moving by its own weight, have since been used as the most delicate tests of the variation of gravity from the equator towards the poles.

† The attractive power to the centre is, on the whole, diminished in mines, because the earth above attracts in the contrary direction.

traction of the corporeal mass of the earth may be taken as the cause of weight.

Again, let the required nature be the polarity of the steel needle, when touched with the magnet. We have these two ways with regard to this nature. Either the touch of the magnet must communicate polarity to the steel towards the north and south, or else it may only excite and prepare it, whilst the actual motion is occasioned by the presence of the earth, which Gilbert considers to be the case, and endeavours to prove with so much labour. The particulars he has inquired into with such ingenious zeal amount to this: 1. An iron bolt placed for a long time towards the north and south acquires polarity from this habit, without the touch of the magnet; as if the earth itself operating but weakly from its distance, (for the surface or outer crust of the earth does not, in his opinion, possess the magnetic power,) yet, by long continued motion, could supply the place of the magnet, excite the iron, and convert and change it when excited. 2. Iron, at a red or white heat, when quenched in a direction parallel to the north and south, also acquires polarity without the touch of the magnet; as if the parts of iron being put in motion by ignition, and afterwards recovering themselves, were at the moment of being quenched more susceptible and sensitive of the power emanating from the earth, than at other times, and, therefore, as it were, excited. But these points, though well observed, do not completely prove his assertion.

An instance of the cross on this point might be as follows. Let a small magnetic globe be taken, and its poles marked, and placed towards the east and west, not towards the north and south, and let it continue thus. Then let an untouched needle be placed over it, and suffered to remain so for six or seven days. Now, the needle, (for this is not disputed,) whilst it remains over the magnet, will leave the poles of the world, and turn to those of the magnet, and, therefore, as long as it remains in the above position will turn to the east and west. But if the needle, when removed from the magnet, and placed upon a pivot, be found immediately to turn to the north and south, or even by degrees to turn thither, then the presence of the earth must be considered as the cause; but if it remains turned as at first towards the east and west, or lose its polarity, then that cause must be suspected, and farther inquiry made.

Again, let the required nature be the corporeal substance of the moon, whether it be rare, fiery, and aërial, (as most of the ancient philosophers have thought,) or solid and dense, (as Gilbert and many of the moderns, with some of the ancients, hold.)* The reasons for this latter opinion are grounded chiefly upon this, that the moon reflects the sun's rays, and that light does not appear capable of being reflected, except by solids. The instance of the cross will, therefore, (if any,) be such as to exhibit reflection by a rare body, such as flame, if it be but sufficiently dense. Now, certainly one of the reasons of twilight is the reflection* of the rays of the sun by the upper part of the atmosphere. We see the sun's rays also reflected on fine evenings, by streaks of moist clouds, with a splendour not less, but perhaps more bright and glorious, than that reflected from the body of the moon, and yet, it is not clear that those clouds have formed into a dense body of water. We see also that the dark air, behind the windows at night, reflects the light of a candle in the same manner as a dense body would do.† The experiment should also be made of causing the sun's rays to fall through a hole upon some dark and bluish flame. The unconfined rays of the sun, when falling on faint flames, do certainly appear to deaden them, and render them more like white smoke than flames. These are the only instances which occur at present of the nature of those of the cross, and better, perhaps, can be found. But it must always be observed, that reflection is not to be expected from flame, unless it be of some depth, for otherwise it becomes nearly transparent. This at least may be considered certain, that light is always either received and transmitted, or reflected by an even surface.

Again, let the required nature be the motion of projectiles (such as darts, arrows, and balls) through the air. The school, in its usual manner, treats this very carelessly, considering it enough to distinguish it by the name of violent motion, from that which they term natural, and as far as regards the first percussion or impulse, satisfies itself by its axiom, "that two bodies cannot exist in one place, or there would be a penetration of dimensions." With regard to this nature we have these two crossways. The motion must arise either from the air carrying the projected body and collecting behind it, like a stream behind boats or the wind behind straws; or from the parts of the body itself not supporting the impression, but pushing themselves forward in succession to ease it. Fracastorius, and nearly all those who have entered into any refined inquiry upon the subject, adopt the first. Nor can it be doubted, that the air has some effect, yet, the other motion is, without doubt, real, as is clear from a vast number of experiments. Amongst

---

* A sufficient proof of its necessary solidity is now afforded by the attraction of the sea, and the moon's motion around the earth.

* Rather the refraction—the sky or air, however, *reflects* the blue rays of light.

† The polished surface of the glass causes the reflection in this case, and not the air; and a hat or other black surface put behind the window in the day time will enable the glass to reflect distinctly for the same reason; namely, that the reflected rays are not mixed and confused with those transmitted from the other side of the window.

others we may take this instance of the cross: namely, that a thin plate or wire of iron rather stiff, or even a reed of a pen split in two, when drawn up and bent between the finger and thumb, will leap forward. For it is clear, that this cannot be attributed to the air's being collected behind the body, because the source of motion is in the centre of the plate or pen, and not in its extremities.

Again, let the required nature be the rapid and powerful motion of the explosion of gunpowder, by which such vast masses are upheaved, and such weights discharged as we observe in large mines and mortars; there are two crossways before us, with regard to this nature. This motion is excited, either by the mere effort of the body expanding itself when inflamed, or by the assisting effort of the crude spirit, which escapes rapidly from fire, and bursts violently from the surrounding flame as from a prison. The school, however, and common opinion, only consider the first effort. For men think that they are great philosophers, when they assert that flame, from the form of the element, is endowed with a kind of necessity of occupying a greater space, than the same body had occupied when in the form of powder, and that thence proceeds the motion in question. In the mean time they do not observe, that although this may be true, on the supposition of flame being generated, yet the generation may be impeded by a weight of sufficient force to compress and suffocate it; so that no such necessity exists as they assert. They are right, indeed, in imagining that the expansion, and the consequent emission or removal of the opposing body, is necessary if flame be once generated; but such a necessity is avoided, if the solid opposing mass suppress the flame before it be generated. And we in fact see that flame, especially at the moment of its generation, is mild and gentle, and requires a hollow space where it can play and try its force. The great violence of the effect, therefore, cannot be attributed to this cause: but the truth is, that the generation of these exploding flames and fiery blasts arises from the conflict of two bodies of a decidedly opposite nature; the one very inflammable, as is the sulphur, the other having an antipathy to flame; namely, the crude spirit of the nitre: so that an extraordinary conflict takes place, whilst the sulphur is becoming inflamed, as far as it can, (for the third body, the willow charcoal, merely incorporates and conveniently unites the two others,) and the spirits of nitre is escaping, as far also as it can, and at the same time expanding itself, (for air, and all crude substances, and water are expanded by heat,) fanning thus, in every direction, the flame of the sulphur by its escape and violence, just as if by invisible bellows.

Two kinds of instances of the cross might here be used: the one of very inflammable substances, such as sulphur and camphire, naphtha, and the like, and their compounds, which take fire more readily and easily than gunpowder, if left to themselves; (and this shows that the effort to catch fire does not of itself produce such a prodigious effect;) the other of substances which avoid and repel flame, such as all salts. For we see that when they are cast into the fire the aqueous spirit escapes with a crackling noise before flame is produced, which also happens, in a less degree, in stiff leaves; from the escape of the aqueous part, before the oily part has caught fire. This is more particularly observed in quicksilver, which is not improperly called mineral water; and which, without any inflammation, nearly equals the force of gunpowder, by simple explosion and expansion, and is said, when mixed with gunpowder, to increase its force.

Again, let the required nature be the transitory nature of flame, and its momentaneous extinction. For to us the nature of flame does not appear to be fixed or settled, but to be generated from moment to moment, and to be every instant extinguished; it being clear that those flames which continue and last, do not owe their continuance to the same mass of flame, but to a continued succession of new flame regularly generated, and that the same identical flame does not continue. This is easily shown by removing the food or source of the flame, when it at once goes out. We have the two following cross-ways with regard to this nature. This momentary nature either arises from the cessation of the cause which first produced it, as in light, sounds, and violent motions, as they are termed, or flame may be capable by its own nature of duration, but is subjected to some violence from the contrary natures which surround it, and is destroyed.

We may, therefore, adopt the following instance of the cross. We see to what a height the flames rise in great conflagrations; for as the base of the flame becomes more extensive, its vertex is more lofty. It appears, then, that the commencement of the extinction takes place at the sides, where the flame is compressed by the air, and is ill at ease. But the centre of the flame, which is untouched by the air, and surrounded by flame, continues the same, and is not extinguished until compressed by degrees by the air attacking it from the sides. All flame, therefore, is pyramidal, having its base near the source, and its vertex pointed, from its being resisted by the air, and not supplied from the source. On the contrary, the smoke, which is narrow at the base, expands in its ascent, and resembles an inverted pyramid; because the air admits the smoke, but compresses the flame; for, let no one dream that the lighted flame is air, since they are clearly heterogeneous.

The instance of the cross will be more accurate, if the experiment can be made by flames of different colours. Take, therefore, a small metal sconce, and place a lighted taper in it. then put it in a basin, and pour a small quantity of spirits of wine round the sconce, so as not to reach its edge, and light the spirit. Now, the flame of the spirit will be blue, and that of the taper yellow; observe, therefore, whether the latter (which can easily be distinguished from the former by its colour, for flames do not mix immediately, as liquids do) continue pyramidal, or tend more to a globular figure, since there is nothing to destroy or compress it. If the latter result be observed, it must be considered as settled, that flame continues positively the same, whilst enclosed within another flame, and not exposed to the resisting force of the air.

Let this suffice for the instances of the cross. We have dwelt the longer upon them in order gradually to teach and accustom mankind to judge of nature by these instances, and enlightening experiments, and not by probable reasons.

37. We will treat of the instances of *divorce* as the fifteenth of our prerogative instances. They indicate the separation of natures of the most common occurrence. They differ, however, from those subjoined to the accompanying instances; for the instances of divorce point out the separation of a particular nature from some concrete substance with which it is usually found in conjunction, whilst the hostile instances point out the total separation of one nature from another. They differ also from the instances of the cross, because they decide nothing, but only inform us that the one nature is capable of being separated from the other. They are of use in exposing false forms, and dissipating hasty theories derived from obvious facts: so that they add ballast and weight, as it were, to the understanding.

For instance, let the required natures be those four which Telesius terms associates, and of the same family, namely, heat, light, rarity, and mobility, or promptitude to motion; yet, many instances of divorce can be discovered between them. Air is rare and easily moved, but neither hot nor light, the moon is light, but not hot, boiling water is warm, but not light, the motion of the needle in the compass is swift and active, and its substance is cold, dense, and opaque; and there are many similar examples.

Again, let the required natures be corporeal nature and natural action. The latter appears incapable of subsisting without some body, yet may we, perhaps, even here find an instance of divorce, as in the magnetic motion, which draws the iron to the magnet, and heavy bodies to the globe of the earth: to which we may add other actions which operate at a distance. For such action takes place in time, by distinct moments, not in an instant; and in space by regular degrees and distances. There is, therefore, some one moment of time and some interval of space, in

which the power or action is suspended betwixt the two bodies creating the motion. Our consideration, then, is reduced to this, whether the bodies which are the extremes of motion prepare or alter the intermediate bodies, so that the power advances from one extreme to the other by succession and actual contact, and in the mean time exists in some intermediate body; or whether there exist in reality nothing but the bodies, the power, and the space? In the case of the rays of light, sounds, and heat, and some other objects which operate at a distance, it is indeed probable that the intermediate bodies are prepared and altered, the more so because a qualified medium is required for their operation. But the magnetic or attractive power admits of an indifferent medium, and it is not impeded in any. But if that power or action is independent of the intermediate body, it follows that it is a natural power or action, existing in a certain time and space without any body, since it exists neither in the extreme nor in the intermediate bodies. Hence the magnetic action may be taken as an instance of divorce of corporeal nature and natural action: to which we may add as a corollary, and an advantage not to be neglected, that it may be taken as a proof of essence and substance being separate and incorporeal, even by those who philosophize according to the senses. For if natural power and action emanating from a body can exist at any time and place entirely without any body, it is nearly a proof that it can also emanate originally from an incorporeal substance. For a corporeal nature appears to be no less necessary for supporting and conveying, than for exciting or generating natural action.

38. Next follow five classes of instances which we are wont to call by the general term of instances *of the lamp*, or of immediate information. They are such as assist the senses. For since every interpretation of nature sets out from the senses, and leads, by a regular, fixed, and well established road, from the perceptions of the senses to those of the understanding, (which are true notions and axioms,) it necessarily follows that, in proportion as the representatives, or ministerings of the senses, are more abundant and accurate, every thing else must be more easy and successful.

The first of these five sets of instances of the lamp strengthen, enlarge, and correct the immediate operations of the senses. The second reduce to the sphere of the senses such matters as are beyond it. The third indicate the continued process or series of such things and motions, as, for the most part, are only observed in their termination, or in periods. The fourth supply the absolute wants of the senses. The fifth excite their attention and observation. and, at the same time, limit the subtilty of things. We will now proceed to speak of them singly.

39. In the sixteenth rank, then, of prerogative instances, we will place the instances of the *door or gate*, by which name we designate such as assist the immediate action of the senses. It is obvious, that sight holds the first rank among the senses, with regard to information, for which reason we must seek principally helps for that sense. These helps appear to be threefold; either to enable it to perceive objects not naturally seen, or to see them from a greater distance, or to see them more accurately and distinctly.

We have an example of the first (not to speak of spectacles and the like, which only correct and remove the infirmity of a deficient sight, and therefore give no further information) in the lately invented microscopes, which exhibit the latent and invisible minutiæ of substances, and their hidden formation and motion, by wonderfully increasing their apparent magnitude. By their assistance we behold, with astonishment, the accurate form and outline of a flea, moss, and animalculæ, as well as their previously invisible colour and motion. It is said also that an apparently straight line, drawn with a pen or pencil, is discovered by such a microscope to be very uneven and curved, because neither the motion of the hand, when assisted by a ruler, nor the impression of ink or colour are really regular, although the irregularities are so minute as not to be perceptible without the assistance of the microscope. Men have (as is usual in new and wonderful discoveries) added a superstitious remark, that the microscope sheds a lustre on the works of nature, and dishonour on those of art; which only means that the tissue of nature is much more delicate than that of art. For the microscope is only of use for minute objects; and Democritus, perhaps, if he had seen it, would have exulted in the thought of a means discovered for seeing his atom, which he affirmed to be entirely invisible. But the inadequacy of these microscopes, for the observation of any but the most minute bodies—and even of those, if parts of a larger body, destroys their utility. For if the invention could be extended to greater bodies, or the minute parts of greater bodies, so that a piece of cloth would appear like a net, and the latent minutiæ and irregularities of gems, liquids, urine, blood, wounds, and many other things could be rendered visible, the greatest advantage would, without doubt, be derived.

We have an instance of the second kind in the telescope, discovered by the wonderful exertions of Galileo: by the assistance of which a nearer intercourse may be opened (as by boats or vessels) between ourselves and the heavenly objects. For by its aid we are assured that the milky way is but a knot or constellation of small stars, clearly defined and separate, which the ancients only conjectured to be the case: whence it appears to be capable of demonstration, that the spaces of the planetary orbits (as they are termed) are not quite destitute of other stars, but that the heaven begins to glitter with stars before we arrive at the starry sphere; although they may be too small to be visible without the telescope. By the telescope, also, we can behold the revolutions of smaller stars round Jupiter, whence it may be conjectured that there are several centres of motion among the stars. By its assistance, also, the irregularity of light and shade on the moon's surface is more clearly observed and determined, so as to allow of a sort of selenography. By the telescope we see the spots in the sun, and other similar phenomena; all of which are most noble discoveries, as far as credit can be safely given to demonstrations of this nature, which are, on this account, very suspicious, namely, that experiment stops at these few, and nothing further has yet been discovered by the same method, among objects equally worthy of consideration.

We have instances of the third kind in measuring rods, astrolabes, and the like, which do not enlarge, but correct and guide the sight. If there be other instances which assist the other senses in their immediate and individual action, yet, if they add nothing further to their information, they are not opposite to our present purpose, and we have therefore said nothing of them.

40. In the seventeenth rank of prerogative instances we will place *citing* instances, (to borrow a term from the tribunals,) because they cite those things to appear, which have not yet appeared. We are wont also to call them invoking instances, and their property is that of reducing to the sphere of the senses objects which do not immediately fall within it.

Objects escape the senses either from their distance, or the intervention of other bodies; or because they are not calculated to make an impression upon the senses; or because they are not in sufficient quantity to strike the senses; or because there is not sufficient time for their acting upon the senses; or because the impression is too violent; or because the senses are previously filled and possessed by the object, so as to leave no room for any new motion. These remarks apply principally to sight and next to touch: which two senses act extensively in giving information, and that too upon general objects, whilst the remaining three inform us only, as it were, by their immediate action, and as to specific objects.

There can be no reduction to the sphere of the senses in the first case, unless, in the place of the object, which cannot be perceived on account of the distance, there be added or substituted some other object, which can excite and strike the sense from a greater distance, as in the communication of intelligence by fires, bells, and the like.

In the second case we effect this reduction by rendering those things which are concealed by the interposition of other bodies, and which cannot easily be laid open, evident to the senses by means of that which lies at the surface, or proceeds from the interior; thus the state of the body is judged of by the pulse, urine, &c.

The third and fourth cases apply to many subjects, and the reduction to the sphere of the senses must be obtained from every quarter in the investigation of things. There are many examples. It is obvious that air, and spirit, and the like, whose whole substance is extremely rare and delicate, can neither be seen nor touched; a reduction therefore to the senses becomes necessary in every investigation relating to such bodies.

Let the required nature, therefore, be the action and motion of the spirit enclosed in tangible bodies. For every tangible body, with which we are acquainted, contains an invisible and intangible spirit, over which it is drawn, and which it seems to clothe. This spirit being emitted from a tangible substance, leaves the body contracted and dry, when retained it softens and melts it, when neither wholly emitted nor retained, it models it, endows it with limbs, assimilates, manifests, organizes it, and the like. All these points are reduced to the sphere of the senses by manifest effects.

For in every tangible and inanimate body the enclosed spirit at first increases, and, as it were, feeds on the tangible parts which are most open and prepared for it; and when it has digested and modified them, and turned them into spirit, it escapes with them. This formation and increase of spirit is rendered sensible by the diminution of weight: for in every desiccation something is lost in quantity, not only of the spirit previously existing in the body, but of the body itself, which was previously tangible, and has been recently changed, for the spirit itself has no weight. The departure or emission of spirit is rendered sensible in the rust of metals, and other putrefactions of a like nature, which stop before they arrive at the rudiments of life, which belong to the third species of process.* In compact bodies the spirit does not find pores and passages for its escape, and is therefore obliged to force out, and drive before it, the tangible parts also, which consequently protrude; whence arises rust, and the like. The contraction of the tangible parts, occasioned by the emission of part of the spirit, (whence arises desiccation,) is rendered sensible by the increased hardness of the substance, and still more by the fissures, contractions, shrivelling, and folds of the bodies thus produced. For, the parts of wood split and contract, skins become shrivelled, and not only that,

but, if the spirit be emitted suddenly by the heat of the fire, become so hastily contracted as to twist and roll themselves up.

On the contrary, when the spirit is retained, and yet expanded and excited by heat, or the like, (which happens in solid and tenacious bodies,) then the bodies are softened, as in hot iron; or flow, as in metals; or melt, as in gums, wax, and the like. The contrary effects of heat, therefore, (hardening some substances and melting others,) are easily reconciled,* because the spirit is emitted in the former, and agitated and retained in the latter; the latter action is that of heat and the spirit, the former that of the tangible parts themselves, after the spirit's emission.

But when the spirit is neither entirely retained nor emitted, but only strives and exercises itself within its limits, and meets with tangible parts, which obey, and readily follow it wherever it leads them; then follows the formation of an organic body, and of limbs, and the other vital actions of vegetables and plants. These are rendered sensible, chiefly by diligent observation of the first beginnings, and rudiments or effects of life in animalculæ sprung from putrefaction, as in the eggs of ants, worms, mosses, frogs after rain, &c. Both a mild heat and a pliant substance, however, are necessary for the production of life, in order that the spirit may neither hastily escape, nor be restrained by the obstinacy of the parts, so as not to be able to bend and model them like wax.

Again, the difference of spirit, which is important and of effect in many points, (as unconnected spirit, branching spirit, branching and cellular spirit, the first of which is that of all inanimate substances, the second of vegetables, and the third of animals,) is placed, as it were, before the eyes, by many reducing instances.

Again, it is clear that the more refined tissue and conformation of things (though forming the whole body of visible or tangible objects) are neither visible nor tangible. Our information, therefore, must here, also, be derived from reduction to the sphere of the senses. But the most radical and primary difference of formation, depends on the abundance or scarcity of matter within the same space or dimensions. For, the other formations, which regard the dissimilarity of the parts contained in the same body, and their collocation and position, are secondary in comparison with the former.

Let the required nature then be the expansion, or coherence of matter in different bodies, or the quantity of matter relative to the dimensions of each. For, there is nothing in nature more true, than the twofold proposition, "That nothing proceeds from nothing," and "that nothing is reduced to nothing," but, that the quantum, or

---

* Rust is now well known to be a chymical combination of oxygen with the metal, and the metal when rusty, acquires additional weight. The theory of spirits to which Bacon frequently recurs is very obscure, especially as applied to inanimate objects. His theory as to the generation of animals, is deduced from the erroneous notion of the possibility of spontaneous generation, (as it was termed.) See the next paragraph but one.

* Limus ut hic durescit, et hæc ut cera liquescit
Uno eodemque igni.--*Virg. Ecl.* viii

sum total of matter, is constant, and is neither increased nor diminished. Nor is it less true, "that out of this given quantity of matter, there is a greater or less quantity contained within the same space or dimensions, according to the difference of bodies;" as, for instance, water contains more than air. So that, if any one were to assert, that a given content of water can be changed into an equal content of air, it is the same as if he were to assert that something can be reduced into nothing. On the contrary, if any one were to assert, that a given content of air can be changed into an equal content of water, it is the same as if he were to assert that something can proceed from nothing. From this abundance, or scarcity of matter, are properly derived the notions of density and rarity, which are taken in various and promiscuous senses.

This third assertion may be considered as being also sufficiently certain; namely, that the greater or less quantity in this or that body, may, by comparison, be reduced to calculation, and exact, or nearly exact proportion. Thus, if one should say that there is such an accumulation of matter in a given quantity of gold, that it would require twenty-one times the quantity in dimension of spirits of wine, to make up the same quantity of matter, it would not be far from the truth.

The accumulation of matter, however, and its relative quantity are rendered sensible by weight. For weight is proportionate to the quantity of matter, as regards the parts of a tangible substance, but spirit, and its quantity of matter, are not to be computed by weight, which spirit rather diminishes than augments.

We have made a tolerably accurate table of weight, in which we have selected the weights and size of all the metals, the principal minerals, stones, liquids, oils, and many other natural and artificial bodies: a very useful proceeding both as regards theory and practice, and which is capable of revealing many unexpected results. Nor is this of little consequence, that it serves to demonstrate that the whole range of the variety of tangible bodies, with which we are acquainted, (we mean tolerably close, and not spongy, hollow bodies, which are for a considerable part filled with air,) does not exceed the ratio of one to twenty-one. So limited is nature, or at least that part of it to which we are most habituated.

We have also thought it deserving our industry, to try if we could arrive at the ratio of intangible or pneumatic bodies to tangible bodies; which we attempted by the following contrivance. We took a vial capable of containing about an ounce, using a small vessel in order to effect the subsequent evaporation with less heat. We filled this vial, almost to the neck, with spirits of wine, selecting it as the tangible body which, by our table, was the rarest, and contained a less quantity of matter in a given space, than all other tangible

bodies which are compact and not hollow. Then we noted exactly the weight of the liquid and vial. We next took a bladder, containing about two pints, and squeezed all the air out of it, as completely as possible, and until the sides of the bladder met. We first, however, rubbed the bladder gently with oil, so as to make it air-tight, by closing its pores with the oil. We tied the bladder tightly round the mouth of the vial, which we had inserted in it, and with a piece of waxed thread to make it fit better and more tightly, and then placed the vial on some hot coals in a brazier. The vapour or steam of the spirit, dilated and become aeriform by the heat, gradually swelled out the bladder and stretched it in every direction like a sail. As soon as that was accomplished, we removed the vial from the fire and placed it on a carpet, that it might not be cracked by the cold: we also pricked the bladder immediately, that the steam might not return to a liquid state by the cessation of heat, and confound the proportions. We then removed the bladder, and again took the weight of the spirit which remained; and so calculated the quantity which had been converted into vapour, or an aeriform shape, and then examined how much space had been occupied by the body in its form of spirits of wine in the vial, and how much on the other hand had been occupied by it in its aeriform shape in the bladder, and subtracted the results; from which it was clear, that the body, thus converted and changed, acquired an expansion of one hundred times beyond its former bulk.

Again, let the required nature be heat or cold, of such a degree as not to be sensible from its weakness. They are rendered sensible by the thermometer as we described it above;* for the cold and heat are not actually perceived by the touch, but heat expands and cold contracts the air. Nor, again, is that expansion or contraction of the air in itself visible, but the air when expanded depresses the water, and when contracted raises it, which is the first reduction to sight.

Again, let the required nature be the mixture of bodies; namely, how much aqueous, oleaginous, or spirituous, ashy or salt parts they contain; or, as a particular example, how much butter, cheese, and whey there is in milk, and the like? These things are rendered sensible by artificial and skilful separations in tangible substances, and the nature of the spirit in them, though not immediately perceptible, is nevertheless discovered by the various motions and efforts of bodies. And, indeed, in this branch men have laboured hard in distillations and artificial separations, but with little more success than in their other experiments now in use; their methods being mere guesses and blind attempts, and more industrious than intelligent; and what is worst of all, without

* See Table of Degrees, No. 38.

any imitation or rivalry of nature, but rather by violent heats and too energetic agents, to the destruction of any delicate conformation, in which principally consist the hidden virtues and sympathies. Nor do men in these separations ever attend to or observe what we have before pointed out; namely, that in attacking bodies by fire, or other methods, many qualities are superinduced by the fire itself, and the other bodies used to effect the separation, which were not originally in the compound. Hence arise most extraordinary fallacies. For the mass of vapour, which is emitted from water by fire, for instance, did not exist as vapour or air in the water, but is chiefly created by the expansion of the water by the heat of the fire.

So, in general, all delicate experiments on natural or artificial bodies, by which the genuine are distinguished from the adulterated, and the better from the more common, should be referred to this division; for they bring that which is not the object of the senses within their sphere. They are, therefore, to be everywhere diligently sought after.

With regard to the fifth cause of objects escaping our senses, it is clear that the action of the sense takes place by motion, and this motion is time. If, therefore, the motion of any body be either so slow, or so swift, as not to be proportioned to the necessary momentum which operates on the senses, the object is not perceived at all; as in the motion of the hour hand, and that again of a musket ball. The motion which is imperceptible by the senses from its slowness, is readily and usually rendered sensible by the accumulation of motion; that which is imperceptible from its velocity, has not, as yet, been well measured; it is necessary, however, that this should be done, in some cases, with a view to a proper investigation of nature.

The sixth case, where the sense is impeded by the power of the object, admits of a reduction to the sensible sphere, either by removing the object to a greater distance, or by deadening its effects by the interposition of a medium, which may weaken, and not destroy the object; or by the admission of its reflection, where the direct impression is too strong, as that of the sun in a basin of water.

The seventh case, where the senses are so overcharged with the object, as to leave no further room, scarcely occurs, except in the smell or taste, and is not of much consequence as regards our present subject. Let what we have said, therefore, suffice with regard to the reduction to the sensible sphere of objects not naturally within its compass.

Sometimes, however, this reduction is not extended to the senses of man, but to those of some other animal, whose senses, in some points, exceed those of man: as (with regard to some scents) to that of the dog, and with regard to light existing imperceptibly in the air, when not illumined from any extraneous source, to the sense of the cat, the owl, and other animals which see by night. For Telesius has well observed that there appears to be an original portion of light even in the air itself, although but slight and meagre, and of no use for the most part to the eyes of men, and those of the generality of animals; because those animals to whose senses this light is proportioned, can see by night, which does not, in all probability, proceed from their seeing either without light, or by any internal light.

Here, too, we would observe, that we at present discuss only the wants of the senses, and their remedies; for their deceptions must be referred to the inquiries appropriated to the senses, and sensible objects; except that important deception, which makes them define objects in their relation to man, and not in their relation to the universe, and which is only corrected by universal reasoning and philosophy.

41. In the eighteenth rank of prerogative instances, we will class the instances *of the road*, which we are also wont to call *itinerant* and jointed instances. They are such as indicate the gradually continued motions of nature. This species of instances escapes rather our observation, than our senses: for men are wonderfully indolent upon this subject, consulting nature in a desultory manner, and at periodic intervals, when bodies have been regularly finished and completed, and not during her work. But if any one were desirous of examining and contemplating the talents and industry of an artificer, he would not merely wish to see the rude materials of his art, and then his work when finished, but rather to be present whilst he is at labour, and proceeding with his work. Something of the same kind should be done with regard to nature. For instance, if any one investigate the vegetation of plants, he should observe from the first sowing of any seed (which can easily be done, by pulling up every day seeds which have been two, three, or four days in the ground, and examining them diligently) how and when the seed begins to swell and break, and be filled, as it were, with spirit; then how it begins to burst the bark and push out fibres, raising itself a little at the same time, unless the ground be very stiff; then how it pushes out these fibres, some downwards for roots, others upwards for the stem; sometimes, also, creeping laterally, if it find the earth open and more yielding on one side, and the like. The same should be done in observing the hatching of eggs, where we may easily see the process of animation and organization, and what parts are formed of the yolk, and what of the white of the egg, and the like. The same may be said of the inquiry into the formation of ani-

.mals from putrefaction; for it would not be so humane to inquire into perfect and terrestrial animals, by cutting the fetus from the womb; but opportunities may perhaps be offered of abortions, animals killed in hunting, and the like. Nature, therefore, must, as it were, be watched, as being more easily observed by night than by day; for contemplations of this kind may be considered as carried on by night, from the minuteness and perpetual burning of our watch-light. The same must be attempted with inanimate objects, which we have ourselves done by inquiring into the opening of liquids by fire. For the mode in which water expands is different from that observed in wine, vinegar, or verjuice, and very different again from that observed in milk and oil, and the like; and this was easily seen, by boiling them with slow heat, in a glass vessel, through which the whole may be clearly perceived. But we merely mention this, intending to treat of it more at large and more closely when we come to the discovery of the latent process; for it should always be remembered that we do not here treat of things themselves, but merely propose examples.

42. In the nineteenth rank of prerogative instances we will class *supplementary* or substitutive instances, which we are also wont to call instances of refuge. They are such as supply information, where the senses are entirely deficient, and we, therefore, have recourse to them when appropriate instances cannot be obtained. This substitution is twofold, either by approximation or by analogy. For instance; there is no known medium, which entirely prevents the effect of the magnet in attracting iron, neither gold, nor silver, nor stone, nor glass, wood, water, oil, cloth, or fibrous bodies, air, flame, or the like. Yet, by accurate experiment, a medium may perhaps be found which would deaden its effect, more than another comparatively and in degree; as, for instance, the magnet would not, perhaps, attract iron through the same thickness of gold as of air, or the same quantity of ignited as of cold silver, and so on: for we have not ourselves made the experiment, but it will suffice as an example. Again, there is no known body which is not susceptible of heat, when brought near the fire. Yet, air becomes warm much sooner than stone. These are examples of substitution by approximation.

Substitution by analogy is useful, but less sure, and, therefore, to be adopted with some judgment. It serves to reduce that which is not the object of the senses to their sphere, not by the perceptible operations of the imperceptible body, but by the consideration of some similar perceptible body. For instance, let the subject for inquiry be the mixture of spirits, which are invisible bodies. There appears to be some relation between bodies and their sources or support. Now,

the source of flame seems to be oil and fat; that of air, water, and watery substances; for flame increases over the exhalation of oil, and air over that of water. One must, therefore, consider the mixture of oil and water, which is manifest to the senses, since that of air and flame in general escapes the senses. But oil and water mix very imperfectly by composition, or stirring, whilst they are exactly and nicely mixed in herbs, blood, and the parts of animals. Something similar, therefore, may take place in the mixture of flame and air in spirituous substances, not bearing mixture very well by simple collision, whilst they appear, however, to be well mixed in the spirits of plants and animals.

Again, if the inquiry do not relate to perfect mixtures of spirits, but merely to their composition, as whether they easily incorporate with each other, or there be rather (as an example) certain winds and exhalations, or other spiritual bodies, which do not mix with common air, but only adhere to and float in it in globules and drops, and are rather broken and pounded by the air, than received into, and incorporated with it; this cannot be perceived in common air, and other aeriform substances, on account of the rarity of the bodies, but an image, as it were, of this process, may be conceived in such liquids as quicksilver, oil, water, and even air, when broken and dissipated it ascends in small portions through water, and also in the thicker kinds of smoke; lastly, in dust, raised and remaining in the air, in all of which there is no incorporation: and the above representation in this respect is not a bad one, if it be first diligently investigated, whether there can be such a difference of nature between spirituous substances, as between liquids, for, then, these images might conveniently be substituted by analogy.

And although we have observed of these supplementary instances, that information is to be derived from them, when appropriate instances are wanting, by way of refuge, yet, we would have it understood, that they are also of great use, when the appropriate instances are at hand, in order to confirm the information afforded by them; of which we will speak more at length, when our subject leads us, in due course, to the supports of induction.

43. In the twentieth rank of prerogative instances we will place *lancing* instances, which we are also wont (but for a different reason) to call twitching instances. We adopt the latter name, because they twitch the understanding, and the former because they pierce nature, whence we style them occasionally the instances of Democritus.* They are such as warn the understanding of the admirable and exquisite subtility of nature, so that it becomes roused and awakened

* Alluding to his theory of atoms.

to attention, observation, and proper inquiry : as, for instance, that a little drop of ink should be drawn out into so many letters; that silver merely gilt on its surface should be stretched to such a length of gilt wire; that a little worm, such as you may find on the skin, should possess both a spirit and a varied conformation of its parts; that a little saffron should imbue a whole tub of water with its colour; that a little musk or aroma should imbue a much greater extent of air with its perfume; that a cloud of smoke should be raised by a little incense; that such accurate differences of sounds as articulate words should be conveyed in all directions through the air, and even penetrate the pores of wood and water, (though they become much weakened;) that they should be moreover reflected, and that with such distinctness and velocity; that light and colour should for such an extent, and so rapidly pass through solid bodies, such as glass and water, with so great and so exquisite a variety of images, and should be refracted and reflected; that the magnet should attract through every description of body, even the most compact; but (what is still more wonderful) that in all these cases the action of one should not impede that of another in a common medium, such as air; and that there should be borne through the air, at the same time, so many images of visible objects, so many impulses of articulation, so many different perfumes, as of the violet, rose, &c., besides cold and heat, and magnetic attractions; all of them, I say, at once, without any impediment from each other, as if each had its paths and peculiar passage set apart for it, without infringing against or meeting each other.

To these lancing instances, however, we are wont, not without some advantage, to add those which we call the limits of such instances. Thus, in the cases we have pointed out, one action does not disturb or impede another of a different nature, yet those of a similar nature subdue and extinguish each other; as the light of the sun does that of the candle, the sound of a cannon that of the voice, a strong perfume a more delicate one, a powerful heat a more gentle one, a plate of iron between the magnet and other iron the effect of a magnet. But the proper place for mentioning these will be also amongst the supports of induction.

44. We have now spoken of the instances which assist the senses, and which are principally of service as regards information; for information begins from the senses. But our whole labour terminates in practice, and as the former is the beginning, so is the latter the end of our subject. The following instances, therefore, will be those which are chiefly useful in practice. They are comprehended in two classes, and are seven in number. We call them all by the general name of practical instances. Now, there are

two defects in practice, and as many divisions of important instances. Practice is either deceptive or too laborious. It is generally deceptive, (especially after a diligent examination of natures,) on account of the power and actions of bodies being ill defined and determined. Now, the powers and actions of the bodies are defined and determined either by space or by time, or by the quantity at a given period, or by the predominance of energy; and if these four circumstances be not well and diligently considered, the sciences may indeed be beautiful in theory, but are of no effect in practice. We call the four instances referred to this class, *mathematical* instances and instances of measure.

Practice is laborious either from the multitude of instruments, or the bulk of matter and substances requisite for any given work. Those instances, therefore, are valuable, which either direct practice to that which is of most consequence to mankind, or lessen the number of instruments, or of matter to be worked upon. We assign to the three instances relating to this class the common name of *propitious* or *benevolent* instances. We will now separately discuss these seven instances, and conclude with them that part of our work which relates to the prerogative or illustrious instances.

45. In the twenty-first rank of prerogative instances, we will place the instances *of the rod or rule*, which we are also wont to call the instances of completion, or non-ultra. For the powers and motions of bodies do not act and take effect through indefinite and accidental, but through limited and certain spaces; and it is of great importance to practice that these should be understood and noted in every nature which is investigated; not only to prevent deception, but to render practice more extensive and efficient. For it is sometimes possible to extend these powers, and bring the distance, as it were, nearer, as in the example of telescopes.

Many powers act and take effect only by actual touch, as in the percussion of bodies; where the one does not remove the other, unless the impelling touch the impelled body. External applications in medicine, as ointment, and plasters, do not exercise their efficacy, except when in contact with the body. Lastly, the objects of touch and taste only strike those senses when in contact with their organs.

Other powers act at a distance, though it be very small, of which but few have, as yet, been noted, although there be more than men suspect: this happens (to take every day-instances) when amber or jet attract straws, bubbles dissolve bubbles, some purgative medicines draw humours from above, and the like. The magnetic power by which iron and the magnet, or two magnets, are attracted together, acts within a definite and narrow sphere; but if there be any magnetic power emanating from the earth, a little below its surface, and affecting the needle in its polarity, it must act at a great distance.

Again, if there be any magnetic force, which acts by sympathy between the globe of the earth and heavy bodies, or between that of the moon and the waters of the sea, (as seems most probable from the particular floods and ebbs which occur twice in the month,) or between the starry sphere and the planets, by which they are summoned and raised to their apogees; these must all operate at very great distances.* Again, some conflagrations and the kindling of flames take at very considerable distances, with particular substances, as they report of the naphtha of Babylon. Heat, too, insinuates itself at wide distances, as does also cold, so that the masses of ice which are broken off and float upon the Northern Ocean, and are borne through the Atlantic to the coast of Canada, become perceptible by the inhabitants, and strike them with cold from a distance. Perfumes also (though here there appears to be always some corporeal emission) act at remarkable distances; as is experienced by persons sailing by the coast of Florida, or parts of Spain, where there are whole woods of lemons, oranges, and other odoriferous plants, or rosemary and marjorum bushes, and the like. Lastly, the rays of light and the impression of sound act at extensive distances.

Yet all these powers, whether acting at a small or great distance, certainly act within definite distances, which are well ascertained by nature: so that there is a limit depending either on the mass or quantity of the bodies, the vigour or faintness of the powers, or the favourable or impeding nature of the medium, all of which should be taken into account and observed. We must also note the boundaries of violent motions, such as missiles, projectiles, wheels, and the like, since they are also manifestly confined to certain limits.

Some motions and virtues are to be found of a directly contrary nature to these, which act in contact, but not at a distance; namely, such as operate at a distance, and not in contact, and again act with less force at a less distance, and the reverse. Sight, for instance, is not easily effective in contact, but requires a medium and distance; although I remember having heard from a person, deserving of credit, that in being cured of a cataract, (which was done by putting a small silver needle within the first coat of the eye, to remove the thin pellicle of the cataract, and force it into a corner of the eye,) he had distinctly seen the needle moving across the pupil. Still, though this may be true, it is clear that large bodies cannot be seen well or distinctly, unless at the vertex of a cone, where the rays from the object meet at some distance from the eye. In old persons, the

eye sees better if the object be moved a little farther, and not nearer. Again, it is certain, that in projectiles the impact is not so violent at too short a distance as a little afterwards.* Such are the observations to be made on the measure of motions as regards distance.

There is another measure of motion in space which must not be passed over, not relating to progressive, but spherical motion: that is, the expansion of bodies into a greater, or their contraction into a lesser sphere. For, in our measure of this motion, we must inquire what degree of compression or extension bodies easily and readily admit of, according to their nature, and at what point they begin to resist it, so as, at last, to bear it no farther; as, when an inflated bladder is compressed, it allows a certain compression of the air, but, if this be increased, the air does not suffer it, and the bladder is burst.

We have proved this by a more delicate experiment. We took a metal bell, of a light and thin sort, such as is used for salt-cellars, and immerged it in a basin of water, so as to carry the air contained in its interior down with it to the bottom of the basin. We had first, however, placed a small globe at the bottom of the basin, over which we placed the bell. The result was, that if the globe were small, compared with the interior of the bell, the air would contract itself, and be compressed without being forced out, but, if it were too large for the air readily to yield to it, the latter became impatient of the pressure, raised the bell partly up, and ascended in bubbles.

To prove, also, the extension (as well as the compression) which air admits of, we adopted the following method. We took a glass egg, with a small hole at one end; we drew out the air by violent suction at this hole, and then closed the hole with the finger, immersed the egg in water, and then removed the finger. The air being constrained by the effort made in suction, and dilated beyond its natural state, and, therefore, striving to recover and contract itself, (so that if the egg had not been immersed in water, it would have drawn in the air with a hissing sound,) now drew in a sufficient quantity of water to allow the air to recover its former dimensions.†

It is well ascertained, that rare bodies (such as air) admit of considerable contraction, as has been before observed; but tangible bodies (such as water) admit of it much less readily, and to a less extent. We investigated the latter point by the following experiment.

We had a leaden globe made, capable of containing about two pints, wine measure, and of tolerable thickness, so as to support considerable

---

* Observe the approximation to Newton's theory.

* Query.

† This passage shows that the pressure of the external atmosphere, which forces the water into the egg, was not in Bacon's time, understood.

pressure. We poured water into it through an aperture, which we afterwards closed with melted lead, as soon as the globe was filled with water, so that the whole became perfectly solid. We next flattened the two opposite sides with a heavy hammer, which necessarily caused the water to occupy a less space, since the sphere is the solid of greatest content; and when hammering failed, from the resistance of the water, we made use of a mill or press, till at last the water, refusing to submit to a greater pressure, exuded, like a fine dew, through the solid lead. We then computed the extent to which the original space had been reduced, and concluded that water admitted such a degree of compression when constrained by great violence.

The more solid, dry, or compact bodies, such as stones, wood, and metals, admit of much less, and, indeed, scarcely any perceptible compression, or expansion, but escape by breaking, slipping forward, or other efforts; as appears in bending wood, or steel for watch-springs, in projectiles, hammering, and many other motions, all of which, together with their degrees, are to be observed and examined in the investigation of nature, either to a certainty, or by estimation, or comparison, as opportunity permits.

46. In the twenty-second rank of prerogative instances, we will place the instances *of the course*, which we were also wont to call water instances; borrowing our expression from the water hour-glass, employed by the ancients instead of those with sand. They are such as measure nature by the moments of time, as the last instances do by the degrees of space. For all motion or natural action takes place in time, more or less rapidly, but still in determined moments, well ascertained by nature. Even those actions which appear to take effect suddenly, and in the twinkling of an eye, (as we express it,) are found to admit of greater or less rapidity.

In the first place, then, we see that the return of the heavenly bodies to the same place, takes place in regular times, as does the flood and ebb of the sea. The descent of heavy bodies towards the earth, and the ascent of light bodies towards the heavenly sphere, take place in definite times, according to the nature of the body, and of the medium through which it moves. The sailing of ships, the motions of animals, the transmission of projectiles, all take place in times, the sums of which can be computed. With regard to heat, we see that boys in winter bathe their hands in the flame without being burned; and conjurors, by quick and regular movements, overturn vessels filled with wine or water, and replace them without spilling the liquid, with several similar instances. The compression, expansion, and eruption of several bodies, takes place more or less rapidly, according to the nature of the body, and its motion, but still in definite moments.

In the explosion of several cannon at once, (which are sometimes heard at the distance of thirty miles,) the sound of those nearest to the spot, is heard before that of the most distant. Even in sight, (whose action is most rapid,) it is clear that a definite time is necessary for its exertion, which is proved by certain objects being invisible from the velocity of their motion, such as a musket ball. For the flight of a ball is too swift to allow an impression of its figure to be conveyed to the sight.

This last instance, and others of a like nature, have sometimes excited in us a most marvellous doubt, no less than whether the image of the sky and stars is perceived as at the actual moment of its existence, or rather a little after, and whether there is not (with regard to the visible appearance of the heavenly bodies) a true and apparent time, as well as a true and apparent place, which is observed by astronomers in parallaxes.* It appeared so incredible to us, that the images or radiations of heavenly bodies could suddenly be conveyed through such immense spaces to the sight, and it seemed that they ought rather to be transmitted in a definite time. That doubt, however, (as far as regards any great difference between the true and apparent time,) was subsequently completely set at rest, when we consider the infinite loss and diminution of size as regards the real and apparent magnitude of a star, occasioned by its distance, and at the same time observed at how great a distance (at least sixty miles) bodies which are merely white can be suddenly seen by us. For there is no doubt, that the light of heavenly bodies not only far surpass the vivid appearance of white, but even the light of any flame (with which we are acquainted) in the vigour of its radiation. The immense velocity of the bodies themselves, which is perceived in their diurnal motion, and has so astonished thinking men, that they have been more ready to believe in the motion of the earth, renders the motion of radiation from them (marvellous as it is in its rapidity) more worthy of belief. That which has weighed most with us, however, is, that if there were any considerable interval of time between the reality and the appearance, the images would often be interrupted and confused by clouds formed in the mean time, and similar disturbances of the medium. Let this suffice with regard to the simple measures of time.

It is not merely the absolute, but still more the relative measure of motions and actions which must be inquired into, for this latter is of great use and application. We perceive that the flame of fire-arms is seen sooner than the sound is heard, although the ball must have struck the air before the flame, which was behind it, could escape: the reason of which is, that light moves with greater

---

* This is a singular approximation to Rœmer's discovery of time being required for the propagation of light.

velocity than sound. We perceive, also, that visible images are received by the sight with greater rapidity than they are dismissed, and for this reason, a violin string touched with the finger appears double or triple, because the new image is received before the former one is dismissed. Hence, also, rings when spinning, appear globular, and a lighted torch, borne rapidly along at night, appears to have a tail. Upon the principle of the inequality of motion, also, Galileo attempted an explanation of the flood and ebb of the sea, supposing the earth to move rapidly, and the water slowly, by which means the water, after accumulating, would at intervals fall back, as is shown in a vessel of water made to move rapidly. He has, however, imagined this on data which cannot be granted, (namely, the earth's motion,) and, besides, does not satisfactorily account for the tide taking place every six hours.

An example of our present point, (the relative measure of motion,) and, at the same time, of its remarkable use of which we have spoken, is conspicuous in mines filled with gunpowder, where immense weights of earth, buildings, and the like, are overthrown and prostrated by a small quantity of powder; the reason of which is decidedly this, that the motion of the expansion of the gunpowder is much more rapid than that of gravity, which would resist it, so that the former has terminated before the latter has commenced. Hence, also, in missiles, a strong blow will not carry them so far as a sharp and rapid one. Nor could a small portion of animal spirit in animals, especially in such vast bodies as those of the whale and elephant, have ever bent or directed such a mass of body, were it not owing to the velocity of the former, and the slowness of the latter in resisting its motion.

In short, this point is one of the principal foundations of the magic experiments, (of which we shall presently speak,) where a small mass of matter overcomes and regulates a much larger, if there be but an anticipation of motion, by the velocity of one before the other is prepared to act.

Finally, the point of the first and last should be observed in all natural actions. Thus, in an infusion of rhubarb, the purgative property is first extracted, and then the astringent; we have experienced something of the same kind in steeping violets in vinegar, which first extracts the sweet and delicate odour of the flower, and then the more earthy part, which disturbs the perfume; so that if the violets be steeped a whole day, a much fainter perfume is extracted than if they were steeped for a quarter of an hour only, and then taken out; and since the odoriferous spirit in the violet is not abundant, let other and fresh violets be steeped in the vinegar every quarter of an hour, as many as six times, when the infusion becomes so strengthened, that although the violets have not altogether remained there for more than one hour and a half, there remains a most pleasing perfume, not inferior to the flower itself, for a whole year. It must be observed, however, that the perfume does not acquire its full strength, till about a month after the infusion. In the distillation of aromatic plants macerated in spirits of wine, it is well known that an aqueous and useless phlegm rises first, then water containing more of the spirit, and lastly, water containing more of the aroma; and many observations of the like kind, well worthy of notice, are to be made in distillations. But let these suffice as examples.

47. In the twenty-third rank of prerogative instances, we will place instances of *quantity*, which we are also wont to call the doses of nature, (borrowing a word from medicine.) They are such as measure the powers by the quantity of bodies, and point out the effect of the quantity in the degree of power. And, in the first place, some powers only subsist in the universal quantity, or such as bears a relation to the conformation and fabric of the universe. Thus the earth is fixed, its parts fall. The waters in the sea flow and ebb, but not in the rivers, except by the admission of the sea. Then, again, almost all particular powers act according to the greater or less quantity of the body. Large masses of water are not easily rendered foul, small are. New wine and beer become ripe and drinkable in small skins, much more readily than in large casks. If an herb be placed in a considerable quantity of liquid, infusion takes place rather than impregnation, if in less, the reverse. A bath, therefore, and a light sprinkling, produce different effects on the human body. Light dew, again, never falls, but is dissipated and incorporated with the air; thus we see that in breathing on gems the slight quantity of moisture, like a small cloud in the air, is immediately dissolved. Again, a piece of the same magnet does not attract so much iron as the whole magnet did. There are some powers where the smallness of the quantity is of more avail; as in boring, a sharp point pierces more readily than a blunt one; the diamond, when pointed, makes an impression on glass, and the like.

Here, too, we must not rest contented with a vague result, but inquire into the exact proportion of quantity requisite for a particular exertion of power. For one would be apt to suppose that the power bears an exact proportion to the quantity; that if a leaden bullet of one ounce, for instance, would fall in a given time, one of two ounces ought to fall twice as rapidly, which is most erroneous. Nor does the same ratio prevail in every kind of power, their difference being considerable. The measure, therefore, must be determined by experiment, and not by probability or conjecture.

Lastly, we must in all our investigations of nature observe what quantity, or dose, of the body is requisite for a given effect, and must at the same time be guarded against estimating it at too much or too little.

48. In the twenty-fourth rank of prerogative instances, we will place *wrestling* instances, which we are also wont to call instances of predominance. They are such as point out the predominance and submission of powers compared with each other, and which of them is the more energetic and superior, or more weak and inferior. For the motions and effects of bodies are compounded, decomposed, and combined, no less than the bodies themselves. We will exhibit, therefore, the principal kinds of motions or active powers, in order that their comparative strength, and thence a demonstration and definition of the instances in question, may be rendered more clear.

Let the first motion be that of the *resistance of matter*, which exists in every particle, and completely prevents its annihilation; so that no conflagration, weight, pressure, violence, or length of time. can reduce even the smallest portion of matter to nothing, or prevent it from being something, and occupying some space, and delivering itself, (whatever straits it be put to,) by changing its form or place, or, if that be impossible, remaining as it is, nor can it ever happen that it should either be nothing or nowhere. This motion is designated by the schools (which generally name and define every thing by its effects and inconveniences, rather than by its inherent cause) by the axiom, "that two bodies cannot exist in the same place," or they call it a motion, "to prevent the penetration of dimensions." It is useless to give examples of this motion, since it exists in every body.

Let the second motion be that which we term the motion of *connexion*, by which bodies do not allow themselves to be separated at any point from the contact of another body, delighting, as it were, in the mutual connexion and contact. This is called by the schools a motion "to prevent a vacuum." It takes place when water is drawn up by suction or a syringe, the flesh by cupping, or when the water remains without escaping from perforated jars, unless the mouth be opened to admit the air, and innumerable instances of a like nature.

Let the third be that which we term the motion of *liberty*; by which bodies strive to deliver themselves from any unnatural pressure or tension, and to restore themselves to the dimensions suited to their mass; and of which, also, there are innumerable examples. Thus, we have examples of their escaping from pressure, in the water in swimming, in the air in flying, in the water again in rowing, and in the air in the undulations of the winds, and in the springs of watches. An exact instance of the motion of compressed air is seen in children's popguns, which they make by scooping out elder branches,

or some such matter, and forcing in a piece of some pulpy root, or the like, at each end; then they force the root or other pellet with a ramrod to the opposite end, from which the lower pellet is emitted and projected with a report, and that before it is touched by the other piece of root or pellet, or by the ramrod. We have examples of their escape from tension, in the motion of the air that remains in glass eggs after suction, in strings, leather, and cloth, which recoil after tension, unless it be long continued. The schools define this by the term of motion "from the form of the element;" injudiciously enough, since this motion is to be found not only in air, water, or fire, but in every species of solid, as wood, iron, lead, cloth, parchment, &c., each of which has its own proper size, and is with difficulty stretched to any other. Since, however, this motion of liberty is the most obvious of all, and to be seen in an infinite number of cases, it will be as well to distinguish it correctly and clearly; for some most carelessly confound this with the two others of resistance and connection; namely, the freedom from pressure with the former, and that from tension with the latter; as if bodies when compressed yielded or expanded to prevent a penetration of dimensions, and, when stretched, rebounded and contracted themselves to prevent a vacuum. But if the air, when compressed, could be brought to the density of water, or wood to that of stone, there would be no need of any penetration of dimensions, and yet the compression would be much greater than they actually admit of. So, if water could be expanded till it became as rare as air, or stone as rare as wood, there would be no need of a vacuum, and yet the expansion would be much greater than they actually admit of. We do not, therefore, arrive at a penetration of dimensions or a vacuum, before the extremes of condensation and rarefaction, whilst the motion we speak of stops and exerts itself much within them, and is nothing more than a desire of bodies to preserve their specific density, (or, if it be preferred, their form,) and not to desert them suddenly, but only to change by degrees, and of their own accord. It is, however, much more necessary to intimate to mankind (because many other points depend upon this) that the violent motion which we call mechanical, and Democritus (who, in explaining his primary motions, is to be ranked even below the middling class of philosophers) termed the motion of a blow, is nothing else than this motion of liberty, namely, a tendency to relaxation from compression. For, in all simple impulsion or flight through the air, the body is not displaced or moved in space, until its parts are placed in an unnatural state, and compressed by the impelling force. When that takes place, the different parts urging the other in succession, the whole is moved, and that with a rotatory as well as pro gressive motion, in order that the parts may, by this means, also, set themselves at liberty, or more readily submit. Let this suffice for the motion in question.

Let the fourth be that which we term the motion of *matter*, and which is opposed to the last. For, in the motion of liberty, bodies abhor, reject, and avoid a new size or volume, or any new expansion or contraction, (for these different terms have the same meaning,) and strive, with all their power, to rebound and resume their former density. On the contrary, in the motion of matter they are anxious to acquire a new volume or dimension, and attempt it willingly and rapidly, and occasionally by a most vigorous effort, as in the example of gunpowder. The most powerful, or, at least, most frequent, though not the only instruments of this motion, are heat and cold. For instance, the air, if expanded by tension, (as by suction in the glass egg,) struggles anxiously to restore itself; but if heat be applied, it strives, on the contrary, to dilate itself, and longs for a larger volume, regularly passing and migrating into it, as into a new form, (as it is termed:) nor, after a certain degree of expansion, is it anxious to return, unless it be invited to do so by the application of cold, which is not indeed a return, but a fresh change. So, also, water, when confined by compression, resists, and wishes to become as it was before, namely, more expanded; but if there happen an intense and continued cold, it changes itself readily and of its own accord, into the condensed state of ice; and if the cold be long continued, without any intervening warmth, (as in grottos and deep caves,) it is changed into crystal or similar matter, and never resumes its form.

Let the fifth be that which we term the motion of *continuity*. We do not understand by this, simple and primary continuity with any other body, (for that is the motion of connexion.) but the continuity of a particular body in itself. For it is most certain, that all bodies abhor a solution of continuity, some more and some less, but all partially. In hard bodies, (such as steel and glass,) the resistance to an interruption of continuity is most powerful and efficacious, whilst, although in liquids it appears to be faint and languid, yet it is not altogether null, but exists in the lowest degree, and shows itself in many experiments, such as bubbles, the round form of drops, in thin threads which drip from roofs, the cohesion of glutinous substances, and the like. It is most conspicuous, however, if an attempt be made to push this separation to still smaller particles. Thus, in mortars, the pestle produces no effect after a certain degree of contusion, water does not penetrate small fissures, and the air itself, notwithstanding its subtilty, does not penetrate the pores of solid vessels at once, but only by long continued insinuation.

Let the sixth be that which we term the motion of *acquisition*, or the motion of *need*. It is that by which bodies placed amongst others of a heterogenous and, as it were, hostile nature, if they meet with the means or opportunity of avoiding them and uniting themselves with others of a more analagous nature, even when these latter are not closely allied to them, immediately seize and, as it were, select them, and appear to consider it as something acquired, (whence we derive the name,) and to have need of these latter bodies. For instance, gold, or any other metal in leaf, does not like the neighbourhood of air; if, therefore, they meet with any tangible and thick substance, (such as the finger, paper, or the like,) they immediately adhere to it, and are not easily torn from it. Paper, too, and cloth, and the like, do not agree with the air, which is inherent and mixed in their pores. They readily, therefore, imbibe water or other liquids, and get rid of the air. Sugar, or a sponge, dipped in water or wine, and though part of it be out of the water or wine, and at some height above it, will yet gradually absorb them.

Hence, an excellent rule is derived for the opening and dissolution of bodies. For, (not to mention corrosive and strong waters, which force their way,) if a body can be found which is more adapted, suited, and friendly to a given solid, than that with which it is by some necessity united, the given solid immediately opens and dissolves itself to receive the former, and excludes or removes the latter.* Nor is the effect or power of this motion confined to contact, for the electric energy (of which Gilbert and others after him have told so many fables) is only the energy excited in a body by gentle friction, and which does not endure the air, but prefers some tangible substance, if there be any at hand.

Let the seventh be that which we term the motion of *greater congregation*, by which bodies are borne towards masses of a similar nature, for instance, heavy bodies towards the earth, light to the sphere of heaven. The schools termed this natural motion, by a superficial consideration of it, because produced by no external visible agent, which made them consider it innate in the substances; or, perhaps, because it does not cease, which is little to be wondered at, since heaven and earth are always present, whilst the causes and sources of many other motions are sometimes absent, and sometimes present. They, therefore, called this perpetual and proper, because it is never interrupted, but instantly takes place when the others are interrupted, and they called the others adscititious. The former, however, is in reality weak and slow, since it yields, and is inferior to the others as long as they act, unless the mass of the body be great; and although this motion have so filled men's minds, as almost to

---

* This is one of the most useful practical methods in chymistry at the present day

have obscured all others, yet they know but little about it, and commit many errors in its estimate.

Let the eighth be that which we term the motion of *lesser congregation*, by which the homogeneous parts in any body separate themselves from the heterogenous and unite together, and whole bodies of a similar substance coalesce and tend towards each other, and are sometimes congregated, attracted, and meet, from some distance; thus, in milk the cream rises after a certain time, and in wine the dregs and tartar sink; which effects are not to be attributed to gravity and levity only, so as to account for the rising of some parts and the sinking of others, but much more to the desire of the homogeneous bodies to meet and unite. This motion differs from that of need in two points: 1st. Because the latter is the stimulus of a malignant and contrary nature; whilst in this of which we treat, (if there be no impediment or restraint,) the parts are united by their affinity, although there be no foreign nature to create a struggle; 2dly. Because the union is closer and more select. For, in the other motion, bodies which have no great affinity unite, if they can but avoid the hostile body, whilst in this, substances which are connected by a decided kindred resemblance, come together and are moulded into one. It is a motion existing in all compound bodies, and would be readily seen in each, if it were not confined and checked by the other affections and necessities of bodies which disturb the union.

This motion is usually confined in the three following manners: by the torpor of the bodies; by the power of the predominating body; by external motion. With regard to the first, it is certain that there is more or less sluggishness in tangible bodies, and an abhorrence of locomotion: so that, unless excited, they prefer remaining contented with their actual state, to placing themselves in a better position. There are three means of breaking through this sluggishness: heat; the active power of a similar body; vivid and powerful motion. With regard to the first, heat is, on this account, defined as that which separates heterogeneous, and draws together homogeneous substances; a definition of the peripatetics, which is justly ridiculed by Gilbert, who says it is as if one were to define man to be that which sows wheat and plants vineyards; being only a definition deduced from effects, and those but partial. But, it is still more to be blamed, because those effects, such as they are, are not a peculiar property of heat, but a mere accident, (for cold, as we shall afterwards show, does the same,) arising from the desire of the homogeneous parts to unite; the heat then assists them in breaking through that sluggishness, which before restrained their desire. With regard to the assistance derived from the power of a similar body, it is most conspicuous in the magnet when armed with steel, for it excites in the steel a power of adhering to steel, as a homogeneous substance, the power of the magnet breaking through the sluggishness of the steel. With regard to the assistance of motion, it is seen in wooden arrows or points, which penetrate more deeply into wood than if they were tipped with iron, from the similarity of the substance, the swiftness of the motion breaking through the sluggishness of the wood; of which two last experiments we have spoken above, in the aphorism on clandestine instances.*

The confinement of the motion of lesser congregation, which arise from the power of the predominant body, is shown in the decomposition of blood and urine by cold. For, as long as these substances are filled with the active spirit, which regulates and restrains each of their component parts, as the predominant ruler of the whole, the several different parts do not collect themselves separately on account of the check; but as soon as that spirit has evaporated, or has been choked by the cold, then the decomposed parts unite, according to their natural desire. Hence, it happens, that all bodies which contain a sharp spirit (as salts, and the like) last, without decomposition, owing to the permanent and durable power of the predominating and imperious spirit.

The confinement of the motion of lesser congregation, which arises from external motion, is very evident in that agitation of bodies, which preserves them from putrefaction. For all putrefaction depends on the congregation of the homogeneous parts, whence, by degrees, there ensues a corruption of the first form, (as it is called,) and the generation of another. For, the decomposition of the original form, which is itself the union of the homogeneous parts, precedes the putrefaction, which prepares the way for the generation of another. This decomposition, if not interrupted, is simple; but if there be various obstacles, putrefactions ensue, which are the rudiments of a new generation. But, if (to come to our present point) a frequent agitation be excited, by external motion, the motion towards union (which is delicate and gentle, and requires to be free from all external influence) is disturbed, and ceases; which we perceive to be the case in innumerable instances. Thus, the daily agitation or flowing of water prevents putrefaction; winds prevent the air from being pestilent; corn, turned about and shaken in granaries, continues clean; in short, every thing which is externally agitated, will, with difficulty, rot internally.

We must not omit that union of the parts of bodies which is the principal cause of induration and desiccation. When the spirit or moisture, which has evaporated into spirit, has escaped

* See Aphorism 25.

2 M 2

from a porous body, (such as wood, bone, parchment, and the like,) the thicker parts are drawn together, and united with a greater effort, and induration or desiccation is the consequence; and this we attribute not so much to the motion of connexion, (in order to prevent a vacuum,) as to this motion of friendship and union.

Union from a distance is rare, and yet is to be met with in more instances than are generally observed. We perceive it when one bubble dissolves another, when medicines attract humours from a similarity of substance, when one string moves another in unison with it on different instruments, and the like. We are of opinion that this motion is very prevalent also in animal spirits, but are quite ignorant of the fact. It is, however, conspicuous in the magnet, and magnetized iron. Whilst speaking of the motions of the magnet, we must plainly distinguish them, for there are four distinct powers or effects of the magnet which should not be confounded, although the wonder and astonishment of mankind has classed them together. 1. The attraction of the magnet to the magnet, or of iron to the magnet, or of magnetized iron to iron. 2. Its polarity towards the north and south, and its variation. 3. Its penetration through gold, glass, stone, and all other substances. 4. The communication of power from the mineral to iron, and from iron to iron, without any communication of the substances. Here, however, we only speak of the first. There is also a singular motion of attraction between quicksilver and gold, so that the gold attracts quicksilver even when made use of in ointment, and those who work surrounded by the vapours of quicksilver are wont to hold a piece of gold in their mouths, to collect the exhalations, which would otherwise attack the heads and bones, and this piece soon grows white.* Let this suffice for the motion of lesser congregation.

Let the ninth be the *magnetic* motion, which although of the nature of that last mentioned, yet, when operating at great distances, and on great masses, deserves a separate inquiry, especially if it neither begin in contact, as most motions of congregation do, nor end by bringing the substances into contact, as all do, but only raise them, and make them swell without any further effect. For if the moon raise the waters, or cause moist substances to swell, or if the starry sphere attract the planets towards their apogees, or the sun confine the planets Mercury and Venus to within a certain distance of his mass;† these motions do not appear capable of being classed under either of those of congregation, but to be, as it were, intermediately and imperfectly congregative, and thus to form a distinct species.

Let the tenth motion be that of *avoidance*, or

that which is opposed to the motion of lesser congregation, by which bodies, with a kind of antipathy, avoid and disperse, and separate themselves from, or refuse to unite themselves with others of a hostile nature. For, although this may sometimes appear to be an accidental motion, necessarily attendant upon that of the lesser congregation, because the homogeneous parts cannot unite, unless the heterogeneous be first removed and excluded; yet it is still to be classed separately, and considered as a distinct species, because, in many cases, the desire of avoidance appears to be more marked than that of union.

It is very conspicuous in the excrements of animals, nor less, perhaps, in objects odious to particular senses, especially the smell and taste. For a fetid smell is rejected by the nose, so as to produce a sympathetic motion of expulsion at the mouth of the stomach; a bitter and rough taste is rejected by the palate or throat, so as to produce a sympathetic concussion and shivering of the head. This motion is visible also in other cases. Thus it is observed in some kinds of antiperistasis, as in the middle region of the air. the cold of which appears to be occasioned by the rejection of cold from the regions of the heavenly bodies; and also in the heat and combustion observed in subterraneous spots, which appear to be owing to the rejection of heat from the centre of the earth. For heat and cold, when in small quantities, mutually destroy each other, whilst in larger quantities, like armies equally matched, they remove and eject each other in open conflict. It is said, also, that cinnamon and other perfumes retain their odour longer when placed near privies and foul places, because they will not unite and mix with stinks. It is well known that quicksilver, which would otherwise reunite into a complete mass, is prevented from so doing by man's spittle, pork, lard, turpentine, and the like, from the little affinity of its parts with those substances, so that when surrounded by them it draws itself back, and its avoidance of these intervening obstacles is greater than its desire of reuniting itself to its homogeneous parts; which is what they term the mortification of quicksilver. Again, the difference in weight of oil and water is not the only reason for their refusing to mix, but it is also owing to the little affinity of the two, for spirits of wine, which are lighter than oil, mix very well with water. A very remarkable instance of the motion in question is seen in nitre, and crude bodies of a like nature, which abhor flame, as may be observed in gunpowder, quicksilver, and gold. The avoidance of one pole of the magnet by iron is not, (as Gilbert has well observed,) strictly speaking, an avoidance, but a conformity, or attraction to a more convenient situation.

Let the eleventh motion be that of *assimilation*, or self-multiplication, or simple generation. by

* Query.
† Observe this approximation to Newton's theory

which latter term we do not mean the simple generation of integral bodies, such as plants or animals, but of homogeneous bodies. By this motion homogeneous bodies convert those which are allied to them, or, at least, well disposed and prepared, into their own substance and nature. Thus flame multiplies itself over vapours and oily substances, and generates fresh flame; the air over water and watery substances multiplies itself and generates fresh air; the vegetable and animal spirit, over the thin particles of a watery or oleaginous spirit contained in its food, multiplies itself and generates fresh spirit; the solid parts of plants and animals, as the leaf, flower, the flesh, bone, and the like, each of them assimilate some part of the juices contained in their food, and generate a successive and daily substance. For let none rave with Paracelsus, who (blinded by his distillations) would have it, that nutrition takes place by mere separation, and that the eye, nose, brain, and liver, lie concealed in bread and meat, the root, leaf, and flower, in the juice of the earth; asserting that just as the artist brings out a leaf, flower, eye, nose, hand, foot, and the like, from a rude mass of stone or wood, by the separation and rejection of what is superfluous; so the great artist within us brings out our several limbs and parts by separation and rejection. But to leave such trifling, it is most certain that all the parts of vegetables and animals, as well the homogeneous as organic, first of all attract those juices contained in their food, which are nearly common, or at least not very different, and then assimilate and convert them into their own nature. Nor does this assimilation, or simple generation, take place in animated bodies only, but the inanimate also participate in the same property, (as we have observed of flame and air,) and that languid spirit, which is contained in every tangible animated substance, is perpetually working upon the coarser parts, and converting them into spirit, which afterwards is exhaled, whence ensues a diminution of weight, and a desiccation of which we have spoken elsewhere.* Nor should we, in speaking of assimilation, neglect to mention the accretion which is usually distinguished from aliment, and which is observed when mud grows into a mass between stones, and is converted into a stony substance, and the scaly substance round the teeth is converted into one no less hard than the teeth themselves; for we are of opinion that there exists in all bodies a desire of assimilation, as well as of uniting with homogeneous masses. Each of these powers, however, is confined, although in different manners, and should be diligently investigated, because they are connected with the revival of old age. Lastly, it is worthy of observation, that in the nine preceding

* See the citing instances, Aphorism 40.

motions, bodies appear to aim at the mere preservation of their nature, whilst in this they attempt its propagation.

Let the twelfth motion be that of *excitement*, which appears to be a species of the last, and is sometimes mentioned by us under that name. It is, like that, a diffusive, communicative, transitive, and multiplying motion; and they agree remarkably in their effect, although they differ in their mode of action, and in their subject-matter. The former proceeds imperiously, and with authority; it orders and compels the assimilated to be converted and changed into the assimilating body. The latter proceeds by art, insinuation, and stealth, inviting and disposing the excited towards the nature of the exciting body. The former both multiplies and transforms bodies and substances; thus a greater quantity of flame, air, spirit, and flesh is formed; but in the latter, the powers only are multiplied and changed, and heat, the magnetic power, and putrefaction, in the above instances, are increased. Heat does not diffuse itself, when heating other bodies, by any communication of the original heat, but only by exciting the parts of the heated body to that motion which is the form of heat, and of which we spoke in the first vintage of the nature of heat. Heat, therefore, is excited much less rapidly and readily in stone or metal, than in air, on account of the inaptitude and sluggishness of those bodies in acquiring that motion, so that it is probable that there may be some substances, towards the centre of the earth, quite incapable of being heated, on account of their density, which may deprive them of the spirit by which the motion of excitement is usually commenced. Thus, also, the magnet creates in the iron a new disposition of its parts, and a conformable motion, without losing any of its virtue. So the leaven of bread, yeast, rennet, and some poisons, excite and invite successive and continued motion in dough, beer, cheese, or the human body; not so much from the power of the exciting, as the predisposition and yielding of the excited body.

Let the thirteenth motion be that of *impression*, which is also a species of motion of assimilation, and the most subtile of diffusive motions. We have thought it right, however, to consider it as a distinct species, on account of its remarkable difference from the two last. For the simple motion of assimilation transforms the bodies themselves, so that if you remove the first agent, you diminish not the effect of those which succeed; thus, neither the first lighting of flame, nor the first conversion into air, are of any importance to the flame or air next generated. So, also, the motion of excitement still continues for a considerable time after the removal of the first agent, as in a heated body on the removal of the original heat, in the excited iron on the removal of the magnet, and in the dough on the removal of the leaven. But the motion of impression, although diffusive and transitive, appears, nevertheless, to depend on the first agent, so that, upon the removal of the latter, the former immediately fails and perishes; for which reason also it takes effect in a moment, or at least a very short space of time. We are wont to call the two former motions the motions of the generation of Jupiter, because when born they continue to exist; and the latter, the motion of the generation of Saturn, because it is immediately devoured and absorbed. It may be seen in three instances; 1. In the rays of light; 2. In the percussions of sounds; 3. In magnetic attractions as regards communication. For, on the removal of light, colours and all its other images disappear, as, on the cessation of the first percussion and the vibration of the body, sound soon fails; and although sounds are agitated by the wind, like waves, yet it is to be observed, that the same sound does not last during the whole time of the reverberation. Thus, when a bell is struck, the sound appears to be continued for a considerable time, and one might easily be led into the mistake of supposing it to float and remain in the air during the whole time, which is most erroneous. For the reverberation is not one identical sound, but the repetition of sounds; which is made manifest by stopping and confining the sonorous body; thus, if a bell be stopped and held tightly, so as to be immovable, the sound fails, and there is no further reverberation; and if a musical string be touched after the first vibration, either with the finger, (as in the harp,) or a quill, (as in the harpsichord,) the sound immediately ceases. If the magnet be removed, the iron falls. The moon, however, cannot be removed from the sea, nor the earth from a heavy falling body, and we can, therefore, make no experiment upon them, but the case is the same.

Let the fourteenth motion be that of *configuration* or *position*, by which bodies appear to desire a peculiar situation, collocation, and configuration with others, rather than union or separation. This is a very abstruse motion, and has not been well investigated; and, in some instances, appears to occur almost without any cause, although we be mistaken in supposing this to be really the case. For if it be asked, why the heavens revolve from east to west, rather than from west to east, or why they turn on poles situated near the Bears, rather than round Orion or any other part of the heaven, such a question appears to be unreasonable, since these phenomena should be received as determinate, and the objects of our experience. There are, indeed, some ultimate and self-existing phenomena in nature, but those which we have just mentioned are not to be referred to that class: for we attribute them to a certain harmony and consent of the universe, which has not yet been properly observed. But if the motion of the earth from west to east be allowed, the same question

may be put, for it must also revolve round certain poles, and why should they be placed where they are, rather than elsewhere? The polarity and variation of the needle come under our present head. There is also observed in both natural and artificial bodies, especially solids rather than fluids, a particular collocation and position of parts, resembling hairs or fibres, which should be diligently investigated, since, without a discovery of them, bodies cannot be conveniently controlled or wrought upon. The eddies observable in liquids by which, when compressed, they successively raise different parts of their mass before they can escape, so as to equalize the pressure, is more correctly assigned to the motion of liberty.

Let the fifteenth motion be that of *transmission*, or of *passage*, by which the powers of bodies are more or less impeded or advanced by the medium, according to the nature of the bodies and their effective powers, and also according to that of the medium. For one medium is adapted to light, another to sound, another to heat and cold, another to magnetic action, and so on with regard to the other actions.

Let the sixteenth be that which we term the *royal* or *political* motion, by which the predominant and governing parts of any body check, subdue, reduce, and regulate the others, and force them to unite, separate, stand still, move, or assume a certain position, not from any inclination of their own, but according to a certain order, and as best suits the convenience of the governing part, so that there is a sort of dominion and civil government exercised by the ruling part over its subjects. This motion is very conspicuous in the spirits of animals, where, as long as it is in force, it tempers all the motion of the other parts. It is found in a less degree in other bodies, as we have observed in blood and urine, which are not decomposed until the spirit, which mixed and retained their parts, has been emitted or extinguished. Nor is this motion peculiar to spirits only, although in most bodies the spirit predominates, owing to its rapid motion and penetration; for the grosser parts predominate in denser bodies, which are not filled with a quick and active spirit, (such as exists in quicksilver or vitriol,) so that unless this check or yoke be thrown off by some contrivance, there is no hope of any transformation of such bodies. And let not any one suppose that we have forgotten our subject, because we speak of predominance in this classification of motions, which is made entirely with the view of assisting the investigation of wrestling instances, or instances of predominance. For we do not now treat of the general predominance of motions or powers, but of that of parts in whole bodies, which constitutes the particular species here considered.

Let the seventeenth motion be the *spontaneous motion of revolution*, by which bodies having a tendency to move, and placed in a favourable situation, enjoy their peculiar nature, pursuing themselves and nothing else, and seeking as it were to embrace themselves. For bodies seem either to move without any limit, or to tend towards a limit, arrived at which, they either revolve according to their peculiar nature, or rest. Those which are favourably situated, and have a tendency to motion, move in a circle with an eternal and unlimited motion; those which are favourably situated and abhor motion, rest. Those which are not favourably situated move in a straight line, (as their shortest path,) in order to unite with others of a congenial nature. This motion of revolution admits of nine differences; 1. With regard to the centre about which the bodies move; 2. The poles round which they move; 3. The circumference or orbit relatively to its distance from the centre; 4. The velocity or greater or less speed with which they revolve; 5. The direction of the motion, as from east to west, or the reverse; 6. The deviation from a perfect circle, by spiral lines at a greater or less distance from the centre; 7. The deviation from the circle by spiral lines at a greater or less distance from the poles; 8. The greater or less distance of these spirals from each other; 9. And, lastly, the variation of the poles, if they be movable; which, however, only affects revolution when circular. The motion in question is, according to common and long received opinion, considered to be that of the heavenly bodies. There exists, however, with regard to this, a considerable dispute between some of the ancients as well as moderns, who have attributed a motion of revolution to the earth. A much more reasonable controversy, perhaps, exists, (if it be not a matter beyond dispute,) whether the motion in question (on the hypothesis of the earth's being fixed) is confined to the heavens, or rather descends and is communicated to the air and water. The rotation of missiles, as in darts, musket balls, and the like, we refer entirely to the motion of liberty.

Let the eighteenth motion be that of *trepidation*, to which (in the sense assigned to it by astronomers) we do not give much credit; but in our serious and general search after the tendencies of natural bodies, this motion occurs and appears worthy of forming a distinct species. It is the motion of an (as it were) eternal captivity; when bodies, for instance, being placed not altogether according to their nature, and yet not exactly ill, constantly tremble, and are restless, not contented with their position, and yet not daring to advance. Such is the motion of the heart and the pulse of animals, and it must necessarily occur in all bodies which are situated in a mean state, between conveniences and inconveniences; so that being removed from their proper position, they strive to escape, are repulsed, and again continue to make the attempt.

Let the nineteenth and last motion be one which can scarcely be termed a motion, and yet is one; and which we may call the motion of *repose*, or of abhorrence of motion. It is by this motion that the earth stands by its own weight, whilst its extremes move towards the middle, not to an imaginary centre, but in order to unite. It is owing to the same tendency, that all bodies of considerable density abhor motion, and their only tendency is not to move, which nature they preserve, although excited and urged in a variety of ways to motion. But if they be compelled to move, yet do they always appear anxious to recover their former state, and to cease from motion, in which respect they certainly appear active, and attempt it with sufficient swiftness and rapidity, as if fatigued and impatient of delay. We can only have a partial representation of this tendency, because with us every tangible substance is not only not condensed to the utmost, but even some spirit is added, owing to the action and concocting influence of the heavenly bodies.

We have now, therefore, exhibited the species or simple elements of the motions, tendencies, and active powers, which are most universal in nature; and no small portion of natural science has been thus sketched out. We do not, however, deny that other instances can, perhaps, be added, and our divisions changed according to some more natural order of things, and also reduced to a less number; in which respect we do not allude to any abstract classification, as if one were to say, that " bodies desire the preservation, exaltation, propagation, or fruition of their nature;" or, that " motion tends to the preservation and benefit either of the universe, (as in the case of those of resistance and connection,) or of extensive wholes, (as in the case of those of the greater congregation, revolution, and abhorrence of motion,) or in particular forms, as in the case of the others. For, although such remarks be just, yet, unless they terminate in matter and construction, according to true definitions, they are speculative and of little use. In the mean time, our classification will suffice, and be of much use in the consideration of the predominance of powers, and examining the wrestling instances which constitute our present subject.

For, of the motions here laid down, some are quite invincible, some more powerful than others, which they confine, check, and modify; others extend to a greater distance, others are more immediate and swift, others strengthen, increase, and accelerate the rest.

The motion of resistance is most adamantine and invincible. We are yet in doubt whether such be the nature of that of connection; for we cannot with certainty determine whether there be a vacuum, either extensive or intermixed with matter. Of one thing, however, we are satisfied, that the reason assigned by Leucippus and Democritus for the introduction of a vacuum, (namely, that the same bodies could not otherwise comprehend and fill greater and less spaces,) is false. For there is clearly a folding of matter, by which it wraps and unwraps itself in space within certain limits, without the intervention of a vacuum. Nor is there two thousand times more of vacuum in air than in gold, as there should be on this hypothesis; a fact demonstrated by the very powerful energies of fluids, (which would otherwise float like fine dust in vacuo,) and many other proofs. The other motions direct and are directed by each other according to their strength, quantity, excitement, emission, or the assistance or impediments they meet with.

For instance, some armed magnets hold and support iron of sixty times their own weight; so far does the motion of lesser congregation predominate over that of the greater; but if the weight be increased, it yields. A lever of a certain strength will raise a given weight, and so far the motion of liberty predominates over that of the greater congregation, but if the weight be greater, the former motion yields. A piece of leather stretched to a certain point does not break, and so far the motion of continuity predominates over that of tension, but if the tension be greater, the leather breaks, and the motion of continuity yields. A certain quantity of water flows through a chink, and so far the motion of greater congregation predominates over that of continuity, but if the chink be smaller, it yields. If a musket be charged with ball and powdered sulphur alone, and fire be applied, the ball is not discharged, in which case the motion of greater congregation overcomes that of matter, but when gunpowder is used, the motion of matter in the sulphur predominates, being assisted by that motion and the motion of avoidance in the nitre; and so of the rest. For wrestling instances (which show the predominance of powers, and in what manner and proportion they predominate and yield) must be searched for with active and industrious diligence.

The methods and nature of this yielding must also be diligently examined; as, for instance, whether the motions completely cease or exert themselves, but are constrained. For, in the bodies with which we are acquainted, there is no real, but an apparent rest, either in the whole or in parts. This apparent rest is occasioned either by equilibrium or the absolute predominance of motions. By equilibrium, as in the scales of the balance, which rest if the weights be equal. By predominance, as in perforated jars, in which the water rests, and is prevented from falling by the predominance of the motion of connection. It is, however, to be observed (as we have said before) how far the yielding motions exert themselves. For, if a man be held stretched out on the ground against his will, with arms and legs bound down, or otherwise confined, and yet strive with all his power to get up, the struggle is not the less, although ineffectual. The real state of the case (namely, whether the yielding motion be, as it were, annihilated by the predominance, or there be rather a continued although an invisible effort) will perhaps appear in the concurrence of motions, although it escape our notice in their conflict. For instance, let an experiment be made with muskets; whether a musket ball, at its utmost range in a straight line, or, as it is commonly called, point blank, strike with less force when projected upwards, where the motion of the blow is simple, than when projected downwards, where the motion of gravity concurs with the blow.

The rules of such instances of predominance as occur, should be collected: such as the following; the more general the desired advantage is, the stronger will be the motion; the motion of connexion, for instance, which relates to the intercourse of the parts of the universe, is more powerful than that of gravity, which relates to the intercourse of dense bodies only. Again, the desire of a private good does not, in general, prevail against that of a public one, except where the quantities are small. Would that such were the case in civil matters!

49. In the twenty-fifth rank of prerogative instances, we will place *suggesting* instances; such as suggest or point out that which is advantageous to mankind; for bare power and knowledge, in themselves, exalt, rather than enrich human nature. We must, therefore, select from the general store, such things as are most useful to mankind. We shall have a better opportunity of discussing these when we treat of the application to practice; besides, in the work of interpretation, we leave room, on every subject, for the human or optative chart; for it is a part of science to make judicious inquiries and wishes.

50. In the twenty-sixth rank of prerogative instances, we will place the *generally useful* instances. They are such as relate to various points, and frequently occur, sparing, by that means, considerable labour and new trials. The proper place for treating of instances and contrivances, will be that in which we speak of the application to practice, and the methods of experiment. All that has hitherto been ascertained, and made use of, will be described in the particular history of each art. At present, we will subjoin a few general examples of the instances in question.

Man acts, then, upon natural bodies (besides merely bringing them together or removing them) by seven principal methods: 1. By the exclusion of all that impedes and disturbs; 2. By compression, extension, agitation, and the like; 3. By heat and cold; 4. By detention in a suitable place; 5. By checking or directing motion; 6. By peculiar harmonies; 7. By a seasonable and proper alternation, series, and succession of all these, or at least of some of them.

I. With regard to the first; common air, which is always at hand, and forces its admission, as also the rays of the heavenly bodies, create much disturbance. Whatever, therefore, tends to exclude them, may well be considered as generally useful. The substance and thickness of vessels in which bodies are placed when prepared for operations may be referred to this head. So, also, may the accurate methods of closing vessels by consolidation, or the *latum sapientiæ*, as the chymists call it. The exclusion of air by means of liquids at the extremity, is also very useful; as, when they pour oil on wine, or the juices of herbs, which, by spreading itself upon the top, like a cover, preserves them uninjured from the air. Powders, also, are serviceable, for, although they contain air mixed up in them, yet they ward off the power of the mass of circumambient air, which is seen in the preservation of grapes, and other fruits, in sand and flour. Wax, honey, pitch, and other resinous bodies, are well used in order to make the exclusion more perfect, and to remove the air and celestial influence. We have sometimes made an experiment, by placing a vessel or other bodies in quicksilver, the most dense of all substances capable of being poured round others. Grottos and subterraneous caves are of great use in keeping off the effects of the sun, and the predatory action of air, and, in the north of Germany, are used for granaries. The depositing of bodies at the bottom of water may be also mentioned here, and I remember having heard of some bottles of wine being let down into a deep well in order to cool them, but left there by chance, carelessness, and forgetfulness, for several years, and then taken out; by which means, the wine not only escaped becoming flat or dead, but was much more excellent in flavour; arising (as it appears) from a more complete mixture of its parts. But, if the case require that bodies should be sunk to the bottom of water, as in rivers, or the sea, and yet should not touch the water, nor be enclosed in sealed vessels, but surrounded only by air, it would be right to use that vessel which has been sometimes employed under water, above ships that have sunk, in order to enable the divers to remain below and breathe occasionally by turns. It was of the following nature. A hollow tub of metal was formed, and sunk so as to have its bottom parallel with the surface of the water; it thus carried down with it to the bottom of the sea all the air contained in the tub. It stood upon three feet, (like a tripod,) being of rather less height than a man, so that when the diver was in want of breath, he could put his head into the hollow of the tub, breathe, and then continue his work. We hear that some sort of boat or vessel has now been invented, capable of carrying men some distance under water.

Any bodies, however, can easily be suspended under some such vessel as we have mentioned, which has occasioned our remarks upon the experiment.

Another advantage of the careful and hermetical closing of bodies is this; not only the admission of external air is prevented, (of which we have treated,) but the spirit of bodies also is prevented from making its escape, which is an internal operation. For any one operating on natural bodies must be certain as to their quantity, and that nothing has evaporated or escaped; since profound alterations take place in bodies, when art prevents the loss or escape of any portion, whilst nature prevents their annihilation. With regard to this circumstance, a false idea has prevailed, (which, if true, would make us despair of preserving quantity without diminution,) namely, that the spirit of bodies, and air when rarefied by a great degree of heat, cannot be so kept in by being enclosed in any vessel, as not to escape by the small pores. Men are led into this idea by common experiments of a cup inverted over water, with a candle or piece of lighted paper in it, by which the water is drawn up, and of those cups which when heated draw up the flesh. For they think that in each experiment the rarefied air escapes, and that its quantity is therefore diminished, by which means the water or flesh rises by the motion of connexion. This is, however, most incorrect. For the air is not diminished in quantity, but contracted in dimensions,* nor does this motion of the rising of the water begin till the flame is extinguished, or the air cooled, so that physicians place cold sponges, moistened with water, on the cups, in order to increase their attraction. There is, therefore, no reason why men should fear much from the ready escape of air: for, although it be true that the most solid bodies have their pores, yet neither air nor spirit readily suffers itself to be rarefied to such an extreme degree; just as water will not escape by a small chink.

II. With regard to the second of the seven above mentioned methods, we must especially observe, that compression and similar violence have a most powerful effect either in producing locomotion, and other motions of the same nature, as may be observed in engines and projectiles, or in destroying the organic body and those qualities which consist entirely in motion, (for all life, and every description of flame and ignition are destroyed by compression, which also injures and deranges every machine;) or in destroying those qualities which consist in position and a coarse difference of parts, as in colours; for the

---

* Part of the air is expanded and escapes, and part is consumed by the flame. When condensed, therefore, by the cold application, it cannot offer sufficient resistance to the external atmosphere to prevent the liquid or flesh from being forced into the glass

colour of a flower when whole differs from that it presents when bruised, and the same may be observed of whole and powdered amber; or in taste, for the taste of a pear before it is ripe and of the same pear when bruised and softened is different, since it becomes perceptibly more sweet. But such violence is of little avail in the more noble transformations and changes of homogeneous bodies, for they do not, by such means, acquire any constantly and permanently new state, but one that is transitory, and always struggling to return to its former habit and freedom. It would not, however, be useless to make some more diligent experiments with regard to this; whether, for instance, the condensation of a perfectly homogeneous body (such as air, water, oil, and the like) or their rarefaction, when effected by violence, can become permanent, fixed, and, as it were, so changed as to become a nature. This might at first be tried by simple perseverance, and then by means of helps and harmonies. It might readily have been attempted, (if we had but thought of it,) when we condensed water (as was mentioned above) by hammering and compression until it burst out. For we ought to have left the flattened globe untouched for some days, and then to have drawn off the water in order to try whether it would have immediately occupied the same dimensions as it did before the condensation. If it had not done so, either immediately or soon afterwards, the condensation would have appeared to have been rendered constant; if not, it would have appeared that a restitution took place, and that the condensation had been transitory. Something of the same kind might have been tried with the glass eggs; the egg should have been sealed up suddenly and firmly, after a complete exhaustion of the air, and should have been allowed to remain so for some days, and it might then have been tried whether, on opening the aperture, the air would be drawn in with a hissing noise, or whether as much water would be drawn into it when immersed, as would have been drawn into it at first, if it had not continued sealed. For it is probable (or at least worth making the experiment) that this might have happened, or might happen, because perseverance has a similar effect upon bodies which are a little less homogeneous. A stick bent together for some time does not rebound, which is not owing to any loss of quantity in the wood during the time, for the same would occur (after a larger time) in a plate of steel, which does not evaporate. If the experiment of simple perseverance should fail, the matter should not be given up, but other means should be employed. For it would be no small advantage, if bodies could be en lued with fixed and constant natures by violence. Air could then be converted into water by condensation, with other similar effects; for man is more the master of violent motions than of any other means.

III. The third of our seven methods is referred to that great practical engine of nature as well as of art, cold and heat. Here man's power limps, as it were, with one leg. For we possess the heat of fire, which is infinitely more powerful and intense than that of the sun (as it reaches us) and that of animals. But we want cold,* except such as we can obtain in winter, in caverns, or by surrounding objects with snow and ice, which, perhaps, may be compared in degree with the noontide heat of the sun in tropical countries, increased by the reflection of mountains and walls. For this degree of heat and cold can be borne for a short period only by animals, yet it is nothing compared with the heat of a burning furnace, or the corresponding degree of cold.† Every thing with us has a tendency to become rarefied, dry, and wasted, and nothing to become condensed or soft, except by mixtures, and, as it were, spurious methods. Instances of cold, therefore, should be searched for most diligently, such as may be found by exposing bodies upon buildings in a hard frost, in subterraneous caverns, by surrounding bodies with snow and ice in deep places excavated for that purpose, by letting bodies down into wells, by burying bodies in quicksilver and metals, by immersing them in streams which petrify wood, by burying them in the earth, (which the Chinese are reported to do with their china, masses of which, made for that purpose, are said to remain in the ground for forty or fifty years, and to be transmitted to their heirs as a sort of artificial mine,) and the like. The condensations which take place in nature by means of cold should also be investigated, that by learning their causes they may be introduced into the arts; such as are observed in the exudation of marble and stones, in the dew upon the panes of glass in a room towards morning after a frosty night, in the formation and the gathering of vapours under the earth into water, whence spring fountains, and the like.

Besides the substances which are cold to the touch, there are others which have also the effect of cold, and condense; they appear, however, to act only upon the bodies of animals, and scarcely any further. Of these we have many instances, in medicines and plasters. Some condense the flesh and tangible parts, such as astringent and inspissating medicines, others the spirits, such as soporifics. There are two modes of condensing

---

* Heat can now be abstracted by a very simple process, till the degree of cold be of almost any required intensity.

† It is impossible to compare a degree of heat with a degree of cold, without the assumption of some arbitrary test, to which the degrees are to be referred. In the next sentence Bacon appears to have taken the power of animal life to support heat or cold as the test, and then the comparison can only be between the degree of heat or of cold that will produce death.

The zero must be arbitrary which divides equally a certain degree of heat from a certain degree of cold.

the spirits, by soporifics or provocatives to sleep; the one by calming the motion, the other by expelling the spirit. The violet, dried roses, lettuces, and other benign or mild remedies, by their friendly and gently cooling vapours, invite the spirits to unite, and restrain their violent and perturbed motion. Rose-water, for instance, applied to the nostrils in fainting fits, causes the resolved and relaxed spirits to recover themselves, and, as it were, cherishes them. But opiates, and the like, banish the spirits by their malignant and hostile quality. If they be applied, therefore, externally, the spirits immediately quit the part, and no longer readily flow into it; but if they be taken internally, their vapour, mounting to the head, expels, in all directions, the spirits contained in the ventricles of the brain, and since these spirits retreat, but cannot escape, they consequently meet and are condensed, and are sometimes completely extinguished and suffocated; although the same opiates, when taken in moderation, by a secondary accident, (the condensation which succeeds their union,) strengthen the spirits, render them more robust, and check their useless and inflammatory motion, by which means they contribute not a little to the cure of diseases, and the prolongation of life.

The preparations of bodies, also, for the reception of cold, should not be omitted, such as that water a little warmed is more easily frozen than that which is quite cold, and the like.

Moreover, since nature supplies cold so sparingly, we must act like the apothecaries, who, when they cannot obtain any simple ingredient, take a succedaneum, or quid pro quo, as they term it, such as aloes for xylobalsamum, cassia for cinnamon. In the same manner we should look diligently about us, to ascertain whether there may be any substitutes for cold, that is to say, in what other manner condensation can be effected, which is the peculiar operation of cold. Such condensations appear hitherto to be of four kinds only. 1. By simple compression, which is of little avail towards permanent condensation, on account of the elasticity of substances, but may still however be of some assistance. 2. By the contraction of the coarser, after the escape or departure of the finer parts of a given body; as is exemplified in induration by fire, and the repeated heating and extinguishing of metals, and the like. 3. By the cohesion of the most solid homogeneous parts of a given body, which were previously separated, and mixed with others less solid, as in the return of sublimated mercury to its simple state, in which it occupies much less space than it did in powder, and the same may be observed of the cleansing of all metals from their dross. 4. By harmony or the application of substances which condense by some latent power. These harmonies are as yet but rarely observed, at which we cannot be surprised, since there is little to hope

for from their investigation, unless the discovery of forms and conformation be attained. With regard to animal bodies, it is not to be questioned that there are many internal and external medicines which condense by harmony, as we have before observed, but this action is rare in inanimate bodies. Written accounts, as well as report, have certainly spoken of a tree in one of the Tercera or Canary Islands (for I do not exactly recollect which) that drips perpetually, so as to supply the inhabitants, in some degree, with water; and Paracelsus says, that the herb called ros solis is filled with dew at noon, whilst the sun gives out its greatest heat, and all other herbs around it are dry. We treat both these accounts as fables; they would, however, if true, be of the most important service, and most worthy of examination. As to the honey-dew, resembling manna, which is found in May on the leaves of the oak, we are of opinion that it is not condensed by any harmony or peculiarity of the oak leaf, but that whilst it falls equally upon other leaves, it is retained and continues on those of the oak, because their texture is closer, and not so porous as that of most of the other leaves.*

With regard to heat, man possesses abundant means and power, but his observation and inquiry are defective in some respects, and those of the greatest importance, notwithstanding the boasting of quacks. For the effects of intense heat are examined and observed, whilst those of a more gentle degree of heat, being of the most frequent occurrence in the paths of nature, are, on that very account, least known. We see, therefore, the furnaces, which are most esteemed, employed in increasing the spirits of bodies to a great extent, as in the strong acids, and some chymical oils; whilst the tangible parts are hardened, and, when the volatile part has escaped, become sometimes fixed; the homogeneous parts are separated, and the heterogeneous incorporated and agglomerated in a coarse lump; and (what is chiefly worthy of remark) the junction of compound bodies, and the more delicate conformations are destroyed and confounded. But the operation of a less violent heat should be tried and investigated, by which more delicate mixtures and regular conformations may be produced and elicited, according to the example of nature, and in imitation of the effect of the sun, which we have alluded to in the aphorism on the instances of alliance. For the works of nature are carried on in much smaller portions, and in more delicate and varied positions than those of fire, as we now employ it. But man will then appear to have really augmented his power, when the works of nature can be imitated *in specie*, perfected in power, and varied in quantity; to which should be added the acceleration in point of time. Rust, for instance, is

* It may often be observed on the leaves of the lime and other trees.

2 N

the result of a long process, but crocus Martis is obtained immediately; and the same may be observed of natural verdigris and ceruse. Crystal is formed slowly, whilst glass is blown immediately: stones increase slowly, whilst bricks are baked immediately, &c. In the mean time (with regard to our present subject) every different species of heat should, with its peculiar effects, be diligently collected and inquired into; that of the heavenly bodies, whether their rays be direct, reflected, or refracted, or condensed by a burning-glass; that of lightning, flame, and ignited charcoal; that of fire of different materials, either open or confined, straitened or overflowing, qualified by the different forms of the furnaces, excited by the bellows, or quiescent, removed to a greater or less distance, or passing through different media; moist heats, such as the balneum Mariæ, and the dunghill; the external and internal heat of animals; dry heats, such as the heat of ashes, lime, warm sand; in short, the nature of every kind of heat, and its degrees.

We should, however, particularly attend to the investigation and discovery of the effects and operations of heat, when made to approach and retire by degrees, regularly, periodically, and by proper intervals of space and time. For this systematical inequality is in truth the daughter of heaven and mother of generation, nor can any great result be expected from a vehement, precipitate, or desultory heat. For this is not only most evident in vegetables, but in the wombs of animals, also, there arises a great inequality of heat, from the motion, sleep, food, and passions of the female. The same inequality prevails in those subterraneous beds where metals and fossils are perpetually forming, which renders yet more remarkable the ignorance of some of the reformed alchymists, who imagined they could attain their object by the equable heat of lamps, or the like, burning uniformly. Let this suffice concerning the operation and effects of heat; nor is it time for us to investigate them thoroughly before the forms and conformations of bodies have been further examined and brought to light. When we have determined upon our models, we may seek, apply, and arrange our instruments.

IV. The fourth mode of action is by continuance, the very steward and almoner, as it were, of nature. We apply the term continuance to the abandonment of a body to itself for an observable time, guarded and protected in the mean while from all external force. For the internal motion then commences to betray and exert itself when the external and adventitious is removed. The effects of time, however, are far more delicate than those of fire. Wine, for instance, cannot be clarified by fire as it is by continuance. Nor are the ashes produced by combustion so fine as the particles dissolved or

wasted by the lapse of ages. The incorporations and mixtures, which are hurried by fire, are very inferior to those obtained by continuance; and the various conformations assumed by bodies left to themselves, such as mouldiness, &c., are put a stop to by fire or a strong heat. It is not, in the mean time, unimportant to remark, that there is a certain degree of violence in the motion of bodies entirely confined. For the confinement impedes the proper motion of the body. Continuance in an open vessel, therefore, is useful for separations, and in one hermetically sealed for mixtures, that in a vessel partly closed, but admitting the air for putrefaction. But instances of the operation and effect of continuance must be collected diligently from every quarter.

V. The direction of motion (which is the fifth method of action) is of no small use. We adopt this term when speaking of a body, which, meeting with another, either arrests, repels, allows, or directs its original motion. This is the case principally in the figure and position of vessels. An upright cone, for instance, promotes the condensation of vapour in alembics, but, when reversed, as in inverted vessels, it assists the refining of sugar. Sometimes a curved form or one alternately contracted and dilated is required. Strainers may be ranged under this head, where the opposed body opens a way for one portion of another substance and impedes the rest. Nor is this process, or any other direction of motion, carried on externally only, but sometimes by one body within another. Thus, pebbles are thrown into water to collect the muddy particles, and syrups are refined by the white of an egg, which glues the grosser particles together so as to facilitate their removal. Telesius, indeed, rashly and ignorantly enough attributes the formation of animals to this cause, by means of the channels and folds of the womb. He ought to have observed a similar formation of the young in eggs, which have no wrinkles or inequalities. One may observe a real result of this direction of motion in casting and modelling.

VI. The effects produced by harmony and aversion (which is the sixth method) are frequently buried in obscurity. For these occult and specific properties, (as they are termed,) the sympathies and antipathies are for the most part but a corruption of philosophy. Nor can we form any great expectation of the discovery of the harmony which exists between natural objects, before that of their forms and simple conformations, for it is nothing more than the symmetry between these forms and conformations.

The greater and more universal species of harmony are not, however, so wholly obscure, and with them, therefore, we must commence. The first and principal distinction between them is this; that some bodies differ considerably in the abundance and rarity of their substance, but correspond in their conformation; others, on the contrary, correspond in the former and differ in the latter. Thus the chymists have well observed, that in their trial of first principles, sulphur and mercury, as it were, pervade the universe; their reasoning about salt, however, is absurd, and merely introduced to comprise earthy, dry, fixed bodies. In the other two, indeed, one of the most universal species of natural harmony manifests itself. Thus there is a correspondence between sulphur, oil, greasy exhalations, flame, and, perhaps, the substance of the stars. On the other hand, there is a like correspondence between mercury, water, aqueous vapour, air, and, perhaps, pure intersidereal ether. Yet do these two quaternions, or great natural tribes (each within its own limits) differ immensely in quantity and density of substance, whilst they generally agree in conformation, as is manifest in many instances. On the other hand, the metals agree in such quantity and density, (especially when compared with vegetables, &c.,) but differ in many respects in conformation. Animals and vegetables, in like manner, vary in their almost infinite modes of conformation, but range within very limited degrees of quantity and density of substance.

The next most general correspondence is that between individual bodies and those which supply them by way of menstruum or support. Inquiry, therefore, must be made as to the climate, soil, and depth at which each metal is generated, and the same of gems, whether produced in rocks or mines; also as to the soil in which particular trees, shrubs, and herbs mostly grow and, as it were, delight; and as to the best species of manure, whether dung, chalk, sea-sand, or ashes, &c., and their different propriety and advantage according to the variety of soils. So also the grafting and setting of trees and plants (as regards the readiness of grafting one particular species on another) depends very much upon harmony, and it would be amusing to try an experiment I have lately heard of, in grafting forest trees, (garden trees alone having hitherto been adopted,) by which means the leaves and fruit are enlarged, and the trees produce more shade. The specific food of animals again should be observed, as well as that which cannot be used. Thus the carnivorous cannot be fed on herbs, for which reason the order of Feuilletans, the experiment having been made, has nearly vanished; human nature being incapable of supporting their regimen, although the human will has more power over the bodily frame than that of other animals. The different kinds of putrefaction from which animals are generated should be noted.

The harmony of principal bodies with those subordinate to them (such indeed may be deemed those we have alluded to above) are sufficiently manifest, to which may be added those that exist between different bodies and their objects, and,

since these latter are more apparent, they may throw great light, when well observed and diligently examined, upon those which are more latent.

The more eternal harmony and aversion, or friendship and enmity, (for superstition and folly have rendered the terms of sympathy and antipathy almost disgusting,) have been either falsely assigned, or mixed with fable, or most rarely discovered from neglect. For if one were to allege that there is an enmity between the vine and the cabbage, because they will not come up well when sown together, there is a sufficient reason for it in the succulent and absorbent nature of each plant, so that the one defrauds the other. Again, if one were to say that there is a harmony and friendship between the corn and the corn-flower, or the wild poppy, because the latter seldom grow anywhere but in cultivated soils, he ought rather to say there is an enmity between them, for the poppy and the corn-flower are produced and created by those juices which the corn has left and rejected, so that the sowing of the corn prepares the ground for their production. And there are a vast number of similar false assertions. As for fables, they must be totally exterminated. There remains then but a scanty supply of such species of harmony as has borne the test of experiment, such as that between the magnet and iron, gold and quicksilver, and the like. In chymical experiments on metals, however, there are some others worthy of notice, but the greatest abundance (where the whole are so few in numbers) is discovered in certain medicines, which, from their occult and specific qualities, (as they are termed,) affect particular limbs, humours, diseases, or constitutions. Nor should we omit the harmony between the motion and phenomena of the moon, and their effects on lower bodies, which may be brought together by an accurate and honest selection from the experiments of agriculture, navigation, and medicine, or of other sciences. By as much as these general instances, however, of more latent harmony are rare, with so much the more diligence are they to be inquired after, through tradition and faithful and honest reports, but without rashness and credulity, with an anxious and, as it were, hesitating degree of reliance. There remains one species of harmony which, though simple in its mode of action, is yet most valuable in its use, and must by no means be omitted, but rather diligently investigated. It is the ready or difficult coition or union of bodies in composition or simple juxta position. For some bodies readily and willingly mix and are incorporated, others tardily and perversely; thus powders mix best with water, chalk and ashes with oils, and the like. Nor are these instances of readiness and aversion to mixture to be alone collected, but others also of the collocation, distribution, and digestion of the parts when mingled, and the predominance after the mixture is complete.

VII. Lastly, there remains the seventh and last of the seven modes of action; namely, that by the alteration and interchange of the other six; out of this it will not be the right time to offer any examples until some deeper investigation shall have taken place of each of the others. The series, or chain of this alternation, in its mode of application to separate effects, is no less powerful in its operation than difficult to be traced. But men are possessed with the most extreme impatience, both of such inquiries and their practical application, although it be the clue of the labyrinth in all greater works. Thus far of the generally useful instances.

51. The twenty-seventh and last place we will assign to the *magical* instances, a term which we apply to those where the matter, or efficient agent, is scanty or small, in comparison with the grandeur of the work or effect produced; so that, even when common, they appear miraculous, some at first sight, others even upon more attentive observation. Nature, however, of herself, supplies these but sparingly. What she will do when her whole store is thrown open, and after the discovery of forms, processes, and conformation, will appear hereafter. As far as we can yet conjecture, these magic effects are produced in three ways, either by self-multiplication, as in fire, and the poisons termed specific, and the motions transferred and multiplied from wheel to wheel; or by the excitement, or, as it were, invitation of another substance, as in the magnet, which excites innumerable needles without losing or diminishing its power, and, again, in leaven, and the like; or, by the excess of rapidity of one species of motion over another, as has been observed in the case of gunpowder, cannon, and mines. The two former require an investigation of harmonies, the latter of a measure of motion. Whether there be any mode of changing bodies per minima, (as it is termed,) and transferring the delicate conformations of matter, which is of importance in all transformations of bodies, so as to enable art to effect, in a short time, that which nature works out by divers expedients, is a point of which we have as yet no indication. But, as we aspire to the extremest and highest results in that which is solid and true, so do we ever detest, and, as far as in us lies, expel all that is empty and vain.

52. Let this suffice as to the respective dignity or prerogatives of instances. But it must be noted, that, in this our organ, we treat of logic, and not of philosophy. Seeing, however, that our logic instructs and informs the understanding, in order that it may not, with the small hooks, as it were, of the mind, catch at and grasp mere abstractions, but rather actually penetrate nature, and discover the properties and effects of bodies, and the determinate laws of their substance, (so that this science of ours springs from the nature of things, as well as from that of the mind;) it is not to be wondered at, if it have been continually interspersed and illustrated with natural observations and experiments, as instances of our method The prerogative instances are, as appears from what has preceded, twenty-seven in number, and are termed, solitary instances, migrating instances. conspicuous instances, clandestine instances, constitutive instances, similar instances, singular instances, deviating instances, bordering instances, instances of power, accompanying and hostile instances, subjunctive instances, instances of alliance, instances of the cross, instances of divorce, instances of the gate, citing instances, instances of the road, supplementary instances, lancing instances, instances of the rod, instances of the course, doses of nature, wrestling instances, suggesting instances, generally useful instances, and magical instances. The advantage, by which these instances excel the more ordinary, regards specifically either theory or practice, or both. With regard to theory, they assist either the senses or the understanding; the senses, as in the five instances of the lamp; the understanding. either by expediting the exclusive mode of arriving at the form, as in solitary instances, or by confining and more immediately indicating the affirmative, as in the migrating, conspicuous, accompanying, and subjunctive instances; or, by elevating the understanding, and leading it to general and common natures, and that either immediately, as in the clandestine and singular instances, and those of alliance; or, very nearly so, as in the constitutive; or, still less so, as in the similar instances; or, by correcting the understanding of its habits, as in the deviating instances; or, by leading to the grand form or fabric of the universe, as in the bordering instances; or, by guarding it from false forms and causes, as in those of the cross and of divorce. With regard to practice, they either point it out, or measure, or elevate it. They point it out, either by showing where we must commence, in order not to repeat the labours of others, as in the instances of power; or, by inducing us to aspire to that which may be possible, as in the suggesting instances: the four mathematical instances measure it. The generally useful and the magical elevate it.

Again, out of these twenty-seven instances, some must be collected immediately, without waiting for a particular investigation of properties. Such are the similar, singular, deviating, and bordering instances, those of power, and of the gate, and suggesting, generally useful, and magical instances. For these either assist and cure the understanding and senses, or furnish our general practice. The remainder are to be collected when we finish our synoptical tables for the work of the interpreter, upon any particular nature. For these instances, honoured and gifted with such prerogatives, are like the soul amid the vulgar crowd of instances, and (as we from the first observed) a few of them are worth a multitude of the others. When, therefore, we are forming our tables, they must be searched out with the greatest zeal, and placed in the table. And, since mention must be made of them in what follows, a treatise upon their nature has necessarily been prefixed. We must next, however, proceed to the supports and corrections of induction, and thence to concretes, the latent process, and latent conformations, and the other matters, which we have enumerated in their order in the twenty-first aphorism, in order that, like good and faithful guardians, we may yield up their fortune to mankind, upon the emancipation and majority of their understanding; from which must necessarily follow an improvement of their estate, and an increase of their power over nature. For, man, by the fall, lost at once his state of innocence and his empire over creation, both of which can be partially recovered, even in this life, the first by religion and faith, the second by the arts and sciences. For creation did not become entirely and utterly rebellious by the curse; but in consequence of the divine decree, "In the sweat of thy brow shalt thou eat bread," she is compelled by our labours, (not assuredly by our disputes or magical ceremonies,) at length, to afford mankind, in some degree, his bread, that is to say, to supply man's daily wants.

END OF NOVUM ORGANUM.

A

PREPARATION

FOR A

NATURAL AND EXPERIMENTAL HISTORY.

A DESCRIPTION

OF

SUCH A NATURAL AND EXPERIMENTAL HISTORY AS SHALL BE SUFFICIENT AND SUITABLY ARRANGED FOR FORMING THE BASIS AND FOUNDATION OF A TRUE PHILOSOPHY.

OUR motive for publishing our Instauration in parts, was that we might make sure of something. A similar reason induces us to subjoin, even now, another small portion of the work, and to publish it with that which has been completed above. It is a description and delineation of such a natural and experimental history as should be arranged for the completing our philosophy, and should comprehend genuine and copious materials, properly adapted to the work of the interpreter who is next to make his appearance. The proper place for this would have been that where we treat of *preparations* in the regular course of our inquiry. Yet does it appear better to anticipate, rather than wait for this proper place, since the history which we design, and will presently describe, is a matter of great magnitude, and not to be effected without vast labour and expense, requiring the combined assistance of many, and being, (to use our former expression,) as it were, a royal work. It occurred, therefore, that it might be worth while to see if any others would undertake it, so that whilst we orderly pursue our design, this complicated and laborious portion of it may, by the joint application of others, be set in order and prepared even in our lifetime, should it so please God; especially, since our own unassisted strength appears scarcely adequate to so great a sphere. For we may, perhaps, by our own power, overcome all that is the actual work of the understanding, but the materials on which it is to work, are so scattered, that they should be sought after and imported from all quarters by factors and merchants. We consider it, moreover, as scarcely worthy of our undertaking ourselves to waste time in that which is open to the industry of almost all. We will, however, perform the principal part, that of laying down, with diligence and accuracy, a model and sketch of such a history as will satisfy our intention, lest, for want of caution, others should waste their time, and direct their efforts by the example of such natural histories as are now in use, thus wandering far from our proposal. In the mean time, that which we have often said must here be specially repeated, namely, that if all the talents of every age had concurred, or shall hereafter concur, if the whole human race had applied, or shall apply itself to philosophy, and the whole globe had consisted, or shall consist of academies, and colleges, and schools of the learned, yet, without such a natural and experimental history as we shall now recommend, it were impossible that any progress worthy of mankind should have been, or should hereafter be made in philosophy and the sciences. But, on the other hand, when it has once been prepared and drawn up, with the addition of such auxiliary and instructive experiments as will occur or be searched out, in the course of interpretation, the investigation of nature and of all the sciences will be a work many years. This, therefore, must be done, or the whole work must be abandoned, for by this method only can the foundation be laid of a genuine and active philosophy; and men will at once perceive, as if roused from a profound sleep, what a difference exists between the dogmatism and fictions of man's wit, and a genuine and active philosophy, and what it is to consult nature herself about nature.

In the first place, then, we will give general precepts as to completing such a history, and will then set a particular species of it before men's eyes, alluding occasionally to the end to which the inquiry must be adapted and referred, as well as to the subject-matter of investigation itself; in order that, the intention being well understood and known beforehand, it may suggest other points that may have escaped us. To this history we are wont to give the name of First, or Mother History.

APHORISMS

ON THE FORMATION OF THE FIRST HISTORY.

APHORISMS.

I. NATURE is placed in three situations, and subject to a threefold government. For she is either free, and left to unfold herself in a regular course, or she is driven from her position by the obstinacy and resistance of matter, and the violence of obstacles, or she is constrained and moulded by human art and labour. The first state applies to the specific nature of bodies; the second to monsters; the third to artificial productions, in which she submits to the yoke imposed on her by man, for without the hand of man they would not have been produced. But from the labour and contrivance of man an entirely new appearance of bodies takes its rise, forming, as it were, another universe or theatre. Natural history, then, is threefold, and treats either of the liberty, the wanderings, or the fetters of nature; so that we may aptly divide it into the histories of generation, pretergeneration, and arts; the latter of which divisions we are also wont to call mechanic or experimental. Yet would we not direct these three to be carried on separately, for why should not the history of monstrosities in every species be combined with that of the species itself? So, also, artificial subjects may sometimes properly enough be treated of together with certain natural species, though, at other times, it is better to separate them. Circumstances, therefore, must guide us, for too rigid a method admits of repetitions and prolixity as much as no method.

II. Natural history being, as we have observed, threefold relative to its subject, is twofold in its application. For it is employed either as a means of arriving at the knowledge of the matters themselves which are consigned to it, or as the elementary material for philosophy, and as the stock or forest, as it were, from which to furnish forth genuine induction. The latter is its present application; its present one, I observe, for it was never before so applied. For neither Aristotle, nor Theophrastus, nor Dioscorides, nor Pliny, nor much less the moderns, ever proposed this as the object of natural history. And the principal point to be attended to is this, that those who shall henceforth take charge of natural history, do perpetually reflect, and impress upon their minds, that they ought not to be subservient to the pleasure or even benefit which may, at this present time, be derived from their narrative, but that they must collect and prepare such and so varied a supply of things, as may be sufficient for the forming of genuine axioms. If they thus reflect, they will themselves lay down their own method for such a history, for the end governs the means.

III. But by as much as this is a matter requiring great pains and labour, by so much the less should it be unnecessarily burdened. There are three points, then, upon which men should be warned to employ but scanty labour, inasmuch as they infinitely increase the bulk of the work, and add but little or nothing to its value.

First, then, let them dismiss antiquity and quotations, or the suffrages of authors, all disputes, controversies, and discordant opinions, and, lastly, all philological disquisitions. Let no author be quoted except on doubtful points, nor controversies entered into except on matter of great importance; and as for the ornaments of language, and comparisons, and the whole treasury of eloquence, and the like puerilities, let them be wholly renounced. Nay, let all which is admitted be propounded briefly and concisely, so as to be nothing less than words. For no one, who is preparing and laying by materials, for building houses or ships, or the like, takes the trouble, as they would in shops, of arranging them elegantly and showing them off to advantage, but rather attends only to their being strong and good, and to their taking up as little room as possible in his warehouse. Let the like be done here.

Secondly, There is not much real use in the lavish abundance of descriptions, painted representations of species, and collections of their varieties with which natural history is adorned. These trifling varieties are the mere sport and wantonness of nature, and approximate to merely individual characteristics, affording a pleasant digression, but a mean and superfluous sort of information as regards science.

Thirdly, We must reject all superstitious narratives, (I do not say prodigious, where faithful and probable accounts can be obtained, but superstitious,) together with the experiments of natural magic. For we would not accustom philosophy in her infancy, whose very nurse is natural history, to old wives' tales. A time may come (after a deeper investigation of nature) when such matters may be lightly touched upon, so as to extract and lay up for use such natural knowledge as may lurk in their dregs, but till then they are to be put aside. In like manner, the experiments of natural magic are to be diligently and rigidly sifted before their adoption, especially those which are wont to be derived from vulgar sympathies and antipathies, owing to the indolence and credulity of both believers and inventors.

It is no slight matter to have thus relieved natural history of these three vanities, which might otherwise have hereafter filled volumes. Nor is this all; for it is as essential to a great work, that that which is admitted be briefly described, as that the superfluous should be rejected, although it must be obvious that this chastened and precise style must afford less pleasure, both to the reader and to the author. But it is ever to be repeated, that the object is to prepare a mere granary and ware house, in which no one is to loiter or dwell for amusement, but only to visit as occasion may require, when any thing is wanted for the work of the interpreter, which follows next in order.

IV. One thing, above all others, is requisite for the history we design; namely, that it be most extensive, and adapted to the extent of the universe. For the world is not to be narrowed down to the measure of the understanding, (as has hitherto been done,) but the understanding is to be expanded, and opened for the admission of the actual representation of the world as it is. The maxim of examining little and pronouncing on that little has ruined every thing. Resuming then our late partition of natural history, into that of generation, pretergeneration, and the arts, we divide the first into five parts: 1. The history of the sky and heavenly bodies. 2. Of meteors and the regions (as they are termed) of the air, that is to say, its division from the moon to the earth's surface, to which division we assign every kind of comet, either superior or inferior, (however the actual fact may be,) for the sake of method. 3. The history of the earth and sea. 4. Of the elements, as they are called, flame or fire, air, water, and earth; considering them, however, under that name, not as the first principles of things, but as forming the larger masses of natural bodies. For natural objects are so distributed, that the quantity or mass of certain bodies throughout the universe is very great, owing to the easy and obvious material texture required for their conformation, whilst the quantity of others is but small and sparingly supplied, the material, being of a diversified and subtile nature, having many specific qualities, and being of an organized construction, such as the different species of natural objects, namely, metals, plants, and animals. We are wont, therefore, to call the former greater colleges, and the latter lesser colleges. The fourth part of our history, then, is of the former, under the name of elements. Nor is

there any confusion between this and the second or third parts, although we have spoken of air, water, and earth in each. For in the second and third they are spoken of as integral parts of the world, and in relation to the creation and configuration of the universe; but in the fourth is contained the history of their own substance and nature, as displayed in the homogeneous parts of each, and not referred to the whole. Lastly, the fifth part of natural history contains the lesser colleges or species, upon which alone natural history has hitherto been chiefly occupied.

As to the history of pretergeneration, we have already observed that it may, with the greatest convenience, be combined with that of generation, including that which is prodigious only, not natural. For we reserve the superstitious history of miracles (such as it may be) for a separate treatise, nor is it to be undertaken immediately, but rather later, when more way shall have been made in the investigation of nature.

We divide the history of the arts, and of nature's course diverted and changed by man, or experimental history, into three parts. For it is derived either, 1. From the mechanical arts; or, 2. From the practical part of the liberal sciences; or, 3. From various practical applications and experiments, which have not yet been classed as a peculiar art, nay, sometimes occur in every day's experience and require no such art. If, then, a history be completed of all these which we have mentioned, namely, generation, pretergeneration, the arts and experiments, nothing appears omitted for preparing the senses to inform the understanding, and we shall no longer dance, as it were, within the narrow circles of the enchanter, but extend our march round the confines of the world itself.

V. Of those parts into which we have divided natural history, that of the arts is the most useful, since it exhibits bodies in motion, and leads more directly to practice. Besides this, it lifts the mask and veil, as it were, from natural objects, which are generally concealed or obscured under a diversity of forms and external appearance. Again, the attacks of art are assuredly the very fetters and miracles of Proteus, which betray the last struggle and efforts of nature. For bodies resist destruction or annihilation, and rather transform themselves into various shapes. The greatest diligence, therefore, is to be bestowed upon this history, however mechanical and illiberal it may appear, laying aside all fastidious arrogance.

Again, amongst the arts those are preferable which control, alter, and prepare natural bodies, and the materials of objects, such as agriculture, cookery, chymistry, dyeing, manufactures of glass, enamel, sugar, gunpowder, fireworks, paper, and the like. There is less use to be derived from those which chiefly consist in a delicate motion of the hands, or of tools, such as weaving, carpentry, architecture, mill and clock-work, and the like; although the latter are by no means to be neglected, both on account of their frequently presenting circumstances tending to the alteration of natural bodies, and also on account of the accurate information they afford of translatitious motion, a point of the greatest importance in many inquiries.

One thing, however, is to be observed and well remembered in this whole collection of arts, namely, to admit not only those experiments which conduce to the direct object of the art, but also those which indirectly occur. For instance, the changing of the lobster or a crab when cooked from a dark to a red colour has nothing to do with cookery, yet this instance is not a bad one in investigating the nature of redness, since the same thing occurs in baked bricks. So, again, the circumstance of meat requiring less time for salting in winter than in summer, is not only useful information to the cook for preparing his meat, but is also a good instance to point out the nature and effect of cold. He therefore will be wonderfully mistaken, who shall think that he has satisfied our object when he has collected these experiments of the arts for the sole purpose of improving each art in particular. For, although we do not by any means despise even this, yet our firm intention is to cause the streams of every species of mechanical experiment to flow from all quarters into the ocean of philosophy. The choice of the most important instances in each (such as should be most abundantly and diligently searched and, as it were, hunted out) must be governed by the prerogative instances.

VI. We must here allude to that which we have treated more at length in the ninety-ninth, one hundred and nineteenth, and one hundred and twentieth aphorisms of the first book, and need now only briefly urge as a precept, namely, that there be admitted into this history, 1. The most common matters, such as one might think it superfluous to insert from their being so well known; 2. Base, illiberal, and filthy matters, (for to the pure every thing is pure, and if money derived from urine be of good odour, much more so is knowledge and information from any quarter,) and also those which are trifling and puerile; lastly, such matters as appear too minute, as being of themselves of no use. For (as has been observed) the subjects to be treated of in this history are not compiled on their own account, nor ought their worth, therefore, to be measured by their intrinsic value, but by their application to other points, and their influence on philosophy.

VII. We moreover recommend that all natural bodies and qualities be, as far as possible, reduced to number, weight, measure, and precise definition; for we are planning actual results and not mere theory; and it is a proper combination of physics and mathematics that generates prac-

tice. The exact return and distances of the planets, therefore, in the history of the heavens, the circumference of the earth, and the extent of its surface compared with that of water, in the history of the earth and sea, the quantity of compression which the air will suffer without any powerful resistance, in the history of air, the quantity by which one metal exceeds another in weight, in that of metals, and a number of like points are to be thoroughly investigated and detailed. When, however, the exact proportions cannot be obtained, recourse must be had to those which are estimated or comparative. Thus, if we distrust the calculations of astronomers as to distances, it may be stated that the moon is within the shadow of the earth, and Mercury above the moon, &c. If mean proportions cannot be had, let extremes be taken, as that the feeblest magnet can raise iron of such a weight compared with its own, and the most powerful sixty times as much as its own weight, which I have myself observed in a very small armed magnet. For we know very well that determinate instances do not readily or often occur, but must be sought after as auxiliary, when chiefly wanted, in the very course of interpretation. If, however, they casually occur, they should be inserted in natural history, provided they do not too much retard its progress.

VIII. With regard to the credit due to the matters admitted into our history, they must either be certain, doubtful, or absolutely false. The first are to be simply stated, the second to be noted with "a report states," or, "they say," or, "I have heard from a person worthy of credit," and the like. For it would be too laborious to enter into the arguments on both sides, and would too much retard the author, nor is it of much consequence towards our present object, since (as we have observed in the hundred and eighteenth aphorism of the first book) the correctness of the axioms will soon discover the errors of experiment, unless they be very general. If, however, there be any instance of greater importance than the rest, either from its use, or the consequences dependent upon it, then the author should certainly be named, and not barely named, but some notice should be taken as to whether he merely heard or copied it, (as is generally the case with Pliny,) or rather affirmed it of his own knowledge; and, also, whether it were a matter within his own time or before it, or whether such as, if true, must necessarily have been witnessed by many; or, lastly, whether the author were vain and trifling, or steady and accurate and the like points, which give weight to testimony. Lastly, those matters which are false, and yet have been much repeated and discussed, such as have gained ground by the lapse of ages, partly owing to neglect, partly to their being used as poetical comparisons; for instance, that the diamond overpowers the magnet, that garlic enervates, that amber attracts every thing but the herb basil, &c. &c., all these ought not to be silently rejected, but expressly proscribed, that they may never trouble science more.

It will not, however, be improper to notice the origin of any fable or absurdity, if it should be traced in the course of inquiry, such as the venereal qualities attributed to the herb satyrium, from its roots bearing some resemblance to the testicles. The real cause of this formation being the growth of a fresh bulbous root every year, which adheres to that of the preceding year, and produces the twin roots, and is proved by the firm, juicy appearance which the new root always presents, whilst the old one is withered and spongy. This last circumstance renders it a matter not worthy of much wonder, that the one root should always sink and the other swim, though this, too, has been considered marvellous, and has added weight to the reputed virtues of the plant.

IX. There now remain certain useful accessories to natural history, for the purpose of bending and adapting it more readily to the labour of the interpreter which is to follow. They are five in number.

In the first place, queries are to be subjoined, (not of causes, but of facts,) in order to challenge and court further inquiry. As, for instance, in the history of the earth and sea, whether the Caspian has any tide, and the period of it? whether there is any southern continent, or only islands? and the like.

Secondly, in relating any new and delicate experiment, the method adopted in making it should be added, in order to allow free scope to the reader's judgment upon the soundness or fallacy of the information derived from it, and also to spur on men's industry in searching for more accurate methods, if such there be.

Thirdly, if there be any particle of doubt or hesitation as to the matter related, we would by no means have it suppressed or passed over, but it should be plainly and clearly set out, by way of note or warning. For we would have our first history written with the most religious particularity, and as though upon oath as to the truth of every syllable, for it is a volume of God's works, and (as far as the majesty of things divine can brook comparison with the lowliness of earthly objects) is, as it were, a second Scripture.

Fourthly, it will be proper to intersperse some observations, as Pliny has done. Thus, in the history of the earth and sea, we may observe, that the figure of the earth, as far as it is known to us, when compared with that of the sea, is narrow and pointed towards the south, broad and expanded towards the north, the contrary to that of the sea: and that vast oceans divide the continents, with channels extended from north to south, not from east to west, except, perhaps,

near the poles. Canons, also, (which are only general and universal observations,) are very properly introduced; as in the history of the heavens, that Venus is never more than forty-six degrees distant from the sun, nor Mercury more than twenty-three; and that the planets, which are placed above the sun, move most slowly when farthest from the earth, those beneath the sun most quickly. Another kind of observation is to be adopted, which has not hitherto been introduced, although of no small importance; namely, that to a list of things which exist, should be subjoined one of those which do not exist, as, in the history of the heavens, that no oblong or triangular star has been discovered, but all are globular, either simply, as the moon, or angular to the sight, but globular in the centre, as the other stars; or bearded to the sight, and globular in the centre, as the sun: or, that the stars are not arranged in any order, that there is no quincunx, square, or other perfect figure, (notwithstanding the names of the delta, crown, cross, wain, &c.,) scarcely in a right line, excepting, perhaps, the belt and sword of Orion.

Fifthly, it will, perhaps, assist the inquirer, though pernicious and destructive to the believer, to review all received opinions, their varieties and sects, briefly and currently as he proceeds, just to waken the intellect, and nothing further.

X. These will form a sufficient store of general precepts; and if they be diligently adhered to, the labour of this our history will both be directed immediately to its object and confined within proper limits. But if, even thus circumscribed and limited, it may, perhaps, appear vast to the feeble-minded, let him cast his eyes upon our libraries, and observe the codes of civil and canon law on the one hand, and the commentaries of doctors and practitioners on the other, and see what difference there is in the bulk and number of volumes. For we, who as faithful scribes do but receive and copy the very laws of nature, not only can, but must by necessity be brief; but opinions, dogmatisms, and theory, are innumerable and endless.

In the distribution of our work we made mention of the cardinal virtues of nature, and observed that a history of them must be completed before we come to the work of interpretation. This we have by no means forgotten, but we reserve it to ourselves, not daring to augur much from the industry of others in the attempt, until men have begun to be a little more acquainted with nature. We next proceed, therefore, to the designation of particular histories.

Pressed, however, by business, we have only leisure sufficient to subjoin a catalogue of particular histories, arranged under their proper heads As soon as time permits, it is our intention to instruct, as it were, by interrogation in each namely, as to the points to be investigated and committed to writing in every history, on account of their conducing to the end in view, and forming particular topics; or rather, (to borrow a metaphor from the civilians,) in this great action or cause, which has been conceded and instituted by special favour and divine providence, and by which mankind are contending for the recovery of their dominion over nature, let us examine nature and the arts themselves upon interrogatives.

A CATALOGUE
OF
PARTICULAR HISTORIES,
ARRANGED UNDER HEADS.

1. A History of the Heavenly bodies; or, an Astronomical History.
2. A History of the Configuration of Heaven and its Parts as it lies towards the Earth and its Parts; or, a Cosmographical History.
3. A History of Comets.
4. A History of Igneous Meteors.
5. A History of Thunderbolts, Flashes of Lightning, Thunders, and Coruscations.
6. A History of Winds, Sudden Blasts, and Undulations of the Air.
7. A History of Rainbows.
8. A History of Clouds as they are seen in the Air above.
9. A History of the Azure Expanse, of Twilight, of two or more Suns or Moons visible at once, of Halos, of the different Colours of the Sun and Moon, and of all that diversity of the Heavenly Bodies to the eye which results from the medium of vision.
10. A History of Rains, common, tempestuous, and extraordinary; also of Cataracts of Heaven, as they are called, and the like.
11. A History of Hail, Snow, Ice, Hoar-frost, Fog, Dew, and the like.
12. A History of all other Substances which fall or are precipitated from on high, and are generated in upper Air.
13. A History of Noises heard on high, if there be any, besides Thunder.
14. A History of the Air as a whole, or relatively to the Structure of the World.
15. A History of Weathers or of the State of Temperature throughout the Year, with reference to variety of clime, and the Accidents of particular Seasons and the periods of the Year; of Floods, Heats, Droughts, and the like.
16. A History of the Earth and Sea, of their Figure and Outline, their Configuration relatively to one another, the manner in which they stretch into one another in broad Tracts or narrow Indentations, the History of the Islands in the Sea, of the Bays of the Sea, of salt inland Lakes, of Isthmuses, and Promontories.
17. The History of the Motions, if there be such, of the Globe of Earth and Sea, and from what Experiments they may be inferred.
18. The History of the greater Motions and Agitations of the Earth and Sea, that is, of Earthquakes, Tremblings of the Earth, and Chasms; of new Islands, of floating Islands, of Divulsions of the parts of the Land by inroads of the Sea, of its Encroachments and Influxes, and, on the other hand, its Recessions; of the Eruption of Fires from the Earth, of sudden Eruptions of Water from the Earth, and the like.
19. A Geographical Natural History, of Mountains, Valleys, Woods, Plains, Sands, Marshes, Lakes, Rivers, Torrents, Fountains, and all their diversities of irrigation, and the like; Leaving out of view Nations, Provinces, Cities, and other parts of Civil Society.
20. A History of the Ebbs and Flows of the Sea, of Undulations, and other Motions of the Sea.
21. A History of the other Accidents of the Sea, its Saltness, diversity of Colours, Depth, of Submarine Rocks, Mountains, and Valleys, and the like.

The following are Histories of the larger Masses in Nature.

22. A History of Flame and Ignited Bodies.
23. A History of the Air in its Substance, not its Configuration.

24. A History of Water in its Substance, not its Configuration.

25. A History of the Earth, and its Varieties in its Substance, not its Configuration.

The following are Histories of Species.

26. A History of the perfect Metals, of Gold, Silver; of Mines, Veins, and Marcasites of the same, also the chymical Actions of Minerals in their natural state,

27. The History of Quicksilver.

28. A History of Fossils; as vitriol, sulphur, &c.

29. A History of Gems; as the diamond, ruby, &c.

30. A History of Stones; as marble, gold-touch-stone, flint, &c.

31. A History of the Magnet.

32. A History of Miscellaneous Substances, which are neither wholly fossil nor vegetable; as salts, amber, ambergris, &c.

33. A Chymical History, regarding Metals and Minerals.

34. A History of Plants, Trees, Fruits, Grapes, and their parts, the Roots, Stalks, Wood, Leaves, Flowers, Fruits, Seeds, Tears, or Exudations, &c.

35. A Chymical History, regarding Vegetables.

36. A History of Fishes, and their Parts and Generation.

37. A History of Volant Creatures, their Parts and Generation.

38. A History of Quadrupeds, their Parts and Generation.

39. A History of Reptiles, Worms, Flies, and other Insects, and of their Parts and Generation.

40. A Chymical History of those Substances which are extracted from Animals.

The following are Histories of Man.

41. A History of the Figure and external Members of Man, his Stature, the Knitting of his Frame, his Countenance and Features; and the varieties of these, according to nation and climate, or any minute diversities.

42. A History of Physiognomy, derived from the former.

43. A History Anatomical, or of the Internal Members of Man, and their Variety, so far as it is found in the Natural Cohesion and Structure of the Parts, and not merely with reference to Diseases and preternatural Accidents.

44. A History of the Homogeneous Parts of Man; as of flesh, bones, membranes, &c.

45. A History of the Humours in Man; as blood, bile, semen, &c.

46. A History of Excrements, Spittle, Urine, Sweats, Fæces, the Hair of the Head, and Hair generally, Nails, and the like.

47. The History of the Faculties of Attraction, Digestion, Retention, Expulsion; the Forma-

tion of the Blood; the Assimilation of Nourishment to the Frame, the Conversion of the Blood and the Flower of it into Spirits, &c.

48. A History of Natural and Involuntary Motions; as the motions of the heart, the motions of the pulse, sneezing, the motions of the lungs, priapism.

49. A History of Motion of a mixed nature, between natural and voluntary; respiration, coughing, making water, stool, &c.

50. A History of Voluntary Motions; as of the organs of articulation or speaking, the motions of the eyes, tongue, jaws, hands, fingers, of swallowing, &c.

51. A History of Sleep and Dreams.

52. A History of different Habits of Body, of fat and lean, of complexions, (as they are called,) &c.

53. A History of the Generation of Man.

54. A History of Conception, Quickening, Gestation in Utero, Birth, &c.

55. A History of the Nourishment of Man, of all Esculents and Potables, and of all Diet, and its Varieties, according to nations, or minor differences.

56. A History of the Augmentation and Growth of the Body, in the whole, or in its parts.

57. A History of the Course of life: of Infancy, Boyhood, Manhood, Old Age; of Longevity, Shortness of Life, and the like, according to nations, or minor differences.

58. A History of Life and Death.

59. A Medical History of Diseases; their symptoms and signs.

60. A Medical History of the Cure, Remedies of, and Liberations from Diseases.

61. A Medical History of those Things which preserve the Body and Health.

62. A Medical History of those Things which belong to the Form and Beauty of the Body, &c.

63. A Medical History of those Things which alter the Body, and belong to Alterative Regimen.

64. A History of Drugs.

65. A Chirurgical History.

66. A Chymical History, with Reference to Medicines.

67. A History of Light and Visible Objects, or optical.

68. A History of Painting, Sculpture, Casts, &c.

69. A History of Hearing and Sounds.

70. A History of Music.

71. A History of Smell and Odours.

72. A History of Taste and Savours.

73. A History of Touch, and its Objects.

74. A History of Venery, as a Species of Touch.

75. A History of Bodily Pains, as a Species of Touch.

76. A History of Pleasure and Pain in general.

77. A History of the Passions; as anger, love, shame, &c.

78. A History of the Intellectual Faculties; the Cogitative Faculty, Fancy, Reason, Memory, &c.
79. A History of Natural Divination.
80. A History of Discernments; or, Discriminations of Occult Qualities.
81. A History of Cookery, and the Arts subservient to it; of the Shambles, of Aviaries, &c.
82. A History of Baking, and the Preparation of Bread, and the subservient Arts, as grinding meal.
83. A History of Wines.
84. A History of the Cellar, and different Kinds of Drinks.
85. A History of Sweetmeats and Confections.
86. A History of Honey.
87. A History of Sugar.
88. A History of Milkmeats.
89. A History of the Bath of Unguents.
90. A Miscellaneous History of the Care of the Person; Shaving, Perfuming, &c.
91. A History of Working in Gold, and the Arts subservient to it.
92. A History of the Preparation of Wool, and the Arts subservient to it.
93. A History of Manufactures of Silk and Satin, and the Arts subservient to them.
94. A History of Manufactures of Linen, Canvass, Cotton, Hair, and other thready Substances, and of the Arts subservient to them.
95. A History of the Preparation of Feathers.
96. A History of Weaving, and the Arts subservient to it.
97. A History of Dyeing.
98. A History of Leather and Tanning, and the Arts subservient to it.
99. A History of Mattrasses and Feather Beds.
100. A History of Working in Iron.
101. A History of the Lapidary Art; or of Stonecutting.
102. A History of Bricks and Tiles.
103. A History of Pottery.
104. A History of Cements and Incrustations.
105. A History of Working in Wood.
106. A History of Lead.
107. A History of Glass and all Vitreous Substances, and of the Manufacture of Glass.
108. A History of Architecture in general.
109. A History of Wagons, Cars, Litters, &c.
110. A Typographical History of Books, Writings, Seals, Ink, Pens, Paper, Parchment, &c.

111. A History of Wax.
112. A History of Osiers.
113. A History of Carpeting, and Manufactures of Straw, Rushes, and the like.
114. A History of Washing, Brushing, &c.
115. A History of Farming, Pasturage, the Managing of Wood, &c.
116. A History of Gardens.
117. A History of Fishing.
118. A History of Hunting and Fowling.
119. A History of the Art of War, and the Arts subservient to it, as the manufacture of arms, bows, arrows, muskets, projectile engines, balistæ, machines, &c.
120. A History of the Nautical Art, and the Trades and Arts subservient to it.
121. A History of Gymnastics, and of all Kinds of Exercise used by Man.
122. A History of Riding.
123. A History of Games of all kinds.
124. A History of Conjurors and Sleight of Hand Men.
125. A Miscellaneous History of different Artificial Substances, as smalt, porcelain, various cements, &c.
126. A History of Salts.
127. A Miscellaneous History of different Machines and Motions.
128. A Miscellaneous History of Common Experiments, which have not yet united into an Art.

Histories also of pure Mathematics ought to be written, although they be rather Observations than Experiments.

129. A History of the Natures and Powers of Numbers.
130. A History of the Natures and Powers of Figures.

It may not be useless to suggest that, as many of the experiments fall under two or more heads, (thus the History of Plants and of the Art of Gardening contains many things common to both,) it will be more convenient to regulate the inquisition by the arts, the arrangement by the bodies. For we pay no great attention to the mechanical arts as such, but only to those of them which contribute to furnish forth philosophy. But these matters will be best disposed of as the cases arise.

THIRD PART

OF THE INSTAURATIO.

A

NATURAL AND EXPERIMENTAL HISTORY,

TO SERVE AS A FOUNDATION FOR PHILOSOPHY:

OR,

PHENOMENA OF THE UNIVERSE;

BEING THE THIRD PART OF THE INSTAURATIO MAGNA.

TO

THE MOST ILLUSTRIOUS AND EXCELLENT PRINCE

CHARLES,

SON AND HEIR TO THE HIGH AND MIGHTY KING JAMES.

I HUMBLY present unto your highness the first-fruits of our Natural History; a thing exceeding little in quantity, like a grain of mustard seed, but yet a pledge of those things which, God willing, shall ensue. For we have bound ourselves, as by a vow, every month that God shall of his goodness please (whose glory it sets forth, as it were in a new canticle or song) to prolong our life, to set out one or more parts of it, according as their length and difficulty shall prove more or less. Others may peradventure (moved by our example) be moved to the like industry; especially when they shall clearly perceive what is in hand. For in a natural history which is good and well set out, are the keys both of sciences and works. God preserve your highness long in safety.

Your highness's humble and devoted servant,

FRAN. ST. ALBAN.

THE TITLES OF THE HISTORIES AND INQUISITIONS DESTINED FOR THE FIRST SIX MONTHS.

THE HISTORY OF WINDS.

THE HISTORY OF DENSITY AND RARITY, AS LIKEWISE OF COITION AND EXPANSION OF MATTER BY SPACES.

THE HISTORY OF HEAVY AND LIGHT.

THE HISTORY OF THE SYMPATHY AND ANTIPATHY OF THINGS.

THE HISTORY OF SULPHUR, MERCURY, AND SALT.

THE HISTORY OF LIFE AND DEATH.

THE

NATURAL AND EXPERIMENTAL HISTORY,

FOR THE MAKING UP OF PHILOSOPHY:

OR,

EXPERIMENTS OF THE UNIVERSE:

WHICH IS THE THIRD PART OF THE INSTAURATIO MAGNA.

MEN are to be entreated, advised, and adjured, even by their fortunes, to submit their minds and seek for knowledge in the greater world; and likewise to cast away so much as the thought of philosophy, or at least to hope but for slender and small fruits thereof, until a diligent and approved natural and experimental history be acquired and made up. For what would these shallow brains of men, and these potent trifles have? There were among the ancients numerous opinions of philosophers, as of Pythagoras, Philolaus, Xenophanes, Heraclitus, Empedocles, Parmenides, Anaxagoras, Leucippus, Democritus, Plato, Aristotle, Tneophrastus, Zeno, and others. All these made up arguments of worlds, as of fables, according to their own fancies, and recited and published those fables; whereof some indeed were more handsome and probable, and some again most harsh. But in our ages, by means of colleges and schools' disciplines, wits are somewhat more restrained; yet have they not quite ceased: Patricius, Telesius, Brunus, Severine, the Dane, Gilbertus, an Englishman, and Campanella, did set foot upon the stage, and acted new fables, neither much applauded, nor of any elegant argument or subject. But do we wonder at these things, as though such sects and opinions might not in an infinite number arise in all ages? For neither is there, nor ever will be any end or limit for these things. One snatches at one thing, another is pleased with another; there is no dry nor clear sight of any thing; every one plays the philosopher out of the small treasures of his own fancy, as it were out of Plato's cave; the more sublime wits more acutely, and with better success; the duller with less success, but equal obstinacy: and not long since, by the discipline of some learned (and, as things go now, excellent) men, sciences are bounded within the limits of some certain authors which they have set down, imposing them upon old men, and instilling them into young. So that now (as Tully cavilled upon Cæsar's consulship)

the star Lyra or Harpe riseth by an edict, and authority is taken for truth, not truth for authority; which kind of order and discipline is very convenient for our present use, but banisheth those which are better. For we both suffer for and emulate our first parents' sin; they desired to be like unto God, and their posterity much more: for we create new worlds, go before nature and command it. We must have all things to be so as may agree with our folly, not to divine wisdom, nor as they are found to be in themselves; neither can I say which we rest most, our wits or the things themselves: but certainly we set the stamps and seals of our own images upon God's creatures and works, and never carefully look upon and acknowledge the Creator's stamps. Therefore, we do not, without cause, again strive for the domination over the creatures. For, whereas, even after the fall of man, he had some kind of domination left him over reluctant creatures, that he might tame and subdue them by true and solid arts; we have, for the most part, lost that, also, through our own insolence, because we will be like unto God, and follow the dictates of our own reason. Wherefore, if there be any humility towards the Creator, any reverence and magnifying of his works, any charity in men, or care to release them out of their necessities and miseries, if there be any love of truth in natural things, hatred of darkness, and a desire of purifying the understanding, men are to be again and again desired that, casting off, or, at least, laying aside for a while the flying and preposterous philosophies, which have set the theses before the hypotheses, or suppositions before solid grounds, have captivated experience, and triumphed over the works of God, they would humbly, and with a certain reverence, draw near and turn over the great volume of the creatures, stop and meditate upon it; and, being cleansed, and free from opinions, handle them choicely and entirely. This is the speech and language that went out into all the ends of the world, and suffered not in the confusion of Babel. Let men learn this, and becoming children again, and infants, not scorn to take A B C thereof in hand, and in finding and searching out the interpretation of it, let them spare no labour, but let them persist and go on, and even die in the quest of it. Seeing, therefore, that in our Instauration we have placed the Natural History (such as it is, in order to our ends) in the third part of the work, we have thought fit to prevent this thing, and fall upon it immediately. For, although in our Organon there are many things of especial consequence to be finished, yet we think it fitting rather to promote or set forward the general work of instauration in many things, than to perfect it in a few; always desiring, with extreme fervency, (such as we are confident God puts in the minds of men,) to have that which was never yet attempted, not to be now attempted in vain. Likewise, there came this thought into my mind, namely, that there are questionless in Europe many capable, free, sublimed, subtile, solid, constant wits; and what if any one endued with such a wit do betake himself to the use and manner of our Organon, and approve of it? yet hath he nothing to do, nor knows not how to address himself to, or fit himself for philosophy.. If it were a thing which might be effected by reading of philosophy books, disputation, or meditation, that man (whosoever it be) might sufficiently and abundantly perform it; but if we remit him, as indeed we do, to natural history, and experi-

ments of arts, he is gravelled, or sticks in the mire; it is not his intention, he hath no time, nor will not be at the charge; yet we must not desire to have men cast off old things before they have gotten new. But after a copious and faithful history of nature and arts is gathered and digested, and, as it were, set and laid open before men's eyes, there is no small hope that such great wits as we have before spoken of, (such as have been in ancient philosophers, and are at this day frequent enough,) having been heretofore of such efficacy, that they could, out of cork, or a little shell, (namely, by thin and frivolous experience,) build certain little boats for philosophy, gallant enough for art and structure, how much more gallant and solid structures will they make when they have found a whole wood, and stuff enough; and that, though they had rather go on in the old way, than make use of our Organon's way, which (in our opinion) is either the only, or the best way. So that the case stands thus: our Organon (though perfect) could not profit much without the Natural History; but our Natural History, without the Organon, might much advance instauration, or renewing of sciences. Wherefore, we have thought it best and most advisedly to fall upon this before any thing else. God, the maker, preserver, and renewer of the universe, guide and protect this work, both in its ascent to his own glory, and in its descent to the good of man, through his good will towards man, by his only begotten Son, God with us!

THE RULE OF THIS PRESENT HISTORY.

THOUGH we have set down, towards the end of that part of our Organon which is come forth, precepts concerning the Natural and Experimental History, yet we have thought good to set down more exactly and briefly the form and rule of this history which we now take in hand. To the titles comprehended in the catalogue, which belong to the concretes, we have added the titles of the abstract natures; of which, as of a reserved history, we made mention in the same place. These are the various figurations of the matter, or forms of the first class; simple motions, sums of motions, measures of motions, and some other things: of these we have made a new alphabet, and placed it at the end of this volume. We have taken titles, (being no way able to take them all,) not according to order, but by choice; those, namely, the inquisition of

which either for use was most of weight, or for abundance of experiments most convenient, or for the obscurity of the thing most difficult and noble, or, by reason of the discrepancy of titles among themselves, most open to examples. In each title, after a kind of an entrance or preface, we presently propound certain particular topics or articles of inquisition, as well to give light to the present inquisition, as to encourage a future. For we are master of questions, but not of things; yet we do not, in the history, precisely observe the order of questions, lest that which is for an aid and assistance should prove a hindrance.

The histories and experiments always hold the first place; and if they set forth any enumeration and series of particular things, they are made up in tables, or if otherwise, they are taken up severally.

Seeing that histories and experiments do oftentimes fail us, especially those which give light, and instances of the cross, by which the understanding may be informed of the true causes of things, we give precepts of new experiments, as far as we can see them fitting in our mind, for that as is to be inquired; and these precepts are designed like histories. For what other means is left to us, who are the first that come into this way? We unfold and make plain the manner of some experiments that are more quaint and subtile, that there may be no error, and that we may stir up others to find out better and more exact ways. We interweave monitions and cautions of the fallacies of things, and of such errors and scruples as may be found in the inquiry, that all fancies, and, as it were, apparitions, may be frighted away, as by an exorcism or spell.

We join thereunto our observations upon history and experiments, that the interpretation of the nature may be the readier.

We interpose some comments, or, as it were, rudiments of the interpretations of causes, sparingly, and rather supposing what may be, than positively defining what is.

We prescribe and set down rules, but movable ones, and, as it were, inchoated axioms which offer themselves unto us as we inquire, not as we decisorily pronounce, for they are profitable, though not altogether true.

Never forgetting the profit of mankind, (though the light be more worthy than those things which be shown by it,) we offer to man's attention and practice certain essays of practice, knowing that men's stupidity is such, and so unhappy, that sometimes they see not and pass over things which lie just in their way.

We set down works and things impossible, or at least which are not yet found out, as they fall under each title; and withal those which are already found out, and are in men's power; and we add to those impossible, and not yet found out things, such as are next to them, and have most affinity with them, that we may stir up and withal encourage human industry.

It appears by the aforesaid things that this present history doth not only supply the place of the third part of the instauration, but also is not a despicable preparation to the fourth, by reason of the titles out of the alphabet and topics, and to the sixth, by reason of the larger observations, commentations, and rules.

THE

ENTRY INTO THE HISTORY OF WINDS.

The winds gave wings to men; for by their assistance men are carried up through the air and fly; not through the air, indeed, but upon the sea; and a wide door is laid open to commerce, and the world is made pervious. They are the besoms which sweep and make clean the earth, which is the seat and habitation of mankind, and they cleanse both it and the air; but they make the sea hurtful, which otherwise is harmless, neither are they some other ways also free from doing hurt. They are, without help of man, able to stir up great and vehement motions, and like hirelings, serve both to sail and grind, and would be useful for many other things, if human care were not wanting. Their natures are reckoned amongst secret and hidden things. Neither is that to be wondered at, seeing the nature and power of the air is unknown, whom the winds do serve and flatter, as Eolus doth Juno in the Poets. They are not primary creatures, nor any of the six days' works, no more than the rest of the meteors actually, but afterborn, by the order of the creation.

2 o 2

PARTICULAR TOPICS;

OR,

ARTICLES OF INQUISITION CONCERNING THE WINDS.

The names of winds.

DESCRIBE or set down the winds according to the seaman's industry; and give them names either new or old, so that you keep yourself constant to them.

Winds are either general or precise, either peculiar or free. I call them general which always blow; precise, those which blow at certain times; attendants or peculiar, those which blow most commonly; free winds, those which blow indifferently or at any time.

General winds.

2. Whether there be any general winds, which are the very self-motion of the air; and if there be any such, in order to what motion, and in what places they blow?

Precise or fixed winds.

3. What winds are anniversary or yearly winds, returning by turns; and in what countries? Whether there be any wind so precisely fixed, that it returns regularly at certain days and hours, like unto the flowing of the sea?

Attending or peculiar winds.

4. What winds are peculiar and ordinary in countries, which observe a certain time in the same countries; which are spring winds, and which are summer winds; which autumnal, which brumal, which equinoctial, which solstitial; which are belonging to the morning, which to noon, which to the evening, and which to the night.

5. What winds are sea winds, and what winds blow from the continent? and mark and set down the differences of the sea and land winds carefully, as well of those which blow at land and sea, as of those which blow from land and sea.

Free winds.

3. Whether winds do not blow from all parts of heaven?

Winds do not vary much more in the parts of heaven from which they blow, than in their own qualities. Some are vehement, some mild, some constant, some mutable; some hot, some cold, some moistening and dissolving; some drying and astringent; some gather clouds and are rainy, and peradventure stormy; some disperse the clouds, and are clear.

Divers qualities of winds.

7. Inquire, and give account, which are the winds of all the forenamed sorts or kinds, and how they vary, according to the regions and places.

There are three local beginnings of winds: either they are thrown and cast down from above, or they spring out of the earth, or they are made up of the very body of the air.

Local beginnings of winds.

8. According to these three beginnings inquire concerning winds; namely, which are thrown down, out of that which they call the middle region of the air; which breathe out of the concavities of the earth, whether they break out together; or whether they breathe out of the earth imperceivably, and scattering, and afterwards gather together, like rivulets into a river. Finally, which are scatteringly engendered from the swellings and dilatations of the neighbouring air?

Neither are the generations of the winds original only, for some there are also accidental, namely, by the compression or restraints of the air, and by the percussions and repercussions of it.

Accidental generations and productions of winds.

9. Inquire concerning these accidental generations of winds; they are not properly generations of winds; for they rather increase and strengthen winds, than produce and excite them.

Hitherto of the community of winds. There are also certain rare and prodigious winds, such as are called tempests, whirlwinds, and storms. These are above ground. There are likewise some that are subterraneal and under ground, whereof some are vaporous and mercurial, they are perceivable in mines; some are sulphurous, they are sent out, getting an issue by earthquakes, or do flame out of fiery mountains.

Extraordinary winds and sudden blasts.

10. Inquire concerning such rare and prodigious winds, and of all miraculous and wonderful things done by winds.

From the several sorts of winds, let the inquisition pass to those things which contribute towards the winds, (for we will so express it, because the word efficient signifies more, and the word concomitant, less than we mean,) and to those things which seem to raise, or to appease the winds.

Things contributing or making for the winds, and raising and appeasing them.

11. Inquire sparingly concerning astrological considerations of winds, neither care thou for the over-curious schemes of the heaven, only do not neglect the more manifest observations of winds rising, about the rising of some stars, or about the eclipses of the luminaries, or conjunctions of planets; nor much less on those which depend on the courses of the sun and moon.

12. What meteors of several sorts do contribute or make for winds, what the earthquakes, what rain, what the skirmishing of winds, one with another? for these things are linked together, and one draws on the other.

13. What the diversity of vapours and exhalations contributes towards the winds? and which of them do most engender winds? and how far the nature of winds doth follow these its materials?

14. What those things which are here upon the earth, or are there done do contribute towards the winds; what the hills and the dissolutions of snow upon them; what those masses of ice which swim upon the sea, and are carried to some place; what the differences of soil and land; (so it be of some large extent;) what ponds, sands, woods, and champion ground; what those things which we men do here, as burning of heath, and the like, doth contribute to the manuring of land, the firing of towns in time of war, the drying up of ponds and lakes: the continual shooting off of guns, the ringing of many bells together in great cities, and the like? These things and acts of ours are but as small straws, yet something they may do.

15. Inquire concerning all manner of raisings, or allaying of winds, but be sparing in fabulous and superstitious causes.

From those things which make for the winds, let the inquisition proceed to inquire of the bounds of the winds, of their height, extension, and continuance.

The bounds of winds.

16. Inquire carefully of the height or elevation of winds, and whether there be any tops of mountains to which the winds do not reach; or whether clouds may be seen sometimes to stand still, and not move, when the winds at the same time blow strongly upon the earth.

17. Inquire diligently of the spaces or rooms which the winds take up at once, and within what bounds they blew. As, for example, if the south wind blew in such a place, whether it be known certainly, that at the same time the north wind blew ten miles off? And, contrariwise, into how narrow and straight bounds the winds may be reduced, so that winds may pass, as it were, through channels, which seems to be done in some whirlwinds.

18. Inquire for how long a time, very much, ordinary, or little time, winds use to continue, and then slack, and, as it were, expire and die. Likewise, how the rising and beginning of winds useth to be; what their languishing or cessation is, whether suddenly, or by degrees, or how?

From the bounds of the winds let your inquisition pass over to the succession of winds, either amongst themselves, or in respect of rain and showers; for when they lead their rings, it were pretty to know the order of their dancing.

Successions of winds.

19. Whether there be any more certain rule or observation concerning the successions of winds one to another, or whether it have any relation to the motion of the sun, or otherwise; if it have any, what manner of one it is?

20. Inquire concerning the succession and the alteration, or taking turns of the winds and rain, seeing it is ordinarily and often seen, that rain lays the wind, and the wind doth disperse the rain.

21. Whether, after a certain term and period of years, the succession of winds begin anew; and if it be so, what that period is, and how long?

From the succession of the winds, let the inquisition pass to their motions; and the motions of the winds are comprehended in seven inquisitions; whereof three are contained in the former articles, four remain as yet untouched. For, we have inquired of the motion of winds divided into the several regions of the heaven; also, of the motion upon three lines, upward, downward, and laterally. Likewise, of the accidental motion of compressions or restraints. There remain the fourth, of progressions or going forward; the fifth, of undulation, or waving; the sixth, of conflict or skirmish; the seventh, in human instruments and engines.

Divers motions of the winds.

22. Seeing progression is always from some certain place or bound, inquire diligently, or as well as thou canst, concerning the place of the first beginning, and, as it were, the spring of any wind. For winds seem to be like unto fame, for, though they make a noise and run up and down, yet they hide their heads amongst the clouds; so is their progress; as, for example, if the vehement northern wind which blew at York such a day, do blow at London two days after.

23. Omit not the inquisition of undulation of

winds. We call undulation of winds that motion by which the wind, in or for a little space of time, rises and abates, as the waves of the water; which turns may easily be apprehended by the hearing of them in houses; and you must so much the rather mark the differences of undulation, or of furrowing between the water and the air, because in the air and winds there wants the motion of gravity or weight, which is a great part of the cause of the waves rising in the water.

24. Inquire carefully concerning the conflict and meeting of winds, which blow at one and the same time: first, whether at the same time there blow several original winds, (for we do not speak of reverberated winds.) which, if it comes to pass, what windings they engender and bring forth in their motion, and also what condensations, and alterations they produce in the body of the air?

25. Whether one wind blow above at the same time as another blows here below with us? For it hath been observed by some, that sometimes the clouds are carried one way, when the weather-cock upon a steeple stands another. Also, that the clouds have been driven by a strong gale, when we, here below, have had a great calm.

26. Make an exact particular description of the motion of the winds in driving on ships with their sails.

27. Let there be a description made of the motion of the winds in the sails of ships, and the sails of windmills, in the flight of hawks and birds; also, in things that are ordinary, and for sport, as of displayed colours, flying dragons, duels with winds, &c.

From the motions of winds, let the inquisition pass to the force and power of them.

Of the power of winds.

28. What winds do or can do concerning currents or tides of waters, in their keeping back, putting forth, or inlets or overflowings.

29. What they do concerning plants and insects, bringing in of locusts, blastings and mildews.

30. What they effect concerning purging or clearing, and infecting of the air, in plagues, sickness, and diseases of beasts.

31. What they effect concerning the conveying to us things (which we call) spiritual, as sounds, rays, and the like.

From the powers of winds let the inquisition pass to the prognostics of winds, not only for the use of predictions, but because they lead us on to the causes : for prognostics do either show us the preparations of things, before they be brought into action; or the beginnings before they appear to the sense.

Prognostics of winds.

32. Let all manner of good prognostics of winds be carefully gathered together, (besides astrological ones, of which we set down formerly how far they are to be inquired after,) and let them either be taken out of meteors, or waters, or instincts of beasts, or any other way.

Lastly, close up the inquisition, with inquiring after the imitations of winds, either in natural or artificial things.

Imitations of winds.

33. Inquire of the imitations of winds in natural things; such as breaths enclosed within the bodies of living creatures, and breaths within the receptacles of distilling vessels.

Inquire concerning made gales, and artificial winds, as bellows, refrigeratories, or coolers in parlours, or dining-rooms, &c.

Let the heads or articles be such. Neither is it unknown to me that it will be impossible to answer to some of these according to the small quantity of experience that we have. But, as in civil causes, a good lawyer knows what interrogatories the cause requires to have witnesses examined upon; but what the witnesses can answer he knows not. The same thing is incident to us in natural history. Let those who came after us endeavour for the rest.

THE HISTORY.

The Names of Winds.

To the first article.

WE give names to winds rather as they are numbered in their order and degrees than by their own antiquity; this we do for memory's and perspicuity's sake. But we add the old words also, because of the assenting voices or opinions of old authors; of which having taken (though with somewhat a doubtful judgment) many things, they will hardly be known, but under such names as themselves have used. Let the general division be this: let cardinal winds be those which blow from corners or angles of the world; semicardinal, those which blow in the half-wards of those; and median winds, those which blow between these half-wards: likewise of those which blow betwixt these half-wards; let those be called major medians which blow in a quadrant or fourth part of these divisions: the lesser medians are all the rest. Now the particular division is that which follows:

Cardinal.	North.
	North and by east.
Med. Maj.	North-north-east, or aquilo.
	North-east, and by north, or meses.
Semicard.	North-east.
	North-east and by east.
Med. Maj.	East-north-east, or cæcias.
	East and by north.
Cardinal.	East, or subsolanus.
	East by south.
Med. Maj.	East-south-east, or vulturnus.
	South-east and by east.
Semicard.	South-east.
	South-east and by south.
Med. Maj.	South-south-east, or phœnicias.
	South and by east.
Cardinal.	South.
	South and by west.
Med. Maj.	South-south-west, or libonotus.
	South-west and by south.
Semicard.	South-west, or libs.
	South-west and by west.
Med. Maj.	West-south-west, or africus.
	West and by south.
Cardinal.	West, or favonius.
	West and by north.
Med. Maj.	West-north-west, or corus.
	North-west and by west.
Semicard.	North-west
	North-west and by north, or thrascias.
Med. Maj.	North-north-west, or circius.
	North and by west.

There are also other names of winds. Apeliotes, the east wind, argestes, the south-west, olympias, the north-west, scyron, the south-east, hellespontius, the east-north-east, for these we care not. Let it suffice that we have given constant and fixed names of winds, according to the order and disposition of the regions of the heavens: we do not set much by the comments of authors, since the authors themselves have little in them.

Free Winds.

To the sixth article.

1. There is not a region of the heaven from whence the winds doth not blow. Yea, if you divide the heaven into as many regions as there be degrees in the horizon, you shall find winds sometimes blowing from every one of them.

2. There are some whole countries where it never rains, or, at least, very seldom; but there is no country where the wind doth not blow, and that frequently.

General Winds.

To the second article.

1. Concerning general winds, experiments are plain; and it is no marvel, seeing that (especially

within the tropics) we may find places condemned among the ancients.

It is certain, that to those who sail between the tropics in a free and open sea, there blows a constant and settled wind (which the seamen call a breeze) from east to west. This wind is not of so little force, but that, partly by its own blowing, and partly by its guiding the current of the sea, it hindereth seamen from coming back again the same way they went to Peru.

2. In our seas in Europe, when it is fair dry weather, and no particular winds stirring, there blows a soft kind of gale from the east, which followeth the sun.

3. Our common observations do admit that the higher clouds are for the most part carried from east to west; and that it is so likewise when here below upon the earth, either there is a great calm, or a contrary wind; and if they do not so always, it is because sometimes particular winds blow aloft which overwhelm this general wind.

A Caution. If there be any such general wind, in order to the motion of the heaven, it is not so firm nor strong but that it gives way to particular winds. But it appears most plainly amongst the tropics, by reason of the larger circles which it makes. And, likewise, it is so when it blows on high, for the same cause, and by reason of its free course. Wherefore, if you will take it without the tropics, and near the earth, (where it blows most gently and slowly,) make trial of it in an open and free air, in an extreme calm, and in high places, and in a body which is very movable, and in the afternoon, for at that time the particular eastern wind blows more sparingly.

Injunction. Observe diligently the vanes and weathercocks upon the tops and towers of churches, whether, in extreme calms, they stand continually towards the west or not.

An indirect experiment.

4. It is certain, that here with us in Europe the eastern wind is drying and sharp; the west wind, contrariwise, moist and nourishing. May not this be by reason that (it being granted that the air moves from east to west) it must of necessity be that the east wind, whose blast goeth the same way, must needs disperse and attenuate the air, whereby the air is made biting and dry; but the western wind, which blows the contrary way, turns the airs back upon itself, and thickens it, whereby it becomes more dull, and, at length, moist.

An indirect experiment.

5. Consider the inquisition of the motion and flowing of waters, whether they move from east to west; for, if the two extremes, heaven and waters, delight in this motion, the air which is in the midst will go near to participate of the same.

Caution. We call the two last experiments indirect, because they do directly show the thing which we aim at but by consequence, which we also gladly admit of when we want direct experiments.

Injunction. That the breeze blows plentifully between the tropics, is most certain; the cause is very ambiguous. The cause may be, because the air moves according to the heaven; but without the tropics almost imperceivably, by reason of the smaller circles which it makes; within the tropics manifestly, because it makes bigger circles. Another cause may be, because all kind of heat dilates and extends the air, and doth not suffer it to be contained in its former place; and by the dilatation of the air, there must needs be an impulsion of the contiguous air which produceth this breeze as the sun goes forward; and that is more evident within the tropics, where the sun is more scorching; without it, is hardly perceived. And this seems to be an instance of the cross, or a decisory instance. To clear this doubt you may inquire, whether the breeze blow in the night or no: for the wheeling of the air continues also in the night, but the heat of the sun does not.

6. But it is most certain that the breeze doth not blow in the night, but in the morning, and when the morning is pretty well spent; yet that instance doth not determine the question, whether the nightly condensation of the air (especially in those countries where the days and nights are not more equal in their length than they are differing in their heat and cold) may dull and confound that natural motion of the air, which is but weak.

If the air participates of the motion of the heaven, it does not only follow that the east wind concurs with the motion of the air, and the west wind strives against it; but also that the north wind blows, as it were, from above, and the south wind as from below here in our hemisphere, where the antarctic pole is under ground, and the arctic pole is elevated! which hath likewise been observed by the ancients, though staggeringly and obscurely: but it agrees very well with our modern experience, because the breeze (which may be a motion of the air) is not a full east, but a north-east wind.

Stayed or Certain Winds.

To the third article. Connexion.

As, in the inquisition of general winds, men have suffered and been in darkness, so they have been troubled with a vertigo or giddiness concerning stayed and certain winds. Of the former, they say nothing; of the latter, they talk up and down at random. This is the more pardonable, the thing being various; for these stayed winds do change and alter according to the places where they be: the same do not blow in Egypt, Greece, and Italy.

1. That there are stayed winds in some places, the very name that is given them doth declare it, as the other name of etesiaes means anniversary or yearly winds.

2. The ancients attributed the cause of the overflowing of Nilus to the blowing of the etesian (that is to say, northern) winds at that time of the year, which did hinder the river's running into the sea, and turned the stream of it back.

3. There are currents in the sea which can neither be attributed to the natural motion of the ocean, nor to the running down from higher places, nor the straitness of the opposite shores, nor to promontories running out into the sea, but are merely guided and governed by these stayed winds.

4. Those who will not have Columbus to have conceived such a strong opinion concerning the West Indies by the relation of a Spanish pilot, and much less believe that he might gather it out of some obscure footsteps of the ancients, have this refuge; that he might conjecture there was some continent in the west by the certain and stayed winds which blew from them towards the shores of Lusitania or Portugal. A doubtful, and not very probable thing, seeing that the voyage of winds will hardly reach so large a distance. In the mean time there is great honour due to this inquisition, if the finding of this new world be due to one of those axioms or observations, whereof it comprehends many.

5. Wheresoever are high and snowy mountains, from thence blow stayed winds, until that time as the snow be melted away.

6. I believe also that from great pools which are full of water in the winter, there blow stayed winds in those seasons, when as they begin to dry up with the heat of the sun. But of this I have no certainty.

7. Wheresoever vapours are engendered in abundance, and that at certain times, be sure that stayed winds will blow there at the same times.

8. If stayed and certain winds blow anywhere, and the cause cannot be found near at hand, assure yourself that those certain winds are strangers, and come from far.

9. It hath been observed, that stayed winds do not blow in the night-time, but do rise about three hours after sunrising. Surely such winds are tired, as it were, with a long journey, that they can scarcely break through the thickness of the night air, but being stirred up again by the rising of the sun, they go forward by little and little.

10. All stayed winds (unless they blow from some neighbouring places) are weak, and yield unto sudden winds.

11. There are many stayed winds which are not perceivable, and which we do not observe, by reason of their weakness, whereby they are over-

thrown by the free winds. Wherefore in the winter they are hardly taken notice of, when the free winds wander most: but are more observable in the summer, when those wandering winds grow weak.

12. In Europe these are the chief stayed winds, north winds from the solstice, and they are both forerunners and followers of the dogstar. West winds from the equinoctial in autumn, east winds from the spring equinoctial; as for the winter solstice, there is little heed to be taken of it, by reason of the varieties.

13. The winds called ornithii, or bird winds, had that name given them because they bring birds out of cold regions beyond the sea, into warm climates; and they belong not to stayed winds, because they for the most part keep no punctual time: and the birds, they for the convenience of them, whether they come sooner or later: and many times when they have begun to blow a little, and turn, the birds being forsaken by it, are drowned in the sea, and sometimes fall into ships.

14. The returns of these certain or stayed winds are not so precise at a day or an hour, as the flowing of the sea is. Some authors do set down a day, but it is rather by conjecture than any constant observation.

Customary or Attending Winds.

Of the fourth and fifth articles. Connexion.

The word of attending wind is ours, and we thought good to give it, that the observation concerning them be not lost, nor confounded. The meaning is this, divide the year if you please (in what country soever you be) into three, four, or five parts, and if any one certain wind blow, then two, three, or four of those parts, and a contrary wind but one; we call that wind which blows most frequently the customary, or attending wind of that country, and likewise of the times.

1. The south and north winds are attendants of the world, for they, with those which are within their sections or divisions, blow oftener over all the world, than either the east or the west.

2. All the free winds (not the customary) are more attendant in the winter than in the summer; but most of all in the autumn and spring.

3. All free winds are attendants rather in the countries without the tropics, and about the polar circles. than within: for in frozen and in torrid countries, for the most part they blow more sparingly, in the middle regions they are more frequent.

4. Also all free winds, especially the strongest and most forcible of them, do blow oftener and more strongly, morning and evening, than at noon and night.

5. Free winds blow frequently in hollow places, and where there be caves, than in solid and firm ground.

Injunction. Human diligence hath almost ceased and stood still in the observation of attending winds in particular places. which, notwithstanding, should not have been, that observation being profitable for many things. I remember, I asked a certain merchant, (a wise and discreet man,) who had made a plantation in Greenland, and had wintered there, why that country was so extreme cold, seeing it stood in a reasonable temperate climate. He said, it was not so great as it was reported; but that the cause was twofold: One was, that the masses and heaps of ice which came out of the Scythian sea were carried thither. The other (which he also thought to be the better reason) was because the west wind there blows many parts of the year, more than the east wind; as also (said he) it doth with us; but there it blows from the continent, and cold, but with us from the sea, and warmish. And (said he) if the east wind should blow here in England so often and constantly as the west wind does there, we should have far colder weather, even equal to that as is there.

6. The west winds are attendants of the *pomeridian* or afternoon hours: for, towards the declining of the sun, the winds blow oftener from the east than from the west.

7. The south wind is attendant on the night; for it rises and blows more strongly in the night, and the north wind in the daytime.

8. But there are many and great differences between winds which are attendant on the sea, and those which are attendant upon the land. That is one of the chief which gave Columbus occasion to find out the new world; namely, that sea winds are not stayed, but land winds are: for the sea abounding in vapours, which are indifferently everywhere, winds are also engendered indifferently everywhere, and with great inconstancy are carried here and there, having no certain beginnings nor sources. But the earth is much unlike for the begetting of winds: some places are more efficacious to engender and increase winds, some less: wherefore they stand most from that part where they have their nourishment, and take their rise from thence.

9. Acosta is unconstant in his own position. He saith that at Peru, and the sea coasts of the south sea, south winds do blow almost the whole year: and he saith in another place, that upon those coasts sea winds do blow chiefliest. But the south wind to them is a land wind, as likewise the north and east wind also, and the west wind is their only sea wind. We must take that which he sets down more certainly; namely, that the south wind is an attending and familiar wind of those countries: unless, peradventure, in the name of the south sea he hath corrupted his meaning, or his speech, meaning the west by the south, which blows from the south sea. But the sea which they call the south sea is not properly the south

sea; but as a second western ocean, being stretched out in the like situation as the Atlantic sea is.

10. Sea winds are questionless more moist than land winds, but yet they are more pure, and will easilier, and with more equality be incorporated with the pure air. For terrestrial winds are ill composed, and smoky. Neither let any one object, that they ought to be grosser by reason of the saltness of the sea. For the nature of terrestrial salt doth not rise in vapours.

11. Sea winds are lukewarm or cold, by reason of the two foresaid qualities, humidity and pureness. For by humidity they mitigate the colds, (for dryness increaseth both heat and cold,) and with their pureness they cool. Therefore without the tropics they are lukewarm, within the tropics they are cold.

12. I believe that sea winds are everywhere attendant upon particular countries, especially such as stand upon the sea-coasts: that is to say, winds blow more frequently from that side where the sea is, by reason of the greater plenty of matter which winds have in the sea, than in the land; unless there be some firm wind blowing from the land, for some peculiar reason. But let no man confound firm or stayed winds with attendant winds: the attendants being always more frequent; but the stayed ones for the most part blowing more seldom. But that is common to them both, namely, to blow from that place from which they receive their nourishment.

13. Sea winds are commonly more vehement than land winds: yet when they cease, the sea is calmer from the shores than near unto them; insomuch that mariners, to avoid calms, will sometimes coast along the shore, rather than launch into the deep.

14. Winds which are called tropei, that is to say, retorted, namely, such as, when they have blown a little way, suddenly turn again, such winds I say blow from the sea towards the shore: but retorted winds and whirlwinds are most commonly in gulfs of seas.

15. Some small gales blow for the most part about all great waters, and they are most felt in a morning; but more about rivers than at sea, because of the difference which is between a land gale and a water gale.

16. In places which are near the sea, trees bow and bend, as shunning the sea air: but that comes not through any averseness to them; but sea winds, by reason of their humidity and thickness, are as it were more heavy and ponderous.

The Qualities and Powers of Winds.

To the seventh, twenty-eighth, twenty-ninth, thirtieth, and thirty-first articles. Connexion.

Concerning the qualities and powers of winds, men have made careless and various observations: we will cull out the most certain, and the rest, as too light, we will leave to the winds themselves.

1. With us the south wind is rainy, and the northern wind clear and fair, the one gathers together and nourishes the clouds; the other scatters and casts them off. Wherefore the poets, when they speak of the deluge, feign the northern wind at that time to be shut up in prison, and the south wind to be sent out with very large commission.

2. The west wind hath with us been held to be the wind which blew in the golden age, the companion of a perpetual spring, and a cherisher of flowers.

3. Paracelsus his scholars, when they sought for a place for their three principles in Juno's temple also, which is the air, placed three, but found no place for the east wind.

They Mercury ascribe to the south winds,
To the rich western blasts the sulphur mines,
And rugged Boreas' blasts the sad salt finds.

4. But with us in England the east wind is thought to be mischievous, so that it goes for a proverb, "that when the wind is in the east, it is neither good for man nor beast."

5. The south wind blows from the presence of the sun, the north from the absence in our hemisphere. The east wind in order to the motion of the air, the west wind from the sea, the east wind from the continent, most commonly in Europe and the western parts of Asia. These are the most radical and essential differences of winds; from which truly and really depend most of the qualities and powers of the winds.

6. The south wind is not so anniversary or yearly, nor so stayed as the northern wind is, but more wandering and free; and when it is stayed, it is so soft and mild that it can scarcely be perceived.

7. The south wind is lower, and more lateral, and blowing of one side; the northern wind is higher and blows from above; we do not mean the polar elevation and depression of which we have spoken formerly; but because the north wind for the most part hath its beginnings higher, and the south wind for the most part nearer to us.

8. The south wind to us is rain, (as we said before,) but in Africa it causes clear weather, but bringing great heat along with it, and not cold, as some have affirmed. In Africa it is pretty healthful, but to us, if the south wind last long with fair weather and without rain, it is very pestilent.

9. The south winds and west winds do not engender vapours, but they blow from those coasts where there is great store of them, by reason of the increase of the sun's heat, which draws forth the vapours, and therefore they are rainy. But if they blow from dry places, which have no vapours in them, they are fair. But, notwithstanding, sometimes they are pure and sometimes turbulent.

10. The south and west winds here with us, seem to be confederate, and are warm and moist,

and on the other side the north and east winds have some affinity between them, being cold and dry.

11. The north and south winds (whereof we have also spoken before) do blow oftener than the east and west winds, because there is a great inequality of vapours in those parts, by reason of the absence and presence of the sun, but to the east and to the west the sun is, as it were, indifferent.

12. The south wind is very healthful when it comes from the sea, but when it blows from the continent it is more unhealthful ; and so, contrariwise, the north wind is suspicious blowing from the sea, from the continent it is healthful. Likewise, the south sea wind is very agreeable with plants and fruits, killing their cankers, or rusts, and other hurtful annoyances.

13. A gentle south wind doth assemble and gather together clouds much, especially if it continue but a short while ; but if it blow too boisterously, or long, it clouds the sky and brings in rain. But especially when it ceases or grows remiss, more than in its beginning, and when it is in its chiefest vigour.

14. When the south wind either begins to blow or ceases, for the most part there are changes of weather, from fair to cloudy, and from hot to cold, and contrariwise. The north wind many times rises and ceases, the former weather remaining and continuing.

15. After hoary frosts and long continued snow, there scarcely blows any other wind than a south wind, there being, as it were, a concoction or digestion made of cold, which then at last dissolves ; neither doth rain also follow ; but this likewise happens in changes or intervals of fair weather.

16. The south wind rises oftener and blows stronger in the night than in the day, especially in winter nights. But the north wind, if it rise in the night, (which is contrary to its custom,) it doth usually last above three days.

17. When the south wind blows, the waves swell higher than when the north wind blows, though it blows with an equal or lesser force.

18. The south wind blowing, the sea becomes blue and more bright than when the north wind blows, which causes it to look darker and blacker.

19. When the air becomes warmer on a sudden, it sometimes betokens rain ; and, again, at other times, when on a sudden it grows colder, it likewise betokens rain. But this happens according to the nature of the winds ; for if the air grow warm whilst the south or east wind blows, there is rain at hand, and likewise when it grows cold during the northern or western blasts.

20. The south wind blows for the most part entire and alone. But the north wind blowing, especially the east-north-east, or the north-west, oftentimes contrary and various, or divers winds blow together, whereby they are broken and disturbed.

21. Beware of a northern wind when you sow seed, neither would I wish any one to inoculate or graft in a southern wind.

22. Leaves fall from trees soonest on the south side, but vine sprouts or stalks bud forth, and grow most that way.

23. In large pasture, shepherds must take care (as Pliny saith) to bring their flocks to the north side, that they may feed against the south. For, if they feed towards the north, they grow lame and blear-eyed, and distempered in their bellies. The northern wind, also, doth so weaken their coupling, that if they couple looking that way, they will for the most part bring forth ewe-lambs. But Pliny doth not stand very stiffly to this opinion, having, as it were, taken it up upon trust and borrowed it.

24. Winds are hurtful to wheat and all manner of grain at three times, namely, at the opening and at the falling of the flower, and when the grain itself is ripe, for then they blow the corn out of the ear, and, at the other two times, either they blast the flower or blow it off.

25. While the south wind blows, men's breath grows ranker, all creatures' appetites decay, pestilent diseases reign, men wax more slow and dull. But when the wind is northwardly, men are more lively, healthful, and greedy after food. Yet the northern wind is hurtful for them that are troubled with the phthisick, cough, gout, or any other sharp defluxions.

26. An east wind is dry, piercing, and mortifying. The west wind moist, meek, and nourishing.

27. If the east wind blow when the spring is any thing forward, it is hurtful to fruits, bringing in of worms and caterpillars, so that the leaves are hardly spared : neither is it very good to grain. Contrariwise, the west wind is very propitious and friendly to herbs, flowers, and all manner of vegetables. And so is the east wind too about the autumnal equinox.

28. Western winds are more vehement than eastern winds, and bow and bend trees more.

29. Rainy weather, which begins when the east wind blows, doth last longer than that which begins when a west wind blows, and may peradventure hold out for a whole day.

30. The east and north wind, when they once begin to blow, blow more constantly ; the south and west wind are more mutable.

31. In an eastern wind all visible things do appear bigger ; but in a western wind all audible things are heard further, as sounds of bells and the like.

32. The east-north-east wind draws clouds to it. It is a proverb amongst the Greeks to compare it to usurers, who by laying out money do swallow it up. It is a vehement and large wind.

which cannot remove clouds so fast, as they will turn back and press upon it. Which is likewise seen in great fires, which grow stronger against the wind.

33. Cardinal or semicardinal winds are not so stormy as the median.

34. Median winds from north to north-east are more fair, from north-east to east more stormy. Likewise from east to south-east more fair, from south-east to south more stormy. Likewise from south to south-west more fair, from south-west to west more stormy. Likewise from west to north-west more fair; from north-west to north more stormy. So that, proceeding according to the order of the heavens, the median winds of the first halfward are always disposed to fair weather, those of the latter halfward to storms and tempests.

35. Thunders and lightnings, and storms, with falling of broken clouds are, when such cold winds as participate of the north do blow, as the north-west, north-north-west, north-north-east, north-east, and east north-east. Wherefore those thunders likely are accompanied with hail.

36. Likewise snowy winds come from the north, but it is from those median winds which are not stormy, as the north-west, and north-east, and by north.

37. Winds gain their natures and properties five ways only: either by the absence or presence of the sun; or by agreeing or disagreeing with the natural motion of the air; or by the diversity of the matter which feedeth them, by which they are engendered; as sea, snow, marishes, or the like; or by the tincture of the countries through which they pass; or by their original local beginnings: on high, under ground, in the middle; all which things the ensuing articles will better declare and explain.

38. All winds have a power to dry, yea, more than the sun itself, because the sun draws out the vapours; but if it be not very fervent, it doth not disperse them; but the wind both draws them out, and carries them away. But the south wind doth this least of any; and both timber and stones sweat more when the south wind blows a little, than when it is calm and lies still.

39. March winds are far more drying than summer winds; insomuch that such as make musical instruments will stay for March winds to dry their stuff they make their instruments of, to make it more porous, and better sounding.

40. All manner of winds purge the air, and cleanse it from all putrefaction, so that such years as are most windy, are most healthful.

41. The sun is like to princes, who sometimes having appointed deputies in some remote countries, the subjects there are more obsequious to those deputies, and yield them more respect than to the prince himself. And so the winds which have their power and origin from the sun, do govern the temperatures of the countries, and the disposition of the air, as much or more than the sun itself. Insomuch that Peru (which, by reason of the nearness of the ocean, the vastness of rivers, and exceeding great and high hills, hath abundance of winds and blasts blowing there) may contend with Europe for a temperate and sweet air.

42. It is no wonder if the force and power of winds be so great, as it is found to be; vehement winds being as inundations, torrents, and flowing of the spacious air, neither (if we attentively heed it) is their power any great matter. They can throw down trees, which, with their tops, like unto spread sails, give them advantage to do it, and are a burden to themselves. Likewise they can blow down weak buildings; strong and firm ones they cannot, without earthquakes join with them. Sometimes they will blow all the snow off the tops of hills, burying the valley that is below them with it; as it befel Solomon in the Sultanian fields. They will also, sometimes, drive in waters, and cause great inundations.

43. Sometimes winds will dry up rivers, and leave the channels bare. For if, after a great drought, a strong wind blows with the current for many days, so that it, as it were, sweeps away the water of the river into the sea, and keeps the sea water from coming in, the river will dry up in many places where it doth not use to be so.

Monition. Turn the poles, and, withal, turn the observations as concerning the north and south. For, the presence and absence of the sun being the cause, it must vary according to the poles. But this may be a constant thing. that there is more sea towards the south, and more land towards the north, which doth not a little help the winds.

Monition. Winds are made or engendered a thousand ways, as by the subsequent inquisition it will appear; so, to fix that observation in a thing so various, is not very easy. Yet, those things which we have set down are, for the most part, most certain.

Local Beginnings of Winds.

To the eighth article. Connexion.

To know the local beginnings of winds, is a thing which requires a deep search and inquisition, seeing that the whence and whither of winds are things noted even in the Scripture, to be abstruse and hidden. Neither do we now speak of the fountains or beginnings of particular winds, (of which more shall be said hereafter,) but of the matrixes of winds in general. Some fetch them from above, some search for them in the deep: but, in the middle, (where they are for the most part engendered,) nobody hardly looks for them: such is the custom of men to inquire after things which are obscure, and omit those things which lie, as it were, in their way. This is certain, that winds are either inbred or strangers; for winds are, as it were, merchants of vapours, which being by them gathered into clouds, they carry out and bring in again into countries, from whence winds are again returned, as it were, by exchange. But let us now inquire concerning native winds, for those which, coming from another place, are strangers, are in another place natives. There are three local beginnings of them: they either breathe, or spring out of the ground, or are cast down from above, or are here made up in the body of the air. Those which are cast down from above, are of a double generation; for they are either cast down before they be formed into clouds, or afterwards composed of rarefied and dispersed clouds. Let us now see what is the history of these things.

1. The poets feigned Eolus his kingdom to be placed under ground in dens and caves, where the winds' prison was, out of which they were at times let-forth.

2. Some philosophical divines, moved by those words of Scripture, "He brings forth the winds out of his treasures," think that the winds come out of some treasuries; namely, places under ground, amongst the mines of minerals. But this is nothing; for the Scripture speaketh likewise of the treasures of snow and hail, which, doubtless, are engendered above.

3. Questionless, in subterraneal places there is great store of air, which it is very likely sometimes breathes out by little and little, and sometimes, again, upon urgent causes, must needs come rushing forth together.

An indirect experiment.

In great droughts, and in the middle of summer, when the ground is cleft and chopped, there breaks out water many times in dry and sandy places; which, if waters (being a gross body) do, though it be but seldom, it is probable that the air (which is a subtile and tenuous body) may often do it.

4. If the air breathes out of the earth by little and little, and scatteringly, it is little perceived at the first; but when many of those small emanations, or comings out, are come together, there is a wind produced, as a river out of several springs. And this seems to be so, because it hath been observed by the ancients, that many winds, in those places where they begin, do at first blow but softly, which afterward grow stronger and increase in their progress like unto rivers.

5. There are some places in the sea, and some lakes also, which swell extremely when there is no wind stirring, which apparently proceeds from some subterraneal wind.

6. There is great quantity of subterraneal spirit required to shake or cleave the earth; less will serve turn for the raising of water. Wherefore earthquakes come but seldom, risings and swellings of waters are more frequent.

7. Likewise it is everywhere taken notice of that waters do somewhat swell and rise before tempests.

8. The weak subterraneal spirit which is breathed out scatteringly is not perceived upon the earth until it be gathered into wind, by reason the earth is full of pores; but when it issues from under the water, it is presently perceived (by reason of the water's continuity) by some manner of swelling.

9. We resolved before that in cavernous and denny places there were attendant winds; insomuch that those winds seem to have their local beginnings out of the earth.

10. In great and rocky hills winds are found to breathe sooner, (namely, before they be perceived in the valleys,) and more frequently, (namely, when it is calm weather in the valleys,) but all mountains and rocks are cavernous and hollow.

11. In Wales, in the county of Denbigh, a mountainous and rocky country, out of certain caves (as Gilbertus relateth) are such vehement eruptions of wind, that clothes or linen laid out there upon any occasion, are blown up, and carried a great way up into the air.

12. In Aber Barry, near Severn in Wales, in a rocky cliff, are certain holes, to which if you lay your ear, you shall hear divers sounds and murmurs of winds under ground.

An indirect experiment.

Acosta hath observed that the towns of Plata and Potosi, in Peru, are not far distant one from the other, and both situated upon a high and hilly ground, so that they differ not in that; and yet Potosi hath a cold and winter-like air, and Plata hath a mild and spring-like temperature, which difference it seems may be attributed to the silver mines which are near Potosi; which showeth that there are breathing-places of the earth, as in relation to hot and cold.

13. If the earth be the first cold thing, according to Parmenides, (whose opinion is not contemptible, seeing cold and density are knit together by a strict knot,) it is no less probable that there are hotter breaths sent out from the central cold of the earth than are cast down from the cold of the higher air.

14. There are certain wells in Dalmatia, and the country of Cyrene, (as some of the ancients record,) into which if you cast a stone, there will presently arise tempests, as if the stone had broken some covering of a place, in which the force of the winds was enclosed.

An indirect experiment.

Ætna and divers other mountains cast out fire; therefore it is likely that air may likewise break forth, especially being dilatated and set into motion by heat in subterraneal places.

15. It hath been noted, that both before and after earthquakes there hath blown certain noxious and foreign winds; as there are certain little smothers usually before and after great firings and burnings.

Monition. The air shut up in the earth is forced to break out for several causes : sometimes a mass of earth, ill joined together, falls into a hollow place of the earth; sometimes waters do ingulf themselves; sometimes the air is extended by subterraneal heats, and seeks for more room : sometimes the earth, which before was solid and vaulted, being by fires turned into ashes, no longer able to bear itself up, falls. And many such like causes.

And so these inquisitions have been made concerning the first local beginning of winds. Now followeth the second origin, or beginning from above, namely, from that which they call the middle region of the air.

Monition. But let no man understand what hath been spoken so far amiss, as if we should deny the rest of the winds also are brought forth of the earth by vapours. But this first kind was of winds which come forth of the earth, being already perfectly framed winds.

16. It hath been observed, that there is a murmuring of woods before we do plainly perceive the winds, whereby it is conjectured that the wind descends from a higher place, which is likewise observed in hills, (as we said before,) but the cause is more ambiguous, by reason of the concavity and hollowness of the hills.

17. Wind follows darted, or (as we call them) shooting stars, and it comes that way as the star hath shot; whereby it appears that the air hath been moved above, before the motion comes to us.

18. The opening of the firmament and dispersion of clouds, are prognostics of wind before they blow here on earth, which also shows that the winds begin above.

19. Small stars are not seen before the rising of winds, though the night be clear and fair; because (it should seem) the air grows thick, and is less transparent, by reason of that matter which afterward is turned into wind.

20. There appear circles about the body of the moon, the sun looks sometimes blood-red at its setting, the moon rises red at her fourth rising : and there are many more prognostics of winds on high, (whereof we will speak in its proper place,) which shows that the matter of the winds is there begun and prepared.

21. In these experiments you must note that difference we speak of, namely, of the twofold generation of winds on high; that is to say, before the gathering together of vapours into a cloud, and after. For the prognostics of circles about, and colours of the sun and moon, have something

of the cloud; but that darting and occultation of the lesser stars is in fair and clear weather.

22. When the wind comes out of a cloud ready formed, either the cloud is totally dispersed, and turned into wind, or it is torn and rent in sunder, and the winds break out, as in a storm.

23. There are many indirect experiments in the world concerning the repercussion by cold. So that, it being certain that there are most extreme colds in the middle region of the air, it is likewise plain that vapours, for the most part, cannot break through that place without being joined and gathered together, or darted, according to the opinion of the ancients, which in this particular is true and sound.

The third local beginning of winds is of those which are engendered here in the lower part of the air, which we also call swellings or overburdenings of the air; a thing very familiar and frequent, yet passed over with silence.

A Commentation. The generation of those winds which are made up in this lower part of the air, is a thing no more obscure than this : namely, that the air newly composed and made up of water, and attenuated and dissolved vapours, joined with the first air, cannot be contained within the same bounds as it was before, but groweth out and is turned, and takes up further room. Yet there are in this two things to be granted : First, that one drop of water turned into air, (whatsoever they fabulously speak of the tenth proportion of the elements,) requires at least a hundred times more room than it had before. Secondly, that a little new air, and moved, added to the old air, shaketh the whole, and sets it into motion ; as we may perceive by a little wind that comes forth of a pair of bellows, or in at a little crevice of a window or wall, that will set all the air which is in a room in motion, as appears by the blazing of the lights which are in the same room.

24. As the dews and mists are engendered here in the lower air, never coming to be clouds, nor penetrating to the middle region of the air : in the like manner are also many winds.

25. A continual gale blows about the sea, and other waters, which is nothing but a small wind newly made up.

26. The rainbow, which is, as it were, the lowest of meteors, and nearest to us, when it doth not appear whole, but curtailed, and, as it were, only some pieces of the horns of it, is dissolved into winds, as often, or rather oftener than into rain.

27. It hath been observed, that there are some winds in countries which are divided and separated by hills, which ordinarily blow on the one side of the hills, and do not reach to the other, whereby it manifestly appears that they are engendered below the height of the said hills.

28. There are an infinite sort of winds that

blow in fair and clear days, and also in countries where it never rains, which are engendered where they blow, and never were clouds, nor did ever ascend in the middle region of the air.

Indirect experiments.

Whosoever shall know how easily a vapour is dissolved into air, and how great a quantity of vapours there are, and how much room a drop of water turned into air takes up more than it did before, (as we said already,) and how little the air will endure to be thrust up together, will, questionless, affirm, that of necessity winds must be everywhere engendered, from the very superficies of the earth, even to the highest parts of the air. For it cannot be, that a great abundance of vapours, when they begin to be dilatated and expanded, can be lifted up to the middle region of the air, without an overburdening of the air, and making a noise by the way.

Accidental Generations of Winds.

To the ninth article.   Connexion.

We call those accidental generations of winds which do not make or beget the impulsive motion of winds, but with compression do sharpen it, by repercussion turn it, by sinuation or winding do agitate and tumble it, which is done by extrinsical causes, and the posture of the adjoining bodies.

1. In places where there are hills which are not very high, bordering upon valleys, and beyond them again higher hills, there is a greater agitation of the air, and sense of winds, than there is in mountainous or plain places.

2. In cities, if there be any place somewhat broader than ordinary and narrow goings out, as portals or porches, and cross streets, winds and fresh gales are there to be perceived.

3. In houses cool roome are made by winds, or happen to be so where the air bloweth through, and comes in on the one side and goeth out at the other. But much more if the air comes in several ways and meets in the corners, and hath one common passage from thence: the vaulting likewise and roundness doth contribute much to coolness, because the air, being moved, is beaten back in every line. Also, the winding of porches is better than if they were built straight out. For a direct blast, though it be not shut up, but hath a tree egress, doth not make the air so unequal and voluminous, and waving, as the meeting at angles and hollow places, and windings round, and the like.

4. After great tempests at sea an accidental wind continues for a time, after the original is laid, which wind is made by the collision and percussion of the air, through the curling of the waves.

5. In gardens commonly there is a repercussion of wind, from the walls and banks, so that one would imagine the wind to come the contrary way from that whence it really comes.

6. If hills enclose a country on the one side, and the wind blows for some space of time from the plain against the hill, by the very repercussion of the hill, either the wind is turned into rain, if it be a moist wind, or into a contrary wind, which will last but a little while.

7. In the turnings of a promontory, mariners do often find changes and alterations of winds.

Extraordinary Winds and sudden Blasts.

To the tenth article.   Connexion.

Some men discourse of extraordinary winds, and derive the causes of them; of clouds breaking, or storms, vortice, typhone, prestere; or, in English, whirlwinds. But they do not relate the thing itself, which must be taken out of chronicles and several histories.

1. Sudden blasts never come in clear weather, but always when the sky is cloudy and the weather rainy. That it may justly be thought that there is a certain eruption made; the blasts driven out and the waters shaken.

2. Storms which come with a mist and a fog, and are called Belluæ, and bear up themselves like a column, are very vehement and dreadful to those who are at sea.

3. The greater typhones, who will take up at some large distance, and sup them, as it were, upward, do happen but seldom, but small whirlwinds come often.

4. All storms and typhones, and great whirlwinds, have a manifest precipitous motion or darting downwards, more than other winds, so as they seem to fall like torrents, and run, as it were, in channels, and be afterwards reverberated by the earth.

5. In meadows, haycocks are sometimes carried on high and spread abroad there like canopies; likewise in fields, cocks of pease, reaped wheat, and clothes laid out to drying, are carried up by whirlwinds as high as tops of trees and houses, and these things are done without any extraordinary force or great vehemency of wind.

6. Also, sometimes there are very small whirlwinds, and within a narrow compass, which happen also in fair, clear weather; so that one that rides may see the dust or straws taken up and turned close by him, yet he himself not feel the wind much, which things are done questionless near unto us, by contrary blasts driving one another back, and causing a circulation of the air by concussion.

7. It is certain, that some winds do leave manifest signs of burning and scorching in plants; but presterem, which is a kind of dark lightning, and hot air without any flame, we will put off to the inquisition of lightning.

Helps to Winds; namely, to Original Winds; for of accidental ones we have inquired before.

To the eleventh, twelfth, thirteenth, fourteenth, and fifteenth articles. Connexion.

Those things which have been spoken by the ancients, concerning winds and their causes, are merely confused and uncertain, and for the most part untrue; and it is no marvel, if they see not clear that look not near. They speak as if wind were somewhat else, or a thing several from moved air; and as if exhalations did generate and make up the whole body of the winds; and as if the matter of winds were only a dry and hot exhalation; and as if the beginning of the motion of winds were but only a casting down and percussion by the cold of the middle region, all fantastical and arbitrary opinions; yet out of such threads they weave long pieces, namely, cobwebs. But all impulsion of the air is wind; and exhalations mixed with the air contribute more to the motion than to the matter; and moist vapours, by a proportionate heat, are easier dissolved into wind than dry exhalations, and many winds are engendered in the lowest region of the air, and breathe out of the earth, besides those which are thrown down and beaten back.

1. The natural wheeling of the air, (as we said in the article of general winds,) without any other external cause, bringing forth winds perceptible within the tropics, where the conversion is in greater circles.

2. Next to the natural motion of the air, before we inquire of the sun, (who is the chief begetter of winds,) let us see whether any thing ought to be attributed to the moon, and other asters, by clear experience.

3. There arise many great and strong winds some hours before the eclipse of the moon; so that, if the moon be eclipsed in the middle of the night, the winds blow the precedent evening; if the moon be eclipsed towards the morning, then the winds blow in the middle of the precedent night.

4. In Peru, which is a very windy country, Acosta observes, that winds blow most when the moon is at the full.

Injunction. It were certainly a thing worthy to be observed, what power the ages and motions of the moon have upon the winds, seeing they have some power over the waters. As, for example, whether the winds be not in a greater commotion in full and new moons, than in her first and last quarters, as we find it to be in the flowings of waters. For, though some do conveniently feign the command of the moon to be over the waters, as the sun and planets over the air, yet it is certain, that the water and the air are very homogeneal bodies, and that the moon, next to the sun, hath most power over all things here below.

5. It hath been observed by men, that about the conjunctions of planets greater winds do blow.

6. At the rising of Orion there rise commonly divers winds and storms. But we must advise whether this be not because Orion rises in such a season of the year as is most effectual for the generation of winds; so that it is rather a concomitant than causing thing. Which may also very well be questioned concerning rain at the rising of the Hyades and the Pleiades, and concerning storms at the rising of Arcturus. And so much concerning the moon and stars.

7. The sun is, questionless, the primary efficient of many winds, working by its heat on a twofold matter, namely, the body of the air, and likewise vapours and exhalations.

8. When the sun is most powerful, it dilatates and extends the air, though it be pure and without any commixion, one-third part, which is no small matter; so that, by mere dilatation, there must needs arise some small wind in the sun's ways; and that rather two or three hours after its rising, than at his first rise.

9. In Europe the nights are hotter, in Peru, three hours in the morning, and all for one cause, namely, by reason of winds and gales ceasing and lying still at those hours.

10. In a vitro calendari, dilatated or extended air beats down the water, as it were, with a breath; but, in a vitro pileato, which is filled only with air, the dilatated air swells the bladder. as a manifest and apparent wind.

11. We have made trial of such a kind of wind in a round tower, every way closed up. For we have placed a hearth or fireplace in the midst of it, laying a fire of charcoal thoroughly kindled upon it, that there might be the less smoke, and on the side of the hearth, at a small distance, hath been a thread hung up with a cross of feathers, to the end that it might easily be moved. So, after a little stay, the heat increasing, and the air dilatating, the thread, and the feather cross which hung upon it, waved up and down in a various motion; and, having made a hole in the window of the tower, there came out a hot breath, which was not continual, but with intermission and waving.

12. Also, the reception of air by cold, after dilatation, begets such a wind, but weaker, by reason of the lesser force of cold. So that, in Peru, under every little shadow, we find not only more coolness than here with us, (by antiperistasis,) but a manifest kind of gale through the reception of air when it comes into the shade. And so much concerning wind occasioned by mere dilatation or reception of air.

13. Winds proceeding from the mere motion of the air, without any commixion of vapours, are but gentle and soft. Let us see what may be said concerning vapoury winds, (we mean such as are engendered by vapours,) which may

be so much more vehement than the other, as a dilatation of a drop of water turned into air exceeds any dilatation of air already made : which it doth by many degrees, as we showed before.

14. The efficient cause of vapoury winds (which are they that commonly blow) is the sun, and its proportionate heat; the matter is vapours and exhalations which are turned and resolved into air. I say air, (and not any thing but air,) yet at the first not very pure.

15. A small heat of the sun doth not raise vapours, and consequently causes no wind.

16. A mean and middle heat of the sun raiseth and excites vapours, but doth not presently dissipate them. Therefore, if there be any great store of them, they gather together into rain, either simply of itself, or joined with wind : if there be but small store of them, they turn only to wind.

17. The sun's heat in its increase, inclines more to the generation of winds, in its decrease to rains.

18. The great and continued heat of the sun attenuates and disperses vapours and sublimes them, and withal equally mixes and incorporates them with the air, whereby the air becomes calm and serene.

19. The more equal and continuate heat of the sun is less apt for the generation of winds; that which is more unequal and intermitted is more apt. Wherefore in sailing into Russia they are less troubled with winds than in the British sea, because of the length of the days; but in Peru under the equinoctial are frequent winds, by reason of the great inequality of heat, taking turns night and day.

20. In vapours is to be considered both the quantity and quality. A small quantity engenders weak winds, a mean or middle store stronger; great store engenders rain, either calm or accompanied with wind.

21. Vapours out of the sea and rivers, and overflown marshes, engender far greater quantity of winds than the exhalations of the earth. But those winds which are engendered on the land and dry places, are more obstinate, and last longer, and are, for the most part, such as are cast down from above. So that the opinion of the ancients in this, is not altogether unprofitable; but only that it pleased them, as in a manner dividing the inheritance, to assign rain to vapours, and to winds exhalations only, which things sound handsomely, but are vain in effect and substance.

22. Winds brought forth out of the resolutions of snow lying upon hills, are of a mean condition between water and land winds; but they incline more to water, yet they are more sharp and movable.

23. The dissolution of snow on snowy hills (as we observed before) always brings constant winds from that part.

24. Also, yearly northern winds about the rising of the dogstar, are held to come from the frozen ocean, and those parts about the arctic circle, where the dissolutions of snow and ice come late when the summer is far spent.

25. Those masses or mountains of ice which are carried towards Canada and Greenland do rather breed cold gales than movable winds.

26. Winds which arise from chalky and sandy grounds, are few and dry, and in hotter countries they are sultry, smoky, and scorching.

27. Winds made of sea vapours do easilier turn back into rain, the water redemanding and claiming its rights; and if this be not granted them, they presently mix with air, and so are quiet. But terrestrial, smoky, and unctuous vapours are both hardlier dissolved and ascend higher, and are more provoked in their motion, and oftentimes penetrate the middle region of the air, and some of them are matter of fiery meteors.

28. It is reported here in England, that in those days that Gascoine was under our jurisdiction, there was a petition offered to the king by his subjects of Bordeaux, and the confines thereof, desiring him to forbid the burning of heath in the counties of Sussex and Southampton, which bred a wind towards the end of April which killed their vines.

29. The meeting of winds, if they be strong, bring forth vehement and whirling winds; if they be soft and moist, they produce rain, and lay the wind.

30. Winds are allayed and restrained five ways. When the air, overburdened and troubled, is freed by the vapours contracting themselves into rain; or when vapours are dispersed and subtilized, whereby they are mixed with the air, and agree fairly with it, and they live quietly; or when vapours or fogs are exalted and carried up on high, so that they cause no disturbance until they be thrown down from the middle region of the air, or do penetrate it; or when vapours, gathered into clouds, are carried away into other countries, by other winds blowing on high, so that for them there is peace in those countries which they fly beyond; or, lastly, when the winds, blowing from their nurseries, languish through a long voyage, finding no new matter to feed on, and so their vehemency forsakes them, and they do as it were expire and die.

31. Rain, for the most part, allayeth winds, especially those which are stormy; as winds, contrariwise, oftentimes keep off rain.

32. Winds do contract themselves into rain, (which is the first of the five, and the chiefest means of allaying them,) either being burdened by the burden itself, when the vapours are copious, or by the contrary motions of winds, so they be calm and mild; or by the opposition of mountains and promontories, which stop the violence of the winds, and, by little and little, turn them

against themselves; or by extreme colds, whereby they are condensed and thickened.

33. Smaller and lighter winds do commonly rise in the morning, and go down with the sun, the condensation of the night air being sufficient to receive them; for air will endure some kind of compression without stirring or tumult.

34. It is thought that the sound of bells will disperse lightning and thunder: in winds it hath not been observed.

Monition. Take advice from the place in prognostics of winds; for there is some connexion of causes and signs.

35. Pliny relates, that the vehemence of a whirlwind may be allayed by sprinkling of vinegar in the encounter of it.

The Bounds of Winds.

To the sixteenth, seventeenth, and eighteenth articles.

1. It is reported of Mount Athos, and likewise of Olympus, that the priests would write in the ashes of the sacrifices which lay upon the altars, built on the tops of those hills, and when they returned the year following, (for the offerings were annual,) they found the same letters undisturbed and uncancelled, though those altars stood not in any temple, but in the open air. Whereby it was manifest, that in such a height there had neither fallen rain nor wind blown.

2. They say that on the top of the Peak of Teneriffe, and on the Andes, betwixt Peru and Chili, snow lieth upon the borders and sides of the hills, but that on the tops of them there is nothing but a quiet and still air, hardly breatheable by reason of its tenuity, which, also, with a kind of acrimony, pricks the eyes and orifice of the stomach, begetting in some a desire to vomit, and in others a flushing and redness.

3. Vapoury winds seem not in any great height, though it be probable that some of them ascend higher than most clouds. Hitherto of the height; now we must consider of the latitude.

4. It is certain that those spaces which winds take up are very various, sometimes they are very large, sometimes little and narrow: winds have been known to have taken up a hundred miles' space with a few hours' difference.

5. Spacious winds (if they be of the free kind) are, for the most part, vehement, and not soft, and more lasting; for they will last almost four-and-twenty hours. They are likewise not so much inclined to rain. Strait or narrow winds, contrariwise, are either soft or stormy, and always short.

6. Fixed and stayed winds are itinerary or travelling, and take up very large spaces.

7. Stormy winds do not extend themselves into any large spaces, though they always go beyond the bounds of the storm itself.

8. Sea winds always blow within narrower spaces than earth winds, as may sometimes be een at sea, namely, a pretty fresh gale in some part of the water, (which may be easily perceived by the crisping of it,) when there is a calm, as smooth as glass, everywhere else.

9. Small whirlwinds (as we said before) will sometimes play before men as they are riding, almost like wind out of a pair of bellows. So much of the latitude; now we must see concerning the lastingness.

10. The vehement winds will last longer at sea, by reason of the sufficient quantity of vapours; at land they will hardly last above a day and a half.

11. Very soft winds will not blow constantly, neither at sea, nor upon the land, above three days.

12. The south wind is not only more lasting than the west, (which we set down in another place,) but likewise what wind soever it be that begins to blow in the morning, useth to be more durable and lasting than that which begins to blow at night.

13. It is certain that winds do rise, and increase by degrees, (unless they be mere storms,) but they allay sooner, sometimes as it were in an instant.

Succession of Winds.

To the nineteenth, twentieth, and twenty-first articles.

1. If the wind doth change according to the motion of the sun, that is, from east to south, from south to west, from west to north, from the north to the east, it doth not return often, or if it doth, it doth it but for a short time. But if it go contrary to the motion of the sun, that is, from the east to the north, from the north to the west, from the west to the south, and from the south to the east, for the most part it is restored to its first quarter, at least before it hath gone round its whole compass and circuit.

2. If rain begins first, and the wind begins to blow afterwards, that wind will outlast the rain; but if the wind blow first, and then is allayed by the rain, the wind for the most part will not rise again; and if it does, there ensues a new rain.

3. If winds do blow variously for a few hours, and as it were to make a trial, and afterward begin to blow constantly, that wind shall continue for many days.

4. If the south wind begin to blow two or three days, sometimes the north wind will blow presently after it. But if the north wind blows as many days, the south wind will not blow, until the wind have blown a little from the east.

5. When the year is declining and winter begins after autumn is past, if the south wind blows in the beginning of winter, and after it comes the north wind, it will be a frosty winter; but if the north wind blow in the beginning of winter, and the south wind come after, it will be a mild and warm winter.

6. Pliny quotes Eudoxus, to show that the order

of winds returns after every four years, which seems not to be true, for revolutions are not so quick. This indeed hath been by some men's diligence observed, that greatest and most notable seasons (for heat, snow, frost, warm winters, and cold summers) for the most part return after the revolution of five-and-thirty years.

The Motion of the Winds.

To the twenty-second, twenty-third, twenty-fourth, twenty-fifth, twenty-sixth, and twenty-seventh articles. Connexion.

Men talk as if the wind were some body of itself, and by its own force did drive and agitate the air. Also, when the wind changes its place, they talk as if it did transport itself into another place. This is the vulgar's opinion; yet the philosophers themselves apply no remedy thereunto, but they likewise stammer at it, and do not any way contradict and oppose these errors.

1. We must therefore inquire concerning the raising of the motion of the winds, and of the direction of it, having already inquired of the local beginnings; and of those winds which have their beginning of motion in their first impulsion, as in those which are cast down from above or blow out of the earth, the raising of their motion is manifest: others descend below their own beginnings; others ascend, and being resisted by the air, become voluminous, especially near the angles of their violence; but of those which are engendered everywhere in this inferior air, (which are the frequentest of all the winds,) the inquisition seems to be somewhat obscure, although it be a vulgar thing, as we have set down in the commentation under the eighth article.

2. We found likewise an image or representation of this in that close tower which we spake of before; for we varied that trial three ways. The first was that which we spake of before; namely, a fire of clear burning coals. The second was a kettle of seething water, the fire being set away, and then the motion of the cross of feathers was more slow and dull. The third was with both fire and kettle; and then the agitation of the cross of feathers was very vehement, so that sometimes it would whirl up and down, as if it had been in a petty whirlwind, the water yielding store of vapours, and the fire which stood by it dissipating and dispersing them.

3. So that the chief cause of exciting motion in the winds is the overcharging of the air by a new addition of air engendered by vapours. Now we must see concerning the direction of the motion, and of the whirling, which is a change of the direction.

4. The nurseries and food of the winds doth govern their progressive motion; which nurseries and feedings are like unto the springs of rivers; namely, the places where there are great store of vapours, for there is the native country of the winds. Then, when they have found a current, where the air makes no resistance, (as water when it finds a falling way,) then, whatsoever semblable matter they find by the way, they take into their fellowship, and mix it with their currents even as rivers do. So that the winds blow always from that side where their nurseries are which feed them.

5. Where there are no notable nurseries in any certain place, the winds stray very much, and do easily change their current, as in the middle of the sea, and large spacious fields.

6. Where there are great nurseries of the winds in one place, but in the way of its progress it hath but small additions, there the winds blow strongly in their beginnings, and by little and little they allay; and contrariwise, where they find good store of matter to feed on by the way, they are weak in the beginning, but gather strength by the way.

7. There are movable nurseries for the winds, namely, in the clouds, which many times are carried far away from the nurseries of vapours of which those clouds were made, by winds blowing high; then the nursery of the wind begins to be in that place where the clouds do begin to be dissolved into wind.

8. But the whirling of winds does not happen, because the wind which blows at first transports itself, but because either that is allayed and spent, or brought into order by another wind; and all this business depends on the various placings of the nurseries of winds, and variety of times, when vapours issuing out of these nurseries are dissolved.

9. If there be nurseries of winds on contrary parts, as one nursery on the south, another on the north side, the strongest wind will prevail; neither will there be contrary winds, but the stronger wind will blow continually, though it be somewhat dulled and tamed by the weaker wind, as it is in rivers, when the flowing of the sea comes in; for the sea's motion prevails, and is the only one, but it is somewhat curbed by the motion of the river; and if it so happen that one of those contrary winds, namely, that which was the strongest, be allayed, then presently the contrary will blow, from that side where it blew before, but lay hidden under the force and power of the greater.

10. As for example, if the nursery be at the north-east, the north-east wind will blow; but if there be two nurseries of winds, namely, another in the north, those winds for some tract of way will blow severally, but after the angle of confluence where they come together they will blow to the north-east, or with some inclination, according as the other nursery shall prove stronger.

11. If there be a nursery of wind on the north side, which may be distant from some country twenty miles, and is the stronger; another on the

east side, which is distant some ten miles, and is weaker; yet the east wind will blow for some hours, and a while after (namely, when its journey is ended) the north wind.

12. If the northern wind blow, and some hill stands in the way of it on the west side, a little while after the north-east wind will blow, compounded by the original, and that which is beaten back again.

13. If there be a nursery of winds in the earth on the northern side, and the breath thereof be carried directly upward, and it find a cold cloud on the west side, which turns it off the contrary way, there will blow a north-east wind.

14. *Monition.* Nurseries of winds in sea and land are constant, so that the spring and beginning of them may be the better perceived; but the nurseries of winds in the clouds are movable, so that in one place there is matter furnished for the winds, and they are formed in another, which makes the direction of motion in winds to be more confused and uncertain.

Those things we have produced for example's sake, the like are after the like manner; and hitherto of the direction of the motion of winds: now we must see concerning the longitude, and, as it were, the itinerary or journey of the winds, though it may seem we have already inquired of this under the notion of the latitude of winds; for latitude may by unlearned men also be taken for longitude, if winds take up more space laterally than they go forward in longitude.

14. If it be true that Columbus could upon the coasts of Portugal judge of the continent of America by the constant winds from the west, truly, the winds can travel a long journey.

15. If it be true that the dissolution of snows about the frozen seas, and Scandia do excite and raise northerly winds in Italy and Greece, &c., in the dogdays, surely these are long journeys.

16. It hath not yet been observed how much sooner a storm does arrive, according to the way it comes, (as for example, if it be an eastern wind,) how much sooner it comes from the east, and how much later from the west. And so much concerning the motion of winds in their progression or going forward: now we must see concerning the undulation or swelling of winds.

17. The undulation or swelling of winds is done in a few moments, so that a wind will (though it be strong) rise and fall by turns, at the least a hundred times in an hour; whereby it appears that the violence of winds is unequal; for neither rivers, though swift, nor currents in the sea, though strong, do rise in waves, unless the blowing of wind be joined thereunto, neither hath the swelling of winds any equality in itself; for like unto the pulse of one's hand, sometimes it beats, and sometimes it intermits.

18 The undulation or swelling of the air dif-

fers from the swelling of waters into waves in this, that in waters, after the waves are risen on high, they of themselves, and their own accord, do again fall to the place of them; whence it comes that (whatsoever poets say when they aggravate tempests, namely, that the waves are raised up to heaven, and again sink down to hell) the descent of the waves do not precipitate much below the plane and superficies of the water. But in the swelling of the air, where the motion of gravity or weight is wanting, the air is thrust down and raised almost in an equal manner. And thus much of undulation. Now we must inquire of the motion of conflict or striving.

19. The conflicts of winds and compounded conflicts we have partly inquired already. It is plain that winds are ubiquitary, especially the mildest of them. Which is likewise manifest by this, that there are few days and hours wherein some gales do not blow in free places, and that inconstantly and variously enough. For winds which do not proceed from greater nurseries are vagabond and voluble, as it were, playing one with the other, sometimes driving forward, and sometimes flying back.

20. It hath been seen sometimes at sea, that winds have come from contrary parts together, which was plainly to be perceived by the perturbation of the water on both sides, and the calmness in the middle between them; but after those contrary winds have met, either there hath followed a general calm of the water everywhere, namely, when the winds have broken and quelled one another equally; or the perturbation of the water hath continued, namely, when the stronger wind hath prevailed.

21. It is certain that, in the mountains of Peru, it hath often chanced that the wind at one time hath blown on the tops of the hills one way, and in the valleys the clean contrary way.

22. It is likewise certain here with us, that the clouds are carried one way, when the wind near us hath blown the contrary way.

23. It is likewise certain, that sometimes the higher clouds will outfly the lower clouds, so that they will go diverse, yea, and contrary ways, as it were in contrary currents.

24. It is likewise certain, that sometimes in the higher part of the air winds have been neither distracted nor moved forward; when here below they have been driven forward with a mad kind of violence, for the space of half a mile.

25. And it is likewise certain, contrariwise, that here below the air hath been very still, when above the clouds have been carried with a fresh and merry gale; but that happen more seldom.

An indirect experiment.

Likewise in waves, sometimes the upper water is swifter, sometimes the lower; and sometimes there are (but that is seldom) several currents of water, of that which is uppermost, and that which lieth beneath.

26. Nor are Virgil's testimonies altogether to be rejected, he being not utterly unskilful in natural philosophy.

> Together rush the east and south-east wind,
> Nor doth wave calling south-west stay behind.

And again:

> I all the winds have seen their battles join.

We have considered of the motions of winds, in the nature of things: we must now consider their motions in human engines; and, first of all, in the sails of ships.

The Motion of Winds in the Sails of Ships.

1. In our greatest Britain ships (for we have chosen those for our pattern) there are four masts, and sometimes five, set up one behind the other, in a direct line drawn through the middle of the ship. Which masts we will name thus:

2. The mainmast, which stands in the middle of the ship; the foremast, the mizenmast, (which is sometimes double,) and the spritmast.

3. Each mast consists of several pieces, which may be lifted up, and fashioned with several knots and joints, or taken away; some have three of them, some only two.

4. The spritsail-mast from the lower joint lies bending over the sea, from that it stands upright; all the other masts stand upright.

5. Upon these masts hang ten sails, and when there be two mizenmasts, twelve; the mainmast and foremast have three tiers of sails, which we will call the mainsail, the topsail, and the main-topsail; the rest have but two, wanting the main-topsail.

6. The sails are stretched out across, near the top of every joint of the mast, by certain beams which we call yards, to which the upper parts of the sails are fastened, the lower parts are fastened with ropes at each corner; the mainsails to the sides of the ship, top and main-topsails to the yards which are next below them.

7. The yard of every mast hangs across, only the yards of the mizenmast hang sloping, one end up, and the other down; in the rest they hang straight across the masts, like unto the letter T.

8. The mainsails of the mainmast, foremast, and boarsprit, are of a quadrangular parallellogram form; the top and main-topsails somewhat sharp, and growing narrow at the top; but the top mizensails are sharp, the lower or mainsails triangular.

9. In a ship of eleven hundred tons, which was one hundred and twelve feet long in the keel, and forty in breadth in the hold; the mainsail of the mainmast was two-and-forty feet deep, and eighty-seven feet broad.

10. The topsail of the same mast was fifty feet deep, and eighty-four feet broad at the bottom, and forty-two at the top.

11. The main-topsail was seven-and-twenty feet deep, and two-and-forty broad at the bottom, and one-and-twenty at the top.

12. The foremast mainsail was forty feet and a half deep, and seventy-two feet broad.

13. The topsail was six-and-forty feet and a half deep, and sixty-nine feet broad at the bottom, and six-and-thirty at the top.

14. The main-topsail was four-and-twenty feet deep, six-and-thirty feet broad at the bottom, and eighteen feet at the top.

15. The mizen-mainsail was on the upper part of the yard one-and-fifty feet broad; in that part which was joined to the yard seventy-two feet; the rest ending in a sharp point.

16. The topsail was thirty feet deep, fifty-seven feet broad at the bottom, and thirty feet at the top.

17. If there be two mizenmasts, the hindermost sails are less than the foremast about the fifth part.

18. The mainsail of the boarsprit was eight-and-twenty feet deep and a half, and sixty feet broad.

19. The topsail five-and-twenty feet and a half deep, and sixty feet broad at the bottom, and thirty at the top.

20. The proportions of masts and sails do vary, not only according to the bigness of ships, but also according to the several uses for which they are built: some for fighting, some for merchandise, some for swiftness, &c. But the proportion of the dimension of sails is no way proportioned to the number of tons whereof the ships consist, seeing a ship of five hundred tons, or thereabout, may bear almost as large a sail as the other we speak of, which was almost as big again. Whence it proceeds that lesser ships are far swifter and speedier than great ones, not only by reason of their lightness, but also by reason of the largeness of their sails, in respect of the body of the ship; for to continue that proportion in bigger ships would be too vast and impossible a thing.

21. Each sail being stretched out at the top, and only tied by the corners at the bottom, the wind must needs cause it to swell, especially about the bottom, where it is slacker.

22. The swelling is far greater in the lower sails than in the upper, because they are not only parallelograms, and the other more pointed at the top, but also because the extent of the yard doth so far exceed the breadth of the ship's sides to which they are fastened, that of necessity, because of the looseness, there must be a great receipt for the wind; so that in the great ship which we proposed for an example, the swelling of the sail in a direct wind may be nine or ten feet inward.

23. By the same reason it also happens that all sails which are swelled by the wind, do gather themselves into a kind of arch or bow, so that of necessity much wind must slip through; insomuch, that in such a ship as we made mention of, that arch may be as high as a man.

24. But in the triangular sail of the mizenmast there must of necessity be a lesser swelling than in the quadrangular; as well because that figure is less capable, as, also, because that in the quadrangular three sides are slack and loose, but in the triangular only two, so that the wind is more sparingly received.

25. The motion of the wind in sails, the nearer it comes to the beak of the ship, the stronger it is, and sets the ship more forward, partly because it is in a place where, because of the sharpness of the beak-head, the waves are easilier cut in sunder; but, chiefly, because the motion at the beak draws on the ship; the motion from the stern and back part of the ship doth but drive it.

26. The motion of the winds in the sails of the upper tier advances more than that in the lower tier, because a violent motion is most violent when it is farthest removed from resistance, as in the wings and sails of windmills; but there is danger of drowning or overturning the ship: wherefore those sails are made narrower at the top, that they should not take in too much wind, and are chiefly made use of when there is not much wind.

27. Sails being placed in a direct line, one behind the other, of necessity those sails which stand behind must steal the wind from the foremost when the wind blows foreright; wherefore, if they be all spread out at once, the force of the wind hath scarce any power but in the mainmast sails, with little help of the lower sails of the boarsprit.

28. The best and most convenient ordering of sails, in a direct wind, is to have the two lower sails of the foremast hoisted up, for there (as we said before) the motion is most effectual; let also the topsail of the mainmast be hoisted up, for there will be so much room left under it, that there may be wind sufficient for the foresails, without any notable stealing of the wind from them.

29. By reason of the hinder sails stealing of the wind away from the foresails, we sail swifter with a side wind than with a fore wind. For with a side wind all the sails may be made use of, for they turn their sides to one another, and so hinder nor rob not one another.

30. Likewise, when a side wind blows, the sails are stifflier stretched out against the wind, which somewhat restrains the wind, and sends it that way as it should blow, whereby it gains some strength. But that wind is most advantageous which blows cornerly between a fore wind and a side wind

31. The lower boarsprit-sail can hardly ever be unuseful, for it cannot be robbed from gathering the wind which way soever it doth blow, either about the ship sides, or under the rest of the sails.

32. There is considerable* in the motion of winds in ships, both the impulsion and direction of them. For that direction, which is made by the helm, doth not belong to the present inquisition, but only as it hath a connexion with the motion of the winds in the sails.

Connexion. As the motion of impulsion or driving forward is in force at the beak, so is the motion of direction in the poop; therefore, for that the lower mizenmast sail is of greatest concernment, for it is, as it were, an assistant to the helm.

33. Seeing the compass is divided into two-and-thirty points, so that the semicircles of it are sixteen points, there may be a progressive sailing, (without any casting aboard, which is used when the wind is clean contrary,) though of the sixteen parts there be but six favourable, and the other ten contrary. But that kind of sailing depends much upon the lower sail of the mizenmast. For whilst the adverse parts of the wind, being more powerful and not to be opposed by the helm alone, would turn the other sails, and the ship itself, against its intended course, that sail being stiffly stretched, favouring the helm, and strengthening its motion, turns the beak into the way of its course.

34. All manner of wind in the sails doth somewhat burden and depress the ship, and so much the more when it blows most from above. So that in the greatest storms, first they lower their yards and take away the upper sails, and if need be, all the rest, cut down the masts, cast their goods into the sea, and their ordnance, &c., to lighten the ship and make it swim and give way to the waves.

35. By this motion of the winds in the sails of ships, (if it be a merry and prosperous gale,) a merchant's ship may sail sixscore Italian miles in four-and-twenty hours; for there are certain packet boats which are built a purpose for swiftness, (that are called caravels,) which will go further. But when the wind is clean contrary, they fly to this last refuge, and a very weak one, to go on their course, namely, to proceed sideway, as the wind will suffer them, out of their course, then turn their way again towards their course, and so proceed in an angular way. By which progression (which is less than creeping, for serpents creep on by crooked turnings, but they make angles) they may, in four-and-twenty hours, go fifteen miles' journey.

Greater Observations.

1. This motion of winds in sails of ships hath

* i. e. to be considered.

three chief heads and fountains of its impulsion, or driving forward, from whence it flows and derives; whence also precepts may be taken to increase and strengthen it.

2. The first spring comes from the quantity of the wind which is received; for questionless more wind helps more than less; wherefore the quantity of wind must be carefully procured, which will be done if, like wise householders, we be good husbands, and take care nothing be stolen from us. Wherefore we must be very careful that no wind may be lost.

3. The wind blows either above the ships or below them, to the very superficies and surface of the sea; and as provident men use to look most after the least things, (for the greater no man can choose but look after,) so we will first look after these lower winds, which questionless cannot perform so much as the higher.

4. As concerning the winds which blow chiefly about the sides of the ships, and under their sails, it is the office of the main boarsprit-sail, which lies low and sloping, to gather them into it, that there may be no waste nor loss of wind; and this of itself does good, and hinders not the wind which fills the other sails. And about this I do not see what can be done more by the industry of man, unless they should perchance fix such low sails out of the middle of the ship, like wings or feathers, two on each side when the wind blows right.

5. But, concerning the bewaring of being robbed, which happens when the hinder sails (in a fore-right wind) steal the wind away from the foresails, (for in a side wind all the sails are set a-work,) I know not what can be added to the care man hath already taken to prevent it, unless when there is a fore wind, there may be made a kind of stairs, or scale of sails, that the hindermost sails of the mizzenmast may be the lowest, the middle ones at the mainmast a little higher, the foremast, at the foremast, highest of all, that one sail may not hinder but rather help the other, delivering and passing over the wind from one to another. And let so much be observed of the first fountain of impulsion.

6. The second fountain of impulsion consists in the manner of striking the sail with the wind, which, if through the contraction of the wind it be acute and swift, will move more; if obtuse and languishing, less.

7. As concerning this, it is of great moment, and much to the purpose, to let the sails have a reasonable extension and swelling; for if they be stretched out stiff, they will, like a wall, beat back the wind; if they be too loose, there will be a weak impulsion.

8. Touching this, human industry hath behaved itself well in some things, though it was more by chance than out of any good judgment. For, in a side wind, they gather up that part of the sail as much as they can which is opposite against the wind: and by that means they set in the wind into that part where it should blow. And this they do and intend. But, in the mean season, this follows, (which, peradventure, they do not perceive,) that the wind is more contracted, and strikes more sharply.

9. What may be added to human industry in this, I cannot perceive, unless the figure of the sails be changed, and some sails be made which shall not swell round, but, like a spur or a triangle, with a mast or piece of timber in that corner of the top, that they may contract the wind more sharply, and cut the outward air more powerfully. And that angle (as we suppose) must not be altogether sharp, but like a short obtuse triangle, that it may have some breadth. Neither do we know what good it would do, if there were, as it were, a sail made in a sail; if, in the middle of a greater sail, there were a kind of a purse, not altogether loose, of canvass, but with ribs of wood, which should take up the wind in the middle of the sail, and bring it into a sharpness.

10. The third fountain or original of impulsion, is in the place where the wind hits, and that is twofold; for, from the fore side of the ship the impulsion is easier and stronger than on the hinder part; and from the upper part of the mast and sail than from the lower part.

11. Neither seems the industry of man to have been ignorant of this, when, in a fore-wind, their greatest hopes have been in their foremasts, and in calms they have have not been careless in hoisting up of their topsails. Neither, for the present, do we find what may be added to human industry in this point, unless concerning the first we should set up two or three foremasts, (the first upright and the rest sloping,) whose sails shall hang downward; and, as for the second, that the foresails should be enlarged at the top, and made less sharp than they usually are: but, in both, we must take heed of the inconvenience of danger, in sinking the ship too much.

The Motion of Winds in other Engines of Man's Invention.

1. The motion of windmills hath no subtilty at all in it; and yet, usually, it is not well explained nor demonstrated. The sails are set right and direct opposite against the wind which bloweth. One side of the sail lies to the wind, the other side by little and little bends itself, and gets itself away from the wind. But the turning and continuance of the motion is always caused by the lower part, namely, that which is farthest from the wind. But the wind, overcasting itself against the engine, is contracted and restrained by the four sails, and is constrained to take its way in four spaces. The wind doth not well endure that compression; wherefore, of necessity it must, as it were, with its elbow hit the sides

of the sails, and so turn them, even as little whirligigs that children play withal, are turned with the fingers.

2 If the sails were extended even and equally, it would be doubtful which way the inclination would be, as in the fall of a staff; but when the nearer side which meets with the wind casts the violence of it upon the lower side and from thence into distances, so that when the lower side receives the wind, like the palm of the hand, or the sail of a ship's boat, presently there is a turning on that side. But this is to be observed, that the beginning of the motion proceeds not from the first impulsion, which is direct and abreast, but from the lateral impulsion, which is after the compression or straitening of the wind.

3. We made some proofs and trials about this, for the increasing of this motion, as well to be assured we had found the cause, as also for use; feigning an imitation of this motion, with paper sails, and the wind of a pair of bellows. We, therefore, added to the side of the lower sail a fold turned in from the wind, that the wind being become a side wind might have somewhat more to beat upon, which did no good, that fold not so much assisting the percussion of the wind, as in consequence hindering the cutting of the air. We placed behind the sails, at some distance, certain obstacles as broad as the diameter of all the sails, that the wind being more compressed might hit the stronger; but this did rather hurt than good, the repercussion dulling the primary motion. Then we made the sails of a double breadth, that the wind might be the more restrained, and there might be a stronger lateral percussion, which at last proved very well; so that the conversion was caused by a far milder gale, and did turn a great deal more swiftly.

Mandate. Peradventure this increase of motion might more conveniently be made by eight sails, than by four, doubling the breath, unless too much weight did overburden the motion; which must have trial made of it.

Mandate. Likewise the length of sails doth much conduce to the motion. For in wheelings a slight violence about the circumference is equivalent to a far greater about the centre. But then this inconvenience follows, that the longer the sails are, the more distant they are at the top, and the wind is so much the less straitened. Peradventure the business would go well if the sails were a little longer and broader towards the top, like the outermost end of an oar. But this we are not sure of.

Motion. If these experiments be made trial of in windmills, care must be taken of the windmill posts, and the foundations of it; for the more the wind is restrained, the more it snakes (though it swiftens the motion of the sails) the whole frame of the mill.

4. It is reported that in some countries there are coaches and wagons which move with the wind; but this must be more diligently looked after.

Mandate. Chariots moving by virtue of the wind can be of no use, unless it be in open places and plains; besides, what will be done if the wind allays? It had been better to have thought of easing the motion of wagons and coaches by sails, which might be set up and taken down, to ease the oxen or horses which draw them, rather than to make a motion by wind alone.

Prognostics of Winds.

To the two-and-thirtieth article. Connexion.

The more divination useth to be polluted by vanity and superstition, so much more is the purer part of it to be received and honoured. But natural divination is sometimes more certain, sometimes more slippery and deceitful, according to the subject with which it hath to do; for if it be of a constant and regular nature, it causeth a certain prediction; if it be of a variable and irregular nature, it may make a casual and deceitful one: yet, in a various subject the prediction will hold true, if it be diligently regulated; peradventure it may not hit upon the very moments, but in the thing itself it will not err much. Likewise, for the times of the event and complement, some predictions will hit right enough, namely, those which are not gathered from the causes, but from the thing itself, already inchoated, but sooner appearing in an apt and fitly disposed matter than in another, as we said before in the topics concerning this two-and-thirtieth article. We will now, therefore, set forth the prognostics of winds, of necessity intermixing some of rain and fair weather, which could not conveniently be separated, remitting the full inquiry of them to their proper titles.

1. If the sun appears hollow at its rising, it will the very same-day yield wind or rain; if it appears as it were a little hollow, it signifies wind: if deeply hollow, rain.

2. If the sun rises pale, or (as we call it) waterish, it betokens rain; if it set so, it betokens wind.

3. If the body of the sun itself appears at its setting of the colour of blood, it betokens great winds for many days.

4. If at sunrising its beams appears rather red than yellow, it signifies wind rather than rain, and the like if they appear so at its setting.

5. If at sunrising or setting its rays appear contracted or shortened, and do not shine out bright, though the weather be not cloudy, it signifies rain rather than wind.

6. If before sunrising there appear some rays as forerunners, it signifies both wind and rain.

7. If the sun at its rising diffuses its rays through the clouds, the middle of the sun remaining still under clouds, it shall signify rain, especially if those beams break out downwards, that the sun appears as it were with a beard. But if the rays break forth out of the middle, or dispersed, and its exterior body, or the out parts of it, be covered with clouds, it foreshows great tempests both of wind and rain.

8. If the sun, when it rises, be encompassed with a circle, let wind be expected from that side on which the circle opens. But if the circle fall off all at one time it will be fair weather.

9. If at the setting of the sun there appears a white circle about it, it signifies some small storm the same night; if black or darkness, much wind the day following.

10. If the clouds look red at sunrising, they are prognostics of wind; if at sunsetting, of a fair ensuing day.

11. If about the rising of the sun clouds do gather themselves about it, they foreshow rough storms that day; but if they be driven back from the rising towards the setting of the sun, they signify fair weather.

12. If at sunrising the clouds be dispersed from the sides of the sun, some southward, and some northward, though the sky be clear about the sun, it foreshows wind.

13. If the sun goes down in a cloud, it foreshows rain the next day; but if it rains at sunsetting it is a token of wind rather. But if the clouds seem to be as it were drawn towards the sun, it signifies both wind and storms.

14. If clouds at the rising of the sun seem not to encompass it, but to lie over it, as if they were about to eclipse it, they foreshow the rising of winds on that side as the clouds incline. And if they do this about noon, they signify both wind and rain.

15. If the clouds have encompassed the sun, the less light they leave it, and the lesser the orb of the sun appears, so much the more raging shall the tempest be; but if there appear a double or treble orb, as though there were two or three suns, the tempest will be so much the more violent for many days.

16. New moons presage the dispositions of the air; but especially the fourth rising of it, as if it were a confirmed new moon. The full moons likewise do presage more than the days which come after

17. By long observation the fifth day of the moon is feared by mariners for stormy.

18. If the new moon do not appear before the fourth day, it foreshows a troubled air for the whole month.

19. If the new moon, at her first appearance, or within a few days, have its lower horn obscure or dusky, or any way blemished, it signifies stormy and tempestuous days before the full moon; if it be ill coloured in the middle, tempests will come about the full of the moon; if it be so about the upper part of the horn, they will be about the decreasing of the moon.

20. If at the fourth rising the moon appear bright, with sharp horns, not lying flat, nor standing upright, but in a middle kind of posture between both, it promises fair weather for the most part until the next new moon.

21. If at the same rising it be red, it portends winds; if dusky or black, rain; but, howsoever, it signifies nothing beyond the full moon.

22. An upright moon is almost always threatening and hurtful, but it chiefly portends winds: but if it have blunt horns, and as it were cut off short, it rather signifies rain.

23. If one horn of the moon be sharp and the other blunt, it signifies wind; if both be blunt, rain.

24. If a circle or halo appear about the moon, it signifies rain rather than wind, unless the moon stands directly within that circle, for then it signifies both.

25. Circles about the moon always foreshow winds on that side where they break; also a notable shining in some part of the circle, signifies winds from that part where the shining is.

26. If the circles about the moon be double or treble, they foreshow horrible and rough tempests, and especially if those circles be not whole, but spotted and divided.

27. Full moons, as concerning the colours and circles, do in a manner foreshow the same things, as the fourth rising, but more present, and not so long delayed.

28. Full moons use to be more clear than the other ages of the moon, and in winter use to be far colder.

29. The moon appearing larger at the going down of the sun, if it be splendent and not dusky, betokens fair weather for many days.

30. Winds almost continually follow the eclipses of the moon, and fair weather the eclipses of the sun; rain comes after neither.

31. From the conjunctions of any of the planets, but only the sun, you may expect winds both before and after; from their conjunctions with the sun, fair weather.

32. At the rising of the Pleiades and Hyades come showers of rain, but calm ones; after the rising of Arcturus and Orion, tempests.

33. Returning and shooting stars (as we call them) signify winds to come from that place whence they run, or are shot; but if they fly from several, or contrary parts, it is a sign of great approaching storms of wind and rain.

34. When such little stars as those which are called Aselli are not seen generally all over the sky, it foreshows great tempests and rain within

some few days; but if they be seen in some places, and not in other some, it foreshows winds only, and that suddenly.

25. The sky, when it is all over bright, in a new moon, or at the fourth rising of it, portends fair weather for many days; if it be all over dark, it foreshows rain; if partly dark and partly fair, it portends wind of that side where the darkness is seen; but if it grow dark on a sudden, without either cloud or mist to dim the brightness of the stars, there are great and rough tempests a-breeding.

36. If an entire circle encloseth a planet, or any of the greater stars, it foreshows wind; if it be a broken circle, winds from those parts where the circle is deficient.

37. When the thunder is more than the lightnings, there will be great winds; but if the lightnings be thick amidst the thundering, it foreshows thick showers, with great drops.

38. Morning thunders signify wind; midday thunders, rain.

39. Bellowing thunders, which do as it were pass along, presage winds; and those which make a sharp and unequal noise, presage storms both of wind and rain.

40. When it lightens in a clear sky, winds are at hand, and rain from the part where it lightens; but if it lightens in diverse parts, there will follow cruel and horrid tempests.

41. If it lightens in the cold quarters of the heavens, namely, the east and north, hail will follow; if in the warmer, namely, south and west, we shall have rain and a warm sky.

42. Great heats after the summer solstice, and commonly with thunder and lightning, and if those come not, there will be wind and rain for many days.

43. The globe of flame, which the ancients called Castor, which is seen by mariners and seafaring men at sea, if there be but one, presages a cruel tempest, (Castor is the dead brother,) and much more, if it stick not close to the mast, but dances up and down; but if they be twins, (and Pollux the living brother be present,) and that when the tempest is high, it is a good presage; but if there be three, (namely, if Helen, the plague of all things, come in,) it will be a more cruel tempest: so that one seems to show the indigested matter of the storm; two, a digested and ripe matter; three or more, an abundance that will hardly be dispersed.

44. If we see the clouds drive very fast when it is a clear sky, we must look for winds from that way from which the clouds are driven; but if they wheel and tumble up together, when the sun draws near to that part in which they are tumbled up together, they will begin to scatter and sever; and if they part most towards the north, it betokens wind: if towards the south, rain.

45. If at sunsetting there arise black and dark clouds, they presage rain; if against the sun, namely, in the east, the same night; if near the sun in the west, the next day, with winds.

46. The clearing of a cloudy sky, if it begins against the wind which then blows, signifies clear, fair weather; with the wind it betokens nothing, but the thing remains uncertain.

47. There are sometimes seen several, as it were, chambers, or joined stories of clouds, one above the other, (so as Gilbertus affirms, he hath seen five of them together,) and always the blackest are lowermost, though sometimes it appears otherwise, because the whitest do more allure the sight. A double conjunction of stories, if it be thick, shows approaching rain, (especially if the lower cloud seem, as it were, big with child;) more conjunctions presage continuance of rage.

48. If clouds spread abroad like fleeces of wool here and there, they foreshow tempests; but if they lie one atop of another, like scales or tiles, they presage drought and clear weather.

49. Feathered clouds, like to the boughs of a palm tree, or the flowers of a rainbow, are prognostics of present rain, or immediately to follow.

50. When hills and hillocks look as though they wore caps, by reason of the clouds lying upon them, and encompassing them, it presages imminent tempests.

51. Amber, or gold colour clouds before sunsetting, that have, as it were, gilded helms or borders, after the sun begins to be quite down, foreshow fair, clear weather.

52. Grayish, and, as it were, clay-coloured clouds, show that rain, with wind, are drawing on.

53. Some petty cloud showing itself suddenly, having not been seen before, and all the sky clear about it, especially if it be in the west, and about noon, shows there is a storm a-coming.

54. Clouds and mists ascending, and going upward, presage rain, and that this be done suddenly, so that they be, as it were, sucked up, they presage rain, but if they fall, and reside in the valleys, they presage fair weather.

55. A big cloud growing white, which the ancients called a white tempest, in summer, is a forerunner of small hail, like comfits, in winter, snow.

56. A fair and clear autumn presages a windy winter; a windy winter a rainy spring; a rainy spring, a clear summer; a clear summer, a windy autumn. So that the year (as the proverb goes) is seldom its own debtor, and the same order of seasons will scarce happen two years together.

57. Fires upon the hearth, when they look paler than they are accustomed, and make a murmuring noise within themselves, do presage tempests. And if the flame rises, bending and turning, it signifies wind chiefly; and when the snuffs of lamps and candles grow like mushrooms with broad heads, it is a sign of rainy weather.

58. Coals shining bright, and sparkling overmuch, signify wind.

59. When the superficies of the sea is calm and smooth in the harbour, and yet murmurs within itself, though it doth not swell, signifies wind.

60. The shores resounding in a calm, and the sound of the sea itself, with a clear noise, and a certain echo, heard plainer and further than ordinary, presages winds.

61. If, in a calm and smooth sea, we espy froth here and there, or white circles or bubbles of water, they are prognostics of winds; and if these presages be very apparent, they foreshow rough tempests.

62. If, in a rough sea, there appear a shining froth, (which they call sea-lungs,) it foreshows a lasting tempest for many days.

63. If the sea swell silently, and rises higher than ordinary within the harbour, or the tide come in sooner than it uses to do, it foretells wind.

64. Sound from the hills, and the murmur of woods growing louder, and a noise in open champion fields, portend wind. Also a prodigious murmuring of the element, without thunder, for the most part, presages winds.

65. Leaves and straws playing on the ground, without any breath of wind that can be felt, and the down of plants flying about, feathers swimming and playing upon the water, signify that wind is near at hand.

66. Waterfowls flying at one another, and flying together in flocks, especially sea-mews and gulls, flying from the sea and lakes, and hastening to the banks and shores, especially if they make a noise and play upon dry land, they are prognostics of winds, especially if they do so in the morning.

67. But, contrariwise, sea-fowls going to the water, and beating with their wings, chattering, and bathing themselves, especially the crow, are all presages of storms.

68. Duckers and ducks cleanse their feathers with their bills against the wind; but geese, with their importunate crying, call for rain.

69. A hern flying high, so that it sometimes flies over a low cloud, signifies wind: but kites, when they fly high, foreshow fair weather.

70. Crows, as it were, barking after a sobbing manner, if they continue in it, do presage winds, but if they catchingly swallow up their voice again, or croak a long time together, it signifies that we shall have some showers.

71. A chattering owl was thought by the ancients to foretell change of weather; if it were fair, rain; if cloudy, fair weather. But, with us, the owl making a clear and free noise, for the most part, signifies fair weather, especially in winter.

72. Birds perching in trees, if they fly to their nests, and give over feeding betimes, it presages tempest. But the hern, standing, as it were, sad and melancholy upon the sand, or a crow walking up and down, do presage wind only.

73. Dolphins playing in a calm sea are thought to presage wind from that way they come; and, if they play and throw up water when the sea is rough, they presage fair weather. And most kinds of fishes swimming on the top of the water, and sometimes leaping, do prognosticate wind.

74. Upon the approach of wind, swine will be so terrified and disturbed, and use such strange actions, that country people say that creature only can see the wind, and perceive the horridness of it.

75. A little before the wind spiders work and spin carefully, as if they prudently forestalled the time, knowing that in windy weather they cannot work.

76. Before rain, the sound of bells is heard further off; but before wind it is heard more unequally, drawing near and going further off, as it doth when the wind blows really.

77. Pliny affirms for a certain, that three-leaved grass creeps together, and raises its leaves against a storm.

78. He says likewise, that vessels, which food is put into, will leave a kind of sweat in cupboards, which presage cruel storms.

Munition. Seeing rain and wind have almost a common matter, and seeing always before rain there is a certain condensation of the air, caused by the new air received into the old, as it appears by the sounding of the shores, and the high flight of herns, and other things; and seeing the wind likewise thickens, (but afterward in rain the air is more drawn together, and in winds, contrariwise, it is enlarged,) of necessity winds must have many prognostics common with the rain. Whereof advise with the prognostics of rain, under their own title.

Imitations of Winds.

To the three-and-thirtieth article. Connexion.

If men could be persuaded not to fix their contemplations overmuch upon a propounded subject, and reject others, as it were, by-the-by; and that they would not subtilize about that subject in infinitum, and for the most part unprofitably, they would not be seized with such a stupor as they are; but, transferring their thoughts, and discoursing, would find many things at a distance, which near at hand are hidden. So that, as in the civil law, so we must likewise in the law of nature, we must carefully proceed to semblable things, and such as have a conformity between them.

1. Bellows with men are Æolus his bags, out of which one may take as much as he needeth. And likewise spaces between, and openings of hills, and crooks of buildings, are but, as it were, large bellows. Bellows are most useful either to kindle fire or for musical organs. The manner of the working of bellows is by sucking in of the air-

to shun vacuity, (as they say,) and to send it out by compression

2. We also use hand fans to make a wind, and to cool, only by driving forward of the air softly.

3. The cooling of summer-rooms we spake of in answer to the ninth article. There may other more curious means be found, especially if the air be drawn in somewhere after the manner of bellows, and let out at another place; but those which are now in use have relation only to mere compression.

4. The breath in man's microcosmos, and in other animals, do very well agree with the winds in the greater world; for they are engendered by humours, and alter with moisture as wind and rain doth, and are dispersed and blow freer by a greater heat. And from them that observation is to be transferred to the winds, namely, that breaths are engendered of matter that yields a tenacious vapour, not easy to be dissolved; as beans, pulse, and fruits; which is so likewise in greater winds.

5. In the distilling of vitriol and other minerals which are most windy, they must have great and large receptacles, otherwise they will break.

6. Wind composed of nitre and gunpowder, breaking out and swelling, the flame doth not only imitate but also exceed winds, which blow abroad in the world, unless they be such as are made by thunder.

7. But the forces of it are pressed in, as in human engines, as guns, mines, and powder-houses set on fire. But it hath not yet been tried whether, in open air, a great heap of gunpowder set on fire would raise a wind for certain hours, by the commotion of the air.

8. There lies hidden a flatuous and expansive spirit in quicksilver, so that it doth (in some men's opinions) imitate gunpowder, and a little of it mixed with gunpowder will make the powder stronger. Likewise, the chymists speak the same of gold, that being prepared some way, it will break out dangerously like to thunder; but these things I never tried.

A greater Observation.

The motion of winds is for most things seen, as it were, in a looking-glass, in the motion of waters.

Great winds are inundations of the air, as we see inundations of waters, both through the augmentation of the quantity. As waters either descend from above, or spring out of the earth, so some winds are cast down, and some rise up. As sometimes in rivers there are contrary motions, one of the flowing of the sea, the other of the current of the river, yet both become one motion, by the prevailing of the flood; so, when contrary winds blow, the greater subdues the lesser. As in the currents of the sea, and of some rivers, it sometimes falls out, that the waves above go con-

trary to the waves below; so in the air, when contrary winds blow together, one flies over the other. As there are cataracts of rain within a narrow space, so there are whirlwinds. As waters, however they go forward, yet, if they be troubled, swell up into waves, sometimes ascending, grow up into heaps, sometimes descending, are as it were furrowed; so the winds do the same, but only want the motion of gravity. There are also other similitudes which may be observed and gathered out of those things which have already been inquired about.

Movable Rules concerning Winds.

Connection.

Rules are either particular or general, both with us are movable; for, as yet, we have not affirmed any thing positively. Particular rules may be taken and gathered almost out of every article. We will cull out some general ones, and those but a few, and add thereunto.

1. Wind is no other thing but moved air; but the air itself moved either by a simple impulsion, or by commixion of vapours.

2. Winds, by a simple impulsion, are caused four ways, either by the natural motion of the air, or by expansion of the air in the sun's ways; or by reception of air thorow a sudden cold, or by the compression of the air by external bodies. There may be also a fifth way, by the agitation and concussion of the air by stars. But let these things be a while silent, or be given ear unto with a sparing belief.

3. Of winds which are made by immixion of vapours, the chief cause is the overburdening of the air by air newly made out of vapours, whereby the mass of the air grows bigger, and seeks new room.

4. A small quantity of air added, causeth a great tumour of the air round about it, so that new air out of the resolution of vapours doth confer more to motion than to matter. But the great body of wind consists in the former air, neither doth the new air drive the old air before it, as if they were several bodies, but being both commixed, they desire larger room.

5. When any other beginning of motion concurs, besides the overburdening of the air, it is an accessory which strengtheneth and increaseth that principal, which is the reason that great and violent winds do seldom rise, by the simple overburdening of the air.

6. Four things are accessory to the overburdening of the air. The breathing out of subterraneal places; the casting down out of (as it is called) the middle region of the air; dissipation made out of a cloud, and the mobility and acrimony of the exhalation itself.

7. The motion of the wind is for the most part lateral; but that which is made by mere over-

burdening, is so from the beginning, that which is made by the expiration of the earth, or repercussion from above, a little while after, unless the eruption, or precipitation, or reverberation, be exceeding violent.

8. Air will endure some compression before it be overburdened, and begins to thrust away the adjoining air, by reason whereof all winds are a little thicker than quiet and calm air.

9. Winds are allayed five ways, either by the conjunction of vapours, or by their sublimation, or by transporting them, or by their being spent.

10. Vapours are conjoined, and so the air itself becomes water, four ways, either by abundance aggravating, or by colds condensing, or by contrary winds compelling, or by obstacles reverberating.

11. Both vapours and exhalations, but wind very frequently from vapours. But there is this difference, that winds which are made of vapours do more easily incorporate themselves into pure air, are sooner allayed, and are not so obstinate as those winds which are engendered of exhalations.

12. The manner and several conditions of heat have no less power in the generation of winds, than the abundance or conditions of the matter.

13. The heat of the sun ought to be so proportioned in the generation of winds, that it may raise them, but not in such abundance as that they gather into rain, nor in so small a quantity, that they may be quite shaken off and dispersed.

14. Winds blow from their nurseries, and the nurseries being disposed several ways, divers winds for the most part blow together, but the strongest either quite overthrows, or turns into its current the weakest.

15. Winds are engendered everywhere, from the very superfices of the earth, up into the middle region of the air, the more frequent below, but the stronger above.

16. The countries which have retaining or trade winds, if they be warm, have them warmer than according to the measure of their climate; if they be cold, they have them colder.

A Human Map, or Optatives, with such things as are next to them concerning Winds.

Optatives.

1. To frame and dispose sails of ships in such a manner, that with less wind they might go a greater journey; a thing very useful to shorten journeys by sea, and save charges.

Next. The next invention precisely in practice I have not as yet found; yet, concerning that, look upon our greater observations upon the six-and-twentieth article.

2. *Optative.* That we could make windmills and their sails in such manner that they may grind more with less wind. A thing very useful for gain.

Next. Look concerning this upon our experiments in the answer to the seven-and-twentieth article, where the thing seems to be, as it were done.

3. *Optative.* To foreknow when winds will rise and allay. A thing useful for navigation and for husbandry, especially for the choosing of times for sea-fights.

Next. To this belong many of those things which are observed in the inquisition, and especially in the answer to the two-and-thirtieth article. But a more careful observation hereafter (if any shall apply their mind to it) will give far more exact prognostics, the cause of the winds being already laid open.

4. *Optative.* To give judgment, and make prognostics by winds, of other things, as, first, whether they be continents or islands in the sea in any place, or rather a free, open sea; a thing very useful for new and unknown voyages.

Next. The next is the observation concerning constant and trade winds; that which Columbus seemed to make use of.

5. *Optative.* Likewise of the plenty or scarcity of corn every year. A thing useful for gain, and buying beforehand, and forestalling, as it is reported of Thales, concerning monopoly of olives.

Next. To this belong some things specified in the inquisition of winds, either hurtful or shaking winds, and the times when they do hurt; to the nine-and-twentieth article.

6. *Optative.* Likewise concerning diseases and plagues every year. A thing useful for the credit of physicians, if they can foretell them, also for the causes and cures of diseases, and some other civil considerations.

Next. To this likewise belong some things set down in the inquisition to the thirtieth article.

Monition. Of predictions by wind concerning corn, fruits, and diseases, look upon histories of husbandry and physic.

7. *Optative.* How to raise winds and to allay them.

Next. Concerning these things there are some superstitious opinions, which do not seem worthy to be inserted into a serious and severe natural history. Nor can I think of any thing that is near in this kind. The design may be this, to look thoroughly into and inquire about the nature of the air; whether any thing may be found, whereof a small quantity put into air may raise and multiply the motion to dilatation, or contraction in the body of the air. For out of this (if it might be done) would follow the raisings and allayings of winds. Such as that experiment of Pliny is, concerning vinegar thrown against the whirlwinds, if it were true. Another design might be, by letting forth of winds out of subterraneal places; if so be they should gather together anywhere in great abundance, as it is a common and approved opinion of the well in Dalmatia; but to know such places of prisons, is very hard and difficult.

8. *Optative.* To work many fine, pleasant, and wonderful conceits by the motion of winds.

Next. We have not leisure to enter into consideration touching these things. Next to it is that common report of the duels of winds. Questionless many such pleasant things might very well be found out, both for motions and sounds of winds.

ENTRANCES

TO THE HISTORIES DESTINED FOR THE NEXT FIVE MONTHS.

THE HISTORY OF DENSITY AND RARITY.

THE ENTRANCE.

It is no marvel if nature be indebted to philosophy and the sciences, seeing it was never yet called upon to give an account, for there never was any diligent and dispensatory inquisition made of the quaintity of the matter, and how that had been distributed into bodies, (in some copiously, in others sparingly,) according to the true, or at least truest accounts that hath been truly received and approved of, that nothing is taken away and lost, or added unto the universal sum. Likewise that place hath been treated upon by some, namely, how it can be loosened or contracted without intermixion or vacuity, according to more or less: but the natures of density and rarity, some have referred to the abundance or scarcity of the matter; another hath laughed at the same; the greatest part, following their author, to discuss and compose the whole matter by that cold and weak distinction of act and power. Those also who attribute them to the reasons of matter, (which is the true opinion,) do neither quite deprive the materia prima, or primary matter of its quantum, or quantity, though for other forms they will have it equal, but here do terminate and end the matter, and seek no further, nor do not perceive what followeth thereby; and either do not touch at all, or at least do not urge home that which hath a regard to infinites, and is, as it were, the basis and ground of natural philosophy.

First, therefore, that which is rightly set down must not be moved nor altered; namely, that there is no transaction made in any transmutation of bodies, either from nothing, or to nothing; but that they are works of the same omnipotence, to create out of nothing, and to reduce unto nothing, and that by course of nature this can never be done. Therefore the sum of the total matter stands still whole, nothing is added, nothing is diminished; yet that this sum is divided by portions amongst the bodies is unquestionable, for there can no man be so much beside himself through any subtile abstractions, as to think that there is as much matter in one vessel of water as in ten vessels of water, nor likewise in one vessel of air as much as in ten vessels of air; but in the same body there is no question but that the abundance of matter is multiplied according to the measure of the body, in divers bodies it is questionable. And if it be demonstrated that one vessel of water turned into air will yield ten vessels of air, (for we take this computation for a received opinion, though that of a hundred-fold be the truer,) it is well; for now they are no more divers bodies, water and air, but the same body of air in ten vessels; but one vessel of air (as it was but now granted) is but only the tenth part of ten vessels. Therefore it cannot be contradicted but that in one vessel of water there is ten times more matter than in one vessel of air: therefore, if one should affirm, that one whole vessel of water could be converted into one vessel of air, it were as much as if one should affirm that something could be reduced to nothing; forasmuch as one tenth part of water would suffice to do it, and the other nine parts must of necessity be reduced to nothing; and, contrariwise, if one should affirm that one vessel of air could be turned into a vessel of water, it would be as much as if he should say, that something could be created out of nothing; for one vessel of air can attain and reach but unto the tenth part of a vessel of water, and the other nine parts must needs proceed from nothing. In the mean time we will plainly acknowledge and confess, that to understand the true means of the reasons and calculations of the how much part of the quantum, or how much of the matter which is in divers bodies, and by what industry and sagacity one may be truly informed thereof, is a high matter to be inquired; but such as the great and largely extended profit which will accrue, thereby will largely recompense. For to know the densities and rarities of the body, and much more, how to procure and effect the condensations and rarefactions, is of great importance and moment both to contemplative and to the practice. Seeing, then, it is a thing (if any there be at all) merely fundamental and universal, we must go carefully and prepared about it, seeing that all philosophy without it is loose and disjointed.

THE HISTORY OF HEAVY AND LIGHT.

THE ENTRANCE.

THE motion of gravity and lightness, the ancients did illustrate with the name of natural motion, for they saw no external efficient, nor no apparent resistance; yea, the motion seemed swifter in its progress. This contemplation, or rather speech, they seasoned with that mathematical phantasy of the staying or stopping of heavy things at the centre of the earth, (although the earth should be bored quite thorow,) and that scholastical invention of the motion of bodies to their several places. Having laid, or set down these things, supposing they had done their parts, they looked no further, but only that which some of them more carefully inquired after, namely, of the centre of gravity in divers figures, and of such things as are carried by water. Neither did any of the modern authors do any thing worth speaking of concerning this, only by adding some few mechanical things, which they had also wrested with their demonstrations; but, laying many words aside, it is most certain that a body cannot suffer but by a body; neither can there be any local motion made, unless it be solicited or set forward, either by the parts of the body itself, which is moved, or by the adjacent bodies, which either touch it or are near unto it, or are, at least, within the orb of its activity. So that Gilbertus did not unknowingly introduce magnetic powers, he also becoming a loadstone, namely, drawing more things by those powers than he should have done, and building a ship, as it were, of a round piece of wood.

THE HISTORY OF THE SYMPATHY AND ANTIPATHY OF THINGS.

THE ENTRANCE.

STRIFE and amity in nature, are the eggers on of motions, and the keys of works. Hence proceeds the union and dissension of bodies; hence the mixion and separation of bodies; hence the high and intimate impressions of virtues, and that which they call joining of actives with passives; finally, they are the great and wonderful works of nature. But this part of philosophy, namely, of the sympathy and antipathy of things, is most impure, which also they call natural magic, and. (which always comes to pass,) where diligence and care hath wanted, there hath hope remained; but the operation thereof in men is merely like unto certain soporiferous medicines, which cast one asleep, and do, moreover, send and infuse into him merry and pleasant dreams. For, first, it casts man's understanding into a sleep, representing unto him specific properties and hidden virtues, whereby men awake no more, nor look after the finding and searching out of true causes, but acquiesce and lie still in these idle ways. Then it insinuates an innumerable company of fictions, like unto dreams; and vain men hope to know the nature by the outward shape and show, and, by extrinsical similitudes, to discover inward properties. Their practice, also, is very like unto their inquiry; for the precepts of natural magic are such as if men should be confident that they could subdue the earth, and eat their bread without the sweat of their brow, and to have power over things by idle and easy applications of bodies; and still they have in their mouths, and, like undertakers or sureties, they call upon the loadstone, and the consent which is between gold and quicksilver; and some few things of this kind they allege for to prove other things, which are not bound by any such like contract. But God hath appointed the best of things to be inquired out, and be wrought by labours and endeavours. We will be a little more careful in searching out the law of nature and the mutual contracts of things, neither favouring miracles, nor making too lowly and straitened an inquisition.

THE HISTORY OF SULPHUR, MERCURY, AND SALT.

THE ENTRANCE.

This triple of principles hath been introduced by the chymists, and, as concerning speculatives, is of them which they bring the best invention. The most subtile and acute of these, and those who are most philosophical, will have the elements' to be earth, water, air, and the sky; and those they will not have to be the matter of things, but the matrixes in which the specifical seeds of things do engender in the nature of a matrix. But, for the materia prima, or primary matter, (which scholars do lay down, as it were, naked and indifferent,) they substitute those three, sulphur, mercury, and salt; out of which all bodies are gathered together and mixed. We do accept of their words, but their opinions are not very sound. Yet that doth not ill agree with their opinion, namely, that we hold two of them, to wit, sulphur and mercury, (taken according to our sense,) to be very first and prime natures, and most inward figurations of matter, and almost chief amongst the forms of the first class. But we may vary the words of sulphur and mercury, and name them otherwise, oily, waterish, fat, crude, inflammable, not inflammable, or the like. For these seem to be two very great things of the three, and which possess and penetrate the universe, for, amongst subterraneal things, they are sulphur and mercury, as they are called; in the vegetable and animal kind, they are oil and water; in the inferior spiritual things, they are air and flame; in the heavenly, the body of a star, and the pure sky; but of this last duality we yet say nothing, though it seem to be a probable deciphering; for, if they mean by salt the fixed part of the body which is not resolved either into flame or smoke, this belongeth to the inquisition of fluid and determinate things. But if we take salt according to the letter, without any parabolical meaning, salt is no third thing from sulphur and mercury, but mixed of both, connexed into one by an acrimonious and sharp spirit; for all manner of salt hath inflammable parts, and other parts, also, which not only will not take fire, but do also abhor it and fly from it: yet the inquisition of salt, being somewhat allied to the inquisition of the other two, and exceeding useful as being a tie and band of both natures, sulphureous and salt, and the very rudiment of life itself, we have thought fitting to comprehend it also within this history and inquisition; but, in the mean time, we give you notice, that those spiritual things, air, water, stars, and sky, we do (as they very well deserve it) reserve them for proper and peculiar inquisitions, and here in this place to set down the history only of tangible, that is to say, mineral or vegetable sulphur and mercury.

THE HISTORY OF LIFE AND DEATH.

THE ENTRANCE.

The entrance to this history will be found in the history itself, which follows next in order.

HISTORY,

NATURAL AND EXPERIMENTAL,

OR

LIFE AND DEATH,

OR, OF

THE PROLONGATION OF LIFE.

TO THE READER.

I AM to give advertisement, that there came forth of late a translation of this book by an unknown person, who, though he wished well to the propagating of his lordship's works, yet he was altogether unacquainted with his lordship's style and manner of expressions, and so published a translation lame and defective in the whole. Whereupon, I thought fit to recommend the same to be translated anew, by a more diligent and zealous pen, which hath since travelled in it; and, though it still comes short of that lively and incomparable spirit and expression, which lived and died with the author, yet, I dare avouch it to be much more warrantable and agreeable than the former. It is true, this book was not intended to have been published in English; but, seeing it hath already been made free of that language, whatsoever benefit or delight may redound from it, I commend the same to the courteous and judicious reader. W. R.

TO THE PRESENT AGE, AND POSTERITY.

GREETING:

Although I had ranked the History of Life and Death as the last amongst my six monthly designations, yet I have thought fit, in respect of the prime use thereof, (in which the least loss of time ought to be esteemed precious,) to invert that order, and to send it forth in the second place. For I have hope, and wish, that it may conduce to a common good; and that the nobler sort of physicians will advance their thoughts, and not employ their times wholly in the sordidness of cures, neither be honoured for necessity only, but that they will become coadjutors and instruments of the Divine omnipotence and clemency in prolonging and renewing the life of man; especially, seeing I prescribe it to be done by safe, and convenient, and civil ways, though hitherto unassayed. For, though we Christians do continually aspire and pant after the land of promise, yet it will be a token of God's favour towards us in our journeyings through this world's wilderness, to have our shoes and garments (I mean those of our frail bodies) little worn or impaired.

FR. ST. ALBANS.

THE HISTORY OF LIFE AND DEATH.

THE PREFACE.

It is an ancient saying and complaint, that life is short and art long; wherefore t behoveth us, who make it our chiefest aim to perfect arts, to take upon us the consideration of prolonging man's life, God, the author of all truth and life, prospering our endeavours. For, though the life of man be nothing else but a mass and accumulation of sins and sorrows, and they that look for an eternal life set but light by a temporary: yet the continuation of works of charity ought not to be contemned, even by us Christians. Besides, the beloved disciple of our Lord survived the other disciples; and many of the fathers of the church, especially of the holy monks and hermits, were long-lived; which shows, that this blessing of long life, so often promised in the old law, had less abatement after our Saviour's days than other earthly blessings had; but to esteem of this as the chiefest good, we are but too prone. Only the inquiry is difficult how to attain the same, and so much the rather, because it is corrupted with false opinions and vain reports: for both those things, which the vulgar physicians talk of, radical moisture and natural heat, are but mere fictions; and the immoderate praises of chymical medicines first puff up with vain hopes, and then fail their admirers.

And as for that death which is caused by suffocation, putrefaction, and several diseases, we speak not of it now, for that pertains to a history of physic; but only of that death which comes by a total decay of the body, and the inconcoction of old age. Nevertheless, the last act of death, and the very extinguishing of life itself, which may so many ways be wrought outwardly and inwardly, (which, notwithstanding, have, as it were, one common porch before it comes to the point of death,) will be pertinent to be inquired of in this treatise; but we reserve that for the last place.

Tha. which may be repaired by degrees, without a total waste of the first stock, is potentially eternal, as the vestal fire. Therefore, when physicians and philosophers saw that living creatures were nourished and their bodies repaired, but that this did last only for a time, and afterwards came old age, and in the end dissolution; they sought death in somewhat which could not properly be repaired, supposing a radical moisture incapable of solid reparation, and which, from the first infancy, received a spurious addition, but no true reparation, whereby it grew daily worse and worse, and, in the end, brought the bad to none at all. This conceit of theirs was both ignorant and vain; for all things in living creatures are in their youth repaired entirely; nay, they are for a time increased in quantity, bettered in quality, so as the matter of reparation might be eternal, if the manner of reparation did not fail. But this is the truth of it. There is in the declining of age an unequal reparation; some parts are repaired easily, others with difficulty and to their loss; so as from that time the bodies of men begin to endure the torments of Mezentius: that the living die in the embraces of the dead; and the parts easily repairable, through their conjunction with the parts hardly repairable, do decay; for the spirits, blood, flesh, and fat are, even after the decline of years, easily repaired; but the drier and more porous parts (as the membranes, all the tunicles, the sinews, arteries, veins, bones, cartilages, most of the bowels, in a word, almost all the organical parts) are hardly repairable, and to their loss. Now, these hardly repairable parts, when they come to their office of repairing the other, which are easily repairable, finding themselves deprived of their wanted ability and strength, cease to perform any longer their proper functions. By which means it comes to pass, that in process of time the whole tends to dissolution; and even those very parts which, in their own nature, are with much ease repairable, yet, through the decay of the organs of reparation, can no more receive reparation, but decline, and in the end utterly fail. And the cause of the termination of life is this, for that the spirits, like a gentle flame, continually preying upon bodies, conspiring with the outward air, which is ever sucking and drying of them, do, in time, destroy the whole fabric of the body, as also the particular engines and organs thereof, and make them unable for the work of reparation. These are the true ways of natural death, well and faithfully to be revolved in our minds; for he that knows not the way of nature, how can he succour her or turn her about?

Therefore, the inquisition ought to be twofold; the one touching the consumption or depredation of the body of man, the other touching the reparation and renovation of the same: to the end, that the former may, as much as is possible, be forbidden and restrained, and the latter comforted. The former of these pertains, especially, to the spirits and outward air, by which the depredation and waste is committed; the latter to the whole race of alimentation or nourishment, whereby the renovation or restitution is made. And, as for the former part, touching consumption, this hath many things common with bodies inanimate, or without life. For such things as the native spirit (which is in all tangible bodies, whether living or without life) and the ambient or external air worketh upon bodies inanimate, the same it attempteth upon animate or living bodies; although the vital spirit superadded, doth partly break and bridle those operations, partly exalt, and advance them wonderfully. For it is most manifest that inanimate bodies (most of them) will endure a long time without any reparation; but bodies animate, without food and reparation, suddenly fall and are extinguished, as the fire is. So, then, our inquisition shall be double. *First*, we will consider the body of man as inanimate, and not repaired by nourishment. *Secondly*, as animate, and repaired by nourishment. Thus, having prefaced these things, we come now to the topic-places of inquisition.

THE

PARTICULAR TOPIC-PLACES,

OR

ARTICLES OF INQUISITION TOUCHING LIFE AND DEATH.

1. FIRST, inquire of nature, durable and not durable, in bodies inanimate or without life, as also in vegetables; but that not in a large or just treatise, but as in a brief or summary only.

2. Also inquire diligently of desiccation, arefaction, and consumption of bodies inanimate, and of vegetables, and of the ways and processes by which they are done: and, further, of inhibiting and delaying of desiccation, arefaction, and consumption, and of the conservation of bodies in their proper state : and, again, of the inteneration, emollition, and recovery of bodies to their former freshness, after they be once dried and withered.

Neither need the inquisition touching these things to be full or exact, seeing they pertain rather to their proper title of nature durable; seeing also, they are not principles in this inquisition, but serve only to give light to the prolongation and instauration of life in living creatures. In which (as was said before) the same things come to pass, but in a particular manner. So, from the inquisition touching bodies inanimate, and vegetables, let the inquisition pass on to other living creatures besides man.

3. Inquire touching the length and shortness of life in living creatures, with the due circumstances which make most for their long or short lives.

4. But because the duration of bodies is twofold, one in identity, or the selfsame substance, the other by a renovation or reparation; whereof the former hath place only in bodies inanimate, the latter in vegetables and living creatures, and is perfected by alimentation or nourishment; therefore, it will be fit to inquire of alimentation, and of the ways and progresses thereof: yet this not exactly, (because it pertains properly to the titles of assimilation and alimentation,) but, as the rest, in progress only.

From the inquisition touching living creatures and bodies repaired by nourishment, pass on to the inquisition touching man. And, now being come to the principal subject of inquisition, the inquisition ought to be, in all points, more precise and accurate.

5. Inquire touching the length and shortness of life in men, according to the ages of the world, the several regions, climates, and places of their nativity and habitation.

6. Inquire touching the length and shortness of life in men, according to their races and families, as if it were a thing hereditary; also, according to their complexions, constitutions, and habits of body, their statures, the manner and time of their growth, and the making and composition of their members.

7. Inquire touching the length and shortness of life in men, according to the time of their nativity, but so as you omit, for the present, all astrological observations, and the figures of

heaven under which they were born, only insist upon the vulgar and manifest observations; as, whether they were born in the seventh, eighth, ninth, or tenth month; also, whether by night or by day, and in what month of the year.

8. Inquire touching the length and shortness of life in men, according to their fare, diet, government of their life, exercises, and the like. For, as for the air in which men live, and make their abode, we account that proper to be inquired of in the abovesaid article, touching the places of their habitation.

9. Inquire touching the length and shortness of life in men, according to their studies, their several courses of life, the affections of the mind, and divers accidents befalling them.

10. Inquire, apart, touching those medicines which are thought to prolong life.

11. Inquire touching the signs and prognostics of long and short life, not those which betoken death at hand, (for they belong to a history of physic,) but those which are seen, and may be observed even in health, whether they be physiognomical signs or any other.

Hitherto have been propounded inquisitions touching length and shortness of life, besides the rules of art, and in a confused manner; now we think to add some, which shall be more art-like, and tending to practice, under the name of intentions. Those intentions are generally three; as for the particular distributions of them, we will propound them when we come to the inquisition itself. The three general intentions are the forbidding of waste and consumption, the perfecting of reparation, and the renewing of oldness.

12. Inquire touching those things which conserve and exempt the body of man from arefaction and consumption, at least, which put off and protract the inclination thereunto.

13. Inquire touching those things which pertain to the whole process of alimentation, (by which the body of man is repaired,) that it may be good, and with the best improvement.

14. Inquire touching those things which purge out the old matter, and supply with new; as also which do intenerate and moisten those parts which are already dried and hardened.

But, because it will be hard to know the ways of death, unless we search out and discover the seat or house, or rather den of death, it will be convenient to make inquisition of this thing; yet not of every kind of death, but of those deaths which are caused by want and indigence of nourishment, not by violence, for they are those deaths only which pertain to a decay of nature, and mere old age.

15. Inquire touching the point of death, and the porches of death leading thereunto from all parts, so as that death be caused by a decay of nature, and not by violence.

16. Lastly, because it is behoveful to know the character and form of old age, which will then be best done if you make a collection of all the differences, both in the state and functions of the body, betwixt youth and old age, that by them you may observe what it is that produceth such manifold effects; let not this inquisition be omitted.

17. Inquire diligently touching the differences in the state of the body, and the faculties of the mind in youth and old age; and whether there be any that remain the same, without alteration or abatement, in old age.

Nature durable, and not durable.

To the first article.   The history.

1. Metals are of that long lasting, that men cannot trace the beginnings of them; and when they do decay, they decay through rust, not through perspiration into air; yet gold decays neither way.

2. Quicksilver, though it be a humid and fluid body, and easily made volatile by fire, yet, (as we have observed,) by age alone, without fire, it neither wasteth nor gathereth rust.

3 Stones, especially the harder sort of them, and many other fossils, are of long lasting, and that though they be exposed to the open air; much more if they be buried in the earth. Notwithstanding, stones gather a kind of nitre, which is to them instead of rust. Precious stones and crystals exceed metals in long lasting; but then they grow dimmer and less orient if they be very old.

4. It is observed that stones lying towards the north do sooner decay with age than those that lie towards the south; and that appears manifestly in pyramids, and churches, and other ancient buildings; contrariwise, in iron, that exposed to the south, gathers rust sooner, and that to the north later; as may be seen in the iron bars of windows, and no marvel, seeing in all putrefaction (as rust is) moisture hastens dissolutions; in all simple arefaction, dryness.

5. In vegetables, (we speak of such as are felled, not growing,) the stocks or bodies of harder trees, and the timber made of them, last divers ages. But then there is difference in the bodies of trees: some trees are, in a manner, spongy, as the elder, in which the pith in the midst is soft, and the outward part harder; but in timber trees, as the oak, the inner part (which they call heart of oak) lasteth longer.

6. The leaves, and flowers, and stalks of plants are but of short lasting, but dissolve into dust, unless they putrefy; the roots are more durable.

7. The bones of living creatures last long, as we may see it of men's bones in charnel-houses; horns, also, last very long; so do teeth, as it is seen in ivory, and the sea-horse teeth.

8. Hides, also, and skins, endure very long, as is evident in old parchment books: paper, like-

wise will last many ages, though not so long as parchment.

9. Such things as have passed the fire last long, as glass and bricks; likewise flesh and fruits that have passed the fire, last longer than raw; and that not only because the baking of the fire forbids putrefaction, but also because the watery humour being drawn forth, the oily humour supports itself the longer.

10. Water of all liquors is soonest drunk up by air; contrariwise, oil latest; which we may see not only in the liquors themselves, but in the liquors mixed with other bodies; for paper wet with water, and so getting some degree of transparency, will soon after wax white, and lose the transparency again, the watery vapour exhaling; but oiled paper will keep the transparency long, the oil not being apt to exhale; and, therefore, they that counterfeit men's hands will lay the oiled paper upon the writing they mean to counterfeit, and then essay to draw the lines.

11. Gums, all of them, last very long; the like do wax and honey.

12. But the equal or unequal use of things conduceth no less to long lasting, or short lasting, than the things themselves; for timber, and stones, and other bodies standing continually in the water, or continually in the air, last longer than if they were sometimes wet, sometimes dry; and so stones continue longer if they be laid towards the same coast of heaven in the building that they lay in the mine. The same is of plants removed, if they be coasted just as they were before.

Observations.

(1.) Let this be laid for a foundation, which is most sure, that there is in every tangible body a spirit, or body pneumatical, enclosed and covered with the tangible parts; and that from this spirit is the beginning of all dissolution and consumption, so as the antidote against them is the detaining of this spirit.

(2.) This spirit is detained two ways; either by a straight enclosure, as it were, in a prison, or by a kind of free and voluntary detention. Again, this voluntary stay is persuaded two ways: either if the spirit be not too movable or eager to depart, or if the external air importune it not too much to come forth. So then, two sorts of substances are durable, hard substances and oily: hard substance binds in the spirits close; oily, partly enticeth the spirit to stay, partly is of that nature that it is not importuned by air; for air is consubstantial to water, and flame to oil; and touching nature durable and not durable in bodies inanimate, thus much.

The History.

13. Herbs of the colder sort die yearly, both in root and stalk, as lettuce, purslane; also wheat, and all kind of corn; yet there are some cold herbs which will last three or four years, as the violet, strawberry, burnet, primrose, and sorrel. But borage and bugloss, which seem so alike when they are alive, differ in their deaths; for borage will last but one year, bugloss will last more.

14. But many hot herbs bear their age and years better; hyssop, thyme, savory, pot marjoram, balm, wormwood, germander, sage, and the like. Fennel dies yearly in the stalk, buds again from the root; but pulse and sweet marjoram can better endure age than winter, for being set in a very warm place and well fenced, they will live more than one year. It is known that a knot of hyssop twice a year shorn hath continued forty years.

15. Bushes and shrubs live threescore years, and some double as much. A vine may attain to threescore years, and continue fruitful in the old age. Rosemary well placed will come also to threescore years: but whitethorn and ivy endure above a hundred years. As for the bramble, the age thereof is not certainly known, because bowing the head to the ground it gets new roots, so as you cannot distinguish the old from the new.

16. Amongst great trees the longest livers are the oak, the holm, wild ash, the elm, the beech tree, the chestnut, the plane tree, ficus ruminalis, the lote tree, the wild olive, the palm tree, and the mulberry tree. Of these some have come to the age of eight hundred years; but the least livers of them do attain to two hundred.

17. But trees odorate, or that have sweet woods, and trees rozenny, last longer in their woods or timber than those abovesaid, but they are not so long-lived as the cypress tree, maple, pine, box, juniper. The cedar being borne out by the vastness of his body, lives well near as long as the former.

18. The ash, fertile and forward in bearing, reacheth to a hundred years and somewhat better; which also the birch, maple, and service tree sometimes do; but the poplar, lime tree, willow, and that which they call the sycamore, and walnut tree, live not so long.

19. The apple tree, pear tree, plum tree, pomegranate tree, citron tree, medlar tree, black cherry tree, cherry tree, may attain to fifty or sixty years; especially if they be cleansed from the moss wherewith some of them are clothed.

20. Generally greatness of body in trees, if other things be equal, hath some congruity with length of life; so hath hardness of substance; and trees bearing mast or nuts are commonly longer livers than trees bearing fruit or berries; likewise trees putting forth their leaves late, and shedding them late again, live longer than those that are early either in leaves or fruit; the like is of wild trees in comparison of orchard trees. And, lastly, in the same kind trees that bear a sour fruit outlive those that bear a sweet fruit.

An Observation.

Aristotle noted well the difference between plants and living creatures, in respect of their nourishment and reparation: namely, that the bodies of living creatures are confined within certain bounds, and that after they become to their full growth, they are continued and preserved by nourishment, but they put forth nothing new except hair and nails, which are counted for no better than excrements; so as the juice of living creatures must of necessity sooner wax old; but in trees, which put forth yearly new boughs, new shoots, new leaves, and new fruits, it comes to pass that all these parts in trees are once a year young and renewed. Now, it being so, that whatsoever is fresh and young draws the nourishment more lively and cheerfully to it than that which is decayed and old, it happens withal, that the stock and body of the tree, through which the sap passeth to the branches, is refreshed and cheered with a more bountiful and vigorous nourishment in the passage than otherwise it would have been. And this appears manifest (though Aristotle noted it not, neither hath he expressed these things so clearly and perspicuously) in hedges, copses, and pollards, when the plashing, shedding, or lopping, comforteth the old stem or stock, and maketh it more flourishing and long-lived.

Desiccation, Prohibiting of Desiccation, and Inteneration of that which is desiccated and dried.

To the second article. The History.

1. Fire and strong heats dry some things and melt others.

> "Limus ut hic durescit, et hæc ut cera liquescit,
> Uno eodemque igne?"

How this clay is hardened, and how this wax is melted, with one and the same thing, fire? It drieth earth, stones, wood, cloth, and skins, and whatsoever is not liquifiable; and it melteth metals, wax, gums, butter, tallow, and the like.

2. Notwithstanding, even in those things which the fire melteth, if it be very vehement and continueth, it doth at last dry them. For metal in a strong fire, (gold only excepted,) the volatile part being gone forth, will become less ponderous and more brittle; and those oily and fat substances in the like fire will burn up, and be dried and parched.

3. Air, especially open air, doth manifestly dry, but not melt; as highways, and the upper part of the earth, moistened with showers, are dried; linen clothes washed, if they be hanged out in the air, are likewise dried; herbs, and leaves, and flowers, laid forth in the shade, are dried. But much more suddenly doth the air this, if it be either enlightened with the sunbeams, (so that they cause no putrefaction,) or if the air be stirred, as when the wind bloweth, or in rooms open on all sides.

4. Age most of all, but yet slowest of all, drieth; as in all bodies which (if they be not prevented by putrefaction) are dry with age. But age is nothing of itself, being only the measure of time; that which causeth the effect is the native spirit of bodies, which sucketh up the moisture of the body, and then, together with it, flieth forth, and the air ambient, which multiplieth itself upon the native spirits and juices of the body, and preyeth upon them.

5. Cold, of all things, most properly drieth; for drying is not caused but by contraction; now, contraction is the proper work of cold. But, because we men have heat in a high degree, namely, that of fire, but cold in a very low degree, no other than that of winter, or perhaps of ice, or of snow, or of nitre; therefore, the drying caused by cold is but weak, and easily resolved. Notwithstanding we see the surface of the earth to be more dried by frost or by March winds than by the sun, seeing the same wind both licketh up the moisture, and affecteth with coldness.

6. Smoke is a drier, as in bacon and neats' tongues, which are hanged up in the chimneys; and perfumes of olibanum or lignum aloes, and the like, dry the brain and cure catarrhs.

7. Salt, after some reasonable continuance, drieth not only on the outside, but in the inside also, as in flesh and fish salted, which, if they have continued any long time, have a manifest hardness within.

8. Hot gums applied to the skin dry and wrinkle it, and some astringent waters also do the same.

9. Spirit of strong waters imitateth the fire in drying, for it will both poach an egg put into it and toast bread.

10. Powders dry like sponges by drinking up the moisture, as it is in sand thrown upon lines new written; also, smoothness and politeness of bodies (which suffer not the vapour of moisture to go in by the pores) dry by accident, because it exposeth it to the air, as it is seen in precious stones, looking-glasses, and blades of swords, upon which if you breathe, you shall see at first a little mist, but soon after it vanisheth like a cloud. And thus much for desiccation or drying.

11. They use at this day, in the east parts of Germany, garners in vaults under ground, wherein they keep wheat and other grains, laying a good quantity of straw both under the grains and about them, to save them from the dampness of the vault, by which device they keep their grains twenty or thirty years. And this doth not only preserve them from fustiness, but (that which pertains more to the present inquisition) preserves them also in that greenness that they are fit and serviceable to make bread. The same is reported to have been in use in Cappadocia and Thracia, and some parts of Spain.

12. The placing of garners on the tops of

houses, with windows towards the east and north, is very commodious. Some, also, make two sollars, an upper and a lower, and the upper sollar hath a hole in it, through which the grain continually descendeth, like sand in an hourglass, and after a few days they throw it up again with shovels, that so it may be in continual motion. Now, it is to be noted that this doth not only prevent the fustiness, but conserveth the greenness, and slacketh the desiccation of it. The cause is that which we noted before; that the discharging of the watery humour, which is quickened by the motion and the winds, preserves the oily humour in his being, which otherwise would fly out together with the watery humour. Also, in some mountains, where the air is very pure, dead carcasses may be kept for a good while without any great decay.

13. Fruits, as pomegranates, citrons, apples, pears, and the like; also, flowers, as roses and lilies, may be kept a long time in earthen vessels close stopped; howsoever, they are not free from the injuries of the outward air, which will affect them with his unequal temper through the sides of the vessel, as it is manifest in heat and cold. Therefore, it will be good to stop the mouths of the vessels carefully, and to bury them within the earth; and it will be as good not to bury them in the earth, but to sink them in the water, so as the place be shady, as in wells or cisterns placed within doors; but those that be sunk in water will do better in glass vessels than in earthen.

14. Generally, those things which are kept in the earth, or in vaults under ground, or in the bottom of a well, will preserve their freshness longer than those things that are kept above ground.

15. They say it hath been observed, that in conservatories of snow, (whether they were in mountains, in natural pits, or in wells made by art for that purpose,) an apple, or chestnut, or nut, by chance falling in, after many months, when the snow hath melted, hath been found in the snow as fresh and fair as if it had been gathered the day before.

16. Country people keep clusters of grapes in meal, which, though it makes them less pleasant to the taste, yet it preserves their moisture and freshness. Also the harder sort of fruits may be kept long, not only in meal, but also in sawdust and in heaps of corn.

17. There is an opinion held, bodies may be preserved fresh in liquors of their own kind, as in their proper menstrua, as to keep grapes in wine, olives in oil.

18. Pomegranates and quinces are kept long, being lightly dipped in sea water or salt water, and some after taken out again, and then dried in the open air, so it be in the shade.

19. Bodies put in wine, oil, or the lees of oil, keep long, much more in honey or spirit of wine, but most of all, as some say, in quicksilver.

20. Fruits enclosed in wax, pitch, plaster, paste, or any the like case or covering, keep green very long.

21. It is manifest that flies, spiders, ants, or the like small creatures, falling by chance into amber, or the gums of trees, and so finding a burial in them, do never after corrupt or rot, although they be soft and tender bodies.

22. Grapes are kept long by being hanged up in bunches; the same is of other fruits. For there is a twofold commodity of this thing; the one, that they are kept without pressing or bruising, which they must needs suffer, if they were laid upon any hard substance; the other, that the air doth encompass them on every side alike.

23. It is observed that putrefaction, no less than desiccation in vegetables, doth not begin in every part alike, but chiefly in that part where, being alive, it did attract nourishment. Therefore some advise to cover the stalks of apples or other fruits with wax or pitch.

24. Great wicks of candles or lamps do sooner consume the tallow or oil than lesser wicks; also wicks of cotton sooner than those of rush or straw, or small twigs; and in staves of torches, those of juniper or fir sooner than those of ash; likewise flame moved and fanned with the wind sooner than that which is still. And, therefore, candles set in a lantern will last longer than in the open air. There is a tradition, that lamps set in sepulchres will last an incredible time.

25. The nature also and preparation of the nourishment conduceth no less to the lasting of lamps and candles, than the nature of the flame; for wax will last longer than tallow, and tallow a little wet longer than tallow dry, and wax candles old made longer than wax candles new made.

26. Trees, if you stir the earth about their root every year, will continue less time; if once in four or perhaps in ten years, much longer; also cutting off the suckers and young shoots will make them live the longer; but dunging them, or laying of marl about their roots, or much watering them, adds to their fertility, but cuts off from their long lasting. And thus much touching the prohibiting of desiccation or consumption.

27. The inteneration or making tender of that which is dried (which is the chief matter) affords but a small number of experiments. And therefore some few experiments which are found in living creatures, and also in man, shall be joined together.

28. Bands of willow, wherewith they use to bind trees, laid in water, grow more flexible; likewise they put boughs of birch (the ends of them) in earthen pots filled with water, to keep

them from withering; and bowls cleft with dryness steeped in water close again.

29. Boots grown hard and obstinate with age, by greasing them before the fire with tallow, wax soft, or being only held before the fire, get some softness. Bladders and parchments hardened also become tender with warm water mixed with tallow or any fat thing, but much the better if they be a little chafed.

30. Trees grown very old, that have stood long without any culture, by digging and opening the earth about the roots of them, seem to grow young again, and put forth young branches.

31. Old draught oxen worn out with labour, being taken from the yoke, and put into fresh pasture, will get young and tender flesh again; insomuch that they will eat as fresh and tender as a steer.

32. A strict emaciating diet of guiacum, biscuit, and the like, (wherewith they use to cure the French pox, old catarrhs, and some kind of dropsies,) doth first bring men to great poverty and leanness, by wasting the juices and humours of the body, which after they begin to be repaired again seem manifestly more vigorous and young. Nay, and I am of opinion, that emaciating diseases afterwards well cured have advanced many in the way of long life.

Observations.

1. Men see clearly, like owls, in the night of their own notions, but in experience, as in the daylight, they wink, and are but half-sighted. They speak much of the elementary quality of siccity or dryness, and of things desiccating, and of the natural periods of bodies in which they are corrupted and consumed; but meanwhile, either in the beginnings, or middle passages, or last acts of desiccation and consumption, they observe nothing that is of moment.

2. Desiccation or consumption in the process thereof is finished by three actions; and all these (as was said before) have their original from the native spirit of bodies.

3. The first action is the attenuation of the moisture into spirit; the second is, the issuing forth or flight of the spirit; the third is, the contraction of the grosser parts of the body immediately after the spirit issued forth. And this last is, that desiccation and induration, which we chiefly handle, the former two consume only.

4. Touching attenuation, the matter is manifest: for the spirit which is enclosed in every tangible body forgets not its nature, but whatsoever it meets withal in the body (in which it is enclosed) that it can digest and master, and turn into itself, that it plainly alters and subdues, and multiplies itself upon it, and begets new spirit. And this evicted by one proof, instead of many; for that those things which are thoroughly dried are lessened in their weight, and become hollow, porous, and resounding from within. Now it is most certain, that the inward spirit of any thing confers nothing to the weight, but rather lightens it; and therefore it must needs be, that the same spirit hath turned into it the moisture and juice of the body which weighed before, by which means the weight is lessened. And this is the first action, the attenuation of the moisture and converting it into spirit.

5. The second action, which is the issuing forth or flight of the spirit, is as manifest also. For that issuing forth, when it is in throngs, is apparent even to the sense, in vapours to the sight, in odours to the smelling; but if it issueth forth slowly, (as when a thing is decayed by age,) then it is not apparent to the sense, but the matter is the same. Again, where composure of the body is either so strait, or so tenacious, that the spirit can find no pores or passages by which to depart, then in the striving to get out, it drives before it the grosser parts of the body, and protrudes them beyond the superfices or surface of the body; as it is in the rust of metals, and mould of all fat things. And this is the second action, the issuing forth or flight of the spirit.

6. The third action is somewhat more obscure, but full as certain; that is, the contraction of the grosser parts after the spirit issued forth. And this appears, first, in that bodies after the spirit issued forth do manifestly shrink, and fill a less room, as it is in the kernels of nuts, which after they are dried, are too little for the shells: and in beams and planchers of houses, which at first lay close together, but after they are dried give, and likewise in bowls, which through drought grow full of crannies, the parts of the bowl contracting themselves together, and after contraction must needs be empty spaces. Secondly, it appears by the wrinkles of bodies dried; for the endeavour of contracting itself is such, that by the contraction it brings the parts nearer together, and so lifts them up; for whatsoever is contracted on the sides, is lifted up in the midst: and this is to be seen in papers and old parchments, and in the skins of living creatures, and in the coats of soft cheeses, all which with age gather wrinkles. Thirdly, this contraction shows itself most in those things which by heat are not only wrinkled, but ruffled and plighted, and, as it were, rolled together, as it is in papers, and parchments, and leaves, brought near the fire; for contraction by age, which is more slow, commonly causeth wrinkles, but contraction by the fire, which is more speedy, causeth plighting. Now in most things where it comes not to wrinkling or plighting, there is simple contraction, and angustiation or straitening, and induration or hardening, and desiccation, as was showed in the first place. But if the issuing forth of the spirit, and absumption or waste of the moisture

be so great that there is not left body sufficient to unite and contract itself, then of necessity contraction must cease, and the body become putrid, and nothing else but a little dust cleaving together, which with a light touch is dispersed, and falleth asunder; as it is in bodies that are rotten, and in paper burnt, and linen made into tinder, and carcasses embalmed after many ages. And this is the third action, the contraction of the grosser parts after the spirit issueth forth.

7. It is to be noted, that fire and heat dry only by accident, for their proper work is to attenuate and dilate the spirit and moisture, and then it follows by accident that the other parts should contract themselves, either for the flying of vacuum alone, or for some other motion withal, whereof we now speak not.

· 8. It is certain that putrefaction taketh its original from the native spirit, no less than arefaction, but it goeth on a far different way; for in putrefaction, the spirit is not simply vapoured forth, but being detained in part, works strange garboils, and the grosser parts are not so much locally contracted, as they congregate themselves to parts of the same nature.

Length and Shortness of Life in living Creatures.

To the first article. The history.

Touching the length and shortness of life in living creatures, the information which may be had is but slender, observation is negligent, and tradition fabulous. In tame creatures their degenerate life corrupteth them, in wild creatures their exposing to all weathers often intercepteth them; neither do those things which may seem concomitants give any furtherance to this information, (the greatness of their bodies, their time of bearing in the womb, the number of their young ones, the time of their growth, and the rest,) in regard that these things are intermixed, and sometimes they concur, sometimes they sever.

1. Man's age (as far as can be gathered by any certain narration) doth exceed the age of all other living creatures, except it be of a very few only, and the concomitants in him are very equally disposed, his stature and proportion large, his bearing in the womb nine months, his fruit commonly one at a birth, his puberty at the age of fourteen years, his time of growing till twenty.

2. The elephant, by undoubted relation, exceeds the ordinary race of man's life, but his bearing in the womb the space of ten years is fabulous; of two years, or at least above one, is certain. Now, his bulk is great, his time of growth until the thirtieth year, his teeth exceeding hard, neither hath it been observed that his blood is the coldest of all creatures; his age hath sometimes reached to two hundred years.

3. Lions are accounted long livers, because many of them have been found toothless, a sign

not so certain, for that may be caused by their strong breath.

4. The bear is a great sleeper, a dull beast, and given to ease, and yet not noted for long life; nay, he has this sign of short life, that his bearing in the womb is but short, scarce full forty days.

5. The fox seems to be well disposed in many things for long life; he is well skinned, feeds on flesh, lives in dens, and yet he is noted not to have that property. Certainly he is a kind of dog, and that kind is but short-lived.

6. The camel is a long liver, a lean creature, and sinewy; so that he doth ordinarily attain to fifty, and sometimes to a hundred years.

7. The horse lives but to a moderate age, scarce to forty years, his ordinary period is twenty years. but, perhaps, he is beholden for this shortness of life to man; for we have now no horses of the sun that live freely, and at pleasure, in good pastures; notwithstanding, the horse grows till he be six years old, and is able for generation in his old age. Besides, the mare goeth longer with her young one than a woman, and brings forth two at a burden more rarely. The ass lives commonly to the horse's age, but the mule outlives them both.

8. The hart is famous amongst men for long life, yet not upon any relation that is undoubted. They tell of a certain hart that was found with a collar about his neck, and that collar hidden with fat. The long life of the hart is the less credible. because he comes to his perfection at the fifth year, and not long after his horns (which he sheds and renews yearly) grow more narrow at the root, and less branched.

9. The dog is but a short liver, he exceeds not the age of twenty years, and, for the most part, lives not to fourteen years; a creature of the hottest temper, and living in extremes, for he is commonly either in vehement motion, or sleeping; besides, the bitch bringeth forth many at a burden, and goeth nine weeks.

10. The ox likewise, for the greatness of his body and strength, is but a short liver, about some sixteen years, and the males live longer than the females: notwithstanding, they bear usually but one at a burden, and go nine months; a creature dull, fleshy, and soon fatted, and living only upon herby substances, without grain.

11. The sheep seldom lives to ten years, though he be a creature of a moderate size, and excellently clad; and, that which may seem a wonder, being a creature with so little a gall, yet he hath the most curled coat of any other, for the hair of no creature is so much curled as wool is. The rams generate not before the third year, and continue able for generation until the eighth. The ewes bear young as long as they live. The sheep is a diseased creature, and rarely lives to his full age.

12. The goat lives to the same age with the sheep, and is not much unlike in other things, though he be a creature more nimble, and of somewhat a firmer flesh, and so should be longer lived; but then he is much more lascivious, and that shortens his life.

13. The sow lives to fifteen years, sometimes to twenty; and though it be a creature of the moistest flesh, yet that seems to make nothing to length of life. Of the wild boar, or sow, we have nothing certain.

14. The cat's age is betwixt six and ten years; a creature nimble and full of spirit, whose seed (as Ælian reports) burneth the female; whereupon, it is said, that the cat conceives with pain, and brings forth with ease. A creature ravenous in eating, rather swallowing down his meat whole than feeding.

15. Hares and coneys attain scarce to seven years, being both creatures generative, and with young ones of several conceptions in their bellies. In this they are unlike, that the coney lives under ground, and the hare above ground. And, again, that the hare is of a more duskish flesh.

16. Birds, for the size of their bodies, are much lesser than beasts; for an eagle or swan is but a small thing in comparison of an ox or horse, and so is an ostrich to an elephant.

17. Birds are excellently well clad, for feathers, for warmth and close sitting to the body, exceed wool and hairs.

18. Birds, though they hatch many young ones together, yet they bear them not all in their bodies at once, but lay their eggs by turns, whereby their fruit hath the more plentiful nourishment whilst it is in their bodies.

19. Birds chew little or nothing, but their meat is found whole in their crops, notwithstanding, they will break the shells of fruit and pick out the kernels; they are thought to be of a very hot and strong concoction.

20. The motion of birds in their flying, is a mixed motion, consisting of a moving of the limbs, and of a kind of carriage, which is the most wholesome kind of exercise.

21. Aristotle noted well touching the generation of birds, (but he transferred it ill to other living creatures,) that the seed of the male confers less to generation than the female, but that it rather affords activity than matter; so that fruitful eggs and unfruitful eggs are hardly distinguished.

22. Birds (almost all of them) come to their full growth the first year, or a little after. It is true, that their feathers, in some kinds, and their bills, in others, show their years; but, for the growth of their bodies, it is not so.

23. The eagle is accounted a long liver, yet his years are not set down; and, it is alleged, as a sign of his long life, that he casts his bill, whereby he grows young again; from whence comes that old proverb, the old age of an eagle. Notwithstanding, perchance, the matter may be thus, that the renewing of the eagle doth not cast his bill, but the casting of his bill is the renewing of the eagle; for, after that his bill is drawn to a great crookedness, the eagle feeds with much difficulty.

24. Vultures are also affirmed to be long livers, insomuch that they extend their life well near to a hundred years. Kites likewise, and so all birds that feed upon flesh, and birds of prey, live long. As for hawks, because they lead a degenerate and servile life, for the delight of men, the term of their natural life is not certainly known; notwithstanding, amongst mewed hawks, some have been found to have lived thirty years, and amongst wild hawks, forty years.

25. The raven, likewise, is reported to live long, sometimes to a hundred years. He feeds on carrion, and flies not often, but rather is a sedentary and melancholic bird, and hath very black flesh. But the crow, like unto him in most things, (except in greatness and voice,) lives not altogether so long, and yet is reckoned amongst the long livers.

26. The swan is certainly found to be a long liver, and exceeds not unfrequently a hundred years. He is a bird excellently plumed, a feeder upon fish, and is always carried, and that in running waters.

27. The goose also may pass amongst the long livers, though his food be commonly grass, and such kind of nourishment, especially the wild goose; whereupon this proverb grew amongst the Germans, Magis senex quam anser nivalis; older than a wild goose.

28. Storks must needs be long livers, if that be true which was anciently observed of them, that they never came to Thebes, because that city was often sacked. This, if it were so, then either they must have the knowledge of more ages than one, or else the old ones must tell their young the history. But there is nothing more frequent than fables.

29. For fables do so abound touching the phœnix, that the truth is utterly lost, if any such bird there be. As for that which was so much admired, that she was ever seen abroad with a great troop of birds about her, it is no such wonder; for the same is usually seen about an owl flying in the daytime, or a parrot let out of a cage.

30. The parrot hath been certainly known to have lived threescore years in England, how old soever he was before he was brought over; a bird eating almost all kinds of meats, chewing his meat, and renewing his bill: likewise curst and mischievous, and of a black flesh.

31. The peacock lives twenty years, but he comes not forth with his argus eyes before he be three years old; a bird slow of pace, having whitish flesh.

32. The dunghill cock is venereous, martial, and but of a short life; a crank bird, having also white flesh.

33. The Indian cock, commonly called the turkey cock, lives not much longer than the dunghill cock; an angry bird, and hath exceeding white flesh.

34. The ringdoves are of the longest sort of livers, insomuch that they attain sometimes to fifty years of age; an airy bird, and both builds and sits on high. But doves and turtles are but short-lived, not exceeding eight years.

35. But pheasants and partridges may live to sixteen years. They are great breeders, but not so white of flesh as the ordinary pullen.

36. The blackbird is reported to be, amongst the lesser birds, one of the longest livers; an unhappy bird, and a good singer.

37. The sparrow is noted to be of a very short life; and it is imputed in the males to their lasciviousness. But the linnet, no bigger in body than the sparrow, hath been observed to have lived twenty years.

38. Of the ostrich we have nothing certain; those that were kept here have been so unfortunate, but no long life appeared by them. Of the bird ibis we find only that he liveth long, but his years are not recorded.

39. The age of fishes is more uncertain than that of terrestrial creatures, because living under the water they are the less observed; many of them breathe not, by which means their vital spirit is more closed in; and, therefore, though they receive some refrigeration by their gills, yet that refrigeration is not so continual as when it is by breathing.

40. They are free from the desiccation and depredation of the air ambient, because they live in the water, yet there is no doubt but the water, ambient, and piercing, and received into the pores of the body, doth more hurt to long life than the air doth.

41. It is affirmed, too, that their blood is not warm. Some of them are great devourers, even of their own kind. Their flesh is softer and more tender than that of terrestrial creatures; they grow exceedingly fat, insomuch that an incredible quantity of oil will be extracted out of one whale.

42. Dolphins are reported to live about thirty years; of which thing a trial was taken in some of them by cutting off their tails: they grow until ten years of age.

43. That which they report of some fishes is strange, that after a certain age their bodies will waste and grow very slender, only their head and tail retaining their former greatness.

44. There were found in Cæsar's fishponds lampreys to have lived threescore years; they were grown so familiar with long use, that Crassus, the orator, solemnly lamented one of them.

45. The pike, amongst fishes living in fresh water, is found to last longest, sometimes to forty years; he is a ravener, of a flesh somewhat dry and firm.

46. But the carp, bream, trench, eel, and the like, are not held to live above ten years.

47. Salmons are quick of growth, short of life; so are trouts; but the perch is slow of growth, long of life.

48. Touching that monstrous bulk of the whale or ork, how long it is weiled by vital spirit, we have received nothing certain; neither yet touching the sea-calf, and sea-hog, and other innumerable fishes.

49. Crocodiles are reported to be exceeding long-lived, and are famous for the times of their growth, for that they, amongst all other creatures, are thought to grow during their whole life. They are of those creatures that lay eggs, ravenous, cruel, and well fenced against the waters. Touching the other kinds of shell-fish, we find nothing certain how long they live.

Observation.

To find out a rule touching length and shortness of life in living creatures is very difficult, by reason of the negligence of observations, and the intermixing of causes. A few things we will set down.

1. There are more kinds of birds found to be long-lived than of beasts; as the eagle, the vulture, the kite, the pelican, the raven, the crow, the swan, the goose, the stork, the crane, the bird called the ibis, the parrot, the ringdove, with the rest, though they come to their full growth within a year, and are less of bodies; surely their clothing is excellent good against the distemperatures of the weather; and, besides, living for the most part in the open air, they are like the inhabitants of pure mountains, which are long-lived. Again, their motion, which (as I elsewhere said) is a mixed motion, compounded of a moving of their limbs and of a carriage in the air, doth less weary and wear them, and it is more wholesome. Neither do they suffer any compression or want of nourishment in their mother's bellies, because the eggs are laid by turns. But the chiefest cause of all I take to be is this, that birds are made more of the substance of the mother than of the father, whereby their spirits are not so eager and hot.

2. It may be a position, that creatures which partake more of the substance of their mother than of their father, are long-lived, as birds are, which was said before. Also, that those which have a longer time of bearing in the womb, do partake more of the substance of their mother, less of the father, and so are longer lived; insomuch, that I am of opinion, that even amongst men, (which I have noted in some,) those that resemble their mothers most are longest lived; and so are the children of old men begotten of young wives, if the fathers be sound, not diseased.

3. The first breeding of creatures is ever material, either to their hurt or benefit. And, therefore, it stands with reason, that the lesser compression, and the more liberal alimentation of the young one in the womb, should confer much to long life. Now, this happens when either the young ones are brought forth successively, as in birds; or when they are single birth, as in creatures bearing but one at a burden.

4. But long bearing in the womb makes for length of life three ways. First, for that the young one partakes more of the substance of the mother, as hath been said. Secondly, that it comes forth more strong and able. Thirdly, that it undergoes the predatory force of the air later. Besides, it shows that nature intendeth to finish their periods by larger circles. Now, though oxen, and sheep, which are borne in the womb about six months, are but short-lived, that happens for other causes.

5. Feeders upon grass and mere herbs are but short livers, and creatures feeding upon flesh, or seeds, or fruits, long livers, as some birds are. As for harts, which are long-lived, they take the one-half of their meat (as men use to say) from above their heads; and the goose, besides grass, findeth something in the water and stubble to feed upon.

6. We suppose that a good clothing of the body maketh much to long life; for it fenceth and armeth against the intemperances of the air, which do wonderfully assail and decay the body; which benefit birds especially have. Now, that sheep, which have so good fleeces, should be so short-lived, that is to be imputed to diseases, whereof that creature is full, and to the bare eating of grass.

7. The seat of the spirits, without doubt, is principally the head, which, though it be usually understood of the animal spirits only, yet this is all in all. Again, it is not to be doubted but the spirits do most of all waste and prey upon the body, so that when they are either in greater plenty, or in greater inflammation and acrimony, there the life is much shortened. And, therefore, I conceive a great cause of long life in birds to be the smallness of their heads in comparison of their bodies; for even men, which have very great heads, I suppose to be the shorter livers.

8. I am of opinion that carriage is, of all other motions, the most helpful to long life, which I also noted before. Now, there are carried waterfowls upon the water, as swans; all birds in their flying, but with a strong endeavour of their limbs; and fishes, of the length of whose lives we have no certainty.

9. Those creatures which are long before they come to their perfection, (not speaking of growth in stature only, but of other steps to maturity, as man puts forth, first, his teeth, next, the signs of puberty, then his beard, and so forward,) are long-lived, for it shows that nature finished her periods by larger circles.

10. Milder creatures are not long-lived, as the sheep and dove; for choler is as the whetstone and spur to many functions in the body.

11. Creatures whose flesh is more duskish, are longer lived than those that have white flesh; for it showeth that the juice of the body is more firm, and less apt to dissipate.

12. In every corruptible body quantity maketh much to the conservation of the whole; for a great fire is longer in quenching, a small portion of water is sooner evaporated, the body of a tree withereth not so fast as a twig. And, therefore, generally, (I speak it of species, not of individuals,) creatures that are large in body are longer lived than those that are small, unless there be some other potent cause to hinder it.

Alimentation or Nourishment; and the way of Nourishing.

To the fourth article. The history.

1. Nourishment ought to be of an inferior nature, and more simple substances than the thing nourished. Plants are nourished with the earth and water, living creatures with plants, man with living creatures. There are also certain creatures feeding upon flesh, and man himself takes plants into a part of his nourishment; but man and creatures feeding upon flesh are scarcely nourished with plants alone; perhaps fruit or grains, baked or boiled, may, with long use, nourish them; but leaves, or plants, or herbs, will not do it, as the order of Foliatanes showed by experience.

2. Over-great affinity or consubstantiality of the nourishment to the thing nourished, proveth not well; creatures feeding upon herbs touch no flesh; and of creatures feeding upon flesh, few of them eat their own kind. As for men which are cannibals, they feed not ordinarily upon man's flesh, but reserve it as a dainty, either to serve their revenge upon their enemies, or to satisfy their appetite at some times. So the ground is best sown with seed growing elsewhere, and men do not use to graft or inoculate upon the same stock.

3. By how much the more the nourishment is better prepared, and approacheth nearer in likeness to the thing nourished, by so much the more are plants more fruitful, and living creatures in better liking and plight; for a young slip or cion is not so well nourished if it be pricked into the ground, as if it be grafted into a stock agreeing with it in nature, and where it finds the nourishment already digested and prepared; neither (as is reported) will the seed of an onion, or some such like, sown in the bare earth, bring forth so large a fruit as if it be put into another onion, which is a new kind of grafting into the root or

under ground. Again, it hath been found out lately, that a slip of a wild tree, as of an elm, oak, ash, or such like, grafted into a stock of the same kind, will bring forth larger leaves than those that grow without grafting. Also men are not nourished so well with raw flesh as with that which hath passed the fire.

4. Living creatures are nourished by the mouth, plants by the root, young ones in the womb by the navel. Birds for a while are nourished with the yolk in the egg, whereof some is found in their crops after they are hatched.

5. All nourishment moveth from the centre to the circumference, or from the inward to the outward; yet it is to be noted, that in trees and plants the nourishment passeth rather by the bark and outward parts, than by the pith and inward parts; for if the bark be pulled off, though but for a small breadth round, they live no more; and the blood in the veins of living creatures doth no less nourish the flesh beneath than the flesh above it.

6. In all alimentation or nourishment there is a twofold action, extusion, and attraction; whereof the former proceeds from the inward function, the latter from the outward.

7. Vegetables assimilate their nourishment simply, without excerning; for gums and tears of trees are rather exuberances than excrements, and knots or knobs are nothing but diseases. But the substance of living creatures is more perceptible of the like; and, therefore, it is conjoined with a kind of disdain, whereby it rejecteth the bad and assimilateth the good.

8. It is a strange thing of the stalks of fruits, that all the nourishment which produceth sometimes such great fruits, should be forced to pass through so narrow necks; for the fruit is never joined to the stocks without some stalk.

9. It is to be noted, that the seeds of living creatures will not be fruitful but when they new shed, but the seeds of plants will be fruitful a long time after they are gathered; yet the slips or cions of trees will not grow unless they be grafted green, neither will the roots keep long fresh unless they be covered with earth.

10. In living creatures there are degrees of nourishment according to their age; in the womb, the young one is nourished with the mother's blood; when it is new-born, with milk; afterwards with meats and drinks: and in old age the most nourishing and savoury meats please best.

Above all, it maketh to the present inquisition, to inquire diligently and attentively whether a man may not receive nourishment from without, at least some other way besides the mouth. We know that baths of milk are used in some hectic fevers, and when the body is brought extreme low, and physicians do provide nourishing glisters. This matter would be well studied; for if nourishment may be made either from without, or some other way than by the stomach, then the weakness of concoction, which is incident to old men, might be recompensed by these helps, and concoction restored to them entire.

Length and Shortness of Life in Man.

To the fifth, sixth, seventh, eighth, ninth, and eleventh articles The History.

1. Before the flood, as the sacred Scriptures relate, men lived many hundred years; yet none of the fathers attained to a full thousand. Neither was this length of life peculiar only to grace or the holy line; for there are reckoned of the fathers, until the flood, eleven generations; but of the sons of Adam, by Cain, only eight generations; so as the posterity of Cain may seem the longer lived. But this length of life, immediately after the flood, was reduced to a moiety, but in the postnati; for Noah, who was born before, equalled the age of his ancestors, and Sem saw the six hundredth year of his life. Afterwards, three generations being run from the flood, the life of man was brought down to a fourth part of the primitive age, that was, to about two hundred years.

2. Abraham lived a hundred and seventy and five years; a man of a high courage, and prosperous in all things. Isaac came to a hundred and eighty years of age; a chaste man, and enjoying more quietness than his father. But Jacob, after many crosses, and a numerous progeny, lasted to the one hundred and forty-seventh year of his life; a patient, gentle, and wise man. Ismael, a military man, lived a hundred and thirty and seven years. Sarah (whose years only amongst women are recorded) died in the hundred and twenty-seventh year of her age; a beautiful and magnanimous woman, a singular good mother and wife, and yet no less famous for her liberty than obsequiousness towards her husband. Joseph, also, a prudent and politic man, passing his youth in affliction, afterwards advanced to the height of honour and prosperity, lived a hundred and ten years. But his brother Levi, older than himself, attained to a hundred and thirty-seven years; a man impatient of contumely and revengeful. Near unto the same age attained the son of Levi; also his grandchild, the father of Aaron and Moses.

3. Moses lived a hundred and twenty years; a stout man, and yet the meekest upon the earth and of a very slow tongue. Howsoever, Moses, in his psalm, pronounceth that the life of man is but seventy years, and if a man have strength, then eighty; which term of man's life standeth firm in many particulars even at this day. Aaron, who was three years the older, died the same year with his brother; a man of a readier speech, of a more facile disposition, and less constant. But Phineas, grandchild of Aaron, (perhaps out of extraordinary grace,) may be collected to have

lived three hundred years; if so be the war of the Israelites against the tribe of Benjamin (in which expedition Phineas consulted with) were performed in the same order of time in which the history hath ranked it; he was a man of a most eminent zeal. Joshua, a martial man and an excellent leader, and evermore victorious, lived to the hundred and tenth year of his life. Caleb was his contemporary, and seemeth to have been of as great years. Ehud, the judge, seems to have been no less than a hundred years old, in regard that after the victory over the Moabites, the Holy Land had rest under his government eighty years; he was a man fierce and undaunted, and one that in a sort neglected his life for the good of his people.

4. Job lived, after the restoration of his happiness, a hundred and forty years, being, before his afflictions, of that age that he had sons at man's estate; a man politic, eloquent, charitable, and the example of patience. Eli, the priest, lived ninety-eight years; a corpulent man, calm of disposition, and indulgent to his children. But Elizæus, the prophet, may seem to have died when he was above a hundred years old; for he is found to have lived after the assumption of Elias sixty years; and at the time of that assumption he was of those years, that the boys mocked him by the name of baldhead; a man vehement and severe, and of an austere life, and a contemner of riches. Also Isaiah, the prophet, seemeth to have been a hundred years old; for he is found to have exercised the function of a prophet seventy years together, the years both of his beginning to prophecy, and of his death, being uncertain; a man of an admirable eloquence, an evangelical prophet, full of the promises of God of the New Testament, as a bottle with sweet wine.

5. Tobias, the elder, lived a hundred and fifty-eight years, the younger a hundred and twenty-seven; merciful men, and great alms-givers. It seems, in the time of the captivity, many of the Jews who returned out of Babylon were of great years, seeing they could remember both temples, (there being no less than seventy years betwixt them,) and wept for the unlikeness of them. Many ages after that, in the time of our Saviour, lived old Simeon, to the age of ninety; a devout man, and full both of hope and expectation. Into the same time also fell Anna, the prophetess, who could not possibly be less than a hundred years old, for she had been seven years a wife, about eighty-four years a widow, besides the years of her virginity, and the time that she lived after her prophecy of our Saviour; she was a holy woman, and passed her days in fastings and prayers.

6. The long lives of men mentioned in heathen authors have no great certainty in them; both for the intermixture of fables, whereunto those kind of relations were very prone, and for their false calculation of years. Certainly of the Egyptians we find nothing of moment in those works that are extant, as touching long life; for their kings which reigned longest did not exceed fifty, or five-and-fifty years; which is no great matter, seeing many at this day attain to those years. But the Arcadian kings are fabulously reported to have lived very long. Surely that country was mountainous, full of flocks of sheep, and brought forth most wholesome food, notwithstanding, seeing Pan was their god, we may conceive that all things about them were panic and vain, and subject to fables.

7. Numa, King of the Romans, lived to eighty years; a man peaceable, contemplative, and much devoted to religion. Marcus Valerius Corvinus saw a hundred years complete, there being betwixt his first and sixth consulship forty-six years; a man valorous, affable, popular, and always fortunate.

8. Solon of Athens, the lawgiver, and one of the seven wise men, lived above eighty years, a man of high courage, but popular, and affected to his country; also learned, given to pleasures, and a soft kind of life. Epimenides, the Cretian, is reported to have lived a hundred and fifty-seven years; the matter is mixed with a prodigious relation, for fifty-seven of those years he is said to have slept in a cave. Half an age after, Xenophon, the Colophonian, lived a hundred and two years, or rather more; for at the age of twenty-five years he left his country, seventy-seven complete years he travelled, and after that returned; but how long he lived after his return appears not; a man no less wandering in mind than in body; for his name was changed for the madness of his opinions, from Xenophanes to Xenomanes; a man, no doubt, of a vast conceit, and that minded nothing but infinitum.

9. Anacreon, the poet, lived eighty years, and somewhat better, a man lascivious, voluptuous, and given to drink. Pindarus, the Theban, lived to eighty years; a poet of a high fancy, singular in his conceits, and a great adorer of the gods. Sophocles, the Athenian, attained to the like age; a lofty tragic poet, given over wholly to writing, and neglectful of his family.

10. Artaxerxes, King of Persia, lived ninety-four years; a man of a dull wit, averse to the despatch of business, desirous of glory, but rather of ease. At the same time lived Agesilaus, King of Sparta, to eighty-four years of age; a moderate prince, as being a philosopher among kings, but, notwithstanding, ambitious, and a warrior, and no less stout in war than in business.

11. Gorgias, the Sicilian, was a hundred and eight years old; a rhetorician, and a great boaster of his faculty, one that taught youth for profit. He had seen many countries, and a little before his death said, that he had done nothing worthy of blame since he was an old man. Protagoras, of Abdera, saw ninety years of age. This man

was likewise a rhetorician, but professed not so much to teach the liberal arts, as the art of governing commonwealths and states; notwithstanding he was a great wanderer in the world, no less than Gorgias. Isocrates, the Athenian, lived ninety-eight years; he was a rhetorician also, but an exceeding modest man, one that shunned the public light, and opened his school only in his own house. Democritus, of Abdera, reached to a hundred and nine years; he was a great philosopher, and, if ever any man amongst the Grecians, a true naturalist, a surveyor of many countries, but much more of nature; also a diligent searcher into experiments, and (as Aristotle objected against him) one that followed similitudes more than the laws of arguments. Diogenes, the Sinopean, lived ninety years; a man that used liberty towards others, but tyranny over himself, a coarse diet, and of much patience. Zeno, of Citium, lacked about two years of a hundred; a man of a high mind, and a contemner of other men's opinions; also of a great acuteness, but yet not troublesome, choosing rather to take men's minds than to enforce them. The like whereof afterwards was in Seneca. Plato, the Athenian, attained to eighty-one years; a man of a great courage, but yet a lover of ease, in his notions sublime, and of a fancy, neat and delicate in his life, rather calm than merry, and one that carried a kind of majesty in his countenance. Theophrastus, the Eressian, arrived at eighty-five years of age; a man sweet for his eloquence, sweet for the variety of his matters, and who selected the pleasant things of philosophy, and let the bitter and harsh go. Carneades, of Cyrena, many years after, came to the like age of eighty-five years; a man of a fluent eloquence, and one who, by the acceptable and pleasant variety of his knowledge, delighted both himself and others. But Orbilius, who lived in Cicero's time, no philosopher or rhetorician, but a grammarian, attained to a hundred years of age; he was first a soldier, then a schoolmaster; a man by nature tart both in his tongue and pen, and severe towards his scholars.

12. Quintius Fabius Maximus was augur sixty-three years, which showed him to be above eighty years of age at his death; though it be true, that in the augurship nobility was more respected than age; a wise man, and a great deliberator, and in all his proceedings moderate, and not without affability severe. Masinissa, King of Numidia, lived ninety years, and being more than eighty-five, got a son; a daring man, and trusting upon his fortune, who in his youth had tasted of the inconstancy of fortune, but in his succeeding age was constantly happy. But Marcus Porcius Cato lived above ninety years of age; a man of an iron body and mind; he had a bitter tongue, and loved to cherish factions; he was given to husbandry, and was to himself and his family a physician.

13. Terentia, Cicero's wife, lived a hundred and three years; a woman afflicted with many crosses; first, with the banishment of her husband, then with the difference betwixt them; lastly, with his last fatal misfortune. She was also oftentimes vexed with the gout. Luceia must needs exceed a hundred by many years, for it is said, that she acted a whole hundred years upon the stage, at first, perhaps, representing the person of some young girl, at last of some decrepit old woman. But Galeria Copiola, a player also, and a dancer, was brought upon the stage as a novice, in what year of her age is not known; but ninety-nine years after, at the dedication of the theatre by Pompey the Great, she was shown upon the stage, not now for an actress, but for a wonder. Neither was this all; for after that, in the solemnities for the health and life of Augustus, she was shown upon the stage the third time.

14. There was another actress, somewhat inferior in age, but much superior in dignity, which lived well near ninety years, I mean Livia Julia Augusta, wife to Augustus Cæsar, and mother to Tiberius. For, if Augustus his life were a play, (as himself would have it, when as upon his death-bed he charged his friends they should give him a plaudit after he was dead,) certainly this lady was an excellent actress, who could carry it so well with her husband by a dissembled obedience, and with her son by power and authority. A woman affable, and yet of a matronal carriage, pragmatical, and unholding her power. But Junia, the wife of Caius Cassius, and sister of Marcus Brutus, was also ninety years old, for she survived the Philippic battle sixty-four years; a magnanimous woman, in her great wealth happy, in the calamity of her husband, and near kinsfolks, and in a long widowhood unhappy, notwithstanding much honoured of all.

15. The year of our Lord seventy-six, falling into the time of Vespasian, is memorable; in which we shall find, as it were, a calendar of long-lived men; for that year there was a taxing: (now, a taxing is the most authentical and truest informer touching the ages of men;) and in that part of Italy, which lieth betwixt the Apennine mountains and the river Po, there were found a hundred and four-and-twenty persons that either equalled or exceeded a hundred years of age: namely, of a hundred years, just fifty-four persons; of a hundred and ten, fifty seven persons; of a hundred and five-and-twenty, two only; of a hundred and thirty, four men; of a hundred and five-and-thirty, or seven-and-thirty, four more; of a hundred and forty, three men. Besides these, Parma in particular afforded five, whereof three fulfilled a hundred and twenty years, and two a hundred and thirty. Brussels afforded one of a hundred and twenty five years old. Placentia one, aged a hundred thirty-and-one. Faventia one woman, aged one hundred thirty-and-two. A certain town, then called Vel-

leiatium, situate in the hills about Placentia, afforded ten, whereof six fulfilled a hundred and ten years of age, four a hundred and twenty. Lastly, Rimini, one of a hundred and fifty years, whose name was Marcus Aponius.

That our catalogue might not be extended too much in length, we have thought fit, as well in those whom we have rehearsed, as in those whom we shall rehearse, to offer none under eighty years of age. Now we have affixed to every one a true and short character or elogy; but of that sort whereunto, in our judgment, length of life (which is not a little subject to the manners and fortunes of men) hath some relation, and that in a twofold respect; either that such kind of men are for the most part long-lived, or that such men may sometimes be of long life, though otherwise not well disposed for it.

16. Amongst the Roman and Grecian emperors, also, the French and Almain, to these our days, which make up the number of well near two hundred princes, there are only four found that lived to eighty years of age; unto whom we may add the two first emperors, Augustus and Tiberius, whereof the latter fulfilled the seventy-and-eighth year, the former the seventy-and-sixth year of his age, and might both, perhaps, have lived to forescore, if Livia and Caius had been pleased. Augustus (as was said) lived seventy-and-six years; a man of moderate disposition, in accomplishing his designs vehement, but otherwise calm and serene; in meat and drink sober, venery intemperate, through all his lifetime happy; and who, about the thirtieth year of his life, had a great and dangerous sickness, insomuch as they despaired of life in him, whom Antonius Musa, the physician, when other physicians had applied hot medicines, as most agreeable to his disease, on the contrary cured with cold medicines, which perchance might be some help to the prolonging of his life. Tiberius lived to be two years older; a man with lean chaps, as Augustus was wont to say, for his speech stuck within his jaws, but was weighty. He was bloody, a drinker, and one that took lust into a part of his diet; notwithstanding a great observer of his health, insomuch that he used to say that he was a fool, that after thirty years of age took advice of a physician. Gordian, the elder, lived eighty years, and yet died a violent death, when he was scarce warm in his empire; a man of a high spirit, and renowned, learned, and a poet, and constantly happy throughout the whole course of his life, save only that he ended his days by a violent death. Valerian, the emperor, was seventy-six years of age before he was taken prisoner by Sapor, King of Persia. After his captivity he lived seven years in reproaches, and then died a violent death also; a man of a poor mind, and not valiant, notwithstanding lifted up in his own, and the opinion of men, but falling

short in the performance. Anastasius, surnamed Dicorut, lived eighty-eight years; he was of a settled mind, but too abject, and superstitious, and fearful. Anicius Justinianus lived to eighty-three years, a man greedy of glory, performing nothing in his own person, but in the valour of his captains happy and renowned, uxorious, and not his own, but suffering others to lead him. Helena, of Britain, mother of Constantine the Great, was fourscore years old; a woman that intermeddled not in matters of state, neither in her husband's nor son's reign, but devoted herself wholly to religion; magnanimous, and perpetually flourishing. Theodora, the empress, (who was sister to Zoes, wife of Monomachus, and reigned alone after her decease,) lived above eighty years; a pragmatical woman, and one that took delight in governing; fortunate in the highest degree, and through her good fortunes credulous.

17. We will proceed now from these secular princes to the princes in the church; St. John, an apostle of our Saviour, and the beloved disciple, lived ninety-three years. He was rightly denoted under the emblem of the eagle, for his piercing sight into the divinity, and was a seraph amongst the apostles, in respect of his burning love. St. Luke, the Evangelist, fulfilled fourscore and four years; an eloquent man, and a traveller, St. Paul's inseparable companion, and a physician. Simeon, the son of Cleophas, called the brother of our Lord, and Bishop of Jerusalem, lived a hundred and twenty years, though he was cut short by martyrdom; a stout man, and constant, and full of good works. Polycarpus, disciple unto the apostles, and Bishop of Smyrna, seemeth to have extended his age to a hundred years and more, though he were also cut off by martyrdom; a man of a high mind, of an heroical patience, and unwearied with labours. Dionysius Areopagita, contemporary to the apostle St. Paul, lived ninety years; he was called the bird of heaven for his high-flying divinity, and was famous, as well for his holy life as for his meditations. Aquila and Priscilla, first St Paul the apostle's hosts, afterwards his fellow-helpers, lived together in a happy and famous wedlock, at least to a hundred years of age apiece, for they were both alive under Pope Xistus the First; a noble pair, and prone to all kind of charity, who amongst other their comforts (which no doubt were great unto the first founders of the church) had this added, to enjoy each other so long in a happy marriage. St. Paul, the hermit, lived a hundred and thirteen years; now, he lived in a cave, his diet was so slender and strict, that it was thought almost impossible to support human nature therewithal; he passed his years only in meditations and soliloquies; yet he was not illiterate, or an idiot, but learned. Saint Anthony, the first founder of monks, or (as some will have it) the restorer only, attained to a hundred and five

years of age; a man devout and contemplative, though not unfit for civil affairs; his life was austere and mortifying, notwithstanding he lived in a kind of glorious solitude, and exercised a command, for he had his monks under him. And, besides, many Christians and philosophers came to visit him as a living image, from which they parted not without some adoration. St. Athanasius exceeded the term of eighty years; a man of an invincible constancy, commanding fame, and not yielding to fortune. He was free towards the great ones, with the people gracious and acceptable, beaten and practised to oppositions, and in delivering himself from them, stout and wise. St. Hierom, by the consent of most writers, exceeded ninety years of age; a man powerful in his pen, and of a manly eloquence, variously learned both in the tongues and sciences; also a traveller, and that lived strictly towards his old age, in an estate private, and not dignified; he bore high spirits, and shined far out of obscurity.

18. The Popes of Rome are in number, to this day, two hundred, forty, and one. Of so great a number, five only have attained to the age of fourscore years or upwards. But, in many of the first popes, their full age was intercepted by the prerogative and crown of martyrdom. John, the twenty-third Pope of Rome, fulfilled the ninetieth year of his age; a man of an unquiet disposition, and one that studied novelty; he altered many things, some to the better, others only to the new, a great accumulator of riches and treasures. Gregory, called the twelfth, created in schism, and not fully acknowledged pope, died at ninety years. Of him, in respect of his short papacy, we find nothing to make a judgment upon. Paul, the third, lived eighty years and one; a temperate man, and of a profound wisdom; he was learned, an astrologer, and one that tended his health carefully, but, after the example of old Eli the priest, over-indulgent to his family. Paul the fourth attained to the age of eighty-three years; a man of a harsh nature, and severe, of a haughty mind, and imperious, prone to anger, his speech was eloquent and ready. Gregory the thirteenth fulfilled the like age of eighty-three years; an absolute good man, sound in mind and body, politic, temperate, full of good works, and an almsgiver.

19. Those that follow are to be more promiscuous in their order, more doubtful in their faith, and more barren of observation. King Arganthenius, who reigned at Cadiz in Spain, lived a hundred and thirty, or, as some would have it, a hundred and forty years, of which he reigned eighty. Concerning his manners, institution of his life, and the time wherein he reigned, there is a general silence. Cynirus, King of Cyprus, living in the island then termed the happy and pleasant island, is affirmed to have attained to a hundred and fifty or sixty years. Two Latin kings in Italy, the father and the son, are reported to have lived, the one eight hundred, the other six hundred years; but this is delivered unto us by certain philologists, who, though otherwise credulous enough, yet themselves have suspected the truth of this matter, or rather condemned it. Others record some Arcadian kings to have lived three hundred years; the country, no doubt, is a place apt for long life, but the relation I suspect to be fabulous. They tell of one Dando, in Illyrium, that lived without the inconveniences of old age, to five hundred years. They tell, also, of the Epians, a part of Ætolia, that the whole nation of them were exceeding long-lived, insomuch that many of them were two hundred years old; and that one principal man amongst them, named Litorius, a man of giantlike stature, could have told three hundred years. It is recorded, that on the top of the mountain Timolus, anciently called Tempsis, many of the inhabitants lived to a hundred and fifty years. We read that the Esseans, amongst the Jews, did usually extend their life to a hundred years. Now, that sect used a single or abstemious diet, after the rule of Pythagoras. Apollonius Tyaneus exceeded a hundred years, his face bewraying no such age; he was an admirable man, of the heathens reputed to have something divine in him, of the Christians held for a sorcerer; in his diet pythagorical, a great traveller, much renowned, and by some adored as a god; nothwithstanding, towards the end of his life, he was subject to many complaints against him, and reproaches, all which he made shift to escape. But, lest his long life should be imputed to his pythagorical diet, and not rather that it was hereditary, his grandfather before him lived a hundred and thirty years. It is undoubted, that Quintus Metellus lived above a hundred years; and that, after several consulships happily administered, in his old age he was made Pontifex Maximus, and exercised those holy duties full two-and-twenty years; in the performance of which rites his voice never failed, nor his hand trembled. It is most certain, that Appius Cæcus was very old, but his years are not extant, the most part whereof he passed after he was blind, yet this misfortune no whit softened him, but that he was able to govern a numerous family, a great retinue and dependence, yea, even the commonwealth itself, with great stoutness. In his extreme old age he was brought in a litter into the senate-house, and vehemently dissuaded the peace with Pyrrhus; the beginning of his oration was very memorable, showing an invincible spirit and strength of mind. "I have, with great grief of mind, (Fathers Conscript,) these many years borne my blindness, but now I could wish that I were deaf also, when I hear you speak to such dishonourable treaties." Marcus Perpenna lived ninety-eight years, surviving all those whose suffrages he had gathered in the

senate-house, being consul, I mean all the senators at that time, as also all those whom, a little after, being consul, he chose into the senate, seven only being excepted. Hiero, King of Sicily, in the time of the second Punic war, lived almost a hundred years; a man moderate both in his government and in his life, a worshipper of the gods, and a religious conserver of friendship, liberal, and constantly fortunate. Statilia, descended of a noble family, in the days of Claudius, lived ninety-nine years. Clodia, the daughter of Osilius, a hundred and fifteen. Xenophilus, an ancient philosopher, of the sect of Pythagoras, attained to a hundred and six years, remaining healthful and vigorous in his old age, and famous amongst the vulgar for his learning. The islanders of Corcyra were anciently accounted long-lived, but now they live after the rate of other men. Hipocrates Cous, the famous physician, lived a hundred and four years, and approved and credited his own art by so long a life; a man that coupled learning and wisdom together, very conversant in experience and observation; one that haunted not after words or methods, but served the very nerves of science, and so propounded them. Demonax, a philosopher, not only in profession, but practice, lived in the days of Adrian, almost to a hundred years; a man of a high mind, and a vanquisher of his own mind, and that truly and without affection; a contemner of the world, and yet civil and courteous. When his friends spake to him about his burial, he said, Take no care for my burial, for stench will bury a carcass. They replied, Is it your mind then to be cast out to birds and dogs? He said, again, Seeing in my lifetime I endeavoured to my uttermost to benefit men, what hurt is it, if, when I am dead, I benefit beasts? Certain Indian people, called Pandoræ, are exceeding long-lived, even to no less than two hundred years. They had a thing more marvellous, that having, when they are boys, an air somewhat whitish, in their old age, before their gray hairs, they grow coalblack, though, indeed, this be everywhere to be seen, that they which have white hair whilst they are boys, in their man's estate, change their hairs into a darker colour. The Seres, another people of India, with their wine of palms, are accounted long livers, even to a hundred and thirty years. Euphranor, the grammarian, grew old in his school and taught scholars when he was above a hundred years old. The elder Ovid, father to the poet, lived ninety years, differing much from the disposition of his son, for he contemned the muses, and dissuaded his son from poetry. Asinius Pollio, intimate with Augustus, exceeded the age of a hundred years; a man of an unreasonable profuseness, eloquent, and a lover of learning, but vehement, proud, cruel, and one that made his private ends the centre of his thoughts. There was an opinion, that Seneca was an ex-

treme old man, no less than a hundred and fourteen years of age, which could not possibly be, it being as improbable that a decrepit old man should be set over Nero's youth, as, on the contrary, it was true, that he was able to manage with great dexterity the affairs of state. Besides, a little before, in the midst of Claudius his reign, he was banished Rome for adulteries committed with some noble ladies, which was a crime no way compatible with so extreme old age. Johannes de Temporibus, among all the men of our latter ages, out of a common fame and vulgar opinion, was reputed long-lived, even to a miracle, or rather even to a fable; his age hath been counted above three hundred years. He was by nation a Frenchman, and followed the wars under Charles the Great. Garcius Aretine, great-grandfather to Petrarch, arrived at the age of a hundred and four years; he had ever enjoyed the benefit of good health, besides, at the last, he felt rather a decay of his strength, than any sickness or malady, which is the true resolution by old age. Amongst the Venetians there have been found not a few long livers, and those of the more eminent sort. Franciscus Donatus, duke; Thomas Contarerus, procurator of Saint Mark; Franciscus Molinus, procurator also of Saint Mark, and others. But, most memorable, is that of Cornarus the Venetian, who, being in his youth of a sickly body, began first to eat and drink by measure to a certain weight, thereby to recover his health; this cure turned by use into a diet, that diet to an extraordinary long life, even of a hundred years and better, without any decay in his senses, and with a constant enjoying of his health. In our age, William Pestel, a Frenchman, lived to a hundred and well nigh twenty years, the top of his beard on the upper lip being black, and not gray at all; a man crazed in his brain, and of a fancy not altogether sound; a great traveller, mathematician, and somewhat stained with heresy.

20. I suppose there is scarce a village with us in England, if it be any whit populous, but it affords some man or woman of fourscore years of age; nay, a few years since, there was in the county of Hereford a May-game, or morrice-dance, consisting of eight men, whose age computed together made up eight hundred years; insomuch that what some of them wanted of a hundred, others exceeded as much.

21. In the hospital of Bethlehem, corruptly called Bedlam, in the suburbs of London, there are found from time to time many mad persons that live to a great age.

22. The ages of nymphs, fawns, and satyrs, whom they make to be indeed mortal, but yet exceedingly long-lived, (a thing which ancient superstition, and the late credulity of some have admitted,) we account but for fables and dreams, especially being that which hath neither con-

sent with philosophy, nor with divinity. And as touching the history of long life in man by individuals, or next unto individuals, thus much. Now we will pass on to observations by certain heads.

23. The running on of ages, and succession of generations, seem to have no whit abated from the length of life. For we see, that from the time of Moses unto these our days, the term of man's life hath stood about fourscore years of age; neither hath it declined (as a man would have thought) by little and little. No doubt there are times in every country wherein men are longer or shorter lived. Longer, for the most part, when the times are barbarous, and men fare less deliciously, and are more given to bodily exercises. Shorter, when the times are more civil, and men abandon themseles to luxury and ease. But these things pass on by their turns, the succession of generations alters it not. The same, no doubt, is in other living creatures, for neither oxen, nor horses, nor sheep, nor any the like, are abridged of their wonted ages at this day. And, therefore, the great abridger of age was the flood; and perhaps some such notable accidents (as particular inundations, long droughts, earthquakes, or the like) may do the same again. And the like reason is in the dimension and stature of bodies, for neither are they lessened by succession of generations; howsoever Virgil (following the vulgar opinion) divined that after-ages would bring forth lesser bodies than the then present. Whereupon, speaking of ploughing up the Æmathian and Æmmensian fields, he saith, Grandiaque effossis mirabitur ossa sepulchris, That after-ages shall admire the great bones digged up in ancient sepulchres. For whereas it is manifested, that there were heretofore men of gigantine statures, (such as for certain have been found in Sicily and elsewhere, in ancient sepulchres and caves,) yet within these last three thousand years, a time whereof we have sure memory, those very places have produced none such, although this thing also hath certain turns and changes, by the civilizing of a nation, no less than the former. And this is the rather to be noted, because men are wholly carried away with an opinion, that there is a continual decay by succession of ages, as well in the term of man's life. as in the stature and strength of his body; and that all things decline and change to the worse.

24. In cold and northern countries men live longer commonly than in hot, which must needs be, in respect the skin is more compact and close, and the juices of the body less dissipable, and the spirits themselves less eager to consume, and in better disposition to repair, and the air (as being little heated by the sunbeams) less predatory. And yet, under the equinoctial line, where the sun passeth to and fro, and causeth a double summer, and double winter, and where the days and nights are more equal, (if other things be concurring,) they live also very long, as in Peru and Taprobane.

25. Islanders are, for the most part, longer lived than those that live in continents; for they live not so long in Russia as in the Orcades, nor so long in Africa, though under the same parallel, as in the Canaries and Terceras; and the Japonians are longer lived than the Chinese, though the Chinese are made upon long life. And this thing is no marvel, seeing the air of the sea doth heat and cherish in cooler regions, and cool in hotter.

26. High situations do rather afford long livers than low, especially if they be not tops of mountains, but rising grounds, as to their general situations; such as was Arcadia in Greece, and that part of Ætolia, where we related them to have lived so long. Now, there would be the same reason for mountains themselves, because of the pureness and clearness of the air, but that they are corrupted by accident, namely, by the vapours rising thither out of the valleys, and resting there; and, therefore, in snowy mountains there is not found any notable long life, not in the Alps, not in the Pyrenean mountains, not in the Apennine; yet in the tops of the mountains running along towards Æthiopia, and the Abyssines, where, by reason of the sands beneath, little or no vapour riseth to the mountains; they live long, even at this very day, attaining many times to a hundred and fifty years.

27. Marshes and fens are propitious to the natives, and malignant to strangers, as touching the lengthening and shortening of their lives; and that which may seem more marvellous, salt marshes, where the sea ebbs and flows, are less wholesome than those of fresh water.

28. The countries which have been observed to produce long livers are these; Arcadia, Ætolia, India on this side Ganges, Brazil, Taprobane, Britain, Ireland, with the islands of the Orcades and Hebrides: for as for Æthiopia, which by one of the ancients is reported to bring forth long livers, it is but a toy.

29. It is a secret; the healthfulness of air. especially in any perfection, is better found by experiment than by discourse or conjecture. You may make a trial by a lock of wool exposed for a few days in the open air, if the weight be not much increased; another by a piece of flesh exposed likewise, if it corrupt not over soon; another by a weatherglass, if the water interchange not too suddenly. Of these, and the like, inquire further.

30. Not only the goodness or pureness of the air, but also the equality of the air, is material to long life. Intermixture of hills and dales is pleasant to the sight, but suspected for long life. A plain, moderately dry, but yet not over barren or

sandy, nor altogether without trees and shade, is very convenient for length of life.

31. Inequality of air (as was even now said) in the place of our dwelling is naught; but change of air by travelling, after one be used unto it, is good, and, therefore, great travellers have been long lived. Also those that have lived perpetually in a little cottage, in the same place, have been long livers; for air accustomed consumeth less, but air changed nourisheth and repaireth more.

32. As the continuation and number of successions (which we said before) makes nothing to the length and shortness of life, so the immediate condition of the parents (as well the father as the mother) without doubt availeth much. For some are begotten of old men, some of young men, some of men of middle age. Again, some are begotten of fathers healthful and well disposed, others of diseased and languishing. Again, some of fathers immediately after repletion, or when they are drunk; others after sleeping, or in the morning. Again, some after a long intermission of Venus, others upon the act repeated. Again, some in the fervency of the father's love, (as it is commonly in bastards,) others after the cooling of it, as in long married couples. The same things may be considered on the part of the mother, unto which must be added the condition of the mother whilst she is with child, as touching her health, as touching her diet, the time of her bearing in the womb, to the tenth month or earlier. To reduce these things to a rule, how far they may concern long life, is hard; and so much the harder, for that those things which a man would conceive to be the best, will fall out to the contrary. For that alacrity in the generation which begets lusty and lively children, will be less profitable to long life, because of the acrimony and inflaming of the spirits. We said before, that to partake more of the mother's blood conduceth to long life. Also we suppose all things in moderation to be best; rather conjugal love than meretricious; the hour for generation to be the morning, a state of body not too lusty or full, and such like. It ought to be well observed, that a strong constitution in the parents, is rather good for them than for the child, especially in the mother. And, therefore, Plato thought ignorantly enough, that the virtue of generations halted, because the woman used not the same exercise both of mind and body with the men. The contrary is rather true; for the difference of virtue betwixt the male and the female is most profitable for the child, and the thinner women yield more towards the nourishment of the child, which also holds in nurses. Neither did the Spartan women, which married not before twenty-two, or, as some say, twenty-five, (and therefore were called manlike women,) bring forth a more generous or long-lived progeny than the Roman, or Athenian, or Theban women did, which were ripe for marriage

at twelve or fourteen years; and if there were any thing eminent in the Spartans, that was rather to be imputed to the parsimony of their diet, than to the late marriages of their women. But this we are taught by experience, that there are some races which are long-lived for a few descents, so that life is like some diseases, a thing hereditary within certain bounds.

33. Fair in face, or skin, or hair, are shorter livers; black, or red, or freckled, longer. Also, too fresh a colour in youth doth less promise long life than paleness. A hard skin is a sign of long life rather than a soft; but we understand not this of a rugged skin, such as they call the goose-skin, which is, as it were, spongy, but of that which is hard and close. A forehead with deep furrows and wrinkles is a better sign than a smooth and plain forehead.

34. The hairs of the head hard, and like bristles, do betoken longer life than those that are soft and delicate. Curled hairs betoken the same thing, if they be hard withal; but the contrary, if they be soft and shining; the like if the curling be rather thick in large bunches.

35. Early or late, baldness is an indifferent thing, seeing many which have been bald betimes have lived long. Also, early gray hairs (howsoever they may seem forerunners of old age approaching) are no sure signs, for many that have grown gray betimes, have lived to great years; nay, hasty gray hairs, without baldness, is a token of long life; contrarily, if they be accompanied with baldness.

36. Hairiness of the upper parts is a sign of short life, and they that have extraordinary much hair on their breasts, live not long; but hairiness of the lower parts, as of the thighs and legs, is a sign of long life.

37. Tallness of stature, (if it be not immoderate,) with convenient making, and not too slender, especially if the body be active withal, is a sign of long life. Also, on the contrary, men of low stature live long, if they be not too active and stirring.

38. In the proportion of the body, they which are short to the waists, with long legs, are longer lived than they which are long to the waists, and have short legs. Also, they which are large in the nether parts, and straight in the upper, (the making of their body rising, as it were, into a sharp figure,) are longer lived than they that have broad shoulders, and are slender downwards.

39. Leanness, where the affections are settled, calm, and peaceable; also, a more fat habit of body, joined with choler, and a disposition stirring and peremptory, signify long life; but corpulency in youth foreshows short life; in age, it is a thing more indifferent.

40. To be long and slow in growing, is a sign of long life; if to a greater stature, the greater

sign; if to a lesser stature, yet a sign; though, contrarily, to grow quickly to a great stature, is an evil sign; if to a small stature, the less evil.

41. Firm flesh, a rawbone body, and veins laying higher than the flesh, betoken long life; the contrary to these, short life.

42. A head somewhat lesser than to the proportion of the body, a moderate neck, not long, nor slender, nor flat, nor too short; wide nostrils, whatsoever the form of the nose be; a large mouth, and ear gristly, not fleshy; teeth strong and contiguous, small or thin set, foretoken long life; and, much more, if some new teeth put forth in our elder years.

43. A broad breast, yet not bearing out, but rather bending inwards; shoulders somewhat crooked, and (as they call such persons) round-backed, a flat belly, a hand large, and with few lines in the palm; a short and round foot, thighs not fleshy, and calves of the legs not hanging over, but neat, are signs of long life.

44. Eyes somewhat large, and the circles of them inclined to greenness; senses not too quick; the pulse in youth slower, towards old age quicker; facility of holding the breath, and longer than usual; the body in youth inclined to be bound, in the decline of years more laxative, are also signs of long life.

45. Concerning the times of nativity, as they refer to long life, nothing has been observed worthy the setting down, save only astrological observations, which we rejected in our topics. A birth at the eighth month is not only long-lived, but not likely to live. Also, winter births are accounted the longer lived.

46. A pythagorical or monastical diet, according to strict rules, and always exactly equal, (as that of Conarus was,) seemeth to be very effectual for long life. Yet, on the contrary, amongst those that live freely, and after the common sort, such as have good stomachs and feed more plentifully, are often the longest lived. The middle diet, which we account the temperate, is commended, and conduceth to good health, but not to long life; for the spare diet begets few spirits, and dull, and so wasteth the body less; and the liberal diet yieldeth more ample nourishment, and so repaireth more; but the middle diet doth neither of both; for, where the extremes are hurtful, there the mean is best; but where the extremes are helpful, there the mean is nothing worth.

Now, to that spare diet there are requisite watching, lest the spirits, being few, should be oppressed with much sleep; little exercise, lest they should exhale; abstinence from venery, lest they should be exhausted; but to the liberal diet, on the other side, are requisite much sleep, frequent exercises, and a seasonable use of venery. Baths and anointings (such as were anciently in use) did rather tend to deliciousness, than to prolonging of life. But of all these things we shall speak more exactly when we come to the inquisition, according to intentions. Meanwhile that of Celsus, who was not only a learned physician, but a wise man. is not to be omitted, who adviseth interchanging and alternation of the diet, but still with an inclination to the more benign; as that a man should sometimes accustom himself to watching, sometimes to sleep, but to sleep oftenest. Again, that he should sometimes give himself to fasting, sometimes to feasting, but to feasting oftenest; that he should sometimes inure himself to great labours of the mind, sometimes to relaxations of the same, but to relaxations oftenest. Certainly this is without all question, that diet well ordered bears the greatest part in the prolongation of life; neither did I ever meet an extreme long-lived man, but being asked of his course, he observed something peculiar; some one thing, some another. I remember an old man, above a hundred years of age, who was produced, as witness, touching an ancient prescription. When he had finished his testimony, the judge familiarly asked him how he came to live so long: He answered, beside expectation, and not without the laughter of the hearers, By eating before I was hungry, and drinking before I was dry. But of these things we shall speak hereafter.

47. A life led in religion, and in holy exercises, seemeth to conduce to long life. There are in this kind of life these things, leisure, admiration, and contemplation of heavenly things, joys not sensual, noble hopes, wholesome fears, sweet sorrows. Lastly, continual renovations by observances, penances, expiations, all which are very powerful to the prolongation of life. Unto which if you add that austere diet which hardeneth the mass of the body, and humbleth the spirits, no marvel if an extraordinary length of life do follow; such was that of Paul, the hermit, Simeon Stelita, the columnar anchorite, and of many other hermits and anchorites.

48. Next to this is the life, led in good letters, such as was that of philosophers, rhetoricians, grammarians. This life is also led in leisure, and in those thoughts, which, seeing they are severed from the affairs of the world, bite not, but rather delight, through their variety and impertinency. They live also at their pleasure, spending their time in such things as like them best, and for the most part in the company of young men, which is ever the most cheerful. But in philosophies there is great difference betwixt the sects, as touching long life; for those philosophies which have in them a touch of superstition, and are conversant in high contemplations, are the best, as the pythagorical and platonic. Also those which did institute a perambulation of the world, and considered the variety of natural things, and had reachless, and high, and magnanimous thoughts, (as of infinitum, of the stars, of the heroical virtues, and such like,)

were good for lengthening of life; such were those of Democritus, Philolaus, Xenophanes, the astrologians and stoics. Also those which had no profound speculation in them, but discoursed calmly on both sides, out of common sense and the received opinions, without any sharp inquisitions, were likewise good; such were those of Carneades and the academics, also of the rhetoricians and grammarians. But, contrary, philosophies conversant in perplexing subtilties, and which pronounced peremptorily, and which examined and wrested all things to the scale of principles. Lastly, which were thorny and narrow were evil; such were those commonly of the peripatetics, and of the schoolmen.

49. The country life also is well fitted for long life; it is much abroad, and in the open air; it is not slothful, but ever in employment; it feedeth upon fresh cates, and unbought; it is without cares and envy.

50. For the military life, we have a good opinion of that whilst a man is young. Certainly many excellent warriors have been long-lived; Corvinus, Camillus, Xenophon, Agesilaus, with others, both ancient and modern. No doubt it furthereth long life, to have all things from our youth to our elder age mend, and grow to the better, that a youth full of crosses may minister sweetness to our old age. We conceive also, that military affections, inflamed with a desire of fighting, and hope of victory, do infuse such a heat into the spirits, as may be profitable for long life.

Medicines for Long Life.
To the tenth article.

The art of physic, which we now have, looks no further commonly than to conservation of health, and cure of diseases. As for those things which tend properly to long life, there is but slight mention, and by the way only. Notwithstanding, we will propound those medicines which are notable in this kind, I mean those which are cordials. For it is consonant to reason, that those things which being taken in cures do defend and fortify the heart, or, more truly, the spirits, against poisons and diseases being transferred with judgment and choice into diet, should have a good effect, in some sort, towards the prolonging of life. This we will do, not heaping them promiscuously together, (as the manner is,) but selecting the best.

1. Gold is given in three forms, either in that which they call aurum potabile, or in wine wherein gold hath been quenched, or in gold in the substance, such as are leaf-gold, and the filings of gold. As for aurum potabile, it is used to be given in desperate or dangerous diseases, and that not without good success. But we suppose that the spirits of the salt, by which the gold is dissolved, do rather minister that virtue which is found in it, than the gold itself,

though this secret be wholly suppressed. Now if the body of gold could be opened with these corrosive waters, or by these corrosive waters (so the venemous quality were wanting) well washed, we conceive it would be no unprofitable medicine.

2. Pearls are taken either in a fine powder, or in a certain mass or dissolution, by the juice of four and new lemons, and they are given sometimes in aromatical confections, sometimes in liquor. The pearl, no doubt, hath some affinity with the shell in which it groweth, and may be of the same quality with the shells of crawfishes.

3. Amongst the transparent precious stones, two only are accounted cordial, the emerald and the jacinth, which are given under the same forms that the pearls are; save only, that the dissolutions of them, as far as we know, are not in use. But we suspect these glassy jewels, lest they should be cutting.

Of these which we have mentioned, how far and in what manner they are helpful, shall be spoken hereafter.

4. Bezoar stone is of approved virtue for refreshing the spirits and procuring a gentle sweat. As for the unicorn's horn, it hath lost the credit with us; yet so as it may keep rank with hartshorn, and the bone in the heart of a hart, and ivory, and such like.

Ambergris is one of the best to appease and comfort the spirits.

5. Hereafter, follow the names only of the simple cordials, seeing their virtues are sufficiently known.

Hot.—Saffron, folium indum, lignum aloes, citron pill or rind, balm, basil, clove-gillyflowers, orange flowers, rosemary, mint, betony, carduus benedictus.

Cold.—Nitre, roses, violets, strawberry leaves, strawberries, juice of sweet lemons, juice of sweet oranges, juice of pearmains, borage, bugloss, burnet, sanders, camphire.

Seeing our speech now is of those things which may be transferred into diet, all hot waters and chymical oils, (which, as a certain trifler saith, are under the planet Mars, and have a furious and destructive force,) as, also, all hot and biting spices are to be rejected, and a consideration to be had how waters and liquors may be made of the former simples; not those phlegmatic distilled waters, nor again those burning waters or spirits of wine, but such as may be more temperate, and yet lively, and sending forth a benign vapour.

6. I make some question touching the frequent letting of blood, whether it conduceth to long life or not; and I am rather in the opinion that it doth, if it be turned into a habit, and other things be well disposed, for it letteth out the old juice of the body and bringeth in new.

I suppose also, that some emaciating diseases, well cured, do profit to long life, for they yield new juice, the old being consumed, and as (he saith) to recover a sickness, is to renew youth. Therefore it were good to make some artificial diseases, which is done by strict and emaciating diets, of which I shall speak hereafter.

The Intentions.

To the twelfth. thirteenth, and fourteenth articles.

Having finished the inquisition according to the subjects, as, namely, of inanimate bodies, vegetables, living creatures, man, I will come now nearer to the matter, and order mine inquisitions by certain intentions, such as are true and proper (as I am wholly persuaded,) and which are the very paths to mortal life. For in this part, nothing that is of worth hath hitherto been inquired, but the contemplations of men have been but simple and non-proficients. For when I hear men on the one side speak of comforting natural heat, and the radical moisture, and of meats which breed good blood, such as may neither be burnt nor phlegmatic, and of the cheering and recreating the spirits, I suppose them to be no bad men which speak these things; but none of these worketh effectually towards the end. But when, on the other side, I hear several discourses touching medicines made of gold, because gold is not subject to corruption; and touching precious stones, to refresh the spirits by their hidden properties and lustre, and that if they could be taken and retained in vessels, the balsams and quintessences of living creatures would make men conceive a proud hope of immortality. And that the flesh of serpents and harts, by a certain consent, are powerful to the renovation of life, because the one casteth his skin, the other his horns; (they should also have added the flesh of eagles, because the eagle changes his bill.) And that a certain man, when he had found an ointment hidden under the ground, and had anointed himself therewith from head to foot, (excepting only the soles of his feet) did, by his anointing, live three hundred years without any disease, save only some tumours in the soles of his feet. And of Artesius, who, when he found his spirit ready to depart, drew into his body the spirit of a certain young man, and thereby made him breathless, but himself lived many years by another man's spirit. And of fortunate hours, according to the figures of heaven, in which medicines are to be gathered and compounded for the prolongation of life; and of the seals of planets, by which virtues may be drawn and fetched down from heaven to prolong life; and such like fabulous and superstitious vanities. I wonder exceedingly that men should so much dote as to suffer themselves to be deluded with these things. And, again, I do pity mankind that they should have the hard fortune to be besieged with such frivolous and senseless apprehensions. But mine intentions do both come home to the matter, and are far from vain and credulous imaginations; being also such, as I conceive, posterity may add much to the matters which satisfy these intentions; but to the intentions themselves, but a little. Notwithstanding there are a few things, and those of very great moment, of which I would have men to be forewarned.

First, We are of that opinion, that we esteem the offices of life to be more worthy than life itself. Therefore, if there be any thing of that kind that may indeed exactly answer our intentions, yet so that the offices and duties of life be thereby hindered, whatsoever it be of this kind, we reject it. Perhaps we may make some light mention of some things, but we insist not upon them. For we make no serious nor diligent discourse, either of leading the life in caves, where the sunbeams and several changes of the air pierce not, like Epimenides his cave; or of perpetual baths, made of liquors prepared; or of shirts and searcloths, so applied, that the body should be always, as it were, in a box; or of thick paintings of the body, after the manner of some barbarous nations; or of an exact ordering of our life and diet, which aimeth only at this, and mindeth nothing else but that a man live, (as was that of Herodicus amongst the ancients, and of Cornarus the Venetian in our days, but with greater moderation,) or of any such prodigy, tediousness, or inconvenience; but we propound such remedies and precepts, by which the offices of life may neither be deserted nor receive any great interruptions or molestations.

Secondly, On the other side, we denounce unto men that they will give over trifling, and not imagine that so great a work as the stopping and turning back the powerful course of nature can be brought to pass by some morning draught, or the taking of some precious drug, but that they would be assured that it must needs be, that this is a work of labour, and consisteth of many remedies, and a fit connexion of them amongst themselves; for no man can be so stupid as to imagine that what was never yet done can be done, but by such ways as were never yet attempted.

Thirdly, We ingeniously profess that some of those things which we shall propound, have not been tried by us by way of experiment, (for our course of life doth not permit that,) but are derived (as we suppose) upon good reasons, out of our principles and grounds, (of which some we set down, others we reserve in our mind,) and are, as it were, cut and digged out of the rock and mine of nature herself. Nevertheless, we have been careful, and that with all providence and circumspection, (seeing the Scripture saith of the body of man, that it is more worth than raiment,) to propound such remedies as may at least be safe, if peradventure they be not fruitful.

Fourthly, We would have men rightly to observe and distinguish that those things which are good for a healthful life, are not always good for a long life; for there are some things which do further the alacrity of the spirits, and the strength and vigour of the functions, which, notwithstanding, do cut off from the sum of life: and there are other things which are profitable to prolongation of life, which, are not without some peril of health, unless this matter be salved by fit remedies; of which, notwithstanding, as occasion shall be offered, we will not omit to give some cautions and monitions.

Lastly, We have thought good to propound sundry remedies according to the several intentions, but the choice of those remedies, and the order of them, to leave to discretion; for to set down exactly which of them agreeth best, with which constitution of body, which with the several courses of life, which with each man's particular age, and how they are to be taken one after another, and how the whole practique of these things is to be administered and governed, would be too long, neither is it fit to be published.

In the topics we propounded three intentions; the prohibiting of consumption, the perfecting of reparation, and the renewing of oldness. But seeing those things which shall be said are nothing less than words, we will deduce these three intentions to ten operations.

1. The first is the operation upon the spirits, that they may renew their vigour.

2. The second operation is upon the exclusion of the air.

3. The third operation is upon the blood, and the sanguifying heat.

4. The fourth operation is upon the juices of the body.

5. The fifth operation is upon the bowels, for their extrusion of aliment.

6. The sixth operation is upon the outer parts, for their attraction of aliment.

7 The seventh operation is upon the aliment itself, for the insinuation thereof.

8. The eighth operation is upon the last act of assimilation.

9. The ninth operation is upon the inteneration of the parts, after they begin to be dried.

10. The tenth operation is upon the purging away of old juice, and supplying of new juice

Of these operations, the four first belong to the first intention, the four next to the second intention, and the two last to the third intention.

But because this part touching the intentions doth tend to practice, under the name of history, we will not only comprise experiments and observations, but also counsels, remedies, explications of causes, assumptions, and whatsoever hath reference hereunto.

I. *The Operation upon the Spirits, that they may remain youthful, and renew their Vigour.*

The history.

1. The spirits are the master workmen of all effects in the body. This is manifest by consen. and by infinite instances.

2. If any man could procure that a young man's spirit could be conveyed into an old man's body; it is not unlikely but this great wheel of the spirits might turn about the lesser wheels of the parts, and so the course of nature become retrograde.

3. In every consumption, whether it be by fire or by age, the more the spirit of the body, or the heat, preyeth upon the moisture, the lesser is the duration of that thing. This occurs everywhere, and is manifest.

4. The spirits are to be put into such a temperament and degree of activity, that they should not (as he saith) drink and guzzle the juices of the body, but sip them only.

5. There are two kinds of flames, the one eager and weak, which consumes slight substances, but hath little power over the harder, as the flame of straw or small sticks: the other strong and constant, which converts hard and obstinate substances; as the flame of hard wood, and such like.

6. The eager flames, and yet less robust, do dry bodies, and render them exhaust and sapless; but the stronger flames do intenerate and melt them.

7. Also in dissipating medicines, some vapour forth the thin part of the tumours or swellings, and these harden the tumour; others potently discuss, and these soften it.

8. Also in purging and absterging medicines, some carry away the fluid humours violently others draw the more obstinate and viscous.

9. The spirits ought to be invested and armed with such a heat, that they may choose rather to stir and undermine hard and obstinate matters, than to discharge and carry away the thin and prepared: for by that means the body becomes green and solid.

10. The spirits are so to be wrought and tempered, that they may be in substance dense, not rare; in heat strong, not eager; in quantity sufficient for the offices of life, not redundant or turgid; in motion appeased, not dancing or unequal.

11. That vapours work powerfully upon the spirits it is manifest by sleep, by drunkenness, by melancholic passions, by letificant medicines, by odours, calling the spirits back again in swoonings and faintings.

12. The spirits are condensed four ways; either by putting them to flight, or by refrigerating and cooling them, or by stroking them, or by quieting them. And first of their condensation, by putting them to flight.

13. Whatsoever putteth to flight on all parts driveth the body into his centre, and so condenseth.

14. To the condensation of the spirits by flight, the most powerful and effectual is opium, and next opiates, and generally all soporiferous things.

15. The force of opium to the condensation of the spirits is exceeding strong, when as perhaps three grains thereof will in a short time so coagulate the spirits, that they return no more, but are extinguished, and become immovable.

16. Opium, and the like, put not the spirits to flight by their coldness, for they have parts manifestly hot, but on the contrary cool by their putting the spirits to flight.

17. The flight of the spirits by opium and opiate medicines is best seen by applying the same outwardly, for the spirits straight withdraw themselves, and will return no more, but the part is mortified, and turns to a gangrene.

18. Opiates in grievous pains, as in the stone, or the cutting off of a limb, mitigate pains most of all, by putting the spirits to flight.

19. Opiates obtain a good effect from a bad cause; for the flight of the spirits is evil, but the condensation of them through their flight is good.

20. The Grecians attributed much both for health and for prolongation of life, as opiates, but the Arabians much more, insomuch that their grand medicines (which they called the god's hands) had opium for their basis and principal ingredient, other things being mixed to abate and correct the noxious qualities thereof; such· were treacle, mithridate, and the rest.

21. Whatsoever is given with good success in the curing of pestilential and malignant diseases, to stop and bridle the spirits, lest they grow turbulent and tumultuous, may very happily be transferred to the prolongation of life; for one thing is effectual unto both, namely, the condensation of the spirits: now, there is nothing better for that than opiates.

22. The Turks find opium, even in a reasonable good quantity, harmless and comfortable, insomuch that they take it before their battle to excite courage; but to us, unless it be in a very small quantity, and with good correctives, it is mortal.

23. Opium and opiates are manifestly found to excite Venus; which shows them to have force to corroborate the spirits.

24. Distilled water out of wild poppy is given with good success in surfeits, agues, and divers diseases; which, no doubt, is a temperate kind of opiate. Neither let any man wonder at the various use of it, for that is familiar to opiates, in regard that the spirits, corroborated and condensed, will rise up against any disease.

25. The Turks use a kind of herb which they call caphe, which they dry and powder, and then drink in warm water, which they say doth not a little sharpen them both in their courage and in their wits; notwithstanding, if it be taken in a large quantity, it affects and disturbs the mind; whereby it is manifest, that it is of the same nature with opiates.

26. There is a root much renowned in all the eastern parts which they call betel, which the Indians and others use to carry in their mouths, and to champ it, and by that champing they are wonderfully enabled both to endure labours, and to overcome sicknesses, and to the act of carnal copulation: it seems to be a kind of stupefactive, because it exceedingly blacks the teeth.

27. Tobacco in our age is immoderately grown into use, and it affects men with a secret kind of delight, insomuch that they who have once inured themselves unto it, can hardly afterwards leave it; and no doubt it hath power to lighten the body, and to shake off weariness. Now, the virtue of it is commonly thought to be, because it opens the passages, and voids humours: but it may more rightly be referred to the condensation of the spirits, for it is a kind of henbane, and manifestly troubles the head as opiates do.

28. There are sometimes humours engendered in the body, which are as it were opiate themselves; as it is in some kind of melancholies, with which if a man be affected it is a sign of very long life.

29. The simple opiates (which are also called stupefactives) are these; opium itself, which is the juice of poppy, both the poppies as well in the herb as in the seed, henbane, mandrake, hemlock, tobacco, nightshade.

30. The compound opiates are, treacle, mithridate, trifera, laudanum, paracelsi, diaconium, diascordium, philonium, pills of houndstongue.

31. From this which hath been said, certain designations or counsels may be deduced for the prolongation of life, according to the present intention, namely, of condensing the spirits by opiates.

32. Let there be, therefore, every year, from adult years of youth, an opiate diet; let it be taken about the end of May, because the spirits in the summer are more loose and attenuated, and there are less dangers from cold humours; let it be some magistral opiate, weaker than those that are commonly in use, both in respect of a smaller quantity of opium, and of a more sparing mixture of extreme hot things; let it be taken in the morning betwixt sleeps. The fare for that time would be more simple and sparing than ordinary, without wine, or spices, or vaporous things. This medicine to be taken only each other day, and to be continued for a fortnight. This designation in our judgment comes home to the intention.

33. Opiates also may be taken not only by the mouth, but also by fumes; but the fumes must be such as may not move the expulsive faculty too strongly, nor force down humours, but only taken

in a weft, may work upon the spirits within the brain. And, therefore, a suffumigation of tobacco, lignum aloes, rosemary leaves dried, and a little myrrh snuffed up in the morning at the mouth and nostrils, would be very good.

34. In grand opiates, such as are treacle, mithridate, and the rest, it would not be amiss (especially in youth) to take rather the distilled waters of them, than themselves in their bodies; for the vapour in distilling doth rise, but the heat of the medicine commonly settleth. Now, distilled waters are good in those virtues which are conveyed by vapours, in other things but weak.

35. There are medicines which have a certain weak and hidden degree, and therefore safe to an opiate virtue; these send forth a slow and copious vapour, but not malignant as opiates do; therefore they put not the spirits to flight, notwithstanding they congregate them, and somewhat thicken them.

36. Medicines, in order to opiates, are principally saffron, next folium indum, ambergris, coriander seed prepared, amomum, pseuda momum, lignum rhodium, orange-flower water, and much more the infusion of the same flowers new gathered in the oil of almonds, nutmegs pricked full of holes and macerated in rosewater.

37. As opiates are to be taken very sparingly, and at certain times, as was said, so these secondaries may be taken familiarly, and in our daily diet, and they will be very effectual to prolongation of life. Certainly an apothecary of Calecute, by the use of amber, is said to have lived a hundred and sixty years, and the noblemen of Barbary through the use thereof are certified to be very long-lived, whereas the mean people are but of short life. And our ancestors, who were longer lived than we, did use saffron much in their cakes, broths, and the like. And touching the first way of condensing the spirits of opiates, and the subordinates thereto, thus much.

38. Now we will inquire of the second way of condensing the spirits by cold, for the proper work of cold is condensation, and it is done without any malignity, or adverse quality; and therefore it is a safer operation than by opiates, though somewhat less powerful, if it be done by turns only as opiates are. But then again, because it may be used familiarly, and in our daily diet with moderation, it is much more powerful for the prolongation of life than by opiates.

39. The refrigeration of the spirits is effected three ways, either by respiration, or by vapours, or by aliment. The first is the best, but, in a sort, out of our power; the second is potent, but yet ready and at hand; the third is weak and somewhat about.

40. Air clear and pure, and which hath no fogginess in it before it be received into the lungs, and which is least exposed to the sunbeams, condenseth the spirits best. Such is found either on the tops of dry mountains, or in champaigns open to the wind, and yet not without some shade.

41. As for the refrigeration and condensation of the spirits by vapours, the root of this operation we place in nitre, as a creature purposely made and chosen for this end, being thereunto led and persuaded by these arguments.

42. Nitre is a kind of cool spice; this is apparent to the sense itself, for it bites the tongue and palate with cold, as spices do with heat, and it is the only thing, as far as we know, that hath this property.

43. Almost all cold things (which are cold properly and not by accident, as opium is) are poor and jejune of spirit; contrarily, things full of spirit are almost all hot, only nitre is found amongst vegetables, which aboundeth with spirit and yet is cold. As for camphire, which is full of spirit, and yet performeth the actions of cold, it cooleth by accident only, as namely, for that by the thinness thereof, without acrimony, it helpeth perspiration and inflammations.

44. In congealing and freezing of liquors (which is lately grown into use) by laying snow and ice on the outside of the vessel, nitre is also added, and no doubt it exciteth and fortifieth the congelation. It is true, that they use also for this work ordinary bay-salt, which doth rather give activity to the coldness of the snow, than cool by itself; but, as I have heard, in the hotter regions, where snow falls not, the congealing is wrought by nitre alone; but this I cannot certainly affirm.

45. It is affirmed that gunpowder, which consisteth principally of nitre, being taken in drink doth conduce to valour, and that it is used oftentimes by mariners and soldiers before they begin their battles, as the Turks do opium.

46. Nitre is given with good success in burning agues, and pestilential fevers, to mitigate and bridle their pernicious heats.

47. It is manifest, that nitre in gunpowder doth mightily abhor the flame, from whence is caused that horrible crack and puffing.

48. Nitre is found to be, as it were, the spirit of the earth; for this is most certain, that any earth, though pure and unmixed with nitrous matter, if it be so laid up and covered, that it be free from the sunbeams, and putteth forth no vegetable, will gather nitre, even in good abundance. By which it is clear, that the spirit of nitre is not only inferior to the spirit of living creatures, but also to the spirit of vegetables.

49. Cattle, which drink of nitrous water, do manifestly grow fat, which is a sign of the cold in nitre.

50. The manuring of the soil is chiefly by nitrous substances; for all dung is nitrous, and this is a sign of the spirit in nitre.

51. From hence it appears, that the spirits of man may be cooled and condensed by the spirit of nitre, and be made more crude and less eager.

And, therefore, as strong wines, and spices, and the like, do burn the spirits and shorten life; so, on the contrary side, nitre doth compose and repress them, and furthereth to life.

52. Nitre may be used with meat, mixed with our salt, to the tenth part of the salt; in broths taken in the morning, for three grains to ten, also in beer; but howsoever it be used, with moderation, it is of prime force to long life.

53. As opium holds the pre-eminence in condensing the spirits, by putting them to flight, and hath withal his subordinates less potent, but more safe, which may be taken both in greater quantity and in more frequent use, of which we have formerly spoken; so also nitre, which condenseth the spirits by cold, and by a kind of frescour, (as we now-a-days speak,) hath also his subordinates.

54. Subordinates to nitre are, all those things which yield an odour somewhat earthy, like the smell of earth, pure and good, newly digged or turned up; of this sort the chief are, borage, buloss, langue de bœuf, burnet, strawberry leaves, and strawberries, frambois, or raspis, raw cucumbers, raw pearmains, vine leaves, and buds, also violets.

55. The next in order, are those which have a certain freshness of smell, but somewhat more inclined to heat, yet not altogether void of that virtue of refreshing by coolness; such as are balm, green citrons, green oranges, rosewater distilled, roasted wardens; also the damask, red, and musk roses.

56. This is to be noted, that subordinates to nitre do commonly confer more to this intension raw, than having passed the fire, because that the spirit of cooling is dissipated by the fire, therefore they are best taken either infused in some liquor, or raw.

57. As the condensation of the spirits by subordinates to opium is, in some sort, performed by odours, so also that which is by subordinates to nitre; therefore the smell of new and pure earth, taken either by following the plough, or by digging, or by weeding, excellently refresheth the spirits. Also the leaves of trees in woods, or hedges, falling towards the middle of autumn, yield a good refreshing to the spirits, but none so good as strawberry leaves dying. Likewise the smell of violets, or wallflowers, or beanflowers, or sweetbrier, or honeysuckles, taken as they grow, in passing by them only, is of the same nature.

58. Nay, and we know a certain great lord who lived long, that had every morning, immediately after sleep, a clod of fresh earth laid in a fair napkin under his nose, that he might take the smell thereof.

59. There is no doubt but the cooling and tempering of the blood by cool things, such as are endive, succory, leverwort, purslain, and the like, do also by consequent cool the spirits. But this is about, whereas vapours cool immediately.

60. And as touching the condensing of the spirits by cold, thus much. The third way of condensing the spirits we said to be by that which we call stroking the spirits. The fourth, by quieting the alacrity and unruliness of them.

61. Such things stroke the spirits as are pleasing and friendly to them, yet they allure them not to go abroad; but rather prevail, that the spirits, contented as it were in their own society, do enjoy themselves, and betake themselves into their proper centre.

61. For these, if you recollect those things which were formerly set down, as subordinates to opium and nitre, there will need no other inquisition.

62. As for the quieting of the unruliness of the spirits, we shall presently speak of that, when we inquire touching their motion. Now then, seeing we have spoken of that condensation of the spirits which pertaineth to their substance, we will come to the temper of heat in them.

63. The heat of the spirits, as we said, ought to be of that kind, that it may be robust, not eager, and may delight rather to master the tough and obstinate, than to carry away the thin and light humours.

64. We must beware of spices, wine, and strong drinks, that our use of them be very temperate, and sometimes discontinued. Also of savory, wild marjorum, pennyroyal, and all such as bite and heat the tongue; for they yield unto the spirits a heat not operative, but predatory.

65. These yield a robust heat, especially elecampane, garlick, carduus benedictus, watercresses, while they are young, germander, angelica, zedoary, vervin, valerian, myrrh, pepperwort, elder flowers, garden chervile. The use of these things, with choice and judgment, sometimes in salads, sometimes in medicines, will satisfy this operation.

66. It falls out well, that the grand opiates will also serve excellently for this operation, in respect that they yield such a heat by composition, which is wished, but not to be found in simples. For the mixing of those excessive hot things, (such as are euphorbium, pellitory of Spain, stavisacre, dragonwort, anacordi, castoreum, aristolochium, opponax, ammoniachum, galbanum, and the like, which of themselves cannot be taken inwardly,) to qualify and abate the stupefactive virtue of the opium, they do make such a constitution of a medicament as we now require; which is excellently seen in this, that treacle and mithridate, and the rest, are not sharp, nor bite the tongue, but are only somewhat bitter, and of strong scent, and at last manifest their heat when they come into the stomach, and in their subsequent operations.

67. There conduces also to the robust heat of the spirits, Venus often excited, rarely performed; and no less some of the affections, of which shall

2 T

he spoken hereafter. So touching the heat of the spirits, analogical to the prolongation of life, thus much.

68. Touching the quantity of the spirits, that they be not exuberant and boiling, but rather sparing, and within a mean, (seeing a small flame doth not devour so much as a great flame,) the inquisition will be short.

69. It seems to be approved by experience, that a spare diet, and almost a pythagorical, such as is either prescribed by the strict rules of a monastical life, or practised by hermits, which have necessity and poverty for their rule, rendereth a man long-lived.

70. Hitherto appertain drinking of water, a hard bed, abstinence from fire, a slender diet, (as, namely, of herbs, fruits, flesh, and fish, rather powdered and salted, than fresh and hot, a hair shirt, frequent fastings, frequent watchings, few sensual pleasures, and such like; for all these diminish the spirits, and reduce them to such a quantity as may be sufficient only for the functions of life, whereby the depredation is the less.

71. But if the diet shall not be altogether so rigorous and mortifying, yet, notwithstanding, shall be always equal and constant to itself, it worketh the same effect. We see it in flames, that a flame somewhat bigger (so it be always alike and quiet) consumeth less of the fuel, than a lesser flame blown with bellows, and by gusts stronger or weaker. That which the regiment and diet of Cornarus, the Venetian, showed plainly, who did eat and drink so many years together by a just weight, whereby he exceeded a hundred years of age, strong in limbs, and entire in his senses.

72. Care also must be taken, that a body, plentifully nourished, and not emaciated by any of these aforesaid diets, omitteth not a seasonable use of Venus, lest the spirits increase too fast, and soften and destroy the body. So then, touching a moderate quantity of spirits, and (as we may say) frugal, thus much.

73. The inquisition, touching bridling the motions of the spirits, followeth next. Motion doth manifestly attenuate and inflame them. This bridling is done by three means; by sleep, by avoiding of vehement labours, immoderate exercise, and, in a word, all lassitude; and by refraining irksome affections. And, first, touching sleep.

74. The fable tells us, that Epimenides slept many years together in a cave, and all that time needed no meat, because the spirits waste not much in sleep.

75. Experience teacheth us that certain creatures, as dormice and bats, sleep in some close places a whole winter together; such is the force of sleep to restrain all vital consumption. That which bees or drones are also thought to do, though

sometimes destitute of honey, and likewise butterflies and other flies.

76. Sleep after dinner (the stomach sending up no unpleasing vapours to the head, as being the first dews of our meat) is good for the spirits, but derogatory and hurtful to all other points of health. Notwithstanding in extreme old age there is the same reason of meat and sleep, for both our meals and our sleeps should be then frequent, but short and little; nay, and towards the last period of old age, a mere rest, and, as it were, a perpetual reposing doth best, especially in winter-time.

77. But as moderate sleep conferreth to long life, so much more if it be quiet and not disturbed.

78. These procure quiet sleep, violets, lettuce, especially boiled, syrup of dried roses, saffron, balm, apples, at our going to bed; a sop of bread in malmsey, especially where musk-roses have been first infused; therefore it would not be amiss to make some pill or a small draught of these things, and to use it familiarly. Also those things which shut the mouth of the stomach close, as coriander seed prepared, quinces and wardens roasted, do induce sound sleep; but above all things in youth, and for those that have sufficient strong stomachs, it will be best to take a good draught of clear cold water when they go to bed. Touching voluntary and procured trances, as also fixed and profound thoughts, so as they be without irksomeness, I have nothing certain; no doubt they make to this intention, and condense the spirits, and that more potently than sleep, seeing they lay asleep, and suspend the senses as much or more. Touching them, let further inquiry be made. So far touching sleep.

79. As for motion and exercise, lassitude hurteth, and so doth all motion and exercise which is too nimble and swift, as running, tennis, fencing, and the like; and, again, when our strength is extended and strained to the uttermost, as dancing, wrestling, and such like; for it is certain, that the spirits being driven into straits, either by the swiftness of the motion, or by the straining of the forces, do afterward become more eager and predatory. On the other side, exercises which stir up a good strong motion, but not over swift, or to our utmost strength, (such as are leaping, shooting, riding, bowling, and the like,) do not hurt, but rather benefit.

We must come now to the affections and passions of the mind, and see which of them are hurtful to long life, which profitable.

80. Great joys attenuate and diffuse the spirits, and shorten life; familiar cheerfulness strengthens the spirits, by calling them forth, and yet not resolving them.

81. Impressions of joy in the sense are naught; ruminations of joy in the memory, or apprehensions of them in hope or fancy, are good.

82. Joy suppressed, or communicated sparingly.

doth more comfort the spirits, than joy poured forth and published.

83. Grief and sadness, if it be void of fear, and afflict not too much, doth rather prolong life; for it contracteth the spirits, and is a kind of condensation.

84. Great fears shorten the life; for though grief and fear do both strengthen the spirit, yet in grief there is a simple contraction; but in fear, by reason of the cares taken for the remedy, and hopes intermixed, there is a turmoil and vexing of the spirits.

85. Anger suppressed is also a kind of vexation, and causeth the spirit to feed upon the juices of the body; but let loose and breaking forth, it helpeth; as those medicines do, which induce a robust heat.

86. Envy is the worst of all passions, and feedeth upon the spirits, and they again upon the body, and so much the more, because it is perpetual, and, as it is said, keepeth no holidays.

87. Pity of another man's misfortune, which is not likely to befall ourselves, is good; but pity, which may reflect with some similitude upon the party pitying, is naught, because it exciteth fear.

88. Light shame hurteth not, seeing it contracteth the spirits a little, and then straight diffuseth them, insomuch that shamefaced persons commonly live long; but shame for some great ignominy, and which afflicteth the mind long, contracteth the spirits even to suffocation, and is pernicious.

89. Love, if it be not unfortunate, and too deeply wounding, is a kind of joy, and is subject to the same laws which we have set down touching joy.

90. Hope is the most beneficial of all the affections, and doth much to the prolongation of life, if it be not too often frustrated, but entertaineth the fancy with an expectation of good; therefore they which fix and propound to themselves some end, as the mark and scope of their life, and continually and by degrees go forward in the same, are, for the most part, long-lived; insomuch that when they are come to the top of their hope, and can go no higher therein, they commonly droop, and live not long after. So that hope is a leaf-joy, which may be beaten out to a great extension, like gold.

91. Admiration and light contemplation are very powerful to the prolonging of life; for they hold the spirits in such things as delight them, and suffer them not to tumultuate, or to carry themselves unquietly and waywardly. And, therefore, all the contemplators of natural things, which had so many and eminent objects to admire, (as Democritus, Plato, Parmenides, Apollonius,) were long-lived; also rhetoricians, which tasted but lightly of things, and studied rather exornation of speech than profundity of matters, were also long-lived; as Gorgias, Protagoras,

Isocrates, Seneca. And, certainly, as old men are for the most part talkative, so talkative men do often grow very old: for it shows a light contemplation, and such as do not much strain the spirits, or vex them; but subtle, and acute, and eager inquisition shortens life, for it tireth the spirit, and wasteth it.

And as touching the motion of the spirits, by the affections of the mind, thus much. Now, we will add certain other general observations touching the spirits, besides the former, which fall not into the precedent distribution.

92. Especial care must be taken that the spirits be not too often resolved; for attenuation goeth before resolution, and the spirit once attenuated doth not very easily retire, or is condensed. Now, resolution is caused by over-great labours, over-vehement affections of the mind, over-great sweats, over-great evacuation, hot baths, and an untemperate and unseasonable use of Venus; also by over-great cares and carpings, and anxious expectations; lastly, by malignant diseases, and intolerable pains and torments of the body; all which, as much as may be, (which our vulgar physicians also advise,) must be avoided.

93. The spirits are delighted both with wonted things and with new. Now, it maketh wonderfully to the conservation of the spirits in vigour, that we neither use wonted things to a satiety and glutting; nor new things, before a quick and strong appetite. And, therefore, both customs are to be broken off with judgment and care, before they breed a fulness; and the appetite after new things to be restrained for a time until it grow more sharp and jocund; and, moreover, the life, as much as may be, so to be ordered, that it may have many renovations, and the spirits, by perpetual conversing in the same actions, may not wax dull. For though it were no ill saying of Seneca's, The fool doth ever begin to live; yet this folly, and many more such, are good for long life.

94. It is to be observed touching the spirits, (though the contrary used to be done,) that when men perceive their spirits to be in good, placid, and healthful state, (that which will be seen by the tranquillity of their mind, and cheerful disposition,) that they cherish them, and not change them; but when in a turbulent and untoward state, (which will also appear by their sadness, lumpishness, and other indisposition of their mind,) that then they straight overwhelm them, and alter them. Now, the spirits are contained in the same state, by a restraining of the affections, temperateness of diet, abstinence from Venus, moderation in labour, indifferent rest and repose, and the contrary to these do alter and overwhelm the spirits; as, namely, vehement affections, profuse feastings, immoderate Venus, difficult labours, earnest studies, and prosecution of business. Yet men are wont, when they are merriest and best

disposed, then to apply themselves to feastings, Venus, labours, endeavours, business, whereas, if they have a regard to long life, (which may seem strange,) they should rather practise the contrary. For we ought to cherish and preserve good spirits; and for the evil disposed spirits to discharge and alter them.

95. Ficinus saith not unwisely, that old men, for the comforting of their spirits, ought often to remember and ruminate upon the acts of their childhood and youth; certainly such a remembrance is a kind of peculiar recreation to every old man: and, therefore, it is a delight to men to enjoy the society of them which have been brought up together with them, and to visit the places of their education. Vespasian did attribute so much to this matter, that when he was emperor, he would by no means be persuaded to leave his father's house, though but mean, lest he should lose the wonted object of his eyes, and the memory of his childhood. And besides, he would drink in a wooden cup tipped with silver, which was his grandmother's, upon festival days.

96. One thing above all is grateful to the spirits, that there be a continual progress to the more benign; therefore we should lead such a youth and manhood, that our old age should find new solaces, whereof the chief is moderate ease: and, therefore, old men in honourable places lay violent hands upon themselves, who retire not to their ease; whereof may be found an eminent example in Cassiodorus, who was of that reputation amongst the gothish Kings of Italy, that he was as the soul of their affairs; afterwards, being near eighty years of age, he betook himself to a monastery, where he ended not his days before he was a hundred years old. But this thing doth require two cautions: one, that they drive not off till their bodies be utterly worn out and diseased; for in such bodies all mutation, though to the more benign, hasteneth death; the other, that they surrender not themselves to a sluggish ease, but that they embrace something which may entertain their thoughts and mind with contentation; in which kind, the chief delights are reading and contemplation, and then the desires of building and planting.

97. Lastly: the same action, endeavour, and labour, undertaken cheerfully and with a good will, doth refresh the spirits, but with an aversation and unwillingness, doth fret and deject them; and therefore it conferreth to long life, either that a man hath the art to institute his life so as it may be free and suitable to his own humour, or else to lay such a command upon his mind, that whatsoever is imposed by fortune, it may rather lead him than drag him.

98. Neither is that to be omitted towards the government of the affections, that especial care be taken of the mouth of the stomach, especially that it be not too much relaxed; for that part hath a greater dominion over the affections, especially the daily affections, than either the heart or brain, only those things excepted which are wrought by potent vapours, as in drunkenness and melancholy.

99. Touching the operation upon the spirits, that they may remain youthful, and renew their vigour thus much, which we have done more accurately, for that there is for the most part amongst physicians, and other authors, touching these operations, a deep silence; but especially, because the operation upon the spirits, and their waxing green again, is the most ready and compendious way to long life, and that for a twofold compendiousness; one, because the spirits work compendiously upon the body; the other, because vapours and the affections work compendiously upon the spirits, so as these attain the end, as it were, in a right line, other things rather in lines circular.

II. *The Operation upon the Exclusion of the Air.*

The History.

1. The exclusion of the air ambient tendeth to length of life two ways; first, for that the external air. next unto the native spirits, howsoever the air may be said to animate the spirit of man, and conferreth not a little to health, doth most of all prey upon the juices of the body, and hasten the desiccation thereof; and therefore the exclusion of it is effectual to length of life.

2. Another effect which followeth the exclusion of air is much more subtile and profound: namely, that the body closed up, and not perspiring by the pores, detaineth the spirits within, and turneth it upon the harder parts of the body, whereby the spirit mollifies and intenerates them.

3. Of this thing, the reason is explained in the desiccation of inanimate bodies, and it is an axiom almost infallible, that the spirit discharged and issuing forth, drieth bodies; detained, melteth and intenerateth them. And it is further to be assumed, that all heat doth properly attenuate and moisten, and contracteth and drieth only by accident.

4. Leading the life in dens and caves, where the air receives not the sunbeams, may be effectual to long life. For the air of itself doth not much towards the depredation of the body, unless it be stirred up by heat. Certainly, if a man shall recall things past to his memory, it will appear that the statures of men have been anciently much greater than those that succeeded, as in Sicily, and some other places: but this kind of men led their lives, for the most part, in caves. Now, length of life, and largeness of limbs, have some affinity; the cave also of Epimenides walks among the fables. I suppose likewise, that the life of columnar anchorites was a thing resembling the life in caves, in respect the sunbeams could not much pierce thither, nor the air receive any great changes or inequalities. This is certain, both the Simeon Stelitas, as well Daniel as Saba, and

other columnar anchorites, have been exceeding long-lived; likewise the anchorites in our days, closed up and immured either within walls or pillars, are often found to be long-lived.

5. Next unto the life in caves, is the life on mountains: for as the beams of the sun do not penetrate into caves, so on the tops of mountains, being destitute of reflection, they are of small force. But this is to be understood of mountains where the air is clear and pure; namely, whether by reason of the dryness of the valleys, clouds and vapours do not ascend, as it is in the mountains which encompass Barbary, where, even at this day, they live many times to a hundred and fifty years, as hath been noted before.

6. And this kind of air of caves and mountains, of its own proper nature, is little or nothing predatory; but air, such as ours is, which is predatory through the heat of the sun, ought as much as is possible to be excluded from the body.

7. But the air is prohibited and excluded two ways: first, by closing the pores: secondly, by filling them up.

8. To the closing of the pores, help coldness of the air, going naked, whereby the skin is made hard, washing in cold water, astringents applied to the skin, such as are mastick, myrrhe, myrtle.

9. But much more may we satisfy this operation by baths, yet those rarely used, (especially in summer,) which are made of astringent mineral waters, such as may safely be used, as waters participating of steel and copperas, for these do potently contract the skin.

10. As for filling up the pores, paintings, and such like unctuous daubings, and (which may most commodiously be used) oil and fat things, do no less conserve the substance of the body, than oil colours and varnish do preserve wood.

11 The ancient Britons painted their bodies with woad, and were exceeding long-lived; the Picts also used paintings, and are thought by some to have derived their name from thence.

12. The Brazilians and Virginians paint themselves at this day, who are (especially the former) very long-lived; insomuch that five years ago, the French Jesuites had speech with some who remembered the building of Fernambuck, which was done a hundred and twenty years since, and they were then at man's estate.

13. Joannes de Temporibus, who is reported to have extended his life to three hundred years, being asked how he preserved himself so long, is said to have answered, By oil without, and by honey within.

14. The Irish, especially the wild Irish, even at this day live very long; certainly they report, that within these few years, the Countess of Desmond lived to a hundred and forty years of age, and bred teeth three times. Now the Irish have a fashion to chafe, and, as it were, to baste themselves with old salt butter against the fire.

15. The same Irish used to wear saffroned linen and shirts, which, though it were at first devised to prevent vermin, yet howsoever I take it to be very useful for lengthening of life; for saffron, of all things that I know, is the best thing for the skin, and the comforting of the flesh, seeing it is both notably astringent, and hath besides an oleosity and subtile heat without any acrimony. I remember a certain Englishman who when he went to sea carried a bag of saffron next his stomach, that he might conceal it, and so escape custom; and whereas he was wont to be always exceeding seasick, at that time he continued very well, and felt no provocation to vomit.

16. Hippocrates adviseth in winter to wear clean linen, and in summer foul linen, and besmeared with oil: the reason may seem to be, because in summer the spirits exhale most, therefore the pores of the skin would be filled up.

17. Hereupon we are of opinion that the use of oil, either of olives or sweet almonds, to anoint the skin therewith, would principally conduce to long life. The anointing would be done every morning when we rise out of bed with oil, in which a little bay-salt and saffron is mixed. But this anointing must be lightly done with wool, or some soft sponge, not laying it on thick, but gently touching and wetting the skin.

18. It is certain that liquors, even the oily themselves, in great quantities draw somewhat from the body; but, contrarily, in small quantities are drunk in by the body; therefore the anointing would be but light as we said, or rather the shirt itself would be besmeared with oil.

19. It may happily be objected that this anointing with oil which we commend (though it were never in use with us, and amongst the Italians is cast off again) was anciently very familiar amongst the Grecians and Romans, and a part of their diet, and yet men were not longer lived in those days than now. But it may rightly be answered, oil was in use only after baths, unless it were perhaps amongst champions; now hot baths are as much contrary to our operation as anointings are congruous, seeing the one opens the passages, the other stops them up; therefore the bath without the anointing following is utterly bad, the anointing without the bath is best of all. Besides, the anointing amongst them was used only for delicacy, or (if you take it at the best) for health, but by no means in order to long life; and therefore they used them with all precious ointments, which were good for deliciousness, but hurtful to our intention, in regard of their heat; so that Virgil seemeth not to have said amiss,

———Nec casiâ liquidi corrumpitur usus olivi.
That odoriferous cassia hath not supplanted the use of neat oil olive.

20. Anointing with oil conduceth to health, both in winter, by the exclusion of the cold air,

and in summer, by detaining the spirits within, and prohibiting the resolution of them, and keeping off the force of the air, which is then most predatory.

21. Seeing the anointing with oil is one of the most potent operations to long life, we have thought good to add some cautions, lest the health should be endangered; they are four, according to the four inconveniences which may follow thereupon.

22. The first inconvenience is, that by repressing sweats it may engender diseases from those excrementitious humours. To this a remedy must be given by purges and clysters, that evacuation may be, duly performed. This is certain, that evacuation by sweats commonly advanceth health, and derogateth from long life, but gentle purges work upon the humours, not upon the spirits as sweat doth.

23. The second inconvenience is, that it may heat the body, and in time inflame it; for the spirits shut in, and not breathing forth, acquire heat. This inconvenience may be prevented, if the diet most usually incline to the colder part, and that at times some proper cooling medicines be taken, of which we shall straight speak in the operation upon the blood.

24. The third is, that it may annoy the head; for all oppletion from without strikes back the vapours, and sends them up into the head. This inconvenience is remedied by purgers, especially clysters, and by shutting the mouth of the stomach strongly with styptics, and by combing and rubbing the head, and by washing it with convenient lees, that something may exhale, and by not omitting competent and good exercises, that something also may perspire by the skin.

25. The fourth inconvenience is a more subtile evil; namely, that the spirit being detained by the closing up of the pores, is likely to multiply itself too much; for when little issueth forth, and new spirit is continually engendered, the spirit increaseth too fast, and so preyeth upon the body more plentifully. But this is not altogether so; for all spirit closed up is dull, (for it is blown and excited with motion as flame is,) and therefore it is less active, and less generative of itself; indeed it is thereby increased in heat, (as flame is,) but slow in motion. And therefore the remedy to this inconvenience must be by cold things, being sometimes mixed with oil, such as are roses and myrtles, for we must altogether disclaim hot things, as we said of cassia.

26. Neither will it be unprofitable to wear next the body garments that have in them some unctuosity, or oleosity, not aquosity, for they will exhaust the body less; such as are those of woollen. rather than those of linen. Certainly it is manifest in the spirits of odours, that if you lay sweet powders amongst linen, they will much sooner lose their smell than amongst woollen.

And therefore linen is to be preferred for delicacy and neatness, but to be suspected for our operation.

27. The wild Irish, as soon as they fall sick, the first thing they do is to take the sheets off their beds, and to wrap themselves in the woollen clothes.

28. Some report that they have found great benefit in the conservation of their health, by wearing scarlet waistcoats next their skin, and under their shirts, as well down to the nether parts as on the upper.

29. It is also to be observed, that air accustomed to the body doth less prey upon it than new air and often changed; and therefore poor people, in small cottages, who live always within the smell of the same chimney, and change not their seats, are commonly longest lived; notwithstanding, to other operations (especially for them whose spirits are not altogether dull) we judge change of air to be very profitable, but a mean must be used which may satisfy on both sides. This may be done by removing our habitation four times a year, at constant and set times, unto convenient seats, that so the body may neither be in too much peregrination, nor in too much station. And touching the operation upon the exclusion of air, and avoiding the predatory force thereof, thus much.

III. *The Operation upon the Blood, and the Sanguifying Heat.*

The history.

1. The following operations answer to the two precedent, and are in the relation of passives and actives; for the two precedent intend this, that the spirits and air in their actions may be the less depredatory. But because the blood is an irrigation or watering of the juices and members, and a preparation to them, therefore we will put the operation upon the blood in the first place: concerning this operation we will propound certain counsels, few in number, but very powerful in virtue: they are three.

2. First, there is no doubt, but that if the blood be brought to a cold temper, it will be so much the less dissipable. But because the cold things which are taken by the mouth agree but ill with many other intentions, therefore it will be best to find out some such things as may be free from these inconveniences.

3. The first is this: let there be brought into use, especially in youth, clysters not purging at all, or absterging, but only cooling, and somewhat opening: those are approved which are made of the juices of lettuce, purslane, liverwort, house-leek, and the mucilage of the seed of fleawort, with some temperate opening decoction, and a little camphire; but in the declining age let the house-leek and purslane be left out, and the juices of borage and endive, and the like. be

put in their rooms. And let these clysters be retained, if it may be for an hour or more.

4. The other is this, let there be in use, especially in summer, baths of fresh water, and but lukewarm, altogether without emollients, as mallows, mercury, milk, and the like; rather take new whey in some good quantity, and roses.

5. But (that which is the principal in this intention and new) we advise that before the bathing, the body be anointed with oil, with some thickness, whereby the quality of the cooling may be received, and the water excluded : yet let not the pores of the body be shut too close, for when the outward cold closeth up the body too strongly, it is so far from furthering coolness, that it rather forbids, and stirs up heat.

6. Like unto this is the use of bladders, with some decoctions and cooling juices, applied to the inferior region of the body, namely, from the ribs to the privy parts : for this also is a kind of bathing, where the body of the liquor is for the most part excluded, and the cooling quality admitted.

7. The third counsel remaineth, which belongeth not to the quality of the blood, but to the substance thereof, that it may be made more firm and less dissipable, and such as the heat of the spirit may have the less power over it.

8. And as for the use of filings of gold, leaf-gold, powder of pearl, precious stones, coral, and the like, we have no opinion of them at this day, unless it be only as they may satisfy this present operation. Certainly, seeing the Arabians, Grecians, and modern physicians, have attributed such virtues to these things, it cannot be altogether nothing, which so great men have observed of them. And, therefore, omitting all fantastical opinions about them, we do verily believe, that if there could be some such things conveyed into the whole mass of the blood in minute and fine portions, over which the spirits and heat should have little or no power, absolutely it would not only resist putrefaction, but arefaction also, and be a most effectual means to the prolongation of life. Nevertheless, in this thing several cautions are to be given ; first, that there be a most exact comminution : secondly, that such hard and solid things be void of all malignant qualities, lest while they be dispersed and lurk in the veins, they breed some illconvenience : thirdly, that they be never taken together with meats, nor in any such manner as they may stick long, lest they beget dangerous obstructions about the mesentery : lastly, that they be taken very rarely, that they may not coagulate and knot together in the veins.

9. Therefore, let the manner of taking them be fasting, in white wine, a little oil of almonds mingled therewith, exercise used immediately upon the taking of them.

10. The simples which may satisfy this operation are, instead of all, gold, pearls, and coral ; for all metals, except gold, are not without some malignant quality in the dissolutions of them, neither will they be beaten to that exquisite fineness that leaf-gold hath. As for all glassy and transparent jewels, we like them not, (as we said before,) for fear of corrosion.

11. But, in our judgment, the safer and more effectual way would be by the use of woods in infusions and decoctions ; for there is in them sufficient to cause firmness of blood, and not the like danger for breeding obstructions ; but especially, because they may be taken in meat and drink, whereby they will find the more easy entrance into the veins, and not be avoided in excrements.

12. The woods fit for this purpose are sanders, the oak, and vine. As for all hot woods or something rosiny, we reject them ; notwithstanding, you may add the woody stalks of rosemary dried, for rosemary is a shrub, and exceedeth in age many trees, also the woody stalks of ivy, but in such quantity as they may not yield an unpleasing taste.

13. Let the woods be taken either boiled in broths, or infused in must or ale before they leave working ; but in broths (as the custom is for guaiacum and the like) they would be infused a good while before the boiling, that the firmer part of the wood, and not that only which lieth loosely, may be drawn forth. As for ash, though it be used for cups, yet we like it not. And touching the operation upon the blood, thus much.

IV. *The Operation upon the Juices of the Body.*

The history.

1. There are two kinds of bodies (as was said before in the inquisition touching inanimates) which are hardly consumed, hard things and fat things, as is seen in metals and stones, and in oil and wax.

2. It must be ordered, therefore, that the juice of the body be somewhat hard, and that it be fat or subroscid.

3. As for hardness, it is caused three ways : by aliment of a firm nature, by cold condensing the skin and flesh, and by exercise, binding and compacting the juices of the body, that they be not soft and frothy.

4. As for the nature of the aliment, it ought to be such as is not easily dissipable, such as are beef, swine's flesh, deer, goat, kid, swan, goose, ringdove, especially if they be a little powdered ; fish is likewise salted and dried, old cheese, and the like.

5. As for the bread, oaten bread or bread with some mixture of pease in it, or rye bread, or barley bread, are more solid than wheat bread, and in wheat bread, the coarse wheat bread is more solid than the pure manchet.

6. The inhabitants of the Orcades, which live upon salted fish, and generally all fish eaters, are long-lived.

7. The monks and hermits which fed sparingly.

and upon dry aliment, attained commonly to a great age.

8. Also, pure water usually drunk, makes the juices of the body less frothy; unto which if, for the dulness of the spirits, (which no doubt in water are but a little penetrative,) you shall add a little nitre, we conceive it would be very good. And touching the firmness of the aliment, thus much.

9. As for the condensation of the skin and flesh by cold: they are longer lived for the most part that live abroad in the open air, than they that live in houses; and the inhabitants of the cold countries, than the inhabitants of the hot.

10. Great store of clothes, either upon the bed or back, do resolve the body.

11. Washing the body in cold water is good for length of life; use of hot baths is naught: touching baths of astringent mineral waters, we have spoken before.

12. As for exercise, an idle life doth manifestly make the flesh soft and dissipable: robust exercise (so it be without overmuch sweating or weariness) maketh it hard and compact. Also exercise within cold water, as swimming, is very good; and generally exercise abroad is better than that within houses.

13. Touching frications, (which are a kind of exercise,) because they do rather call forth the aliment that hardens the flesh, we will inquire hereafter in the due place.

14. Having now spoken of hardening the juices of the body, we are to come next to the oleosity and fatness of them, which is a more perfect and potent intention than induration, because it hath no inconvenience or evil annexed. For all those things which pertain to the hardening of the juices are of that nature, that while they prohibit the absumption of the aliment, they also hinder the operation of the same; whereby it happens, that the same things are both propitious and adverse to length of life; but those things which pertain to making the juices oily and roscid, help on both sides, for they render the aliment both less dissipable, and more reparable.

15. But, whereas we say that the juice of the body ought to be roscid and fat, it is to be noted that we mean it not of a visible fat, but of a dewiness dispersed, or (if you will call it) radical in the very substance of the body.

16. Neither again let any man think, that oil, or the fat of meat or marrow, do engender the like, and satisfy our intention: for those things which are once perfect are not brought back again; but the aliments ought to be such, which after digestion and maturation, do then in the end engender oleosity in the juices.

17. Neither again let any man think, that oil or fat by itself and simple is hard of dissipation; but in mixture it doth not retain the same nature: for as oil by itself is much more longer in consuming than water, so in paper or linen, it sticketh longer, and is later dried, as we noted before.

18. To the irroration of the body, roasted meats or baked meats are more effectual than boiled meats, and all preparation of meat with water is inconvenient; besides oil is more plentifully extracted out of dried bodies than out of moist bodies.

19. Generally, to the irroration of the body much use of sweet things is profitable, as of sugar, honey, sweet almonds, pineapples, pistachios, dates, raisins of the sun, corans, figs, and the like. Contrarily, all sour, and very salt, and very biting things are opposite to the generation of roscid juice.

20. Neither would we be thought to favour the Maenichees, or their diet, though we commend the frequent use of all kinds of seeds, kernels, and roots in meats or sauces, considering all bread (and bread is that which maketh the meat firm) is made either of seeds or roots.

21. But there is nothing makes so much to the irroration of the body as the quality of the drink, which is the convoy of the meat; therefore, let there be in use such drinks as without all acrimony or sourness are notwithstanding subtile; such are those wines which are (as the old woman said in Plautus) vetustate edentula, toothless with age, and ale of the same kind.

22. Mead (as we suppose) would not be ill if it were strong and old; but because all honey hath in it some sharp parts, (as appears by that sharp water which the chymists extract out of it, which will dissolve metals,) it were better to take the same portion of sugar, not lightly infused into it, but so incorporated as honey useth to be in mead, and to keep it to the age of a year, or at least six months, whereby the water may lose the crudity, and the sugar acquire subtilty.

23. Now, ancientness in wine or beer hath this in it, that it engenders subtilty in the parts of the liquor, and acrimony in the spirits, whereof the first is profitable, and the second hurtful. Now, to rectify this evil commixture, let there be put into the vessel, before the wine be separated from the must, swine's flesh or deer's flesh well boiled, that the spirits of the wine may have whereupon to ruminate and feed, and so lay aside their mordacity.

24. In like manner, if ale should be made not only with the grains of wheat, barley, oats, pease, and the like, but also should admit a part (suppose a third part to these grains) of some fat roots, such as are potado roots, pith of artichokes, burre roots, or some other sweet and esculent roots; we suppose it would be a more useful drink for long life than the ale made of grains only.

Also, such things as have very thin parts, yet, notwithstanding, are without all acrimony or mordacity, are very good salads; which virtue we find to be in some few of the flowers, namely, flowers of ivy, which, infused in vinegar, are pleasant even to the taste, marigold leaves, which are used in broths, and flowers of betony. And, touching the operation upon the juices of the body, thus much.

V. *The Operation upon the Bowels of their Extrusion of Aliment.*

The history.

1. What those things are which comfort the principal bowels, which are the fountains of concoctions, namely, the stomach, liver, heart, and brain, to perform their functions well, (whereby aliment is distributed into the parts, spirits are dispersed, and the reparation of the whole body is accomplished,) may be derived from physicians, and from their prescripts and advices.

2. Touching the spleen, gall, kidneys, mesenteries, guts, and lungs, we speak not, for these are members ministering to the principal, and whereas speech is made touching health, they require sometimes a most special consideration, because each of these have their diseases, which, unless they be cured, will have influence upon the principal members. But, as touching the prolongation of life, and reparation by aliments, and retardation of the incoction of old age; if the concoctions and those principal bowels be well disposed, the rest will commonly follow according to one's wish.

3. And as for those things which, according to the different state of every man's body, may be transferred into his diet, and the regiment of his life, he may collect them out of the books of physicians, which have written of the comforting and preserving the four principal members; for conservation of health hath commonly need of no more than some short courses of physic, but length of life cannot be hoped without an orderly diet, and a constant race of sovereign medicines. But we will propound some few, and those the most select and prime directions.

4. The stomach (which, as they say, is the master of the house, and whose strength and goodness is fundamental to the other concoctions) ought so to be guarded and confirmed that it may be without intemperateness hot; next, astricted or bound, not loose; furthermore, clean, not surcharged with foul humours, and yet (in regard it is nourished from itself, and not from the veins) not altogether empty or hungry; lastly, it is to be kept ever in appetite, because appetite sharpens digestion.

5. I wonder much how that same calidum bibere, to drink warm drink, (which was in use amongst the ancients,) is laid down again. I knew a physician that was very famous, who, in the beginning of dinner and supper, would usually eat a few spoonfuls of very warm broth with much greediness, and then would presently wish that it were out again, saying, he had no need of the broth, but only of the warmth.

6. I do verily conceive it good that the first draught either of wine, or ale, or any other drink (to which a man is most accustomed) be taken at supper warm.

7. Wine in which gold hath been quenched, I conceive, would be very good once in a meal; not that I believe the gold conferreth any virtue thereunto, but that I know that the quenching of all metals in any kind of liquor doth leave a most potent astriction. Now, I choose gold, because, besides that astriction which I desire, it leaveth nothing behind it of a metalline impression.

8. I am of opinion that the sops of bread dipped in wine, taken at the midst of the meal, are better than wine itself, especially if there were infused into the wine in which the sops were dipped, rosemary and citron pill, and that with sugar, that it may not slip too fast.

9. It is certain that the use of quinces is good to strengthen the stomach, but we take them to be better if they be used in that which they call quiddeny of quinces, than in the bodies of the quinces themselves, because they lie heavy in the stomach. But those quiddenies are best taken, after meals, alone; before meals, dipped in vinegar.

10. Such things as are good for the stomach above other simples are these, rosemary, elecampane, mastic, wormwood, sage, mint.

11. I allow pills of aloes, mastic, and saffron, winter-time, taken before dinner, but so as the aloes be not only oftentimes washed in rose-water, but also in vinegar in which tragacanth hath been infused, and after that be macerated for a few hours in oil of sweet almonds new drawn, before it be made into pills.

12. Wine or ale, wherein wormwood has been infused, with a little elecampane and yellow sanders, will do well, taken at times, and that especially in winter.

13. But in summer, a draught of white wine allayed with strawberry water, in which wine, powder of pearls, and of the shells of crawfishes exquisitely beaten, and (which may, perhaps, seem strange) a little chalk have been infused, doth excellently refresh and strengthen the stomach.

14. But, generally, all draughts in the morning (which are but too frequently used) of cooling things, as of juices, decoctions, whey, barley waters, and the like, are to be avoided, and nothing is to be put into the stomach fasting which is purely cold. These things are better given, if need require, either at five in the afternoon, or else an hour after a light breakfast.

15. Often fastings are bad for long life; besides, all thirst is to be avoided, and the stomach is to be kept clean, but always moist.

16. Oil of olives new and good, in which a

little mithridate hath been dissolved, anointed upon the backbone, just against the mouth of the stomach, doth wonderfully comfort the stomach.

17. A small bag filled with locks of scarlet wool steeped in red wine, in which myrtle, and citron pill, and a little saffron have been infused, may be always worn upon the stomach. And touching those things which comfort the stomach, thus much, seeing many of those things also which serve for other operations are helpful to this.

18. The liver, if it be preserved from torrefaction or desiccation, and from obstruction, it needeth no more; for that looseness of it which begets aquosities is plainly a disease, but the other two, old age approaching induceth.

19. Hereunto appertain most especially those things which are set down in the operation upon the blood; we will add a very few things more, but those selected.

20. Principally, let there be in use the wine of sweet pomegranates; or, if that cannot be had, the juice of them newly pressed; let it be taken in the morning with a little sugar, and into the glass into which the expression is made put a small piece of citron pill, green, and three or four whole cloves; let this be taken from February till the end of April.

21. Bring also into use, above all other herbs, water-cresses, but young, not old; they may be used either raw in sallets, or in broths, or in drinks; and after that take spoonwort.

22. Aloes, however washed or corrected, is hurtful for the liver, and therefore it is never to be taken ordinarily. Contrariwise, rhubarb is sovereign for the liver, so that these three cautions be interposed: First, that it be taken before meat, lest it dry the body too much, or leave some impressions of the stypicity thereof. Secondly, that it be macerated an hour or two in oil of sweet almonds new drawn, with rosewater, before it be infused in liquor, or given in the proper substance. Thirdly, that it be taken by turns, one while simple, another while with tartar, or a little bay-salt, that it carry not away the lighter parts only, and make the mass of the humours the more obstinate.

23. I allow wine, or some decoction with steel, to be taken three or four times in the year, to open the more strong obstructions; yet so that a draught of two or three spoonfuls of oil of sweet almonds, new drawn, ever go before, and the motion of the body, especially of the arms and sides, constantly follow.

24 Sweetened liquors, and that with some fatness, are principally, and not a little effectual to prevent the arefaction, and saltness, and torrefaction; and, in a word, the oldness of the liver, especially if they be well incorporated with age. They are made of sweet fruits and roots; as, namely, the wines and julips of raisins of the sun new, jujubes, dried figs, dates, parsnips, potatoes, and the like, with the mixture of liquorice sometimes. Also, a julip of the Indian grain, (which they call maize,) with the mixture of some sweet things, doth much to the same end. But it is to be noted, that the intention of preserving the liver in a kind of softness and fatness, is much more powerful than that other which pertains to the opening of the liver, which rather tendeth to health, than to length of life, saving that obstruction which induceth torrefaction, is as opposite to long life as those other arefactions.

25. I commend the roots of succory, spinage, and beets cleared of their piths, and boiled till they be tender in water, with a third part of white wine, for ordinary sallets, to be eaten with oil and vinegar. Also asparagus, pith of artichokes, and burroots boiled and served in after the same manner. Also broths in the spring-time of vine-buds, and the green blades of wheat. And touching the preserving of the liver, thus much.

26. The heart receiveth benefit or harm most from the air which we breathe, from vapours, and from the affections. Now, many of those things which have been formerly spoken, touching the spirits, may be transferred hither; but that undigested mass of cordials collected by physicians avails little to our intention; notwithstanding, those things which are found to be good against poisons, may, with good judgment, be given to strengthen and fortify the heart, especially if they be of that kind, that they do not so much resist the particular poisons, as arm the heart and spirits against poison in general. And touching these several cordials, you may repair to the table already set down.

27. The goodness of the air is better known by experience than by signs. We hold that air to be best where the country is level and plain, and that lieth open on all sides, so that the soil be dry, and yet not barren or sandy; which puts forth wild thyme, and eyebright, and a kind of marjoram, and here and there stalks of calamint; which is not altogether void of wood, but conveniently set with some trees for shade, where the sweetbrier-rose smelleth something musky and aromatically. If there be rivers, we suppose them rather hurtful than good, unless they be very small, and clear, and gravelly.

28. It is certain, that the morning air is more lively and refreshing than the evening air, though the latter be preferred out of delicacy.

29. We conceive also, that the air stirred with a gentle wind, is more wholesome than the air of a serene and calm sky; but the best is, the wind blowing from the west in the morning, and from the north in the afternoon.

30. Odours are especially profitable for the comforting of the heart, yet not so, as though a good odour were the prerogative of a good air; for it is certain, that as there are some pestilential

airs which smell not so ill as others that are less hurtful; so, on the contrary, there are some airs most wholesome and friendly to the spirits, which either smell not at all, or are less pleasing and fragrant to the sense. And generally, when the air is good, odours should be taken but now and then; for a continual odour, though never so good, is burdensome to the spirits.

31. We commend, above all others, (as we have touched before,) odour of plants growing, and not plucked, taken in the open air; the principal of that kind are, violets, gilliflowers, pinks, bean-flowers, lime tree blossoms, vine-buds, honeysuckles, yellow wallflowers, musk-roses, (for other roses growing are fast of their smells,) strawberry leaves, especially dying, sweetbrier, principally in the early spring, wild mint, lavender flowered; and in the hotter countries, orange tree, citron tree, myrtle, laurel. Therefore, to walk or sit near the breath of these plants, would not be neglected.

32. For the comforting of the heart, we prefer cool smells before hot smells; therefore, the best perfume is, either in the morning, or about the heat of the day, to take an equal portion of vinegar, rose-water, and claret wine, and to pour them upon a firepan somewhat heated.

33. Neither let us be thought to sacrifice to our mother the earth, though we advise that, in digging or ploughing the earth for health, a quantity of claret wine be poured thereon.

34. Orange-flower water, pure and good, with a small portion of rose-water, and brisk wine, snuffed up into the nostrils, or put into the nostrils with a syringe, after the manner of an errhine, (but not too frequently,) is very good.

35. But champing, (though we have no betel,) or holding in the mouth only of such things as cheer the spirits, (even daily done,) is exceeding comfortable. Therefore, for that purpose make grains, or little cakes of ambergris, musk, lignum aloes, lignum rhodium, orras powder, and roses; and let those grains or cakes be made up with rose-water which hath passed through a little Indian balsam.

36. The vapours which, arising from things inwardly taken, do fortify and cherish the heart, ought to have these three properties, that they be friendly, clear, and cooling; for hot vapours are naught, and wine itself, which is thought to have only a heating vapour, is not altogether void of an opiate quality. Now we call these vapours clear, which have more of the vapours than of the exhalation, and which are not smoky, or fuliginous, or unctuous, but moist and equal.

37. Out of that unprofitable rabble of cordials a few ought to be taken into daily diet; instead of all, ambergris, saffron, and the grain of Kermes, of the hotter sort. Roots of bugloss and borage, citrons, sweet lemons, and pearmains, of the colder sort. Also, that way which we said, both gold and pearls work a good effect, not only within the veins, but in their passage, and about the parts near the heart; namely, by cooling, without any malignant quality.

38. Of bezoar-stone we believe well, because of many trials; but then the manner of taking it ought to be such, as the virtue thereof may more easily be communicated to the spirits. Therefore, we approve not the taking of it in broths or syrups, or in rose-water, or any such like; but only in wine, cinnamon-water, or the like distilled water, but that weak or small, not burning or strong.

39. Of the affections we have spoken before: we only add this, that every noble, and resolute, and (as they call it) heroical desire, strengtheneth and enlargeth the powers of the heart. And touching the heart, thus much.

40. As for the brain, where the seat and court of the animal spirits is kept, those things which were inquired before touching opium, and nitre, and the subordinates to them both; also touching the procuring of placid sleep, may likewise be referred hither. This also is most certain, that the brain is in some sort in the custody of the stomach; and, therefore, those things which comfort and strengthen the stomach, do help the brain by consent, and may no less be transferred hither. We will add a few observations, three outward, one inward.

41. We would have bathing of the feet to be often used, at least once in a week; and the bath to be made of lye with bay-salt, and a little sage, camomile, fennel, sweet marjoram, and pepperwort, with the leaves of angelica green.

42. We commend also a fume or suffumigation every morning of dried rosemary, bay leaves dried, and lignum aloes; for all sweet gums oppress the head.

43. Especially care must be taken that no hot things be applied to the head outwardly; such are all kind of spices, the very nutmeg not excepted; for those hot things, we debase them to the soles of the feet, and would have them applied there only; but a light anointing of the head with oil, mixed with roses, myrtle, and a little salt and saffron, we much commend.

44. Not forgetting those things which we have before delivered touching opiates, nitre, and the like, which so much condense the spirits; we think it not impertinent to that effect that once in fourteen days broth be taken in the morning with three or four grains of castoreum, and a little angelica seed, and calamus, which both fortify the brain, and in that aforesaid density of the substance of the spirits, (so necessary to long life,) add also a vivacity of motion and vigour to them.

45. In handling the comforters of the four principal bowels we have propounded those things which are both proper and choice, and may

safely and conveniently be transferred into diets and regiment of life; for variety of medicines is the daughter of ignorance; and it is not more true, that many dishes have caused many diseases, as the proverb is, than this is true, that many medicines have caused few cures. And touching the operation upon the principal bowels for their extrusion of aliment, thus much.

VI. *The Operation upon the Outward Parts for their Attraction of Aliment.*

The history.

1. Although a good concoction performed by the inward parts be the principal towards a perfect alimentation, yet the actions of the outward parts ought also to concur; that like as the inward faculty sendeth forth and extrudeth the aliment, so the faculty of the outward parts may call forth, and attract the same; and the more weak the faculty of concoction shall be, the more need is there of a concurring help of the attractive faculty.

2. A strong attraction of the outward parts is chiefly caused by the motion of the body, by which the parts being heated and comforted, do more cheerfully call forth and attract the aliment unto themselves.

3. But this is most of all to be foreseen and avoided, that the same motion and heat which calls the new juice to the members, doth not again despoil the member of that juice wherewith it had been before refreshed.

4. Frications used in the morning serve especially to this intention; but this must evermore accompany them, that after the frication, the part being lightly anointed with oil, lest the attrition of the outward parts make them by perspiration dry and juiceless.

5. The next is exercise, (by which the parts confricate and chafe themselves,) so it be moderate, and which (as was noted before) is not swift, nor to the utmost strength, nor unto weariness. But in exercise and frication there is the same reason and caution, that the body may not perspire, or exhale too much. Therefore exercise is better in the open air than in the house, and better in winter than in summer. And, again, exercise is not only to be concluded with unction, as frication is, but in vehement exercises unction is to be used both in the beginning and in the end, as it was anciently to champions.

6. That exercise may resolve either the spirits or the juices as little as may be, it is necessary that it be used when the stomach is not altogether empty; and, therefore, that it may not be used upon a full stomach, (which doth much concern health,) nor yet upon an empty stomach, (which doth no less concern long life,) it is best to take a breakfast in the morning, not of any physical drugs, or of any liquors, or of raisins, or of figs, or the like, but of plain meat and drink; yet that very light, and in moderate quantity.

7. Exercises used for the irrigation of the members, ought to be equal to all the members; not (as Socrates said) that the legs should move, and the arms should rest, or on the contrary; but that all the parts may participate of the motion. And it is altogether requisite to long life, that the body should never abide long in one posture, but that every half hour, at least, it change the posture, saving only in sleep.

8. Those things which are used to mortification, may be transferred to vivification; for both hair-shirts, and scourgings, and all vexations of the outward parts, do fortify the attractive force of them.

9. Cardan commends nettling, even to let out melancholy; but of this we have no experience. And, besides, we have no good opinion of it, lest, through the venomous quality of the nettle, it may with often use breed itches, and other diseases of the skin. And touching the operation upon the outward parts for their attraction of aliment, thus much.

VII. *The Operation upon the Aliment itself, for the Insinuation thereof.*

The history.

1. The vulgar reproof touching many dishes, doth rather become a severe reformer, than a physician; or, howsoever it may be good for preservation of health, yet it is hurtful to length of life, by reason that a various mixture of aliments, and somewhat heterogeneous, finds a passage into the veins and juices of the body more lively and cheerfully, than a simple and homogeneous diet doth; besides, it is more forcible to stir up appetite, which is the spur of digestion. Therefore we allow both a full table, and a continual changing of dishes, according to the seasons of the year, or upon other occasions.

2. Also that opinion of the simplicity of meats without sauces, is but a simplicity of judgment; for good and well chosen sauces are the most wholesome preparation of meats, and conduce both to health and to long life.

3. It must be ordered, that with meats hard of digestion be conjoined strong liquors, and sauces that may penetrate and make way; but with meats more easy of digestion, smaller liquors, and fat sauces.

4. Whereas we advised before, that the first draught at supper should be taken warm; now we add, that for the preparation of the stomach, a good draught of that liquor (to which every man is most accustomed) be taken warm half an hour before meat also, but a little spiced, to please the taste.

5. The preparation of meats, and bread, and drinks, that they may be rightly handled, and in

order to this intention, is of exceeding great moment, howsoever it may seem a mechanical thing, and savouring of the kitchen and buttery; yet it is of more consequence than those fables of gold, and precious stones, and the like.

6. The moistening of the juices of the body by a moist preparation of the aliment, is a childish thing, it may be somewhat available against the fervours of diseases, but it is altogether averse to roscid alimentation. Therefore, boiling of meats, as concerning our intention, is far inferior to roasting, and baking, and the like.

7. Roasting ought to be with a quick fire, and soon despatched, not with a dull fire and in long time.

8. All solid fleshes ought to be served in not altogether fresh, but somewhat powdered or corned; the less salt may be spent at the table with them, or none at all; for salt incorporated with the meat before, is better distributed in the body than eaten with it at the table.

9. There would be brought into use several and good macerations and infusions of meats in convenient liquors, before the roasting of them, tho like whereof are sometime in use before they bake them, and in the pickles of some fishes.

10. But beatings, and as it were scourgings, of flesh meats before they be boiled, would work no small matter. We see it is confessed, that partridges and pheasants killed with a hawk, also bucks and stags killed in hunting, if they stand not out too long, eat better even to the taste, and some fishes scourged and beaten become more tender and wholesome; also hard and sour pears, and some other fruits, grow sweet with rolling them. It were good to practise some such beating and bruising of the harder kinds of fleshes before they be brought to the fire, and this would be one of the best preparations of all.

11. Bread a little leavened and very little salted is best, and which is baked in an oven thoroughly heated, and not with a faint heat.

12. The preparation of drinks, in order to long life, shall not exceed one precept; and as touching water drinkers, we have nothing to say: such a diet (as we said before) may prolong life to an indifferent term, but to no eminent length; but in other drinks that are full of spirit, (such as are wine, ale, mead, and the like,) this one thing is to be observed and pursued as the sum of all, That the parts of the liquor may be exceeding thin and subtile, and the spirit exceeding mild. This is hard to be done by age alone, for that makes the parts a little more subtile, but the spirits much more sharp and eager; therefore, of the infusions in the vessels of some fat substance, which may restrain the acrimony of the spirits, counsel hath been given before. There is also another way without infusion or mixture; this is, that the liquor might be continually agitated, either by carriage upon the water, or by carriage by land, or by hanging the vessels upon lines, and daily stirring them, or some such other way; for it is certain, that this local motion doth both subtilize the parts, and doth so incorporate and compact the spirits with the parts, that they have no leisure to turn to sourness, which is a kind of putrefaction.

But in extreme old age such a preparation of meats is to be made, as may be almost in the middle way to chylous. And touching the distillations of meats, they are mere toys, for the nutritive part, at least the best of it, doth not ascend in vapours.

14. The incorporating of meat and drink before they meet in the stomach, is a degree to chylous; therefore let chickens, or partridges, or pheasants, or the like, be taken and boiled in water, with a little salt, then let them be cleansed and dried, afterward let them be infused in must or ale before it hath done working, with a little sugar.

Also grazies of meat, and the mincings of them small, well seasoned, are good for old persons; and the rather, for that they are destituted of the office of their teeth in chewing, which is a principal kind of preparation.

16. And as for the helps of that defect, (namely, of the strength of teeth to grind the meat,) there are three things which may conduce thereunto. First, that new teeth may put forth; that which seems altogether difficult, and cannot be accomplished without an inward and powerful restauration of the body. Secondly, that the jaws be so confirmed by due astringents, that they may in some sort supply the office of the teeth; which may possibly be effected. Thirdly, that the meat be so prepared, that there shall be no need of chewing, which remedy is at hand.

17. We have some thought also touching the quantity of the meat and drink, that the same taken in a larger quantity at some times, is good for the irrigation of the body; therefore both great feastings, and free drinkings, are not altogether to be inhibited. And touching the operation upon the aliments, and the preparation of them, thus much.

VIII. *The Operation upon the last Act of Assimilation.*

Touching the last act of assimilation, (unto which the three operations immediately preceding chiefly tend,) our advice shall be brief and single, and the thing itself rather needs explication than any various rules.

1. It is certain, that all bodies are endued with some desire of assimilating those things which are next them. This the rare and pneumatical bodies, as flame, spirit, air, perform generously and with alacrity; on the contrary, those that carry a gross and tangible bulk about them do but weakly, in regard that the desire of assimilating

other things is bound in by a stronger desire of rest, and containing themselves from motion.

2. Again, it is certain that the desire of assimilating being bound, as we said, in a gross body, and made ineffectual, is somewhat freed and stirred up by the heat and neighbouring spirit, so that it is then actuated; which is the only cause why inanimates assimilate not, and animates assimilate.

3. This also is certain, that the harder the consistence of the body is, the more doth that body stand in need of a greater heat to prick forward the assimilation; which falls out ill for old men, because in them the parts are more obstinate, and the heat weaker, and therefore either the obstinacy of their parts is to be softened or their heat increased. And, as touching the malacissation or mollifying of the members, we shall speak afterward, having also formerly propounded many things which pertain to the prohibiting and preventing of this kind of hardness. For the other, touching the increasing of the heat, we will now deliver a single precept, after we have first assumed this axiom.

4. The act of assimilation (which, as we said, is excited by the heat circumfused) is a motion exceeding accurate, subtile, and in little; now, all such motions do then come to their vigour, when the local motion wholly ceaseth which disturbeth it. For the motion of separation into homogeneal parts, which is in milk, that the cream should swim above, and the whey sink to the bottom, will never work, if the milk be never so little agitated; neither will any putrefaction proceed in water or mixed bodies, if the same be in continual local motion. So, then, from this assumption we will conclude this for the present inquisition.

5. The act itself of assimilation, is chiefly accomplished in sleep and rest, especially towards the morning, the distribution being finished. Therefore, we have nothing else to advise but that men keep themselves hot in their sleep; and further, that towards the morning there be used some anointing, or shirt tincted with oil, such as may gently stir up heat, and after that to fall asleep again. And, touching the last act of assimilation, thus much.

IX. *The Operation upon the Inteneration of that which begins to be arefied, or the Malacissation of the Body.*

We have inquired formerly touching the inteneration from within, which is done by many windings and circuits, as well of alimentation as of detaining the spirit from issuing forth, and, therefore, is accomplished slowly. Now, we are to inquire touching that inteneration which is from without, and is affected, as it were, suddenly; or touching the malacissation and supplying of the body.

1. In the fable of restoring Pelias to youth again, Medea, when she feigned to do it, propounded this way of accomplishing the same; that the old man's body should be cut into several pieces, and then boiled in a caldron with certain medicaments. There may, perhaps, some boiling be required to this matter, but the cutting into pieces is not needful.

2. Notwithstanding, this cutting into pieces seems in some sort to be used, not with a knife, but with judgment. For, whereas the consistence of the bowels and parts is very diverse, it is needful that the inteneration of them both be not effected the same way, but that there be a cure designed of each in particular, besides those things which pertain to the inteneration of the whole mass of the body; of which, notwithstanding, in the first place.

3. This operation (if, perhaps, it be within our power) is most likely to be done by baths, unctions, and the like, concerning which, these things that follow are to be observed.

4. We must not be too forward in hoping to accomplish this matter, from the examples of those things which we see done in the imbibitions and macerations of inanimates, by which they are intenerated, whereof we introduced some instances before: for this kind of operation is more easy upon inanimates, because they attract and suck in the liquor; but upon the bodies of living creatures it is harder, because in them the motion rather tendeth outward, and to the circumference.

5. Therefore, the emollient baths which are in use do little good, but on the contrary hurt, because they rather draw forth than make entrance, and resolve the structure of the body, rather than consolidate it.

6. The baths and unctions which may serve to the present operation, (namely, of intenerating the body truly and really,) ought to have three properties.

7. The first and principal is, that they consist of those things which, in their whole substance, are like unto the body and flesh of man, and which have a feeding and nursing virtue from without.

8. The second is, that they be mixed with such things as, through the subtilty of their parts, may make entrance, and so insinuate and convey their nourishing virtue into the body.

9. The third is, that they receive some mixture (though much inferior to the rest) of such things as are astringent; I mean not sour or tart things, but unctuous and comforting, that while the other two do operate, the exhaling out of the body, which destroyeth the virtue of the things intenerating, may, as much as possible, be prohibited; and the motion to the inward parts, by the astriction of the skin, and closing of the passages, may be promoted and furthered.

10. That which is most consubstantial to the body of man is warm blood, either of man, or of some other living creature. But the device of Ficinus, touching the sucking of blood out of the arm of a wholesome young man, for the restoration of strength, in old men, is very frivolous; for that which nourisheth from within, ought no way to be equal or homogeneal to the body nourished, but in some sort inferior and subordinate, that it may be converted. But in things applied outwardly, by how much the substance is liker, by so much the consent is better.

11. It hath been anciently received, that a bath made of the blood of infants will cure the leprosy, and heal the flesh already putrefied; insomuch that this thing hath begot envy towards some kings from the common people.

12. It is reported that Heraclitus, for cure of the dropsy, was put into the warm belly of an ox newly slain.

13. They use the blood of kitlings warm to cure the disease called St. Anthony's Fire, and to restore the flesh and skin.

14. An arm, or other member newly cut off, or that, upon some other occasion, will not leave bleeding, is with good success put into the belly of some creatures newly ripped up, for it worketh potently to stanch the blood; the blood of the member cut off, by consent sucking in, and vehemently drawing to itself the warm blood of the creature slain, whereby itself is stopped, and retireth.

15. It is much used in extreme and desperate diseases to cut in two young pigeons yet living, and apply them to the soles of the feet, and to shift them one after another, whereby sometimes there followeth a wonderful ease. This is imputed vulgarly, as if they should draw down the malignity of the disease: but, howsoever, this application goeth to the head, and comforteth the animal spirit.

16. But these bloody baths and unctions seem to us sluttish and odious: let us search out some others, which perhaps have less loathsomeness in them, and yet no less benefit.

17. Next unto warm blood, things alike in substance to the body of a man are nutritives; fat fleshes of oxen, swine, deer, oysters amongst fishes, milk, butter, yolks of eggs, flower of wheat, sweet wine, either sugared, or before it be fined.

18. Such things as we would have mixed to make impression, are instead of all salts, especially bay-salt: also wine (when it is full of spirit) maketh entrance, and is an excellent convoy.

19. Astringents of that kind which we described, namely, unctuous and comfortable things, are saffron, mastic, myrrh, and myrtle-berries.

20. Of these parts, in our judgment, may very well be made such a bath as we design: physicians and posterity will find out better things hereafter.

21. But the operation will be much better, and more powerful, if such a bath as we have propounded (which we hold to be the principal matter) be attended with a fourfold course and order.

22. First, that there go before the bath a frication of the body, and an anointing with oil, with some thickening substance, that the virtue and moistening heat of the bath may pierce the body, and not the watery part of the liquor; then let the bath follow, for the space of some two hours. After the bath, let the body be emplastered with mastick, myrrhe, tragacanth, diapalma, and saffron, that the perspiration of the body may (as much as possible) be inhibited, till the supple matter be by degrees turned into solid. This to be continued for the space of twenty-four hours, or more. Lastly, the emplastering being removed, let there be an anointing with oil mixed with salt and saffron, and let this bath, together with the emplastering and unction (as before) be renewed every fifth day. This malacissation, or supplying of the body, be continued for one whole month.

23. Also during the time of this malacissation, we hold it useful and proper, and according to our intention, that men nourish their bodies well, and keep out of the cold air, and drink nothing but warm drink.

24. Now, this is one of those things (as we warned in general in the beginning) whereof we have made no trial by experiment, but only set it down out of our aiming and leveling at the end. For having set up the mark, we deliver the light to others.

25. Neither ought the warmths and cherishing of living bodies to be neglected. Ficinus saith, and that seriously enough, That the laying of the young maid in David's bosom was wholesome for him, but it came too late. He should also have added, that the young maid, after the manner of the Persian virgins, ought to have been anointed with myrrh, and such like, not for deliciousness, but to increase the virtue of this cherishing by a living body.

26. Barbarossa, in his extreme old age, by the advice of a physician, a Jew, did continually apply young boys to his stomach and belly, for warmth and cherishing. Also some old men lay whelps (creatures of the hottest kind) close to their stomachs every night.

27. There hath gone a report, almost undoubted, and that under several names, of certain men that had great noses, who, being weary of the derision of people, have cut off the bunches or gillocks of their noses, and then making a wide gash in their arms, have held their noses in the place for a certain time, and so brought forth fair and comely noses; which, if it be true, it shows

plainly the consent of flesh and flesh, especially in live fleshes.

28. Touching the particular inteneration of the principal bowels, the stomach, lungs, liver, heart, brain, marrow of the backbone, guts, reins, gall, veins, arteries, nerves, cartilages, bones, the inquisition and direction would be too long, seeing we now set not forth a practice, but certain indications to the practice.

X. *The Operation upon the purging away of old Juice, and supplying of new Juice; or of Renovation by Turns.*

The history.

Although those things which we shall here set down have been, for the most part, spoken of before; yet because this operation is one of the principal, we will handle them over again more at large.

1. It is certain, that draught oxen, which have been worn out with working, being put into fresh and rich pastures, will gather tender and young flesh again; and this will appear even to the taste and palate; so that the inteneration of flesh is no hard matter. Now, it is likely that this inteneration of the flesh being often repeated, will in time reach to the inteneration of the bones and membranes, and like parts of the body.

2. It is certain, that diets which are now much in use, principally of guaiacum, and of sarsaparilla, china, and sassafras, if they be continued for any time, and according to strict rules, do first attenuate the whole juice of the body, and after consume it, and drink it up. Which is most manifest, because that by these diets the French pox, when it is grown even to a hardness, and hath eaten up and corrupted the very marrow of the body, may be effectually cured. And, further, because it is manifest, that men who, by these diets, are brought to be extreme lean, pale, and, as it were, ghosts, will soon after become fat, well coloured, and apparently young again. Wherefore we are absolutely of opinion, that such kind of diets in the decline of age, being used every year, would be very useful to our intention; like the old skin or spoil of serpents.

3. We do confidently affirm (neither let any man reckon us among those heretics which were called Cathari) that often purges, and made even familiar to the body, are more available to long life than exercises and sweats. And this must needs be so, if that be held which is already laid for a ground, that unctions of the body, and oppletion of the passages from without, and exclusion of air. and detaining of the spirit within the mass of the body, do much conduce to long life. For it is most certain, that by sweats and outward perspirations, not only the humours and excrementitious vapours are exhaled and consumed, but together with them the juices also, and good spirits, which are not so easily repaired; but in

purges (unless they be very immoderate) it is not so, seeing they work principally upon the humours. But, the best purges for this intention are those which are taken immediately before meat, because they dry the body less; and, therefore, they must be of those purges which do least trouble the belly.

These intentions of the operations which we have propounded (as we conceive) are most true, the remedies faithful to the intentions. Neither is it credible to he told (although not a few of these remedies may seem but vulgar) with what care and choice they have been examined by us, that they might be (the intention not at all impeached) both safe and effectual. Experience, no doubt, will both verify and promote these matters. And such, in all things, are the works of every prudent counsel, that they are admirable in their effects, excellent also in their order, but seeming vulgar in the way and means.

The Porches of Death.

We are now to inquire touching the porches of death, that is, touching those things which happen unto men at the point of death, both a little before and after; that seeing there are many paths which lead to death, it may be understood in what common way they all end, especially in those deaths which are caused by indigence of nature, rather than by violence; although something of this latter also must be inserted, because of the connexion of things.

The history.

1. The living spirit stands in need of three things that it may subsist; convenient motion, temperate refrigeration, and fit aliment. Flame seems to stand in need but of two of these, namely, motion and aliment, because flame is a simple substance, the spirit a compounded, insomuch that if it approach somewhat too near to a flamy nature, it overthroweth itself.

2. Also flame by a greater and stronger flame is extinguished and slain, as Aristotle well noted, much more the spirit.

3. Flame, if it be much compressed and straitened, is extinguished; as we may see in a candle having a glass cast over it, for the air being dilated by the heat doth contrude and thrust together the flame, and so lesseneth it, and in the end extinguisheth it; and fires on hearths will not flame, if the fuel be thrust close together, without any space for the flame to break forth.

4. Also things fired are extinguished with compression; as if you press a burning coal hard with the tongs, or the foot, it is straight extinguished.

5. But to come to the spirit; if blood or phlegm get into the ventricles of the brain, it causeth sudden death, because the spirit hath no room to move itself.

6. Also a great blow on the head induceth sud-

den death, the spirits being straitened within the ventricles of the brain.

7. Opium, and other strong stupefactives, do coagulate the spirit, and deprive it of the motion.

8. A venomous vapour, totally abhorred by the spirit, causeth sudden death; as in deadly poisons, which work (as they call it) by a special malignity; for they strike a loathing into the spirit, that the spirit will no more move itself, nor rise against a thing so much detested.

9. Also extreme drunkenness, or extreme feeding, sometimes cause sudden death, seeing the spirit is not only oppressed with over-much condensing, or the malignity of the vapour, (as in opium and malignant poisons,) but also with the abundance of the vapours.

10. Extreme grief or fear, especially if they be sudden, (as it is in a sad and unexpected message,) cause sudden death.

11. Not only over-much compression, but also over-much dilatation of the spirit, is deadly.

12. Joys excessive and sudden have bereft many of their lives.

13. In greater evacuations, as when they cut men for the dropsy, the waters flow forth abundantly, much more in great and sudden fluxes of blood, oftentimes present death followeth; and this happens by the mere flight of vacuum within the body, all the parts moving to fill the empty places; and, amongst the rest, the spirits themselves. For, as for slow fluxes of blood, this matter pertains to the indigence of nourishment, not to the diffusion of the spirits. And touching the motion of the spirit so far, either compressed or diffused, that it bringeth death, thus much.

14. We must come next to the want of refrigeration. Stopping of the breath causeth sudden death; as in all suffocation or strangling. Now, it seems this matter is not so much to be referred to the impediment of motion as to the impediment of refrigeration; for air over-hot, though attracted freely, doth no less suffocate than if breathing were hindered: as it is in them who have been sometimes suffocated with burning coals, or with charcoal, or with walls new plastered in close chambers where a fire is made; which kind of death is reported to have been the end of the Emperor Jovinian. The like happeneth from dry baths over-heated, which was practised in the killing of Fausta, wife to Constantine the Great.

15. It is a very small time which nature taketh to repeat the breathing, and in which she desireth to expel the foggy air drawn into the lungs, and to take in new, scarce the third part of a minute.

16. Again, the beating of the pulse, and the motion of the systole and diastole of the heart, are three times quicker than that of breathing; insomuch that if it were possible that that motion of the heart could be stopped without stopping the breath, death would follow more speedily thereupon than by strangling.

17. Notwithstanding, use and custom prevail much in this natural action of breathing; as it is in the Delian divers and fishers for pearl, who by long use can hold their breaths at least ten times longer than other men can do.

18. Amongst living creatures, even of those that have lungs, there are some that are able to hold their breaths a long time, and others that cannot hold them so long, according as they need more or less refrigeration.

19. Fishes need less refrigeration than terrestrial creatures, yet some they need, and take it by their gills. And as terrestrial creatures cannot bear the air that is too hot, or too close, so fishes are suffocated in waters if they be totally and long frozen.

20. If the spirit be assaulted by another heat greater than itself, it is dissipated and destroyed; for it cannot bear the proper heat without refrigeration, much less can it bear another heat which is far stronger. This is to be seen in burning fevers, where the heat of the putrefied humours doth exceed the native heat, even to extinction or dissipation.

21. The want also and use of sleep is referred to refrigeration; for motion doth attenuate and rarefy the spirit, and doth sharpen and increase the heat thereof: contrarily, sleep settleth and restraineth the motion and gadding of the same; for though sleep doth strengthen and advance the actions of the parts and of the lifeless spirits, and all that motion which is to the circumference of the body, yet it doth in great part quiet and still the proper motion of the living spirit. Now, sleep is regularly due unto human nature once within four-and-twenty hours, and that for six, or five hours at the least; though there are, even in this kind, sometimes miracles of nature; as it is recorded of Mæcenas, that he slept not for a long time before his death. And as touching the want of refrigeration for conserving of the spirit, thus much.

22. As concerning the third indigence, namely, of aliment, it seems to pertain rather to the parts, than to the living spirit; for a man may easily believe that the living spirit subsisteth in identity, not by succession or renovation. And as for the reasonable soul in men, it is above all question, that it is not engendered of the soul of the parents, nor is repaired, nor can die. They speak of the natural spirit of living creatures, and also of vegetables, which differs from that other soul essentially and formally; for out of the confusion of these, that same transmigration of souls, and innumerable other devices of heathens and heretics have proceeded.

23. The body of man doth regularly require renovation by aliment every day, and a body in health can scarce endure fasting three days together; notwithstanding, use and custom will do much, even in this case; but in sickness fasting

is less grievous to the body. Also, sleep doth supply somewhat to nourishment; and on the other side, exercise doth require it more abundantly. Likewise there have some been found who sustained themselves (almost to a miracle in nature) a very long time without meat or drink.

24. Dead bodies, if they be not intercepted by putrefaction, will subsist a long time without any notable absumption; but living bodies, not above three days, (as we said,) unless they be repaired by nourishment; which showeth that quick absumption to be the work of the living spirit, which either repairs itself, or puts the parts into a necessity of being repaired, or both. This is testified by that also which was noted a little before, namely, that living creatures may subsist somewhat the longer without aliment, if they sleep: now, sleep is nothing else but a reception and retirement of the living spirit into itself.

25. An abundant and continual effluxion of blood, which sometimes happeneth in the hæmorrhoids, sometimes in vomiting of blood, the inward veins being unlocked or broken, sometimes by wounds, causeth sudden death, in regard that the blood of the veins ministereth to the arteries, and the blood of the arteries to the spirit.

26. The quantity of meat and drink which a man, eating two meals a day, receiveth into his body, is not small; much more than he voideth again either by stool, or by urine, or by sweating. You will say, no marvel, seeing the remainder goeth into the juices and substance of the body. It is true; but consider, then, that this addition is made twice a day, and yet the body aboundeth not much. In like manner, though the spirit be repaired, yet it grows not excessively in the quantity.

27. It doth no good to have the aliment ready, in a degree removed, but to have it of that kind, and so prepared and supplied, that the spirit may work upon it; for the staff of a torch alone will not maintain the flame, unless it be fed with wax, neither can men live upon herbs alone. And from thence comes the inconcoction of old age, that though there be flesh and blood, yet the spirit is become so penurious and thin, and the juices and blood so heartless and obstinate, that they hold no proportion to alimentation.

28. Let us now cast up the accounts of the needs and indigences according to the ordinary and usual course of nature. The spirit hath need of opening and moving itself in the ventricles of the brain and nerves even continually, of the motion of the heart every third part of a moment, of breathing every moment, of sleep and nourishment once within three days, of the power of nourishment commonly till eighty years be past; and if any of these indigences be neglected, death ensueth. So there are plainly three porches of

death; destitution of the spirit in the motion, in the refrigeration, in the aliment.

It is an error to think that the living spirit is perpetually generated and extinguished as flame is, and abideth not any notable time; for even flame itself is not thus out of its own proper nature, but because it liveth amongst enemies; for flame within flame endureth. Now, the living spirit liveth amongst friends, and all due obsequiousness. So then, as, flame is a momentary substance, air is a fixed substance, the living spirit is betwixt both.

Touching the extinguishing of the spirit by the destruction of the organs (which is caused by diseases and violence) we inquire not now, as we foretold in the beginning, although that also endeth in the same three porches. And touching the form of death itself, thus much.

29. There are two great forerunners of death, the one sent from the head, the other from the heart; convulsion, and the extreme labour of the pulse: for as for the deadly hiccough, it is a kind of convulsion. But the deadly labour of the pulse hath that unusual swiftness, because the heart at the point of death doth so tremble, that the systole and diastole thereof are almost confounded. There is also conjoined in the pulse a weakness and lowness, and oftentimes a great intermission, because the motion of the heart faileth, and is not able to rise against the assault stoutly or constantly.

30. The immediate preceding signs of death are, great unquietness and tossing in the bed, fumbling with the hands, catching and grasping hard, gnashing with the teeth, speaking hollow, trembling of the nether lip, paleness of the face, the memory confused, speechless, cold sweats, the body shooting in length, lifting up the white of the eye, changing of the whole visage, (as the nose sharp, eyes hollow, cheeks fallen,) contraction and doubling of the coldness in the extreme parts of the body, in some, shedding of blood, or sperm, shrieking, breathing thick and short, falling of the nether chap, and such like.

31. There follow death a privation of all sense and motion, as well of the heart and arteries, as of the nerves and joints, an inability of the body to support itself upright, stiffness of the nerves and parts, extreme coldness of the whole body, after a little while putrefaction and stinking.

Eels, serpents, and the insecta, will move a long time in every part after they are cut asunder, insomuch that country people think that the parts strive to join together again. Also birds will flutter a great while after their heads are pulled off; and the hearts of living creatures will pant a long time after they are plucked out. I remember I have seen the heart of one that was bowelled, as suffering for high treason, that being cast into the fire, leaped at the first at least a foot and half in height, and after, by degrees, lower and lower, for the space, as I remember, of seven or eight minutes. There is also an ancient and credible tradition of an ox lowing after his bowels were plucked out. But there is a more certain tradition of a man, who being under the executioner's hand for high treason, after his heart was plucked out, and in the executioner's hand, was heard to utter three or four words of prayer; which therefore we said to be more credible than that of the ox in sacrifice, because the friends of the party suffering do usually give a reward to the executioner to despatch his office with the more speed, that they may the sooner be rid of their pain; but in sacrifices, we see no cause why the priest should be so speedy in his office.

33. For reviving those again which fall into sudden swoonings and catalepsies of astonishments, (in which fits many, without help, would utterly expire,) these things are used, putting into their mouths water distilled of wine, which they call hot waters, and cordial waters, bending the body forward, stopping the mouth and nostrils hard, bending or wringing the fingers, pulling the hairs of the beard or head, rubbing of the parts, especially the face and legs, sudden casting of cold water upon the face, shrieking out aloud and suddenly, putting rose-water to the nostrils, with vinegar in faintings; burning of feathers, or cloth, in the suffocation of the mother; but especially a frying-pan heated red-hot, is good in apoplexies; also a close embracing of the body hath helped some.

34. There have been many examples of men in show dead, either laid out upon the cold floor, or carried forth to burial; nay, of some buried in the earth; which notwithstanding have lived again, which hath been found in those that were buried (the earth being afterwards opened) by the bruising and wounding of their head, through the struggling of the body within the coffin; whereof the most recent and memorable example was that of Joannes Scotus, called the subtile, and a schoolman, who being digged up again by his servant, (unfortunately absent at his burial, and who knew his master's manner in such fits,) was found in that state: and the like happened in our days in the person of a player, buried at Cambridge. I remember to have heard of a certain gentleman that would needs make trial, in curiosity, what men did feel that were hanged; so he fastened the cord about his neck, raising himself upon a stool, and then letting himself fall, thinking it should be in his power to recover the stool at his pleasure, which he failed in, but was helped by a friend then present. He was asked afterward what he felt; he said he felt no pain, but first he thought he saw before his eyes a great fire, and burning; then he thought he saw all black, and dark; lastly, it turned to a pale blue, or sea-water green; which colour is also often seen by them which fall into swoonings. I have heard also of a physician, yet living, who recovered a man to life which had hanged himself, and had hanged half an hour, by frications and hot baths; and the same physician did profess, that he made no doubt to recover any man that had hanged so long, so his neck were not broken with the first swing.

The Difference of Youth and Old Age.
To the sixteenth article.

1. The ladder of man's body is this, to be conceived, to be quickened in the womb, to be born, to suck, to be weaned, to feed upon pap, to put forth teeth the first time about the second year of age, to begin to go, to begin to speak, to put forth teeth the second time about seven years of age, to come to puberty about twelve or fourteen years of age, to be able for generation, and the flowing of the menstrua, to have hairs about the legs and arm-holes, to put forth a beard; and thus long, and sometimes later, to grow in stature, or to come to full years of strength and agility, to grow gray and bald; the menstrua ceasing, and ability to generation, to grow decrepit, and a monster with three legs, to die. Meanwhile, the mind also hath certain periods, but they cannot be described by years, as to decay in the memory, and the like, of which hereafter.

2. The differences of youth and old age are these: a young man's skin is smooth and plain, an old man's dry and wrinkled, especially about the forehead and eyes; a young man's flesh is tender and soft, an old man's hard; a young man hath strength and agility, an old man feels decay in his strength, and is slow of motion; a young man hath good digestion, an old man bad; a young man's bowels are soft and succulent, an old man's salt and parched; a young man's body is erect and straight, an old man's bowing and crooked; a young man's limbs are steady, an old man's weak and trembling; the humours in a young man are choleric, and his blood inclined to heat, in an old man phlegmatic and melancholic, and his blood inclined to coldness; a young man ready for the act of Venus, an old man slow unto it; in a young man the juices of his body are more roscid, in an old man more crude and waterish; the spirit in a young man plentiful and boiling, in an old man scarce and jejune; a young man's spirit is dense and vigorous, an old man's eager and rare; a young man his senses quick and entire, an old man dull and decayed; a young man's teeth are strong and entire, an old man's weak, worn, and fallen out; a young man's hair is coloured, an old man's (of what colour soever it were) gray; a young man hath hair, an old man baldness; a young man's pulse is stronger and quicker, an old man's more confused and slower; the diseases of young men are more acute and curable, of old men longer, and hard

to cure; a young man's wounds soon close, an old man's later; a young man's cheeks are of a fresh colour, an old man's pale, or with a black blood; a young man is less troubled with rheums, an old man more. Neither do we know in what things old men do improve, as touching their body, save only sometimes in fatness; whereof the reason is soon given, because old men's bodies do neither perspire well nor assimilate well. Now, fatness is nothing else but exuberance of nourishment above that which is voided by excrement, or which is perfectly assimilated. Also, some old men improve in the appetite of feeding, by reason of the acid humours, though old men digest worst. And all these things which we have said, physicians negligently enough will refer to the diminution of the natural heat and radical moisture, which are things of no worth for use. This is certain, dryness in the coming on of years doth forego coldness; and bodies, when they come to the top and strength of heat, do decline in dryness, and after that follows coldness.

3. Now we are to consider the affections of the mind. I remember when I was a young man. at Poictiers in France, I conversed familiarly with a certain Frenchman, a witty young man, but something talkative, who afterwards grew to be a very eminent man; he was wont to inveigh against the manners of old men, and would say, that if their minds could be seen as their bodies are, they would appear no less deformed. Besides, being in love with his own wit, he would maintain, that the vices of old men's minds have some correspondence, and were parallel to the putrefactions of their bodies: for the dryness of their skin, he would bring in impudence; for the hardness of their bowels, unmercifulness; for the lippitude of their eyes, an evil eye, and envy; for the casting down of their eyes, and bowing their body towards the earth, atheism; (for, saith he, they look no more up to heaven as they are wont;) for the trembling of their members, irresolutions of their decrees and light inconstancy; for the bending of their fingers, as it were to catch, rapacity and covetousness; for the buckling of their knees, fearfulness; for their wrinkles, craftiness and obliquity; and other things which I have forgotten. But, to be serious, a young man is modest and shamefaced, an old man's forehead is hardened; a young man is full of bounty and mercy, an old man's heart is brawny; a young man is affected with a laudable emulation, an old man with a malignant envy; a young man is inclined to religion and devotion, by reason of his fervency and inexperience of evil, an old man cooleth in piety through the coldness of his charity, and long conversation in evil, and likewise through the difficulty of his belief; a young man's desires are vehement, an old man's moderate; a young man is light and movable, an old

man more grave and constant; a young man is given to liberality, and beneficence, and humanity, an old man to covetousness, wisdom for his own self, and seeking his own ends; a young man is confident and full of hope, an old man diffident, and given to suspect most things; a young man is gentle and obsequious, an old man froward and disdainful; a young man is sincere and open-hearted, an old man cautelous and close; a young man is given to desire great things, an old man to regard things necessary; a young man thinks well of the present times, an old man preferreth times past before them; a young man reverenceth his superiors, an old man is more forward to tax them; and many other things, which pertain rather to manners than the present inquisition. Notwithstanding, old men, as in some things they improve in their bodies, so also in their minds, unless they be altogether out of date; namely, that as they are less apt for invention, so they excel in judgment, and prefer safe things, and sound things, before specious. Also, they improve in garrulity and ostentation, for they seek the fruit of speech while they are less able for action. So as it was not absurd that the poets feigned old Tython to be turned into a grasshopper.

MOVABLE CANONS OF THE DURATION OF LIFE AND FORM OF DEATH.

CANON I.

Consumption is not caused, unless that which is departed with by one body passeth into another.

THE EXPLICATION.

There is in nature no annihilating, or reducing to nothing. Therefore, that which is consumed is either resolved into air, or turned into some body adjacent. So we see a spider, or fly, or ant in amber, entombed in a more stately monument than kings are; to be laid up for eternity, although they be but tender things, and soon dissipated. But the matter is this, that there is no air by, into which they should be resolved, and the substance of the amber is so heterogeneous, that it receives nothing of them. The like we conceive would be if a stick, or root, or some such thing were buried in quicksilver; also wax, and honey, and gums, have the same operation, but in part only.

CANON II.

There is in every tangible body a spirit, covered and encompassed with the grosser parts of the body, and from it all consumption and dissolution hath the beginning.

THE EXPLICATION.

No body known unto us here in the upper part of the earth is without a spirit, either by attenuation and concoction from the heat of the heavenly bodies, or by some other way; for the concavities of tangible things receive not vacuum, but either air, or the proper spirit of the thing. And this spirit whereof we speak, is not from virtue, or energy, or act, or a trifle, but plainly a body, rare and invisible; notwithstanding, circumscribed by place, quantitative, real. Neither, again, is that spirit air, (no more than wine is water,) but a body rarefied, of kin to air, though much different from it. Now, the grosser parts of bodies (being dull things, and not apt for motion) would last a long time; but the spirit is that which troubleth, and plucketh, and undermineth them, and converteth the moisture of the body, and whatsoever it is able to digest, into new spirit; and then as well the pre-existing spirit of the body, as that newly made, fly away together by degrees. This is best seen by the diminution of the weight in bodies dried through perspiration; for neither all that which is issued forth was spirit when the body was ponderous, neither was it not spirit when it issued forth.

CANON III.

The spirit issuing forth drieth; detained and working within either melteth, or putrefieth, or vivifieth.

THE EXPLICATION.

There are four processes of the spirit; to arefaction, to colloquation, putrefaction, to generation of bodies. Arefaction is not the proper work of the spirit, but of the grosser parts after the spirit issued forth; for then they contract themselves partly by their flight of vacuum, partly by the union of the homogeneals; as appears in all things which are arefied by age, and in the drier sort of bodies which have passed the fire; as bricks, charcoal, bread. Colloquation is the mere work of the spirit; neither is it done, but when they are excited by heat; for when the spirits, dilating themselves, yet not getting forth, do insinuate and disperse themselves among the grosser parts, and so make them soft and apt to run, as it is in the metals and wax; for metals, and all tenacious things, are apt to inhibit the spirit; that being excited, it issueth not forth. Putrefaction is a mixed work of the spirits, and of the grosser parts; for the spirit (which before restrained and bridled the parts of the thing) being partly issued forth, and partly enfeebled, all things in the body do dissolve and return to their homogeneities, or (if you will) to their elements; that which was spirit in it is congregated to itself, whereby things putrefied begin to have an ill savour; the oily parts to themselves, whereby things putrefied have that slipperiness and unctuosity; the watery parts also to themselves, the dregs to themselves; whence followeth that confusion in bodies putrefied. But generation or vivification is a work also mixed of the spirit and grosser parts, but in a far different manner; for the spirit is totally detained, but it swelleth and moveth locally; and the grosser parts are not dissolved, but follow the motion of the spirit; and are, as it were, blown out by it, and extruded into divers figures, from whence cometh that generation and organization; and, therefore, vivification is always done in a matter tenacious and clammy, and again yielding and soft, that there may be both a detention of the spirit, and also a gentle cession of the parts, according as the spirit forms them. And this is seen in the matter, as well of all vegetables, as of living creatures, whether they be engendered of putrefaction, or of sperm, for in all these things there is manifestly seen a matter hard to break through, easy to yield.

CANON IV.

In all living creatures there are two kinds of spirits: liveless spirits, such as are in bodies inanimate; and a vital spirit superadded.

THE EXPLICATION.

It was said before, that to procure long life, the body of man must be considered; first, as inanimate, and not repaired by nourishment; secondly, as animate, and repaired by nourishment. For the former, consideration gives laws touching consumption, the latter touching reparation. Therefore we must know, that there are in human flesh bones, membranes, organs; finally, in all the parts such spirits diffused in the substance of them while they are alive, as there are in the same things (flesh, bones, membranes, and the rest) separated and dead, such as also remain in a carcass; but the vital spirit, although it ruleth them, and hath some consent with them, yet it is far differing from them, being integral, and subsisting by itself. Now, there are two special differences betwixt the liveless spirits and the vital spirits. The one, that the liveless spirits are not continued to themselves, but are, as it were, cut off and encompassed with a gross body, which intercepts them, as air is mixed with snow or froth; but the vital spirit is all continued to itself by certain conduit pipes through which it passeth, and is not totally intercepted. And this spirit is twofold also; the one branched, only passing through small pipes, and, as it were, strings, the other hath a cellar also, so as it is not only continued to itself, but also congregated in a hollow space in reasonable good quantity, according to the analogy of the body; and in that cell is the fountain of the rivulets which branch from thence. The cell is chiefly in the ventricles of the brain, which in the ignobler sort of creatures are but narrow, insomuch that the spirits in them seem scattered over their whole body, rather than celled;

as may be seen in serpents, eels, and flies, whereof every of their parts move along after they are cut asunder. Birds also leap a good while after their heads are pulled off, because they have little heads and little cells. But the nobler sort of creatures have those ventricles larger, and man the largest of all. The other difference betwixt the spirits is, that the vital spirit hath a kind of enkindling, and is like a wind or breath compounded of flame and air, as the juices of living creatures have both oil and water. And this enkindling ministereth peculiar motions and faculties; for the smoke which is inflammable, even before the flame conceived, is hot, thin, and movable, and yet it is quite another thing after it is become flame; but the enkindling of the vital spirits is by many degrees gentler than the softest flame, as of spirit of wine, or otherwise; and, besides, it is in great part mixed with an aerial substance, that it should be a mystery or miracle, both of a flammeous and aereous nature.

CANON V.

The natural actions are proper to the several parts, but it is the vital spirit that excites and sharpens them.

THE EXPLICATION.

The actions or functions which are in the several members, follow the nature of the members themselves, (attraction, retention, digestion, assimilation, separation, excretion, perspiration, even sense itself,) according to the propriety of the several organs, (the stomach, liver, heart, spleen, gall, brain, eye, ear, and the rest,) yet none of these actions would ever have been actuated but by the vigour and presence of the vital spirit, and heat thereof; as one iron would not have drawn another iron, unless it had been excited by the loadstone; nor an egg would ever have brought forth a bird, unless the substance of the hen had been actuated by the treading of the cock.

CANON VI.

The liveless spirits are next consubstantial to air; the vital spirits approach more to the substance of flame.

THE EXPLICATION.

The explication of the precedent fourth canon is also a declaration of this present canon. But yet further, from hence it is, that all fat and oily things continue long in their being. For neither doth the air much pluck them, neither do they much desire to join themselves with air. As for that conceit, it is altogether vain, that flame should be air set on fire, seeing flame and air are no less heterogeneal, than oil and water. But whereas it is said in the canon, that the vital spirits approach more to the substance of flame; it must be understood, that they do this more than the liveless spirits, not that they are more flamy than air.

CANON VII.

The spirit hath two desires, one of multiplying itself, the other of flying forth, and congregating itself with the connaturals.

THE EXPLICATION.

The canon is understood of the liveless spirits; for as for the second desire, the vital spirit doth most of all abhor flying forth of the body, for it finds no connatural here below to join withal. Perhaps it may sometimes fly to the outward parts of the body, to meet that which it loveth; but the flying forth, as I said, it abhorreth. But in the liveless spirits each of these two desires holdeth. For to the former this belongeth, every spirit seated amongst the grosser parts dwelleth unhappily; and, therefore, when it finds not a like unto itself, it doth so much the more labour to create and make a like, as being in a great solitude, and endeavour earnestly to multiply itself, and to prey upon the volatile of the grosser parts, that it may be increased in quantity. As for the second desire of flying forth, and betaking itself to the air, it is certain, that all light things (which are ever movable) do willingly go unto their likes near unto them, as a drop of water is carried to a drop, flame to flame; but much more this is done in the flying forth of spirit into the air ambient, because it is not carried to a particle like unto itself, but also as unto the globe of the connaturals. Meanwhile this is to be noted, that the going forth, and flight of the spirit into air is a redoubled action, partly out of the appetite of the spirit, partly out of the appetite of the air, for the common air is a needy thing, and receiveth all things speedily, as spirits, odours, beams, sounds, and the like.

CANON VIII.

Spirit detained, if it have no possibility of begetting new spirits, intenerateth the grosser parts.

THE EXPLICATION.

Generation of new spirit is not accomplished but upon those things which are in some degree near to the spirit, such as are humid bodies. And, therefore, if the grosser parts (amongst which the spirit converseth) be in a remote degree, although the spirit cannot convert them, yet (as much as it can) it weakeneth, and softeneth, and subdueth them, that seeing it cannot increase in quantity, yet it will dwell more at large, and live amongst good neighbours and friends. Now, this aphorism is most useful to our end, because it tendeth to the inteneration of the obstinate parts by the detention of the spirit.

CANON IX.

The inteneration of the harder parts cometh to good effect when the spirit neither flieth forth, nor begetteth new spirit.

THE EXPLICATION.

This canon solveth the knot and difficulty in the operation of intenerating by the detention of the spirit; for if the spirit not flying forth wasteth all within, there is nothing gotten to the inteneration of the parts in their subsistence, but rather they are dissolved and corrupted. Therefore, together with the detention, the spirits ought to be cooled and restrained, that they may not be too active.

CANON X.

The heat of the spirit, to keep the body fresh and green, ought to be robust, not eager.

THE EXPLICATION.

Also, this canon pertaineth to the solving of the knot aforesaid, but it is of a much larger extent, for it setteth down of what temperament the heat in the body ought to be for the obtaining of long life. Now, this is useful, whether the spirits be detained, or whether they be not. For, howsoever, the heat of the spirits, must be such, as it may rather turn itself upon the hard parts, than waste the soft; for the one desiccateth, the other intenerateth. Besides, the same thing is available to the well perfecting of assimilation; for such a heat doth excellently excite the faculty of assimilation, and withal doth excellently prepare the matter to be assimilated. Now, the properties of this kind of heat ought to be these. First, that it be slow, and heat not suddenly. Secondly, that it be not very intense, but moderate. Thirdly, that it be equal, not incomposed; namely, intending and remitting itself. Fourthly, that if this heat meet any thing to resist it, it be not easily suffocated or languish. The operation is exceeding subtile; but seeing it is one of the most useful, it is not to be deserted. Now, in those remedies which we propounded to invest the spirits with a robust heat, or that which we call operative, not predatory, we have in some sort satisfied this matter.

CANON XI.

The condensing of the spirits in their substance is available to long life.

THE EXPLICATION.

This canon is subordinate to the next precedent; for the spirit condensed receiveth all those four properties of heat whereof we speak; but the ways of condensing them are set down in the first of the ten operations.

CANON XII.

The spirit in great quantity hasteneth more to flying forth, and preyeth upon the body more than in small quantity.

THE EXPLICATION.

This canon is clear of itself, seeing mere quantity doth regularly increase virtue. And it is to be seen in flames, that the bigger they are the stronger they break forth, and the more speedily they consume. And, therefore, over-great plenty, or exuberance of the spirits, is altogether hurtful to long life: neither need one wish a greater store of spirits, than what is sufficient for the functions of life, and the office of a good reparation.

CANON XIII.

The spirit equally dispersed, maketh less haste to fly forth, and preyeth less upon the body, than unequally placed.

THE EXPLICATION.

Not only abundance of spirits, in respect of the whole, is hurtful to the duration of things, but also the same abundance, unevenly placed, is, in like manner, hurtful; and, therefore, the more the spirit is shred and inserted by small portions, the less it preyeth; for dissolution ever beginneth at that part where the spirit is loser. And, therefore, both exercise and frications conduce much to long life, for agitation doth fineliest diffuse and commix things by small portions.

CANON XIV.

The inordinate and subsultory motion of the spirits doth more hasten to going forth, and doth prey upon the body more than the constant and equal.

THE EXPLICATION.

The inanimates this canon holds for certain, for inequality is the mother of dissolution; but in animates (because not only the consumption is considered, but the reparation, and reparation proceedeth by the appetites of things, and appetite is sharpened by variety) it holdeth not rigorously; but it is so far forth to be received, that this variety be rather an alternation or interchange, than a confusion; and, as it were, constant in inconsistency.

CANON XV.

The spirit in a body of a solid composure is detained, though unwillingly.

THE EXPLICATION.

All things do abhor a solution of their continuity, but yet in proportion to their density or rarity; for the more rare the bodies be the more do they suffe. themselves to be thrust into small and narrow passages; for water will go into a passage which dust will not go into, and air which water will not go into; nay, flame and spirit which air will not go into. Notwithstanding, of this thing there are some bounds, for the spirit is not so much transported with the desire of going forth, that it will suffer itself to be too much discontinued, or be driven into over-straight pores and passages; and, therefore, if the spirit be encompassed with a hard body, or else with an unctuous and tenacious, (which is not easily divided,) it is plainly bound, and, as I may say, imprisoned, and layeth down the appetite of going out; wherefore we see that metals and stones require a long time for their spirit to go forth, unless either the spirit be excited by the fire, or the grosser parts be dissevered with corroding and strong waters. The like reason is there of tenacious bodies, such as are gums, save only that they are melted by a more gentle heat; and therefore the juices of the body hard, a close and compact skin, and the like, (which are procured by the dryness of the aliment, and by exercise, and by the coldness of the air,) are good for long life, because they detain the spirit in close prison, that it goeth not forth

CANON XVI.

In oily and fat things the spirit is detained willingly, though they be not tenacious.

THE EXPLICATION.

The spirit, if it be not irritated by the antipathy of the body enclosing it, nor fed by the over-much likeness of that body, nor solicited nor invited by the external body, it makes no great stir to get out; all which are wanting to oily bodies, for they are neither so pressing upon the spirits as hard bodies, nor so near as watery bodies, neither have they any good agreement with the air ambient.

CANON XVII.

The speedy flying forth of the watery humour conserves the oily the longer in his being.

THE EXPLICATION.

We said before, that the watery humours, as being consubstantial to the air, fly forth soonest; the oily later, as having small agreement with the air. Now, whereas these two humours are in most bodies, it comes to pass that the watery doth in a sort betray the oily, for that issuing forth insensibly carrieth this together with it. Therefore, there is nothing more furthereth the conservation of bodies, than a gentle drying of them, which causeth the watery humour to expire, and inviteth not the oily; for then the oily enjoyeth the proper nature. And this tendeth not only to the inhibiting of putrefaction, (though that also followeth,) but to the conservation of greenness. Hence it is, that gentle frications, and moderate exercises, causing rather perspiration than sweating, conduce much to long life.

CANON XVIII.

Air excluded conferreth to long life, if other inconveniences be avoided.

THE EXPLICATION.

We said a little before, that the flying forth of the spirit is a redoubled action, from the appetite of the spirit, and of the air; and, therefore, if either of these be taken out of the way, there is not a little gained. Notwithstanding, divers inconveniences follow hereupon, which how they may be prevented we have showed in the second of our operations.

CANON XIX.

Youthful spirits inserted into an old body, might soon turn nature's course back again.

THE EXPLICATION.

The nature of the spirits is as the uppermost wheel, which turneth about the other wheels in the body of man; and therefore in the intention of long life, that ought to be first placed. Hereunto may be added, that there is an easier and more expedite way to alter the spirits, than to other operations. For the operation upon the spirits is twofold; the one by aliments, which is slow, and as it were, about; the other, (and that twofold,) which is sudden, and goeth directly to the spirits, namely, by vapours, or by the affections.

CANON XX.

Juices of the body hard and roscid are good for long life.

THE EXPLICATION.

The reason is plain, seeing we showed before, that hard things, and oily or roscid, are hardly dissipated; notwithstanding, there is difference, (as we also noted in the tenth operation,) that juice somewhat hard is indeed less dissipable, but then it is withal less reparable; therefore, a convenience is interlaced with an inconvenience, and for this cause no wonderful matter will be achieved by this. But roscid juice will admit both operations; therefore this would be principally endeavoured.

CANON XXI.

Whatsoever is of thin parts to penetrate, and yet hath no acrimony to bite, begetteth roscid juices.

THE EXPLICATION.

This canon is more hard to practise than to understand. For it is manifest, whatsoever penetrateth well, but yet with a sting or tooth, (as do all sharp and sour things,) it leaveth behind it, wheresoever it goeth, some mark or print of dryness and cleaving, so that it hardeneth the juices, and chappeth the parts; contrarily, whatsoever things penetrate through their thinness merely, as it were by stealth, and by way of insinuation without violence, they bedew and water in their passage. Of which sort we have recounted many in the fourth and seventh operations.

CANON XXII.

Assimilation is best done when all local motion is expended.

THE EXPLICATION.

This canon we have sufficiently explained in our discourse upon the eighth operation.

CANON XXIII.

Alimentation from without, at least some other way than by the stomach, is most profitable for long life, if it can be done.

THE EXPLICATION.

We see that all things which are done by nutrition ask a long time, but those which are done by embracing of the like (as it is in infusions) require no long time. And, therefore, alimentation from without would be of principal use; and so much the more, because the faculties of concoction decay in old age; so that if there could be some auxiliary nutritions by bathing, unctions, or else by clysters, these things in conjunction might do much, which single are less available.

CANON XXIV.

Where the concoction is weak to thrust forth the aliment, there the outward parts should be strengthened to call forth the aliment.

THE EXPLICATION.

That which is propounded in this canon, is not the same thing with the former, for it is one thing for the outward aliment to be attracted inward, another for the inward aliment to be attracted outward; yet herein they concur, that they both help the weakness of the inward concoctions, though by divers ways.

CANON XXV.

All sudden renovation of the body is wrought either by the spirit, or by malacissations.

THE EXPLICATION.

There are two things in the body, spirits and parts; to both these the way by nutrition is long and about; but it is a short way to the spirits by vapours, and by the affections, and to the parts by malacissations. But this is diligently to be noted, that by no means we confound alimentation from without with malacissation; for the intention of malacissation is not to nourish the parts, but only to make them more fit to be nourished.

CANON XXVI.

Malacissation is wrought by consubstantials, by imprinters, and by closers up.

THE EXPLICATION.

The reason is manifest, for that consubstantials do properly supple the body, imprinters do carry in, closers up do retain and bridle the perspiration, which is a motion opposite to malacissation. And, therefore, (as we described in the ninth operation,) malacissation cannot well be done at once, but in a course or order. First, by excluding the liquor by thickness; for an outward and gross infusion doth not well compact the body; that which entereth must be subtile, and a kind of vapour. Secondly, by intenerating by the consent of consubstantials : for bodies upon the touch of those things which have good agreement with them, open themselves, and relax their pores. Thirdly, imprinters are convoys, and insinuate into the parts the consubstantials, and the mixture of gentle astringents doth somewhat restrain the perspiration. But then, in the fourth place, follows that great astriction and closure up of the body by emplasteration, and then afterwards by inunction, until the supple be turned into solid, as we said in the proper place.

CANON XXVII.

Frequent renovation of the parts reparable, watereth and reneweth the less reparable also.

THE EXPLICATION.

We said in the preface to this history, that the way of death was this, that the parts reparable died in the fellowship of the parts less reparable ; so that in the reparation of these same less reparable parts, all our forces would be employed. And, therefore, being admonished by Aristotle's observation touching plants, namely, that the putting forth of new shoots and branches refresheth the body of the tree in the passage; we conceive the like reason might be, if the flesh and blood in the body of man were often renewed, that thereby the bones themselves, and membranes, and other parts, which in their own nature are less reparable, partly by the cheerful passage of the juices, partly by that new clothing of the young flesh and blood, might be watered and renewed.

CANON XXVIII.

Refrigeration, or cooling of the body, which passeth some other ways than by the stomach, is useful for long life.

THE EXPLICATION.

The reason is at hand; for seeing a refrigeration not temperate, but powerful, (especially of the blood,) is above all things necessary to long life; this can by no means be effected from within as much as is requisite, without the destruction of the stomach and bowels.

CANON XXIX.

That intermixing, or entangling, that as well consumption as reparation are the works of heat, is the greatest obstacle to long life.

THE EXPLICATION.

Almost all great works are destroyed by the natures of things intermixed, when as that which helpeth in one respect, hurteth in another; therefore men must proceed herein by a sound judgment, and a discreet practice. For our part, we have done so far as the matter will bear, and our memory serveth us, by separating benign heats from hurtful, and the remedies which tend to both.

CANON XXX.

Curing of diseases is effected by temporary medicines; but lengthening of life requireth observation of diets.

THE EXPLICATION.

Those things which come by accident, as soon as the causes are removed, cease again: but the continual course of nature, like a running river, requires a continual rowing and sailing against the stream, therefore we must work regularly by diets. Now, diets are of two kinds; set diets, which are to be observed at certain times, and familiar diet, which is to be admitted into our daily repast. But the set diets are the more potent, that is, a course of medicines for a time; for those things which are of so great virtue that they are able to turn nature back again, are, for the most part, more strong, and more speedily altering, than those which may without danger be received into a continual use. Now, in the remedies set down in our intentions, you shall find only three set diets, the opiate diet, the diet malacissant or supplying, and the diet emaciant and renewing. But amongst those which we prescribed for familiar diet, and to be used daily, the most efficacious are these that follow, which also come not far short of the virtue of set diets. Nitre, and the subordinates to nitre; the regiment of the affections, and course of our life; refrigerators which pass not by the stomach; drinks roscidating, or engendering oily juices; besprinkling of the blood with some firmer matter, as pearls, certain woods, competent unctions to keep out the air and to keep in the spirit. Heaters from without, during the assimilation after sleep; avoiding of those things which inflame the spirit, and put it into an eager heat, as wine and spices. Lastly, a moderate and seasonable use of those things which endue the spirits with a robust heat, as saffron, crosses, garlic, elecampane, and compound opiates.

CANON XXXI.

The living spirit is instantly extinguished, if it be deprived either of motion, or of refrigeration, or of aliment.

THE EXPLICATION.

Namely, these are those three which before we called the porches of death, and they are the proper and immediate passions of the spirit. For all the organs of the principal parts serve hereunto, that these three offices be performed; and again, all destruction of the organs which is deadly brings the matter to this point, that one or more of these three fail. Therefore all other things are the divers ways to death, but they end in these three. Now, the whole fabric of the parts is the organ of the spirit, as the spirit is the organ of the reasonable soul, which is incorporeous and divine.

CANON XXXII.

Flame is a momentary substance, air a fixed; the living spirit in creatures is of a middle nature.

THE EXPLICATION.

This matter stands in need both of a higher indagation, and of a longer explication than is pertinent to the present inquisition. Meanwhile we must know this, that flame is almost every moment generated and extinguished; so that it is continued only by succession; but air is a fixed body, and is not dissolved; for though air begets new air out of watery moisture, yet, notwithstanding, the old air still remains; whence cometh that superoneration of the air whereof we have spoken in the title De Ventis. But spirit is participant of both natures, both of flame and air, even as the nourishments thereof are, as well oil, which is homogeneous to flame, as water, which is homogeneous to air; for the spirit is not nourished either of oily alone, or of watery alone, but of both together; and though air doth not agree well with flame, nor oil with water, yet in a mixed body they agree well enough. Also the spirit hath from the air his easy and delicate impressions and yieldings, and from the flame his noble and potent motions and activities. In like manner the duration of spirit is a mixed thing, being neither so momentary as that of flame, nor so fixed as that of air. And so much the rather it followeth not the condition of flame, for that flame itself is extinguished by accident, namely, by contraries, and enemies environing it; but spirit is not subject to the like conditions and necessities. Now, the spirit is repaired from the lively and florid blood of the small arteries which are inserted into the brain; but this reparation is done by a peculiar manner, of which we speak not now.

END OF THIRD PART OF THE INSTAURATIO.

THE FOURTH PART

OF THE GREAT INSTAURATION.

SCALING LADDER OF THE INTELLECT; OR, THREAD OF THE LABYRINTH.

It would be difficult to find fault with tnose who affirm that " nothing is known," if they had tempered the rigour of their decision by a softening explanation. For, should any one contend, that science rightly interpreted is a knowledge of things through their causes, and that the knowledge of causes constantly expands, and by gradual and successive concatenation rises, as it were, to the very loftiest parts of nature, so that the knowledge of particular existences cannot be properly possessed without an accurate comprehension of the whole of things; it is not easy to discover, what can reasonably be observed in reply. For it is not reasonable to allege, that the true knowledge of any thing is to be attained before the mind has a correct conception of its causes: and to claim for human nature such a correct conception universally, might justly be pronounced perhaps not a little rash, or rather the proof of an ill-balanced mind. They, however, of whom we are writing, shrink not from thus desecrating the oracles of the senses, which must lead to a total recklessness. Nay, to speak the truth, had they even spared their false accusations, the very controversy itself appears to originate in an unreasonable and contentious spirit; since, independently of that rigid truth to which they refer, there still remains such a wide field for human exertion, that it would be preposterous, if not symptomatic of an unsettled and disturbed intellect, in the anxious grasping at distant extremes, to overlook such utilities as are obvious and near at hand. For, however they may seek, by introducing their distinction of true and probable, to subvert the certainty of science, without at the same time superseding the use or practically affecting the pursuit of it, yet, in destroying the hope of effectually investigating truth, they have cut the very sinews of human industry, and by a promiscuous license of disquisition converted what should have been the labour of discovery, into a mere exercise of talent and disputation.

We cannot, however, deny, that if there be any fellowship between the ancients and ourselves, it is principally as connected with this species of philosophy : as we concur in many things which they have judiciously observed and stated about the varying nature of the senses, the weakness of human judgment, and the propriety of withholding or suspending assent; to which we might add innumerable other remarks of a similar tendency. So that the only difference between them and ourselves is, that they affirm " nothing can be perfectly known by any method whatever; we, that " nothing can be perfectly known by the methods which mankind have hitherto pursued." Of this fellowship we are not at all ashamed. For the aggregate, if it consists not of those alone who lay down the above-mentioned dogma as their peremptory and unchangeable opinion, but of such also as indirectly maintain it under the forms of objection and interrogatory, or by their indignant complaints about the obscurity of things, confess, and, as it were, proclaim it aloud, or suffer it only to transpire from their secret thoughts in occasional and ambiguous whispers; the aggregate, I say, comprises, you will find, the far most illustrious and profound of the ancient thinkers, with whom no modern need blush to be associated ; a few of them may, perhaps, too magisterially have assumed to decide the matter, yet this tone of authority prevailed only during the late dark ages, and now maintains its ground simply through a spirit of party, the invéteracy of habit, or mere carelessness and neglect.

Yet, in the fellowship here spoken of, it is easy to discover that, agreeing as we do with the great men alluded to, as to the premises of our opinions, in our conclusions we differ from them most widely. Our discrepancies may, indeed, at first sight, appear to be but inconsiderable ; they asserting the absolute, and we the modified incompetency of the human intellect; but the practical result is this, that as they neither point out, nor, in fact, profess to expect any remedy for the defect in question, they wholly give up the business; and thus, by denying the certainty of the senses, pluck up science from its very foundation; whereas, we, by the introduction of a new method, endeavour to regulate and correct the aberrations both of the senses and of the intellect. The consequence is, that they, thinking the die finally cast, turn aside to the uncontrolled and fascinating ramblings of genius; while we, by our different view of the subject, are constrained to enter upon an arduous and distant province, which we unceasingly pray we may administer to the advantage and happiness of mankind. The introductory part of our progress we described in our second book, which, having entered, in the third we treated on the phenomena of the universe, and on history, plunging into and traversing the woodlands, as it were, of nature, here overshadowed (as by foliage) with the infinite variety of experiments; there perplexed and entangled (as by thorns and briers) with the subtilty of acute commentations.

And now, perhaps, by our advance from the woods to the foot of the mountains, we have reached a more disengaged, but yet a more arduous station. For, from history we shall proceed by a firm and sure track, new indeed, and hitherto unexplored, to universals. To these paths of contemplation, in truth, might appositely be applied the celebrated and often quoted illustration of the "double road of active life," of which one branch, at first even and level, conducted the traveller to places precipitous and impassable; the other, though steep and rough at the entrance, terminated in perfect smoothness. In a similar manner, he who, in the very outset of his inqui-

ries, lays firm hold of certain fixed principles in the science, and, with immovable reliance upon them, disentangles (as he will with little effort) what he handles, if he advances steadily onward, not flinching out of excess either of self-confidence or of self-distrust from the object of his pursuit, will find he is journeying in the first of these two tracks; and if he can endure to suspend his judgment, and to mount gradually, and to climb by regular succession the height of things, like so many tops of mountains, with persevering and indefatigable patience, he will in due time attain the very uppermost elevations of nature, where his station will be serene, his prospects delightful, and his descent to all the practical arts by a gentle slope perfectly easy.

It is therefore, our purpose, as in the second book we laid down the precepts of genuine and legitimate disquisition, so in this to propound and establish, with reference to the variety of subjects, illustrative examples; and that in the form which we think most agreeable to truth, and regard as approved and authorized. Yet, we do not alter the customary fashion, as well to all the constituent parts of this formula on absolute necessity, as if they were universally indispensable and inviolable: for we do not hold, that the industry and the happiness of man are to be indissolubly bound, as it were, to a single pillar. Nothing, indeed, need prevent those who possess great leisure, or have surmounted the difficulties infallibly encountered in the beginning of the experiment, from carrying onward the process here pointed out. On the contrary, it is our firm conviction that true art is always capable of advancing.

F. W.

THE FIFTH PART

OF THE GREAT INSTAURATION.

PRECURSORS; OR, ANTICIPATIONS OF THE SECOND PHILOSOPHY.

THAT person, in our judgment, showed at once both his patriotism and his discretion, who, when he was asked, " whether he had given to his fellow-citizens the best code of laws," replied, " the best which they could bear." And, certainly, those who are not satisfied with merely thinking rightly, (which is little better, indeed, than dreaming rightly, if they do not labour to realize and effectuate the object of their meditations,) will pursue not what may be abstractedly the best, but the best of such things as appear most likely to be approved. We, however, do not feel ourselves privileged, notwithstanding our great affection for the human commonwealth, our common country, to adopt this legislatorial principle of selection; for we have no authority arbitrarily to prescribe laws to man's intellect, or the general nature of things. It is our office, as faithful secretaries, to receive and note down as such have been enacted by the voice of nature herself; and our trustiness must stand acquitted, whether they are accepted, or by the suffrage of general opinions rejected. Still we do not abandon the hope, that, in times yet to come, individuals may arise who will both be able to comprehend and digest the choicest of those things, and solicitous also to carry them to perfection; and, with this confidence, we will never, by God's help, desist (so long as we live) from directing our attention thitherward, and opening their fountains and uses, and investigating the lines of the roads leading to them.

Yet, anxious as we are with respect to the subjects of general interest and common concern, in aspiring to the greater, we do not condemn the inferior, for those are frequently at a distance, while these are at hand and around us, nor though we offer (as we think) more valuable things, do we therefore put our veto upon things received and ancient, or seek to cover their estimation with the multitude. On the contrary, we earnestly wish them to be amplified and improved, and held in increased. regard; as it is no part of our ambition to withdraw men, either all, or altogether, or all at once, from what is established and current. But as an arrow, or other missile, while carried directly onward, still, nevertheless, during its progress incessantly whirls about in rapid rotation; so we, while hurrying forward to more distant objects, are carried round and round by these popular and prevalent opinions. And, therefore, we do not hesitate to avail ourselves of the fair services of this common reason and these popular proofs; and shall place whatever conclusions have been discovered or decided through their medium (which may, indeed, have much of truth and utility in them) on an equal footing with the rest; at the same time protesting against any inferences thence to be drawn in derogation of what we have above stated about the incompetency of both this reason and of these proofs. We have rather, in fact, thrown out the preceding hints, as it were, occasionally, for the sake of such as, feeling their progress impeded by an actual want either of talent or of leisure, wish to confine themselves within the ancient tracts and precincts of science, or, at least, not to venture beyond their immediately contiguous domains; since we conceive that the same speculations may (like tents or resting-places on the way) minister ease and rest to such as, in pursuance of our plan, seek the true interpretation of nature, and find it; and may, at the same time, in some slight degree, promote the welfare of man, and infuse into his mind ideas somewhat more closely connected with the true nature of things, This result, however, we are far from anticipating in confidence of any faculty which we ourselves possess, but we entertain no doubt that any one even of moderate abilities, yet ripened mind, who is both willing and able to lay aside his idols, and to institute his inquiries anew, and to investigate with attention, perseverance, and freedom from prejudice, the truths and computations of natural history, will, of himself, by his genuine and native powers, and by his own simple anticipations penetrate more profoundly into nature than he would be capable of doing by the most extensive course of reading, by indefinite abstract speculations, or by continual and repeated disputations; though he may not have brought the ordinary engines into action, or have adopted the prescribed formula of interpretation.

In this, however, we do not wish to be considered as demanding for our own dogma the authority which we have withheld from those of the ancients. We would rather, indeed, testify and proclaim, that we are far from wishing to be ourselves peremptorily bound by what we are about to bring forward, of whatever character it may be, to the maintenance of the whole of our secondary and inductive philosophy. This result of our meditations we have determined to offer loosely, and unconfined by the circumscription of method; deeming this a form both better adapted to sciences newly springing up as from an old stock, and more suitable to a writer whose present object it is not to constitute an art from combined, but to institute a free investigation of individual existences.   F. W.

MISCELLANEOUS TRACTS.

[TRANSLATED FROM THE LATIN.]

OF THE EBB AND FLOW OF THE SEA.

THE investigation of the causes of the ebb and flow of the sea, attempted by the ancients and then neglected, resumed by the moderns, but rather frittered away than vigorously agitated in a variety of opinions, is generally, with a hasty anticipation, directed to the moon, because of certain correspondences between that motion, and the motion of that orb. But to a careful inquirer certain traces of the truth are apparent, which may lead to surer conclusions. Wherefore, to proceed without confusion, we must first distinguish the motions of the sea, which, though thoughtlessly enough multiplied by some, are in reality found to be only five; of these one alone is eccentric, the rest regular. We may mention first the wandering and various motions of what are called currents: the second is the great six-hours motion of the sea, by which the waters alternately advance to the shore, and retire twice a day, not with exact precision, but with a variation, constituting monthly periods. The third is the monthly motion itself, which is nothing but a cycle of the diurnal motion periodically recurring: the fourth is the half-monthly motion, formed by the increase of the tides at new and full moon, more than at half-moon: the fifth is the motion, once in six months, by which, at the equinoxes, the tides are increased in a more marked and signal manner.

It is the second, the great six-hours or diurnal motion, which we propose for the present as the principal subject and aim of our discourse, treating of the others only incidentally and so far as they contribute to the explanation of that motion.

First, then, as relates to the motion of currents, there is no doubt that to form it the waters are either confined by narrow passages, or liberated by open spaces, or hasten as with relaxed rein, down declivities, or rush against and ascend elevations, or glide along a smooth, level bottom, or are ruffled by furrows and irregularities in the channel, or fall into other currents, or mix with them and become subject to the same influences, or are affected by the annual or trade winds, which return at regular periods of the year. That in consequence of these and similar causes, they vary their states of flow and eddy, both as relates to extending and widening the motion itself, and to the velocity and measure of the motion; and thus produce what we term currents. Thus, in the seas the depth of the basin or channel, the occurrence of whirlpools or submarine rocks, the curvature of the shore, gulfs, bays, the various position of islands, and the like, have great effect, acting powerfully on the waters, their paths, and agitations in all possible directions, eastward and westward, and in like manner northward and southward; wherever, in fact, such obstacles, open spaces, and declivities exist in their respective formations. Let us then set aside this particular, and, so to speak, casual motion of the waters, lest it should introduce confusion in the inquisition which we now pursue. For no one can raise and support a denial of the statement which we are presently to make, concerning the natural and *catholic* motions of the seas, by opposing to it this motion of the currents, as not at all consistent with our positions. For the currents are mere compressions of the water, or extrications of it from compression: and are, as as we have said, partial, and relative to the local form of the land or water, or the action of the winds. And what we have said is the more necessary to be recollected and carefully noted, because that universal movement of the ocean of which we now treat is so gentle and slight, as to be entirely overcome by the impulse of the currents, to fall into their order, and to give way, be agitated, and mastered by their violence. That this is the case is manifest particularly from this fact, that the motion of ebb and flow, simply, is not perceptible in midsea, especially in seas broad and vast, but only at the shores. It is, therefore, not at all surprising, that, as inferior in force, it disappears, and is as it were annihilated amidst the currents; except that where the currents are favourable, it lends them some aid and impetuosity, and, on the contrary, where they

523

are adverse considerably restrains them. Waiving then the motion of the currents, we proceed to the four regular motions; that in the six hours, in the month, in the half month, and in six months, of which the sexhorary motion alone seems to produce and develope the ordinary tide, the monthly to determine that motion and define its renewal; the half-monthly and half-yearly to increase and strengthen it. For the ebb and flow, which cover and quit again a certain extent of shore, both vary at various hours, and according to the momentum and quantity of the water; whence these three other motions are rendered more perceptible.

We must, therefore, contemplate, singly and specifically, as we purposed, the motion of ebb and flow. And, first, it is necessary to grant that this motion, the subject of inquiry, is one of these two: either the motion of an *elevation* and *depression*, or the motion of a *progression* of the waters. The motion of elevation and depression we understand to be such, as is found in boiling water, mounting and subsiding alternately in a caldron: the motion of progression to be such as is observed in water carried in a basin, which quitting the one side, is projected to the opposite. Now, that the motion we treat of is not of the former sort, is in the first place suggested by this fact, that in different parts of the world the tides vary according to the times, so that in certain places there are floods and accumulations of the mass of waters, in others at the same hours ebb and diminutions. Now, the waters, if they did not travel from place to place, but rose ebullient from the bottom, ought to rise everywhere at once, and to subside together. For we see those two other motions, the monthly and half monthly, in full movement and operation at the same periods throughout the globe. For the waves increase at the equinoxes in all parts, not in certain places under the equator, or in others under the tropics: and the same is true of the half-monthly motion. For, everywhere over the world, the waters are elevated at new moon and full moon, nowhere at half-moon. The waters, therefore, are manifestly raised, and again depressed in these two motions, and like the heavenly bodies have their apogees and perigees. But in the ebb and flow of the sea, which we now discuss, the contrary takes place, an unequivocal sign of progressive motion. Besides, ere we set down the flow of the sea as an elevation of the waters, we ought to consider a little more carefully how that elevation can take place. For the swelling must either be produced by an augmentation of the mass of waters, or from an extension or rarefaction of fluid in that mass, or from simple elevation of the mass or body. The third supposition we must dismiss entirely. For if the water united in the same body were lifted up, a vacuum would necessarily be left between the earth and the under face of the water, there being no body ready to succeed

and supply its place. If there were a fresh quantity of water added, it must be by flowing and eruption from the earth. If there were dilatation only, this must take place either by solution into greater rarity, or by a tendency to approach another body, which, as it were, evokes the waters, attracts them, and lifts them to greater elevation. And, doubtless, that state of the waters, whether considered as ebullition, or rarefaction, or harmony with some one or other of the heavenly bodies, cannot seem incredible, that is, to a moderate extent, and on the supposition of the lapse of considerable time, in which such swellings and accretions may gather and accumulate. Therefore the difference observable between the ordinary, and the half-monthly tide, or the most copious of all, the half-yearly one, in which the addition to the mass of waters is not equal to the difference between ordinary ebb and flow, and has besides a large interval of time insensibly to form, may, on the hypothesis of *elevation* and *depression*, be consistently explained. But that so great a mass of water should burst forth as to explain that difference which is found between the ebb and flow, and that this should take place with such extreme rapidity, namely, twice a day, as if the earth, according to the fantastic notion of Apollonius, performed respiration, and breathed waters every six hours, and then again inhaled them, is very hard to believe. And let no man be misled by the unimportant fact that in some places wells are said to have a simultaneous motion with the ebb and flow of the sea, whence one might conjecture, that waters enclosed in the entrails of the earth boil up in like manner, in which case that swelling of the waters cannot be attributed to a progressive motion. For the answer is an easy one, that the flow of the sea by its encroachment may perforate and gorge many hollow and loose places of the earth, turn the course of subterraneous waters, or cause a reverberation of the enclosed air, which by a continued series of impulsions may raise the water in this sort of wells. Accordingly, this does not take place in all wells, nor even in many, which ought to be the case if the entire mass of waters had a property of periodically boiling up, and a harmony with the tide. But, on the contrary, this rarely happens, so as to be regarded almost as a miracle, because, in fact, such apertures and spiracles as reach from wells to the sea, without circuity or impediment, are very rarely found; nor is it unimportant to mention, what some relate, that in deep pits situated not far from the sea, the air becomes thick and suffocating at the time of ebb, from which it may seem manifest, not that the waters boil up, (for none are seen to do so,) but that the air is reverberated. No doubt, there is another objection, not despicable, but of great weight, every way deserving of an answer, one which had been the subject of careful observation,

EBB AND FLOW.

and that not incidentally, but a thing especially and of purpose inquired into and discovered, namely, that the water at the opposite shores of Europe and of Florida ebb at the same hours from both shores, and do not quit the shore of Europe when they roll to the shore of Florida, like water (as we have said before) agitated in a basin, but are manifestly raised and depressed at either shore at once. But a clear solution of this objection will be seen in the observations which shall presently be made about the path and progression of the ocean; the substance, however, is this; that the waters, setting out in their course from the Indian ocean, and obstructed by the remora of the continents of the old and new world, are impelled along the Atlantic from south to north; so that it is no wonder if they are driven against either shore equally at the same time, as waters are wont to be, which are propelled from the sea into estuaries and up the channels of rivers, evidently showing that the motion of the sea is progressive as respects the rivers, and yet that it at once inundates both shores. Notwithstanding, according to our custom we freely confess, and would have men observe and remember, that if it is found in experience that the tide advances at the same time on the coast of China and Peru, as on that of Europe and Florida, this our opinion, that ebb and flow is a progressive motion of the sea, must be repudiated.

For if the flow of the sea takes place at the same time at the opposite shores, as well of the Pacific or Southern Ocean as of the Atlantic Ocean, there are not in the universe any shores remaining, at which a corresponding ebb, at the same time, might afford a satisfactory solution of the objection. But we propose with confidence of a trial of this by experiment, to whose test we submit our cause: for we are clearly of opinion, that were the general result of a trial of this fact through the world known to us, this compact of nature would be found effected on sufficiently reciprocal conditions, namely, that at any given hour as much reflux took place in some parts of the world as flow in others. Therefore, from what we have stated, this motion of ebb and flow may be affirmed progressive.

Now follows the inquiry, from what cause and what combination of things this motion of ebb and flow arises and is presented to view. For all the great movements (if these be regular and perpetual) are not isolated, or (to use here an expression of the astronomers) ferine, but have something in nature with which they move harmoniously. Therefore those motions, as well as the half-monthly one of increase as the monthly of reparation, appear to accord with the motion of the moon; and again the half-monthly, or equinoctial, with the motion of the sun; also the elevations and depressions of the water, with the approximation and revolution in the orbits of the heavenly bodies. Notwithstanding, it will not immediately follow from this, and we would have men note the observation, that those things which agree in their periods and curriculum of time, or even in their mode of relation, are of a nature subjected the one to the other, and stand respectively as cause and effect. Thus we do not go so far as to affirm, that the motions of the sun ought to be set down as the causes of the inferior motions which are analogous to them; or that the sun and moon (as is commonly said) have dominion over these motions of the sea, although such notions are easily insinuated into our minds from veneration of the heavenly bodies; but in that very half-monthly motion, if it be rightly noted, it were a new and surprising kind of subjection to influence, that the tides at new and at full moon should be affected in the same manner, when the moon is affected in contrary ways; and many other things might be instanced, destroying similar fancies of this sort of dominant influence, and leading to this inference, that those correspondences arise from the catholic affections of matter, from the primary concatenation of causes, and connexion of things; not as if such were governed the one by the other, but both flowed from the same sources and from joint causes. Notwithstanding this, however, it remains true, as we have said, that nature delights in harmony, and scarcely admits of any thing isolated or solitary. We must therefore look, in treating of the sexhorary ebb and flow of the sea, with what other motions it is found to agree and harmonize. And first we must inquire with respect to the moon, in what manner that motion blends relations or natures with the moon. But this we do not see prevail except in the monthly repairing of the moon, for the periodical course of six hours has no affinity with the monthly course; nor again are the tides found to follow any affections of the moon. For, whether the moon be crescent or waning, whether she be under the earth or above the earth, whether her elevation above the horizon be higher or lower, whether her position be in the zenith or elsewhere, in none of these relations do the ebb and flow of the tide correspond with her.

Therefore, leaving the moon, let us inquire concerning other correspondences; and from all the motions of the heavenly bodies, it is certain that the diurnal motion is the shortest, and is accomplished in the least period of time, that is, in the space of twenty-four hours. It is therefore in harmony with this, that the motion of which we inquire, which is yet three times shorter than the diurnal one, should be referred immediately to that motion which is the shortest of the heavenly ones. But this notion has no great weight with us in this matter. Another hypothesis has more influence with us, that this motion is so distributed, that, though the motion of the waters is slower by innumerable degrees, still it

is referable to a common measure. For the space
of six hours is a quarter of the diurnal motion,
which space (as we said) is found in that motion
of the sea, with a difference coinciding with the
measure of the moon's motion. Whereupon this
belief sinks deep into our mind, and looks as it
were an oracular truth, that this motion is of the
same kind with the diurnal motion. With this,
therefore, as a basis, we shall proceed to a
thorough inquiry: and we think that the whole
subject is exhausted in three points of investigation.

The first is, whether that diurnal motion is confined within the regions of heaven, or descends,
and penetrates to the lower parts? The second
is, whether the seas move regularly from east to
west, as the heaven does? The third, whence and
how that six hours' motion of the tides takes place
which coincides with a quarter of the diurnal motion, with a difference falling in with the measure
of the moon's motion. Now, as relates to the
first inquiry, we think that the motion of rotation,
or of turning from east to west, is not properly a
motion merely of the heavenly bodies, but manifestly of the universe, and a primary motion in all
the great fluids, found to prevail from the highest
part of heaven to the lowest part of the waters,
in direction the same in all, in impulse, that
is, in rapidity and slowness, widely different; in
such wise, however, that in an order not in the
least confused, the rapidity is diminished in proportion as the bodies approach the globe of the earth.
Now this, it seems, may be taken as a probable
reason for supposing that that motion is not
limited to the heavens, because it prevails and is
in force through so great a depth of heaven as
lies between the starry heaven and the moon,
(a space much more extensive than that between
the moon and the earth,) with a regular diminution;
so that it is probable that nature does not at any
point abruptly break off a harmonious motion of
this kind, diffused through such vast spheres and
gradually lessening. And that this is so in the
heavenly bodies is evinced by two inconsistencies,
which follow from the opposite hypothesis. For,
since the planets visibly perform a diurnal motion,
unless we are to suppose that motion natural and
self-moved in all the planets, we must unavoida-
bly have recourse for an explanation either to the
supposition of the primum mobile, which is evidently opposed to nature; or to the rotation of
the earth, which is a notion extravagant enough,
if we look to the methods of nature. Therefore,
the motion exists in the heavenly bodies. And,
quitting heaven, that motion is most distinctly
visible in the inferior comets; which, though
lower than the orb of the moon, evidently move
from east to west. For, though they have their
solitary and eccentric motions, yet in performing
them they for a time have a common movement,
and are borne along with the motion of the ether,
and with the same conversion: but in the tropics
they are not generally so confined, nor move in
the regular course, but sometimes straggle towards the poles, yet, nevertheless, pursue their
rotatory motion from east to west. And thus this
motion, though it suffers great diminution, since
the nearer it descends towards earth the conversion is performed in smaller circles, and more
slowly, still remains powerful, so as to traverse
great distances in a short time. For these comets
are carried round the whole circumference, both
of the earth and the lower atmosphere, in the
space of twenty-four hours, with an excess of
one or two hours more. But after, by a continued
descent, it has reached these regions upon which
the earth acts, this motion, not only by the communication of the earth's nature and influence,
which represses and lowers circular motion, but
also by a substantial immission of the particles
of its matter, by means of vapours and gross exhalations, becomes infinitely relaxed, and almost
falls off, yet it is not therefore wholly annihilated
or ceases, but remains feeble and verging to imperceptible. For mariners now begin to confess that
between the tropics, where, in the open sea, the motion of the air is best perceived; and where the air
itself, as well as heaven, revolves in a larger circle,
and therefore more rapidly, that a perennial and
gentle breeze blows from east to west, insomuch
that those who wish to use the south-west wind
often seek and avail themselves of it outside the
tropics. Consequently, this motion is not extinguished, but becomes languid and obscure, so as to
be scarcely perceptible outside the tropics. Yet,
even outside the tropics, in our own part of the
globe, Europe, at sea, in serene and peaceful
weather, there is observed a certain wind, which
is of the same species; we may even conjecture
that what we experience here in Europe, where
the east wind is sharp and dry, and, on the contrary, the south-west winds are cherishing and humid, does not depend merely on the circumstance
that the one blows from a continent, the other from
the ocean, but on this, that the breath of the east
wind, since it is in the same train with the proper
motion of the air, accelerates and heightens that
motion, and therefore disperses and rarefies the
air, but that of the west wind, which is in the
contrary direction to the motion of the air, makes it
rebound upon itself, and become inspissated. Nor
ought this to be neglected, which is admitted
into the number of common observations, that
the clouds which are in motion in the upper part
of the air generally move from east to west;
while the winds about the earth's surface generally blow at the same time the contrary way.
And if they do not this always, the reason is
this, that there are sometimes opposite winds,
some acting on the high, others on the lowest
exhalations. Now, those blowing on high, if
they be adverse, confound the real motion of the

air. It is sufficiently clear, then, that the motion is not confined within the limits of heaven.

Then follows in order the second inquisition: whether the waters move regularly from east to west. Now, when we speak of waters, we mean those accumulations or masses of waters which are such large portions of nature as to have a relation of harmony to the fabric and system of the universe. And we are fully of opinion that the same motion is natural to, and inherent in, the body of waters, but is slower than in the air; though, on account of the grossness of the body, it is more palpable and manifest. Of this we shall content ourselves with three selected from many experimental proofs, but these weighty and marked ones, which prove that this is so.

The first is, that there is found a manifest motion and flow of waters from the Indian Ocean, even to the Atlantic, and that more swift and strong towards the Straits of Magellan, when an outlet is opened to them westwards; and a great current also on the other side of the world from the Northern Ocean to the British Sea. And these currents of waters manifestly roll from east to west; in which fact we must note in the first place, that in those two places alone the seas find thoroughfares, and can describe in flowing a complete circle: whereas, on the contrary, at the central regions of the globe, by the two ramparts of the old and new world, they are thrown off and driven (as it were into the estuaries of rivers) into the basins of the Atlantic and Pacific, the two oceans extending between the south and north, and open to the motion of a current from east to west. So that the true course of the waters is most safely inferred from the extremities of the globe, as we have stated, where they meet with no impediment, but sweep round in full circuit. And the first experiment is thus, the second is the following.

Let us suppose that the tide takes place at the mouth of the Straits of Gibraltar at any given hour: it is certain that the tide sets in at Cape St. Vincent later in the day than at the mouth of the Straits—at Cape Finisterre later than at Cape St. Vincent,—at King's Island later than at Cape Finisterre,—at the Island Heek later than at King's Island,—at the entrance of the English channel later than at Heek,—at the shore of Normandy later than at the entrance of the channel. Thus far in regular order: but at Graveling, as if by an entire inversion of the order, and that with a great leap, as it were, at the same hour, with a velocity like that which it has at the mouth of the Straits of Gibraltar. This second observation we apply to, and compare with the first. For we think, as has already been said, that in the Indian and northern oceans the true currents of the waters, that is, from the east to the west, are open and unimpeded, but in the channels of the Atlantic and Southern Oceans imprisoned and cross-ing, and reverberated by the interposition of lands, which extend both ways longitudinally from south to north; and nowhere but toward their extremities afford a free canal to the waters. But that strong direction of the waters, which is caused by the Indian Ocean towards the north, and in the opposite direction from the North Sea towards the South, differ infinitely in the extent of sea, affected on account of the different force and quantity of waters. But that this should take place is unavoidable. For the two great islands of the old and new world have the same figures, and are so stretched out as to broaden to the north, and taper to the south. The seas, therefore, on the contrary, towards the south occupy a vast space, but to the north a small one, at the back of Asia, Africa, and America: consequently, that great mass of waters which is discharged from the Indian Ocean, and is refracted into the Atlantic, is capable of forcing or propelling the course of the waters in a continued movement nearly to the British Sea, which is a part of the line described northwards. But that much smaller portion of the waters which issues from the north sea, and which has also a free passage westwards at the back of America, is not strong enough to turn the course of the waters southwards, except towards that point which we mentioned, namely, about the British Sea. Now, in these opposite currents, there must be some goal where they meet and contend, and where within short space the order of advance is suddenly changed, as we have said occurs about Graveling—the focus of the currents from the Indian and Northern Oceans, and that a certain ocean stream is formed by opposite currents on the coast of Holland has been noted by numbers, not only from the inversion of the hour of the tide, which we have stated, but also from the peculiar visible effect. Now, if this is so, we return to the position, that it must needs be, that in proportion as the parts and shores of the Atlantic extend southwards and approach the Indian Sea, in the same proportion the tide is prior, and early in the order of approach, and in proportion as you go northwards, (as far as their common goal,) where they are forced back by the antagonist stream of the Northern Ocean, they are backward and late. Now, that this is the case, the observation of the progression from the Straits of Gibraltar to the British Sea manifestly proves. Wherefore we think that the tide about the shores of Africa is at an earlier hour than that of the Straits of Gibraltar, and, in reversed order, the tide about Norway earlier than the tide about Sweden—but this we have not ascertained by experiment or testimony.

A third experiment is the following: The seas confined by land on one side, which we call bays, if they stretch out with any inclination from east to west, which is in the same line of impetus with the true motion of the waters have heavy and powerful tides; but if in the opposite direction, weak and scarcely perceptible. For the Red Sea hath a considerable tide; and the Persian Gulf, with a yet more entire westward direction, a still stronger. But the Mediterranean, the greatest of all gulfs, and its parts, the Tuscan, Pontic, and Propontic Seas, and in like manner the Baltic, all which tend eastward, are almost destitute of tide, or have only languid ones. But this difference is most conspicuous in certain parts of the Mediterranean, which, so long as they tend eastwards or turn towards the north, as in the Tuscan Sea and the others we have mentioned, are pacific and without much tide. But, after getting a westerly direction, which takes place in the Adriatic, it requires a remarkably large tide. To which we may also add this, that in the Mediterranean the slight reflux which is found begins from the ocean, the flow from the opposite direction, so that the water follows rather a course from the east than the natural refluence of the ocean. The three instances only we shall use for the present, in reference to this second inquiry.

There may be added to these another species of proof, agreeing with those already advanced, but of a more difficult nature. It is this: that an argument may be sought for proof of this motion from east to west, not only from the consenting motion of the heavens, of which we have already spoken,—where this motion is, as it were, in full flower and strength,—but also from the earth when it seems wholly to cease; so that it is really a direction of the universe, and pervades all things from the zenith to the interior parts of the earth. Now, we apprehend that this conversion takes place from east to west (as in reality it is found to do) upon the south and north poles. And Gilbertus has, with great care and accuracy, accomplished for us this discovery, that the whole earth and nature, so far as we call it terrestrial, have an inclination or popularity not softened down, but rigid, and, as Gilbertus himself calls it, robust, latent, but betraying itself in many nice experiments towards the north and south. And this observation we thus modify and correct, that this ought to be asserted only of the exterior formation about the surface of the earth, and ought not to be extended to the bowels of the earth; for that the earth is a magnet was at one time conceived,—a light imagination,—for it cannot be that the inward parts of the earth resemble any substance which the eye of man hath seen: since all the substances among which we live are loosened, subdued, or broken up by the sun and heavenly bodies, so that they cannot possibly agree with those which have had their seat in a place where the influence of the heavenly bodies does not penetrate;—but, which is our present subject, the more superficial crusts or formations of the earth appear to agree with the conversions of the sun. air. and waters, as far as solid and fixed bodies can agree with liquid and fluid—that is, not that they move towards the poles, but are pointed and turned towards the poles. For since every revolving sphere, which has fixed poles, participates of the nature of movable and fixed; after, by its consistency or self-determining nature, the rotatory force is bound up, still the force and tendency to direct itself remains, is augmented and gathered into one; so that direction and verticity to the poles in hard bodies is the same with the revolution on their poles in fluids.

The third inquiry remains. Whence and how ariseth that reciprocal action of the tides, once in six hours, which coincides with a quarter of the diurnal motion, with that difference to which we have adverted. To understand this, let us suppose that the whole globe was covered with water, as in the general deluge; we conceive the waters, as forming a complete and unbroken globe, would always roll in a progression from east to west each day to a certain extent: not certainly a great space, on account of the remission and deliberation of that motion as it approaches the earth, seeing the waters were nowhere obstructed or confined. Let us suppose, again, that the whole land was an island, and that it extended longitudinally between south and north, which confirmation and position most restrain and obstruct the motion from east to west; we think that the waters would keep on in their direct and natural course for a certain time, but, reverberated by the shores of that island, would roll back in equal intervals; that there would be, therefore, only one influx of the sea a day, and in like manner only one reflux, and that to each of these about twelve hours would be apportioned. And let us now suppose what is true and matter-of-fact, that the land is divided into two islands, those, namely, of the new and old world; for Australia, by its position, does not much alter the effect; as neither does Greenland nor Nova Zembla, and that these two islands extend through nearly three zones of the world, between which two oceans, the Atlantic and Southern, flow, and these nowhere find a thoroughfare, except towards the poles; we think it necessarily follows, that these two ramparts impart and communicate the character or double reaction to the entire mass of waters. Whence arises that motion in the quarter of a day,—so that the waters being cooped in on both sides, the ebb and flow of the sea would become visible twice a day, since there is a double advance, and also a double recoil. Now, if these two islands were extended through the waters like cylinders or columns, of equal dimensions, and with rectilinear shores, that motion might be easily perceptible, and might be pointed out to any one, which now seems to be perplexed and obscured by so great a variety of position of land and sea. For it is not difficult to form some conjecture what degree of velocity it is proper to ascribe to that motion of the waters, and what distances it may describe in one day. For, if there be selected, in order to form a judgment of this matter, some of those coasts which are less mountainous, or low lying, and which are contiguous to the open sea, and then the measure of the space of the globe interjacent between the extreme points of the flux and reflux, and that space be quadrupled on account of the four movements of the tide each day, and that number again doubled on account of the tides at the opposite shores of the same ocean; and to this number there be something added over and above on account of the height of the shores, which always rise to a certain elevation above the channel of the sea; that calculation will give the space which this sphere of water, were it free from obstruction, and moving in progression round the enveloped globe of earth, would describe in one day, which certainly would not be great.

Now, with respect to that difference which coincides with the measure of the moon's motion, and forms the period of a lunar month; we think that the explanation is this, that the period of six hours is not the exact measure of this reaction, just as the diurnal motion of any of the planets is not accomplished in twenty-four hours precisely, and least of all that of the moon. Wherefore, the measure of the ebb and flow of the tide is not a quarter of the motion of the fixed stars, which is twenty-four hours, but a quarter of the diurnal motion of the moon.

DIRECTIONS.

Let it be inquired, whether the hour of the tide on the coast of Africa be before the hour of tide about the Straits of Gibraltar. Let it be inquired whether the hour of the tide about Norway is before the hour of the tide about Sweden, and that, in like manner, before the hour of the tide at Graveling?

Let it be inquired, whether the hour of the tide on the coast of Brazil be before the hour of the tide on the coast of New Spain and Florida?

Let it be inquired, whether the hour of the tide at the shores of China is not found nearly the same with the hour of tide on the coast of Peru, and with the hour of reflux on the coast of Africa and Florida?

Let it be inquired, how far the hour of tide on the coast of Peru differs from the hour of tide at the coast of New Spain; and particularly what are the differences of the hour of tide at either shore of the Isthmus of Darien, in America; again, how far the hour of tide on the coast of Peru corresponds with the hour of tide on the coast of China?

Let it be inquired respecting the largeness of the tides on different coasts, not merely respecting their periods or hours. For, although the largeness of tides is generally caused by the depressions of the shores, yet, notwithstanding, they are closely connected with the true principle of the motion of the sea, according as it is favourable or adverse.

Let inquiry be made with respect to the Caspian sea, which is formed by considerable bodies of water locked up, without any outlet into the ocean, if they are subject to ebb and flow, and what? our conjecture being that the waters of the Caspian Sea may have one tide a day, not two, and such that the eastern shores of it are deserted by the sea, while the western are overflowed.

And let inquiry be made, whether the increase of the tide at new and full moons and at the equinoxes, takes place at the same time in different parts of the world, (and when we say at the same time, we do not mean at the same hour, for the hours vary, according to the rapidity of the waters' motion towards the shores, as we have said,) but in the same day.

Limits. The inquiry is not extended to a full explanation of the harmony of the monthly motion of the sea with the moon's motion, whether that takes place from a subordinate or a joint cause.

Relations. The present inquiry is connected with the inquiry whether the earth revolves with the diurnal motion of the heavens. For if the tide is, so to speak, the last stage of the gradual diminution of the diurnal motion, it will follow, that the globe of the earth is immovable, or at least that its motion is slower by far than that of the water. W. G. G

THE ABECEDARIUM NATURÆ,

BY ARCHBISHOP TENNISON.

PUBLISHED IN THE BACONIANA, 1679.

THE SAME IN ENGLISH BY THE PUBLISHER.

A Fragment of a Book written by the Lord Verulam, and entitled, The Alphabet of Nature.

SEEING so many things are produced by the earth and waters; so many things pass through the air, and are received by it; so many things are changed and dissolved by fire; other inquisitions would be less perspicuous, unless the nature of those masses which so often occur, were well known and explained. To these we add inquisitions concerning celestial bodies, and meteors, seeing they are some of greater masses, and of the number of catholic bodies.[*]

Greater Masses.

The sixty-seventh inquisition. The threefold Tau, or concerning the earth.

The sixty-eighth inquisition. The threefold Upsilon, or concerning the water.

The sixty-ninth inquisition. The threefold Phi, or concerning the air.

The seventieth inquisition. The threefold Chi, or concerning the fire.

The seventy-first inquisition. The threefold Psi, or concerning celestial bodies.

The seventy-second inquisition. The threefold Omega, or concerning meteors.

Conditions of Entities.

There yet remain, as subjects of our inquiry, in our alphabet, the conditions of beings, which seem, as it were, transcendentals, and such as touch very little of the body of nature. Yet, by that manner of inquisition which we use, they will considerably illustrate the other objects.

First, therefore; seeing (as Democritus excellently observed) the nature of things is in the plenty of matter, and variety of individuals large, and (as he affirmeth) infinite; but in its coitions and species so finite, that it may seem narrow and poor; seeing so few species are found, either in actual being or impossibility, that they scarce make up a muster of a thousand; and seeing

[*] See the distribution, in l. 2, c. 3, de Augm. Scient. p. 134, 135, 136. Ed. Lugd. Bat. l. 3, c. 4, p. 231. And c. 4. Globi Intellect. p. 88, 89.

negatives subjoined to affirmatives, conduce much to the information of the understanding: it is fit that an inquisition be made concerning being, and not being. That is the seventy-third in order, and reckoned the fourfold Alpha.

Conditions of beings. The fourfold Alpha; or, concerning being, and not being.

Now, possible and impossible, are nothing else but conditions potential to being, or not potential to being. Of this the seventy-fourth inquisition consists, and is accounted the fourfold Beta.

Conditions of beings. The fourfold Beta; or, concerning possible and impossible.

Also, much, little; rare, ordinary; are conditions potential to being in quantity. Of them let the seventy-fifth inquisition consist, and be accounted the fourfold Gamma.

Conditions of beings. The fourfold Gamma; or, concerning much and little.

Durable and transitory, eternal and momentary, are potential to being in duration. Of these let the seventy-sixth inquisition consist, and be called the fourfold Delta.

Conditions of beings. The fourfold Delta; or, concerning durable and transitory.

Natural and monstrous, are potential to being, either by the course of nature, or by its deviations from it. Of these let the seventy-seventh inquisition consist, which is accounted the fourfold Epsilon.

Conditions of beings. The fourfold Epsilon; or, concerning what is natural or monstrous.

Natural and artificial, are potential to being, either with or without the operation of man. Of these let the seventy-eighth inquisition consist, and be accounted the fourfold Zeta.

Conditions of beings. The fourfold Zeta; or, of that which is natural and artificial.

We have not subjoined examples in the explication of the order of this our alphabet: for the inquisitions themselves contain the whole array of examples.

It is by no means intended, that the titles, according to which the order of this alphabet is disposed, should have so much authority given to them, as to be taken for true and fixed partitions of things. That were to profess we already knew the things after which we inquire; for no man does truly dispose of things into their several classes, who does not beforehand very well understand the nature of them. It is sufficient, if these titles be conveniently adapted to the order of inquiry; the thing which is at present designed.

The Rule or Form of the Alphabet.

After this manner we compose and dispose our alphabet:

We begin solely with history and experiments. These, if they exhibit an enumeration and series of particular things, are disposed into tables; otherwise, they are taken separately and by themselves.

But, seeing we are often at a loss for history and experiments, especially such as are luciferous, or instructive, and, as we call them, instances of the cross;[*] by which the understanding might be helped in the knowledge of the true causes of things: we propose the task of making new experiments. These may serve as a history in design. For what else is to be done by us who are but breaking the ice?

For the mode of any more abstruse experiment, we explain it, lest any mistake arise about it; and to the intent, also, that we may excite others to excogitate better methods.

Also, we interspect certain admonitions and cautions concerning such fallacies of things, and errors in invention, as we meet with in our way.

We subjoin our observations upon history and experiments, that the interpretation of nature may be the more in readiness and at hand.

Likewise, we lay down canons (but not such as are fixed and determined) and axioms which are, as it were, in embryo: such as offer themselves to us in the quality of inquirers, and not of judges. Such canons and axioms are profitable, though they appear not yet manifest, and upon all accounts true.

Lastly: we meditate sometimes certain essays of interpretation, though such as are low and of small advance, and by no means to be honoured (in our opinion) with the very name of interpretation.

For, what need have we of arrogance or imposture, seeing we have so often professed that we have not such a supply of history and experiments as is needful; and that, without these, the interpretation of nature cannot be brought to perfection. Wherefore, it is enough for us if we are not wanting to the beginning of things.

Now, for the sake of perspicuity and order, we prepare our way by avenues, which are a kind of prefaces to our inquisitions. Likewise, we interpose bonds of connection, that our inquisitions may not seem abrupt and disjointed.

Also, we suggest for use some hints of practice. Furthermore, we propose wishes of such things as are hitherto only desired and not had, together with those things which border on them, for the exciting the industry of man's mind.

Neither are we ignorant that those inquisitions are sometimes mutually entangled; so that some things of which we inquire, even the same things belong to several titles. But we will observe such measure, that (as far as may be) we may shun both the nauseousness of repetition, and the trouble of rejection, submitting, notwithstanding, to either of these, when, in an argument so obscure, there is necessity of so doing, in order to the more intelligible teaching of it.

This is the form and rule of our alphabet.

May God, the creator, preserver, and renewer of the universe, protect and govern this work, both in its ascent to his glory, and in its descent to the good of mankind, for the sake of his mercy and good will to men, through his only Son, Immanuel, God with us.

---

[*] See Nov. Organ., L. 2., Aph. 36.

CATALOGUE OF BODIES, ATTRACTIVE AND NOT ATTRACTIVE.

BY ARCHBISHOP TENNISON.

PUBLISHED IN THE BACONIANA, 1678.

IF there be made a turn-pin of any metal, after the fashion of a magnetic needle, and amber be applied to one end of it, after having been gently rubbed, the pin will turn.

Amber heated by the fire, be it warmish, hot, or set on fire, it does not draw.

A little bar of iron red-hot, flame, a lighted candle, a hot coal, put nigh sheaves (or straws) or turn-pins, (or compass needles,) do not draw.

Amber, in a greater mass, if it be polite, draws, though not rubbed: in a lesser quantity, and in a less polite mass, it draws not without rubbing.

Crystal, lapis specularis, glass, and other such electric bodies, if burned, or scorched, draw not.

Pitch, the softer rosin, benjoin, asphaltum, camphire, galbanum, ammoniac, storax, assa, these draw not at all when the air is hot: but when it is cooler, they draw weakly, and so that we can just perceive them to do so.

Reeking air, blown-up amber, &c., from the mouth, or from a moister atmosphere, choketh the attractive virtue.

If a paper, or a piece of linen, be put between amber and chaff, there is no motion, or attraction made.

Amber, or other electrics, warmed by the sun-beams, have not their attractive virtue so awakened, as by rubbing.

Amber rubbed, and exposed to the beams of the sun, retains its attractive force the longer; and does not so soon lose it, as it would do in the shadow.

Heat derived from a burning-glass to amber, &c., does not help its attraction.

Sulphur, and hard wax, set on fire, do not draw.

Amber, when, immediately after rubbing, it is applied to a shiver, or a compass-needle, draws best of all.

The electric virtue is as vigorous, for a time, in its retention, as it was in its first attraction.

Flame (amber being put within the sphere of its activity) is not drawn by it.

A drop of water, amber being applied towards it, is drawn into a cone.

If electric bodies be rubbed too hard, their attraction is thereby hindered.

Those bodies, which in a clear sky do scarce draw, in a thick air move not at all.

Water put upon amber choketh its attractive force, though it draweth the water itself.

Fat* so encompassing amber, that it toucheth it, takes away its attraction; but being so put betwixt it and the object to be drawn, as not to touch it, it doth not take it away.

Oil put upon amber, hinders not its motion: neither doth amber, rubbed with the finger moistened with oil, lose its attractive virtue.

Amber, jeats, and the like, do more strongly excite, and longer retain the objects they draw, although the rubbing be but little. But diamonds, crystal, glass, ought to be rubbed longer, that they may appear hot, ere they be used for attraction.

Flames nigh to amber, though the distance be very small, are not drawn by it.

Amber, &c., draw the smoke of a lamp newly extinguished.

Amber draws smoke more strongly when it comes forth, and is more gross; and more weakly, when it ascends and becomes thinner.

A body drawn by electric bodies, is not manifestly altered, but only leans itself upon them.

* For by Sarca, I suppose, he meaneth Sarcia.

INQUISITION OF THE CONVERSIONS OF BODIES.

TRANSLATED BY A. BLAIR, ESQ., 1830.

Inquisition of the Conversions, Transmutations, Multiplications, and Productions of Bodies.

EARTH, by fire, is converted into bricks, which are of the nature of stones, and which we use for building, like stones. So with tiles.

Naphtha, which was that bituminous cement, wherewith the walls of Babylon were built, by time acquires exceedingly great hardness and firmness, equal to stone.

In clayey lands, where are pebbles and gravel, you shall find huge stones, concreted of pebbles and gravel, with stony matter interposed, as hard, or truly harder, than the pebbles themselves.

There are certain springs of water, wherein if you immerse wood, it shall be turned into the nature of stone; so as that the part sunk in the water shall become stone, the part above the water shall remain wood.

The viscous matter about the kidneys and bladder, in the human body, is converted into a pebble or stony matter. A stone, also, is often found in the gall-bladder; and sometimes, but this is most rare, in the vena porta.

Quære, how much time is required, that the matter of earth, in stone-quarries, may be converted into the stony nature?

Water, as there is reason to think, is changed into crystal; which may be seen in many caverns, where the crystal hangs in drops.

You may have an experiment of wood, or the stalks of plants, buried in quicksilver, whether they will harden, and, as it were, petrify, or no.

Report has much prevailed of a stone bred in the head of an old and great toad.

It is related that a certain nobleman, digging in the bed of his pool, found an egg turned into stone, the white and yolk retaining their proper colour; but the shell brightly sparkling, like a diamond exquisitely cut in faces.

Make experiment of some bodies, let down near to the bottom of a well, as wood, or other softer substances; but let them not touch the water, lest they rot.

They say that the white of an egg, through long insolation, or exposure in the sunbeams, has contracted the hardness of a stone.

Mud, in water, is converted in the shells of fishes, as in muscles,—(the fish) which are found in pools of fresh water, that flow not, and are covered with moss. But the substance of those shells is exceedingly delicate, clear, and glistening.

THE MASCULINE BIRTH OF TIME;

OR, THE

GREAT INSTAURATION OF MAN'S DOMINION OVER THE UNIVERSE

To God the Father, God the Word, God the Holy Ghost, I address my most humbled and ardent prayers, that, mindful of the miseries of man, and of this pilgrimage of life, of which the days are few and evil, they would open up yet new sources of refreshment from the fountains of good, for the alleviation of our sorrows; and, also, that things divine may not in this be prejudiced by things human, nor from the opening up of the passages of sense, and the kindling of greater natural light, any infidelity or darkness may arise in our minds towards the mysteries of God; but rather that, by the understanding cleansed and purified from fantastic and vain ideas, yet wholly submissive and subjected to the divine oracles, those things which are of faith may be rendered to faith.

W. G. G.

TRANSLATION OF

THE MASCULINE BIRTH OF TIME;

OR,

THREE BOOKS CONCERNING THE INTERPRETATION OF NATURE.

1. THE PURIFICATION AND APPLICATION OF THE MIND.
2. THE LIGHT OF NATURE, OR METHOD OF INTERPRETATION.
3. NATURE ILLUMINATED, OR THE TRUTH OF THINGS.

C. I. *Legitimate Mode of Statement.*

I find, my son, that men in showing forth, and no less in concealing the knowledge which they think they have acquired, have not acted in a spirit of good faith and of duty. No less mischievous, though perhaps less shameful, is the error of those who, with good intentions, but little wisdom, are ignorant of the art and rules proper for setting forth their several subjects. We do not intend, however, to begin a complaint of either this perversity or ignorance in the expounders of knowledge. Had they, by unskilful teaching, broken down the weight of the subjects taught, it might, no doubt, have been matter of just indignation. But, in teaching inaptitude, it was natural to expect absurdity. I, however, far different from such instructors, intend to impart to you not fictions of imagination or shadows of words; not a mixture of religion; not certain commonplace observations, or certain well-known experiments adjusted to conformity with fanciful theories, but to bind, and place at your command, nature with her offspring about her; and can this be supposed a theme fit to be debased by pretension or unskilfulness, or other defective treatment. So may I exist, my son, and so may I extend the now deplorably narrow limits of man's dominion over the universe to the permitted boundaries, (which is the only object of my prayers among human things,) as I shall disclose to you these things with the fullest conviction, with the deepest forecast of my mind, and after the profoundest research into the present state of knowledge, in the method of all others the most legitimate. "And what," you will say, "is this legitimate method? Have done with artifice and circumlocution; show me the naked truth of your design, that I may be able to form a judgment for myself." I would, my dearest son, that matters were in such a state with you as to render this possible. Do you suppose that when all the entrances and passages to the minds of all men are infested and obstructed with the darkest idols, and these deep-seated and burned in, as it were, into their substance, that clear and smooth spaces can be found for receiving the true and natural rays of objects? A new process must be instituted, by which to insinuate ourselves into minds so entirely obstructed. For as the delusions of the insane are removed by art and ingenuity, but aggravated by violence and opposition, so must we adapt ourselves here to the universal insanity. What! do even those less difficult requisites pertaining to the legitimate method of delivering knowledge, appear to you such light and easy matters? That it be ingenuous, that is, afford no handle or occasion for error; that it have a certain native and inseparable quality, both to conciliate belief, and repel the injuries of time, so that the knowledge so delivered, like a vigorous and healthy plant, may daily shoot and thrive; that it appear to place itself in, and adapt itself to the situation of its proper and reasonable reader: whether I shall show in the sequel all these qualities or not, I appeal to futurity.   W. G. G.

534

THE HISTORY AND FIRST INQUISITION OF

SOUND AND HEARING,

AND

TOUCHING THE FORM OF SOUND, AND THE SECRET PROCESS OF SOUND, OR THE WOOD OF SOUND AND HEARING.

Of the generation of sound, and the first percussion.

Of the lasting of sound, and of the perishing and extinction of sounds.

Of the confusion and perturbation of sounds.

Of the accessory aids and impediments of sounds.

Of the stay of sound, and the diversity of mediums.

Of the penetration of sounds.

Of the carriage of sounds, and their direction or spreading, and of the area which sound fills, together and severally.

Of the variety of the bodies, which yield sound; and the instruments; and of the species of sounds which occur.

Of the multiplication, majoration, diminution, and fraction of sounds.

Of the repercussion of sounds, and echo.

Of the consent and dissents of audibles and visibles, and of other (so called) spiritual species.

Of the quickness of the generation and extinction of sound, and the time in which they are effected.

Of the affinity or non-affinity which sound hath with the motion, local and perceptible, of the air in which it is carried.

Of the communication of the air percussed and elided, with the ambient air, and bodies, or their spirits.

Of the forming or articulation of sound.

Of the very impression of sounds upon the sense.

Of the organ of hearing, and its disposition and indisposition, helps, and hindrances.

The inquiry into sound and hearing I have thought well forthwith to set on foot; for it advantageth the understanding, and, as it were, makes matter of its health, that the contemplations of the spiritual species, as they call them, and of operations at distance, he mixed with the contemplation of those things, which work by communication only of the substance to the touch. Again, the observations concerning sounds have brought forth to us the art of music. But it is customary, and as it were invariable, when trials and observations have grown into art, that the mathematic and practic is pursued, the physic is left. Moreover, optic fareth some whit better: for not only the art of painting, and beauty, and symmetry are propounded unto optic, but the contemplation of all visibles; but unto music, only musical tones. Therefore we do inquire of sounds.

Of the Generation of Sound, and the First Percussion.

The collision, or elision, as they speak, meaning thereby some section or cutting of the air, which they will have to be the cause of sound, imports neither the form, nor the secret process of sound, but is a term of ignorance and superficial contemplation.

Sound is diffused and moves with so small an impulse in its generation; also so far, and that in round, not much depending on the first direction; withal so smoothly, without any evident motion, found either by flame, or by feathers and straws, or in any other manner; that it seems altogether hard that the form of sound should be any cutting, or local and perceptible motion of the air, howsoever this may hold the part of the efficient.

For that sound is so suddenly generated, and straightway dies, it seems necessary that either its generation do a little thrust the air from its nature, and its perishing restore it, as in the compressions of waters, whereas a body cast into the water makes many circles in the waters, that come of the water at first compressed, afterward restoring itself into its proper consistence and dimension; (which we have used to call the motion of liberty;) or that, contrariwise, the generation of sound be an impression pleasant and kindly, that winneth upon the air, and whereunto the air freely stirreth itself, and that its extinction be from some enmity, which suffers not the air longer to enjoy that agitation and impression; as in the generation of the very body of flame, wherein the generation of the flame appears to be made with alacrity, but by the air and other environing adversaries presently to be destroyed.

The whistling which is made by the mouth,

535

without use of a whistle, may be effected by sucking in of the breath toward the inner parts of the mouth, not only by expelling of the breath outwards; and clearly all sucking of the air inwards gives a sound, which seems exceeding worthy of remark: because the sound is generated against the perceptible motion of the air, so as the first impulsion of the air appears plainly to be the remote efficient, and no part of the form of sound.

In like manner, if there be an egg of glass taken, and the air through a small hole forcibly sucked out; then the hole stopped with wax, and it be laid by for a time; if afterwards the wax be removed from the hole, you shall hear plainly the hissing of the air entering into the egg, being drawn, to wit, by the inner air, after forcible rarefaction, restoring itself. So as in this trial also, sound is generated contrarily to the perceptible motion of the air.

In like manner, in the toy that is called a jew's-harp, holding the sides betwixt the teeth, the little tongue of iron is drawn outwards and jarred, when it flies back inwards against the air that is in the mouth, and thence is a sound created.

And in these three trials it may not be doubted but that sound is generated by the percussion of the air inwards towards the mouth on the egg of glass.

Sound is generated by percussions. The percussion is either of air against air, or of a hard body against the air, or of a hard body against a hard body.

The instance of the percussion of air against air chiefly prevails in the human voice, and in the voices of birds and of other animals; next in musical wind instruments; also in ordnance, greater and less, where the percussion that gives the sound is generated chiefly by the percussion of the confined air that issues from the mouth of the piece against the outer air; for the bullet wherewith it is charged makes not much to the noise. Neither is the percussion of a soft body against a soft body only seen in the percussion of air against air, but also of air against flame, as in the raising of a flame with bellows; also flames amongst themselves, when one drives another, yield a certain roaring; but whether the air assist here may be further inquired. Also, all flame that suddenly taketh, if it be of any greatness, makes a sound, rather, as I think, in displacing of the air than of itself. Also in eruptions, there is percussion made of the spirit breaking out against the air adjacent; as in the cracklings made by dry leaves, or bay-salt, and many other things, when cast into the fire; and in thunder, either by the spirit breaking out from the cloud, or wallowing and tossed to and fro, as in the more hollow and lengthened rolling of thunder; also we see in sport that a fresh rose-leaf gathered together so as it shall contain air, and struck upon the back of the hand, or upon the forehead, cracks by eruption of the air.

Instances of the percussion of a hard body against the air, are seen in musical stringed instruments; in the whistling of an arrow, as it flies through the air; in the beating of the air, although it strike not any hard body; also, in regals, their sound is given by the air striking against water; in the pipe they call the nightingale-pipe, which gives a sound continually tumbling; in water agitated and restoring itself again; and in the toys wherewith children please themselves, (they call them cocks,) in imitation of the voices of birds; likewise in other hydraulics.

Instances of the percussion of a hard body against a hard body, are found either simply, or with communication of some air enclosed beside that air, which is cut or elided between the hard bodies percussed; simply, as in all hammering or knocking of hard bodies, with communication of air penned in, as in bells and drums.

A stone cast forcibly into the water gives a sound; as do the drops of rain falling upon the water, and no less wave dashing against wave, in which there is percussion betwixt a hard body and water.

It seemeth to be constant in the generation of all sound, that there are certain parts of air, and that air is required between the bodies percussed; which air, in the percussion of a hard body against the air, and of a hard body against a hard body, appears manifestly to be cut or elided. I judge that flame should suffice for this in the stead of air, as if in the midst of a great flame a bell should be rung, or stones knocked together; but in the percussion of air against air this elision or separation appears more dark, but the air seems only to be beaten and driven, and that in a soft voice, very gently. But it seems, even in this kind, to need that there be some elision of the air percussed by the air percussing: for even in air moved by a fan, the air from the side of the fan, and when air is blown out of bellows, the blast of air from the mouth, divides the other air. But concerning this kind of elision of the air, which happens when the percussion of air against air createth sound, as in the voice, let inquiry be made further.

It is well doubted, whether the percussion that produces sound, when the air is percussed by a string, or otherwise, be from the beginning, when the string starting back percusses the air, or a little after, the air, to wit, being compressed by the first percussion, and thereafter acting the part, as it were, of a hard body.

When sound is yielded by the percussion of air against air, it is required that there be an imprisoning or penning of the air in some concave, as in whistling by the mouth, in pipes, in the viol, in the voice; which is divided, where the air is penned in the hollow of the mouth or throat. In the percussion of a hard body against air is required hardness of the body and quick motion, and sometimes communication with a concave, as in the cittern, lute, beating of the air, &c.. but in the percussion of a hard body against a hard body, the hollow, or the quick motion, is less required.

There is a talk of a white gunpowder, which should give percussion without noise. It is sure that nitre, which is white, is of great force for expulsion, yet in such wise as the speedy kindling doth much enhance both the percussion and the noise; but the quick kindling is caused specially by the coal of willows, which is black. Therefore, if a composition were made of sulphur and nitre, and a modicum of camphor, it is like that the kindling would be slower, and the percussion not so jarring and sharp; whence much might be diminished of the sound, but with loss too in the strength of the percussion. To be further inquired.

Of the Lasting of Sound, and its Perishing and Extinction.

The lasting of the sound of a bell that is struck, or of a string, which seems to be prolonged, and gradually to fade, comes not rightly of the first percussion, but the trembling of the body percussed generates in the air continually new sound. For, if that trembling be checked, and the bell or string stayed, the sound quickly dies; as in virginals, where, if the quill be dropped so that it touch the string, the sound ceases.

A bell hanging in the air gives a far louder and more enduring sound if it be chimed upon with a hammer on the outside, than if it stood fixed, and were in like manner chimed upon with a hammer. And of the more enduring sound the reason is rendered already, because it trembleth longer. But that even the first sound in the hanging bell is more resounding, in the standing less, would be further inquired.

Likewise a drinking cup of silver or of glass that is fillipped, if it be left alone, gives a sound louder and more lasting; but if the foot of the cup be steadied with the other hand, a far duller, and of shorter stay.

The sound which is yielded in the viol or cittern is plainly not made by the percussion between the finger, or the quill, and the string, or between the finger, or the quill, and the air, but by the finger impelling, and thereafter the string flying back, and in that recoil percussing the air. Therefore, when the string is moved with a bow, not by the finger, or a quill, the sound can be continued at pleasure, through the roughness of the bow, which is a little smeared with rosin: whence it slides not on the string, nor once strikes it, but holds and continually tortureth it, out of which motion the sound is maintained.

It can be taken for an argument, that sound is manifestly some kind of local motion in the air. that it so suddenly fails; because, in all cutting or impulsion of the air, the air quite recovers and restores itself, which also water doth through many circles, albeit not so speedily as the air.

Of the Confusion and Perturbation of Sounds.

In the act of sight, visibles from one part impede not visibles from other parts; but all the visibles which offer themselves from every part, lands, waters, woods, the sun, buildings, men, are at once represented to the eyes. But, if so many voices or sounds did at once issue from several parts, the hearing should be plainly confounded, nor might distinctly perceive them.

The greater sound confoundeth the less, that it should not be heard; but spiritual species, as they speak of a diverse kind from sound, confuse not sound, but altogether and at once hang in the air, the one little or nothing troubling the other; as light, or colour, heat and cold, smells, magnetic virtues; all these together can hang in the air, nor yet do greatly hinder or disturb sounds.

The cause wherefore many visibles are at once represented unto the eyes, the one not confounding the other, would seem to be none other but this: that visibles are not seen except in a right line, but sounds are heard even in a line oblique, or arcuate. Therefore, as many objects in the area of the sphere of sight, as are conveyed, there be so many cones of beams, nor ever one cone doth coincide with another; neither do the vertices of the cones meet in the same point, because they are carried by right lines. But sounds, which are carried by lines, both right and arcuate, can meet easily in one point, and so are confused. The same seemeth to be the cause wherefore a more bright colour drowns not a more dim colour; nevertheless, a greater light obscures and hides a weaker light, because light is perceived in an arched line, like as sound. For, although the very flame of a candle be not seen except in a right line, yet does the light that is everywhere spread round attain to the sight in lines, arched in respect of the body of the candle: the like is the case of the sun, or flame. Now, if it be objected that neither is light itself seen except in a right line from air illuminated, it is true; but I think that this as well happens to sound: for neither is sound heard unless in right lines from some part of the sphere of sound, whither the first pulsation arrives. But colour, which is nothing other than the image unequally reflected of the light, spreadeth around so weak species, that it little or nothing tinges the air adjacent, unless where the colours are conveyed in right lines between the object and the eye.

Let there be a trial made with a double recorder, in which let there be two fipples, at each end one, so as they may be played in unison: the hollow pipe being of a double length, and continued in one; let two together play the same tune at either end, and let it be noted whether the sound be confused, or amplified, or dulled.

Let there be two hollow trunks taken, and joined together crosswise, so as they shall open the one into the other, in the place where they are joined; and let two speak into the direct and transverse trunk, and let the ears of two be in like manner applied to the opposite ends, and observe whether the voices confuse one another.

Of the accessary Aids and Impediments of Sound; of the Stay of Sound; and the Diversity of Mediums.

I remember in a chamber in Cambridge that was something ruinous, that a pillar of iron was erected for a prop, of the thickness perhaps of a thumb's breadth and a half; and that this pillar, being struck with a stick or otherwise, made a little flat noise in the chamber wherein the pillar stood, but in the chamber beneath a resounding boom.

To inquire, which bodies, and of what solidity and thickness, altogether debar and shut out sound; as, also, which more or less dull, although they intercept it not wholly. For as yet is it not known which mediums interposed be more propitious, which more adverse. Therefore, let there be trial made in gold, stone, glass, cloth, water, oil, and of the thickness of each. Hereof is all need to inquire further.

Air is the aptest, and, as it were, the sole medium of sound. Again, the moister air (I judge) better conveyeth sound than the drier; but in a fog what happeneth I remember not. Also, the night air better than by day; but this can be ascribed to the silence.

Inquire touching the medium of flame, what its operation shall be in respect of sound; whether, to wit, a flame of some thickness altogether stop and intercept sound, or at least deaden it more than the air. This can be seen in bonfires.

Also, to inquire concerning the medium of air vehemently agitated. For, although wind carry sound, yet I deem that any vehement wind doth somewhat trouble sound, so as it shall be heard less far, even with the wind, than in still weather, of which let there be more inquiry made.

To see what sound brass or iron, red-hot, yields, struck with a hammer, compared to that which it gives cold.

Of the Penetration of Sounds.

The aëtites, or eagle stone, hath like a kernel or yolk of the stone, which being shaken makes a flat sound; so a hawk's bell, [stopped,] but a much clearer if there be a chink.

Let inquiry be made of divers, if they hear at all under water, especially that is of any deep-

ness; and let this be distinctly inquired, not only whether they hear any sound at all from above, which is made in the air, but also, whether they hear the percussion of the body of the water within the water, where no air is. I have made this trial in a bath; a pail of a good size with the mouth turned over was, in such wise, pressed evenly down, as it carried the air fairly down with it, in its hollow, below the water, to the depth of a hand-breath; and in this manner the pail was held down with the hands, that it should not overturn nor rise: then a diver put his head within the pail, and did speak: his voice was heard, speaking; and even his speech was articulately distinguished, but wonderfully shrill, and almost like a whistling, as the voice useth to be heard in a play of puppets.

Let it be exactly inquired, so as it be clearly rendered positive whether sound can be generated, except there be air betwixt the percussing and the percussed body. As, if two pebbles hanging by a string be let down into a basin of water, or a river, and shaken, so as they shall strike together in the midst of the water; or let an open pair of tongs be thrust down into the water, and there knapped; and let it be noted whether they give a sound, and what. I do suppose that divers, in swimming, make no noise under the water; unless there may perchance be some, by the succession of motion under the surface of the water, and the water thence striking the air.

There is no doubt but in bladders tied, and not quite full, and shaken, there is a sound given, namely, of the liquor contained in them, and no less a sound is given on letting down a stone into water, when it strikes the bottom of the vessel. But in the former trial air is intermingled; in the second, the percussion of the bottom of the vessel by the stone communicates with the air without the vessel. But, after the first percussion, it needeth not that there be air intermediate through the whole area of the sphere deferent; for that is shown by the trial of one speaking in a pail under the water, where part of the deferent from the water is not air, but the wood of the pail, and the water; whence the sound is sharpened, and minished, and lost.

But, because it is manifest that sound passes through and penetrates hard bodies, (as potters' earth and glass;) and it is also most certain (although hitherto concealed from men's observation) that there is, in every tangible body, some pneumatical part, besides the gross parts intermixed, it is to be considered whether penetration of sound of this kind come not thence, for that the pneumatical or aerial parts of the tangible body communicate with the outer air.

Take a vessel of silver, and another of wood, full of water; take a pair of iron tongs, and knap them in the water in the vessels, at the distance of a thumb's breadth, perhaps, or more, from the bottom: you shall hear the sound of the tongs knapped in the vessel of silver much more resounding than in the wooden one. Whereas, if the two vessels were empty, and you knapped the tongs at the same distance, there should be little difference, or none. Whence it appears, first, that where is no air that can be elided, but only water, sound is given; next, that the sound given by the percussion communicates better with the vessel through water than through air. The mouth being close shut, there is made a murmur (such as dumb persons use to make) by the throat; if the nostrils likewise be fast closed, no murmur can be made. Whence it appears, that that sound by the throat is not effected unless through the opening which lies between the throat and the nostrils.

Of the Carriage of Sounds, and their Direction or Spreading; and of the Area which Sound fills, together and severally.

All sound is diffused in a sphere from the place of the percussion, and fills the whole area of this sphere to a certain limit, upwards, downwards, sideways, and every way.

Throughout this orb the sound is loudest close to the stroke; thence, in the proportion of the distance, it grows more faint, until it vanishes. The limits of this sphere are extended some little by reason of the quickness of hearing; yet is there something uttermost, whither, to the most delicate sense, sound reaches not.

There is something, I think, in the direction of the first impulsion; for, if a man should stand in an open pulpit in the fields, and shout, the voice, I judge, should be further heard forwards from the speaker than behind. So, if ordnance, or a harquebuss be discharged, I judge that the sound shall be further heard before the ordnance or harquebuss than behind it.

Whether there be any thing in the ascension of sound upwards, or in the descension of sound downwards, which may further sound, or make it cease nearer, doth not appear. The sound is indeed well heard, if one speak from a high window or turret, by those who stand upon the ground; and, contrariwise, being uttered by those that stand upon the ground from the window or turret, but by whether more easily, or further off, let better inquiry be made.

Pulpits are used for speaking in assemblies, and generals did usually speak standing upon mounds of sods; yet is it is no wise hence confirmed that sound easilier descends than it rises, since the cause hereof may be the liberty of the air in the higher place, not thronged or hindered, as below amongst the crowd, but not the readier motion downwards. Therefore, let not the contemplation stay in this instance, but let a trial be made where other things are equal.

The power of the sound is received whole in every part of the air, not the whole in the whole air, unless where the opening or passage is exceedingly strait. For if one stand in any place utterly closed, so as the sound may not penetrate at all, and that in any part soever of a sphere of sound, and there be a small opening made, the articulate voice shall enter through that opening, and in fine through as many openings as you shall choose to make through the whole round of the sphere of sound: so as it is manifest that that whole articulation of sound is conveyed entire in these minutest parts of the air, not less than if the air were at large on every side.

It is, however, to be observed whether sounds proceeding from the greater pulsations of the air (such as are made by the discharge of ordnance) become not more exile when they enter by those small apertures; for it may be that the subtilties of sound shall enter unconfused, but the whole crash, or roar, not so well.

The rays of visible bodies do not strike the sense, unless they be conveyed through the medium in straight lines, and the interposition of any opaque, in a right line, intercepts the sight, although every thing else be on all sides wholly open. But sound, if there be a dilatation or passage, whether by arching over, or by inverted arching downwards, or laterally, or even by winding, perishes not, but arrives. Nevertheless, I judge that sound is more strongly carried in straight lines, betwixt the pulsations and the ear, and that by its archings and windings it is somewhat broken; as, if there be a wall betwixt the speaker and the hearer, I think that the voice shall not be so well heard as if the wall were away. I judge, too, that if the speaker or the hearer be placed at a little distance from the wall, the voice shall be better heard than nigh unto the wall, because the arching so much the less departs from a right line. But this also would be further inquired.

If the ear be laid to the one end of any tube or long hollow trunk, and a voice speak softly at the other opening of the tube, such a voice shall be heard, which, being as softly spoken in the air at large, should not arrive, nor be heard. Whence it is clear, that that confining of the air helps to the conveying of the voice, without confusion.

It is also a common opinion, that, other things being equal, the voice is better heard within doors than abroad; but whether the voice be better heard when the ear is out of doors, and the voice within the house; or contrariwise, when the voice is out of doors, and the ear within the house, may be further inquired; albeit herein also the opinion is received, that what is abroad is better heard within doors, than what is within, abroad.

It is common to hearing and sight, and, indeed, in a certain measure, to the other senses, that the attention of the perceiving mind, and express direction to perceiving, help somewhat to perceiving, as when one looks steadfastly, or (as they say) pricks his ears.

Sounds are not carried so far, articulate and distinct, as their species, and a confused coil of them; for the hum of voices can be heard where the articulate words themselves are not heard; and a confused tinkling of music, when the harmony itself or tune is not heard.

Sound is preserved, at the best, in a hollow trunk. Therefore let there be taken a hollow trunk of a good length, and let it be put out from the window of a lower chamber; let one speak by thrusting of his head out of the window, at one end of the trunk, as softly as ever he may: let another lay his ear to the other end of the trunk, standing below upon the ground: let this be done in like wise reversely, by speaking from below, and laying to of the ear above, and from this trial let a judgment be made, whether the voice ascend or descend more easily, or even alike. They deliver for certain, that there be some places and buildings so vaulted, that if one stand in a certain part of the chamber, and speak, he can be better heard at some distance than near.

All harmony appeareth to sound somewhat fuller and deeper at a little remoteness from the place of the sound than near; so as something should seem to happen to hearing about sound, like as happeneth to sight about visible species, that some removal from the organ of the sense furthereth the perception of the sense. But in that opinion may be twofold error. First, because in the act of sight there be, perhaps, beams required from the object to the pupil, which there cannot be where the object toucheth the pupil, which between the hearing and the sound is not required. But much rather, because to seeing is light needed. But an object touching the pupil intercepts the light: whereas nothing of this kind befalls to hearing. And, in the second place, because to sight there needeth not always a medium; forasmuch as, in the removing of cataracts of the eyes, the little silver needle wherewith the cataracts are removed, even when it moveth upon the pupil within the coat of the eye, is excellently seen.

In objects of sight, if the eye be placed in the dark, and the object in the light, it shall do well; but if the object be placed in the dark, and the eye in the light, you shall not see. So, if a thin veil or net-work be cast over the eyes, the object is well seen; if upon the object, it confounds sight. And albeit, that perhaps neither of these agreeth to sound and hearing, yet may they advertise us that trials be made, whether the ear set against the hollow trunk, if the sound be made at a distance in the air at large, or conversely, the sound be produced at the hollow trunk, the ear being placed at a distance in the air at large, favour more the perception of the sense.

Of the Variety of the Bodies which yield Sound; and the Instruments; and of the Species of Sounds which occur.

The kinds of sounds appear to receive such a division: loud, soft, sharp or treble, base; musical, unmusical; interior or whispering, exterior or sounding; simple, compounded, original, reflected; so as they are divisions six.

The stronger the first pulsation shall be, and the dilatation the more free, and without let, the greater is the sound given: the weaker the percussion, and more disturbed the dilatation, the less.

Treble sounds are carried as far, and perchance farther than base. Let this be better inquired.

Accordingly as the concave of a bell shall be greater, it giveth a baser sound; the less, the more treble.

The bigger a string, the baser sound it shall yield; the less, the more treble.

A string, the more tightly strained, the more treble sound shall it yield; the looser, the baser: so as a little bigger string more tightly strained, and a less more slackly, shall give the same note.

In trumpets, in like wise, in flutes, horns, and recorders, pipes, also in the mouth of a man whistling, the more narrow and straight they are, they give the more treble sound; the wider, or more open, the baser.

In flutes, the air, issuing by a hole nearer the breath, yields a more treble sound; by one more distant, a baser: so a little bigger flute by the nearer hole, and a smaller by the more removed, may give the same note.

In some stringed instruments (as in the viol, citterns, and the like) men have found a skill for the straining of the strings, beyond the first straining, so as compressing them with the fingers lower down or higher up, they strain them to the alteration of the note.

If a drinking-cup of glass or silver be taken and fillipped, if the water stand higher in the cup, and the cup be fuller, it will give a more treble sound; if lower, and the cup be more empty, a baser.

In a hollow pipe, such as they use for shooting of birds, if one whistle with the mouth, setting the mouth to one end of the tube, the sound is dulled, truly, to the bystander; but if the ear be laid to the other end, it gives a most sharp sound, so as it shall hardly be borne.

Let there be a trial made with a trunk, in the part where the ear is laid, narrow, in the part where the mouth is set, wider, and conversely; whether the sound be rendered more treble or baser, after the manner of mirrors, which contract or enlarge the objects of sight.

Of the Multiplication, Majoration, Diminution, and Fraction of Sound.

It would be seen in what, how, way, manner, sound can be artificially magnified and multiplied.

Mirrors do effect both in sight. Now, the sudden reflection of sound seems to turn to augmentation; for if the voice and echo be yielded together, need is that the sound be not distinguished, but magnified. Therefore, sounds upon rivers are greater, the water resounding and blending itself with the original sound.

I have also noted that when a round-house is made in water-conduits, then a long vault, and then a greater chamber, (such as is to be seen in the fields by Charing Cross near London,) if you cry at the window or slit of the round-house, and one stand by the window of the greater chamber, a far more fearful roaring is heard than by one standing where the cry is made.

I bethink me that in the play of puppets, the speaking is such as it is heard distinctly, but far sharper and more exile than in the air at large; as happens in mirrors that render letters far smaller than they are in the ordinary medium: so as sound appears plainly possible by art to be both amplified and rendered more exile.

Children hold the horn of a bent bow betwixt their teeth, and with an arrow strike the string, whence is produced a more resounding sound, and a far greater boom, than if the bow were not held in the teeth; which they ascribe to the consent which the bones of the teeth have with the bone of hearing; since, conversely also, by a certain harsh sound in the hearing, the teeth too be set on edge.

In like manner, let a lance touch the wood of the belly of an harp, especially of the hole in it at the hollow end, and be held with the teeth at the other end, and the harp struck; the sound is made greater by taking hold with the teeth, that is to say, to him that so taketh hold.

It is most assured (however unnoted) that the force, which after the first percussion carries on balls, or arrows, or darts, and the like, is situated in the minute parts of the body discharged, and not in the air continually carrying it, like a boat in the water. This being premised, it may be considered whether sound might not be lessened in ordnance or a harquebuss, without much weakening of the percussion, in this manner. Let there be a harquebuss made with a barrel of a pretty strength, so as it break not easily; in the barrel let there be four or five holes made, not like chinks, but round, about the middle of the barrel. The percussion hath already gotten its force, excepting so far as by reason of the length of the barrel it may be increased; but the percussion of the air at the mouth of the harquebuss, which generates the sound, will be much attenuated by the emission of sound through those holes in the middle of the barrel, before that the air enclosed arrive at the mouth of the harquebuss. Therefore it is probable that the sound and boom shall by many parts be diminished.

Of the Repercussion of Sounds and Echo.

The repercussion of sounds (which we call echo) can be taken for an argument that sound is not a local motion of the air; for if it were, the repercussion should be made in manner conformable to the original, as happens in all corporeal repercussions. But in sound, wherein such an exact generation is required, as in the voice, which hath so many organs, and in musical instruments, which be curiously framed, the things which yield the repercussed sound have nothing such, but are merely rude, having almost nothing save this, that sound passes not through them.

Of the Consents and Dissents of Audibles and Visibles, and of other so called Spiritual Species.

They agree in these:

Both are diffused in a spherical compass or orb, and fill the whole area of that sphere, and are carried to very distant spaces, and wax faint by degrees, according to the distance of the object, then vanish. Both carry their figurations and differences into minute portions of their orb, entire and unconfused, so as they are perceived through small crannies no otherwise than in an open place.

Both are of exceedingly sudden and swift generation and dilatation, and conversely they are extinguished, and perish suddenly and quickly.

Both take and convey minute and exquisite differences, as of colours, figures, motions, distances, in visibles; of articulate voices, of musical tones, and of their swift changes and trepidation, in audibles.

Both, in their virtue and force, appear neither to emit any corporeal substance into their mediums or their orb, nor even to give forth or provoke a local perceptible motion in their mediums, but to convey certain spiritual species, of which the nature and manner is unknown.

Both appear to be not generative of any other virtue or quality besides their proper virtue, and so far to work, being else barren.

Both in their proper action appear, as if corporeally, to work three things. The first, that the stronger object drowns and confounds the weaker; as the light of the sun, the light of a candle, the report of ordnance, the voice. The second, that the more excellent object destroys the weaker sense; as the light of the sun, the eye, a violent sound close at the ear, the hearing. The third, that both are repercussed, as in mirrors and the echo.

Neither doth the object of the one confound or hinder the object of the other; as light or colour, sound, or contrariwise.

Both affect the sense in animals, and that by objects in greater or less degrees grateful or odious: but they affect also after their own manner inanimates proportionate, and having (as seemeth) a conformity with the organs of the senses; as colours, a mirror, that is crystalline like the eye; sounds, the places of reverberation, which seem, likewise, to resemble the bone and cavern of the ear.

Both work diversely, accordingly as they have their mediums well or ill disposed.

To both the medium the most conducible and propitious is the air. In both the stretching of the sense, and, as it were, its erection to perceiving, availeth somewhat in more nice objects.

They differ in these:

The species of visibles appear to be as if emissions of beams from the visible body, almost like odours. But the species of audibles appear more to partake of a local motion, like the percussions which are made in the air: that whereas bodies for the most part work in two manners, by communication of their nature, or by an impression or signature of their motion, that diffusion in visibles appeareth more to partake of the former manner; in audibles, of the latter.

The dilatation of sounds appears to be more evidently carried by the air than of visibles. For I judge that a vehement wind shall not so much hinder any visible afar off, as a sound; I understand the wind blowing contrary.

It is a notable difference, whence also many less differences flow, that visibles (original light excepted) are not carried but by right lines, whilst sounds are carried by arcuate lines.

Hence it happens, that visibles confound not one another, that are represented together: sounds contrarily. Hence it happens, that the solidity of the substance seems not greatly to hinder sight, provided only the positions of the parts of the body be after a simple order and with straight passages, as in glass, water, crystal, diamond; but a little silk or linen cloth breaks the sight, though they be bodies very thin and porous; but cloths of this kind little or nothing hinder hearing, which those solids do exceedingly. Hence it happens, that unto the reverberation of visibles a small mirror suffices, or like transpicuous body, let it be only placed in a right line, where the visibles pass; but unto making of the reverberation of echo, it needeth also to confine the sound from the side, because it is carried to all sides. The visible object is further carried, in proportion, than sound.

Visibles, too nearly approached to the eye, are not so well seen as at some little distance, so as the beams may meet in a more acute angle; but in hearing, the nearer the better. But herein there may be twofold error. The first, because to seeing there is required light; but if the object be brought very near to the eye, this is shut out. For I have heard of one trustworthy, which was cured of cataracts of the eyes, when the little silver needle moved over the very pupil of his eye, and did touch it, he, without any medium, (that silver needle being far narrower than the pupil itself of the eye,) saw perfectly the needle. The second, that the cave of the ear is distinctly interposed before the organ of hearing, so as, being without, the sound is altogether unable to touch the bone and membrane of hearing.

The species of sight are more swiftly conveyed than sounds, as appeareth in the flash and report of guns; also in lightning and thunder, where the thunder is heard after a while.

I conceive also that the species of sound do hang longer in the air than visibles. For, although neither do these perish on the instant, as we see in a ring spinning, and lute-strings fillipped, and in twilight and the like; yet I deem that sounds, for that they are carried by the wind, stay longer.

The beams of light being gathered, induce heat also, which is an action diverse from the visible quality. In like manner, if it be true that shouts have cast down birds flying over, that is also an action exceedingly diverse from the audible quality.

There seemeth not in visibles to be found an object as odious, and noisome to the sense, as in audibles; but they affect it more evenly; for things foul to sight rather offend by moving of the fancy concerning foul things than of themselves; but in audibles the grating of a saw that is sharpened, and other like sounds, cause a horror; and a discordant note in music is straightways refused and loathed.

It is not assured, that there is refraction in sounds, as in beams. But, doubtless, sounds do rebound: but that is to be ascribed to reflection. For, I do not think, if sounds pass through diverse mediums, as air, cloth, wood, that there be one place of the sound, where it is carried, another where it is heard, which is the property of refraction; but refraction seems to depend upon action, in right lines, which pertains not to sound.

But contraction of sound, and its dilatation, according to the disposition of the medium, happens, undoubtedly, as in the speaking of puppets, and under water: the sound is contracted within that cell, which abroad is dispersed; as by mirrors visibles are dilated and contracted.

A tremulous medium (as smoke in visibles) makes the visible objects also to tremble; but in sounds nothing such is yet found, unless, perchance, the rise and fall by winds. For the trembling in the nightingale-pipe is trembling of the percussion, not of the medium.

Going from great light into the dark, or out of the dark into the light, the sight is some little confused; but whether the like be after very loud noises, or a great silence, would be inquired.

Of the Quickness of the Generation and Extinction of Sound, and the time in which they are effected.

All sound is exceeding quickly generated, and quickly perishes. But the swiftness of its motion and of its differences, appears a thing not so wonderful. For the motion of the fingers upon a lute, or of the breath in the pipe or flute, are found to be exceedingly swift: and the tongue itself (no very exquisite organ) goes through as many motions as letters; but that sounds should not only be so speedily generated but that they should also, by their momentary force and impression, as it were, suddenly fill so great space, is matter worthy of the highest admiration. For instance, a man in the middle of a field, speaking aloud, is heard for a quarter of a mile, in a round, and that in articulate words, and these hanging in every little portion of the air, and all in a space of time far less, perhaps, than a minute.

To inquire of the space of time in which sound is conveyed. It can be found thus. Let a man stand in a steeple by night; let another stand in the field, a mile off, perhaps, or as far as the bell can be heard, and let him have ready a torch lighted, but covered. Then let him in the steeple strike the bell: then let the other, who stands in the plain, as soon as he hears it, lift the torch: in this way, by the space of time between the striking of the bell and the seeing of the torch, shall he that stands in the steeple discover the time of the motion of the sound.

In guns, the flame is seen sooner than the report is heard, although the flame follow the discharging of the ball; so as the flash issues later, but sooner strikes the sense. Whence it is rightly gathered, that the beams visible are more speedily diffused, and arrive, than the species or impressions of sound.

Of the Affinity, or Non-affinity, which Sound hath with the Motion, local and perceptible, of the Air in which it is carried.

Sound doth not appear manifestly and actually to shake and trouble the air, as doth wind; but the motions of sound appear to be effected by spiritual species; for thus we must speak, until something more assured shall be found.

So as I conceive that a very loud sound of one shouting, at a little distance from the very motion of the breath, shall scarcely stir any trembling aspen leaf, or straw, or flame.

But in greater pulsations there is found a very bodily and actual motion of the air; but whether that proceed from the motion itself which generates sound, or from a collateral cause, or some concomitants, appeareth not. Thunder-claps sometimes make glass windows to tremble, and even walls: I think, also, that ordnance let off, or explosions of mines, do the same.

And I remember, if I mistake not, that there is, at King's College, in Cambridge, a certain wooden building, in which there hang bells, and that when the bells ring, it is shaken. But whatsoever that hidden motion be, which is sound, it appears that neither is it engendered without perceptible motion in the first pulsation, and that again by the perceptible motion of the air it is carried or hindered.

A word quietly uttered, which at a distance perhaps of thirty feet can be heard, will yet hardly stir the flame of a candle, that is held within a foot of the mouth; whilst blowing a little strongly with the mouth, shall make the flame to waver, at a much greater distance.

The sound of bells, and the like, comes louder, and goes off more dully, as the wind blows towards the ear, or against the sound. The same happens in a shout, which being uttered against the wind, is not heard so far.

It is delivered, that through vast shouts of numbers applauding and cries of rejoicing, the air has been so broken or rarefied, that birds flying over have fallen down. There runs an opinion that the noise of many bells ringing in populous cities is good against thunder and pestilence.

Some places and buildings are certainly reported to be so vaulted, that if one speak in them, and (as the report hath it) against the wall, in one part of the building, his words shall be better heard at some distance from the voice than close at hand.

I have observed, sitting in a coach with one side of the boot down, and the other up, that a beggar crying on the closed side of the coach hath seemed to cry on the open side; so as the voice was plainly repercussed, and went round, or at the least, whilst it sounded on all sides, it seemed to be heard on that side, on which it did best reach the sense.

If a candle be held to the wind-hole of a drum, and the drum be beat, the flame is shaken and extinguished. The same happens in winding of a hunter's horn, if the candle be brought near the mouth of the horn, &c.

Even the exquisite differences which sound takes, and carries them with it, show that these delicate affections are not continued local motions. For seals, in a matter fitly prepared, make exquisite impressions; so as in the generation of sound this same, perhaps, might happen. But the dilatation and continuance sort not, especially in liquids: but those exquisite differences we understand of articulate voices and musical tones.

But of this matter altogether (*videlicet,* what relation and correspondency sound has to the local motion of the air) let inquiry be more diligently made; not by the way, *whether?* (which sort of question in matters of this kind has ruined all,) but by the way, *how far?* and that not by arguments discursive, but by opposite experiments and crucial instances.

Of the Communication of the Air percussed and elided with the ambient Air, and Bodies, or their Spirits.

In the striking of a bell, the sound given by chiming upon the bell with a hammer on the outside, and by the tongue within, is of the same tone. So that the sound yielded by the chiming upon the outside, cannot be generated by the collision of the air between the hammer and the outside of the bell, since it is according to the concave of the bell within. And if it were a flat plate of brass, and not concave, the sound should, I think, be different.

If there be a rift in the bell, it gives a hoarse sound, not pleasant or grateful.

It would be known how the thickness of the percussed body may affect the sound, and how far forth: as if, of the same concave, one bell should be thicker, another thinner. I have proved in a bell of gold, that it gave an excellent sound, nothing worse, yea, better, than a bell of silver or of brass. But money of gold rings not so well as money of silver.

Empty casks yield a deep and resounding sound, full ones a dull and dead sound. But in the viol, and the lute, and other such, although the first percussion be between the string and the exterior air, yet that air straight communicates with the air in the belly, or concave of the viol or lute. Wherefore, in instruments of this kind is ever some perforation made, that the outward air may communicate with the confined air, without which, the sound would be dull and dead.

Let there be a trial made of the nightingale-pipe, that it be filled with oil, and not with water; and let it be noted, how much softer or more obtuse the sound shall be.

When sound is created between the breath and the percussed air, as in a pipe, or flute, it is yet so produced, as it hath some communication with the body of the flute, or pipe. For there is one sound produced in a trumpet of wood, another in one of brass; another, I judge, if the trumpet were lined within, or perhaps even covered, on the outside, with silk or cloth: one perchance if the trumpet were wet, another if dry. I conceive, likewise, in virginals, or the viol, if the board upon which the strings are strained were of brass, or of silver, it should yield a somewhat different sound. But of all these things let there be better inquiry.

Further, in respect of the communication, it would be inquired, what the diversity and inequality of bodies may do; as if three bells should be made to hang, the one within the other, with some space of air interposed, and the outer bell were chimed upon with a hammer, what sound it should give, in respect of a single bell.

Let a bell be covered on the outside with cloth or silk, and let it be noted, when the bell is struck by the tongue within, what that covering shall do to the sound.

If there were in a viol a plate of brass, or of silver, pierced with holes, in place of that of wood, it would be seen what this shall do to the sound.

There are used in Denmark, and are even brought hither, drums of brass, not of wood, less than those of wood, and they give, I think, a louder sound.

The agitation of the air by great winds shall not, I think, yield much sound, if woods, waves, buildings, or the like be away; yet is it received that, before tempests, there be some murmurings made in woods, albeit to the sense the blast be not yet perceived, nor do the leaves stir.*

* Three chapters are deficient, which there wanted leisure to completing.

GENERAL INDEX.

THE END.